TRANSECT URBANISM

READINGS IN HUMAN ECOLOGY

MOULE & POLYZOIDES

TRANSECT URBANISM

READINGS IN HUMAN ECOLOGY

Edited by
ANDRÉS DUANY
and BRIAN FALK

ORO EDITIONS

CENTER FOR APPLIED TRANSECT STUDIES

ORO EDITIONS
Publishers of architecture, art, and design

Gordon goff: publisher
www.oroeditions.com
info@oroeditions.com

Published by ORO Editions

10 9 8 7 6 5 4 3 2 First edition
ISBN: 978-1-951541-01-9

Color separations and printing: oro group ltd.
Printed in China.

ORO Editions makes a continuous effort to minimize the overall carbon footprint of its publications. As part of this goal, ORO Editions, in association withGglobal Releaf, arranges to plant trees to replace those used in the manufacturing of the paper produced for its books. Global Releaf is an international campaign run by american forests, one of the world's oldest nonprofit conservation organizations. Global Releaf is American forests' education and action program that helps individuals, organizations, agencies, and corporations improve the local and global environment by planting and caring for trees.

PREFACE

PART ONE: IMAGES

PART TWO: TEXTS

Dedicated to Sandy Sorlien,
who has been a leader and martyr, the Joan of Arc of the Transect.

ACKNOWLEDGMENTS

The editors wish to thank the many contributors to this book. Many others have created images and essays that regretfully could not be included here, but who have also advanced the understanding and implementation of the Rural-to-Urban Transect.

Sandy Sorlien was perhaps the Transect's greatest champion for several years, serving as managing editor of the previous version of the SmartCode and as the former technical director of the Center for Applied Transect Studies. Among the others who have made significant contributions to the practice are Hazel Borys, Nathan Norris, and Ann Daigle. We are also grateful to Susan Henderson and Matthew Lambert, who have worked to update the SmartCode in recent years.

Several people contributed to the design and layout of this book over the years. All were employees of DPZ CoDesign, which donated their time and expertise to this project. Of special note is Joanne Braga, who did the majority of the final graphic layout.

CENTER FOR APPLIED TRANSECT STUDIES

The Center for Applied Transect Studies promotes understanding of the built environment as part of the natural environment, through the planning methodology of the Rural-to-Urban Transect. CATS supports interdisciplinary research, publication, tools, and training for the design, coding, building, and documentation of resilient communities.

A PERSONAL INTRODUCTION

ANDRÉS DUANY

The essays of this collection take care of themselves. They are compelling, technically clear, and committed to a concept essential to urbanism. But I am not quite convinced that the importance of the Rural-to-Urban Transect is transmitted effectively through them. For me, personally, it took years of slow dawning to understand that an alternative theory or urbanism is fully embedded in this idea. On the other hand, many have been quicker to understand. Some of them leapt from confusion to expertise—perhaps because they were intellectually ravenous for a theory to explain what could be observed in the most thriving places.

Yet, I cannot help but be grateful for the experience of my own slow understanding...and so I here retell the story in the hope that it provides a portal for some of the less technically inclined.

My education began in 1980, while living in a shack on the dunes of Grayton Beach, the village near the site that was to become Seaside. My younger brother Douglas (then age 26) said, "Let me show you something." We waded chest deep into the Gulf waters and then slowly walked back. Feeling the loose sand and then the seaweed underfoot, he asked me to notice the transition to the hard-packed tidal beach, alive with the bubbles of breathing crabs amongst dried-out seaweed, then to walk up the slope to the loose sand of the first dune, and down to the trough where the blocking of the wind had allowed the first scraggly land plants to take hold. Then a long walk up a second dune and down to the second trough—this one brownish with organic material—and more diverse plant species. In a hollow pooled with rainwater, Douglas said, "In antiquity this would have been considered a sacred place, the dwelling of a minor god." I looked around—up at the branches, down at the fallen leaves becoming soil, and I could sense the life: the birds, insects, the lizards and mammals. It was extraordinarily beautiful—I mean this in both the conceptual sense, and also with the subjectivity of human aesthetics. The colors and patterns were perfectly harmonious. Douglas said, "Nature is incapable of vulgarity."

At that time, Douglas was a well-read amateur with an aptitude for discerning natural patterns, which he later contributed to the landscaping of Seaside. He has never lost the sensibility that filled us that day, but had the introduction been years later, after he studied at Harvard and become semi-professionalized, it might not have occurred to him to "waste our time" with that little walk. We might have sat down over whiskeys and just talked about the ideas.

Like most people, I knew about habitats and symbiosis, but I had not made the correlation between symbiosis and beauty. That was the foundation of what I later understood to be a symptom of the natural law that is fundamental to the ethic underlying the Transect. What did stick was a high regard for the pantheism of place, that has increased ever since. Today such places of environmental symbiosis are more ethically binding than the exemplary miracles of the Christian saints.

Lizz and I were staying at that cottage in Grayton Beach with the job of designing Seaside. Seaside manifests ideas that have been exhaustively reported—but not the crucial element of the natural landscape. With Douglas' advice, Seaside was one of the first instances of an urban landscape with natural hydrology and native species. This, with its reintroduction of vernacular building, has provided the visual "branding" of Seaside. But those—the landscape, the architecture and all the rest—are stories told elsewhere.[1] The walk is what led to this volume.

Ten years later, while idling in Miami Beach, I remarked to Douglas that I found its particular urban grid somewhat disorienting. He said, "Let me show you how to understand it." We began another linear walk—an urban one this time—from Ocean Drive on the east crossing the city to West Avenue. He said, "Instead of understanding the urbanism as a collection of monuments or images randomly visited, learn to walk cities across their grain in both directions in a disciplined manner—walk a transect." This was the first time I had heard the term.

We duly crossed each of the avenues in sequence. They then appeared distinct: a memorable declension of function and character. While all of them are straight and all run north-south, I could see how, in comparison, they were specialized and discernibly different from each other. Since that walk I have never again been confused by Miami Beach.

Ever since, when first arriving in a city I avoid the kind of tour that takes you randomly from one great spot to another (the Peter Hall system), or along a single route (the Bill Hillier system). Both can disrupt the understanding of the subtleties of the urban pattern. I tell my hosts, "Don't run me around like a cockroach in the kitchen, zigzagging from one morsel to another. I want to understand it rationally first. Let's walk along various transects." And so the transect became for me a tool to understand the city.

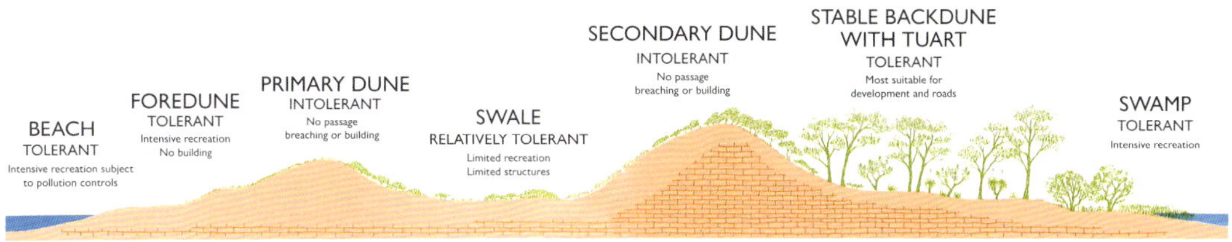

GEORGE SEDDON

This is a classic diagram by George Seddon, the pioneering Australian environmentalist. It closely parallels the first transect walk taken at Grayton Beach, with the Gulf on the left and the sequence leading to the "dwelling of a minor god" on the right, after the last dune line.

GOOGLE EARTH 2019

This image of the South Beach neighborhood in Miami Beach shows the north-south parallel avenues, crossed in the second transect walk taken from Ocean Drive on the right to West Avenue on the left. Notice the similarity of the avenues, and thus the confusion they might cause.

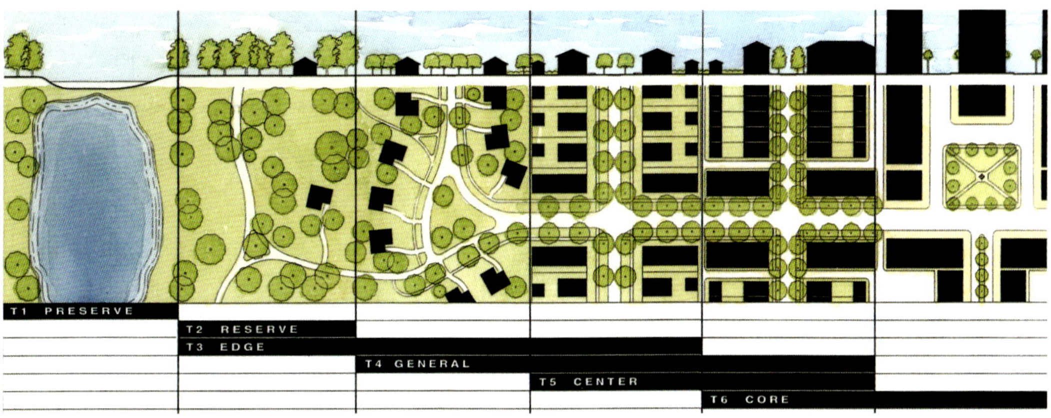

DUANY PLATER-ZYBERK

This is a diagram of the Rural-to-Urban Transect, which combines the natural and the social. That this phenomenon is common across time and culture (as shown by the breadth of images that follow) argues that it may be a natural law, defined as, "observable in nature and thus ethically binding." The most famous appearance of the natural law argument occurs in the Declaration of Independence, in which the signers claim that according to the "Laws of Nature," they "hold these truths to be self-evident," that all men have the right to "Life, Liberty and the pursuit of Happiness."

Then, one day, I envisioned an urban transect and a natural transect together. That was the early 90's in Northern Virginia, for a new town called Haymount. It came up as an idea (seductive to the environmentalists present) that the trees toward the edges of the town would provide fodder, while those on the main street would provide shade to the pedestrians and not drop berries on them and their cars. That small step took us to look at other variables coincident—or symbiotic—with the conventions of density, building height, degree of commercial use, etc., which differentiate urbanism. It was our first time with two "incompatible" concepts: the natural and the cultural technically blended in a controlled declension. I even happened to remember the extraordinarily elegant term of "transect."

Over the years the idea grew into an integrated declension of the urban and the natural, from wilderness to urban core. Later in a month-long jag, everything fell into place. For projecting and analyzing urbanism, as a series of symbiotic habitats where the elements in the silos of a dozen specialists could be allocated rationally, rather than under mining or overwhelming each other.

Henceforth, in the public consultation process that accompanies New Urbanism, we were able to avoid forbidding things for what they intrinsically were, and began to allocate them to the habitats where they belong symbiotically. You cannot (not yet) tell Americans that they are wrong to want something; but they will accept that it must be allocated to a zone where it does not undermine the preferences of others.

From then on, a set of remarkable volunteers—Sandy Sorlien principal among them—insightful, clever, experienced, and hard-working, contributed to the development of the Rural-to-Urban Transect as a general theory for analysis and projection.

The shared discipline was the common sense of symbiosis. It turned out that the problems that made urban design so contentious or kitsch were usually the result of whatever was not symbiotic with its habitat.

When the SmartCode was already at v9.0, it was a breakthrough that I stumbled, in my mental (and physical) library, upon Ian McHarg's *Design With Nature*. In 1960 he had shown a transect as part of a protocol for selecting locations for urban development. (See page 33.) But I noticed that nowhere in his theory did he have a proposition as to what was to be built once nature had revealed the appropriate sites for development. Those projects of McHarg's that I knew in Florida, Texas, and North Carolina remained well-landscaped suburban sprawl, with all the negative social and ecological consequences of functionally segregated zoning reconnected by inevitable automobile trips that, later, the New Urbanism would counter. No wonder I had not remembered McHarg! But the new Transect finally conjoined the natural and urban seamlessly and with a single unified theory, while McHarg had stopped at the edge of nature with his projects, as in the current Landscape Urbanism. Nature persists wherever possible, rusticating the denser zones that do not ever become urban. This is well-covered in the last piece of this collection.

We began illustrating codes when I ran across a little diagram by Patrick Geddes—who had worked 50 years before McHarg. It was called the "Valley Section." It diagrammed habitats from a coastal plain to a highland—what would now be called a watershed. In little drawings he had correlated each habitat with human activity: a forest to be logged, a woodland to be hunted, a hillside to be mined, a prairie to become fodder. This diagram had once been famous. Until the 60's it was the basis of much environmental insight. But it had one flaw: the relationship of humanity to nature was one of exploitation, typical of the 19th century (and in defense of Geddes, let us not forget that both Genesis and Darwin—those old adversaries—did put humans at the top of the heap).

But exploitation could hardly be more politically incorrect today. So by 1970 this synthesizing diagram had been banished—which is why we had not known of it. It was discovered late but it was exciting, as "our" Transect had the highest level of intellectual support from history, even if that modernist premium assigned to absolute innovation was thereby lost.

But New Urbanists are not ideologues. As evidence, see how many have participated in the development of the great toolkit that the Transect has become. The image section in this book confirms that.

This was fortuitous, as some fellow professionals had a problem with the Transect's association with my firm, DPZ CoDESIGN. Now, authorship was diffused—and furthering the absence of single authorship is a purpose of this publication. As a matter of policy the form-based codes and techniques that we have been developing are immediately posted as freeware. Especially through the SmartCode, the Transect technology has spread widely.

It is time now with this book to explain the universality of this taxonomic engine; to showcase the many firms and colleagues who work with the Transect technology; and most important to show that there were predecessors and simultaneous discoveries—that it wasn't the concoction of DPZ. And if no explicit precedent, it was innate in the work of Krier, Unwin, Schinkel, Vitruvius, and others, as shown by their illustrations. To this may be added the photographic evidence of the existence of the Transect in the structure of cities—even unplanned cities. It seems that the Transect is confirmed as an instance of immanence as a natural law.

1. Thadani, Dhiru A., *Visions of Seaside*, 2013.

A TECHNICAL INTRODUCTION

ANDRÉS DUANY

I have in my office a bookshelf reserved for the publications I use as reference. They typically display clear language and good graphics, and they provide practical advice on creating communities that are compact, diverse, and walkable. These are superb publications, and there are considerably more of them on this shelf than there were just 10 years ago.

More than a few urbanists know what they are doing (at long last!). And there is ever more evidence of this happy phenomenon. Editions of New Urban News identify hundreds of neighborhood-scale communities under construction and seeking permitting.

One would hope this published knowhow and the number of built projects would make obsolete Jane Jacobs' statement that "The pseudoscience of planning seems almost neurotic in its determination to imitate empiric failure and ignore empiric success."

Alas…apparently not. Each New Urbanist project encounters resistance unabated. Each requires a tremendous educational and political effort, as if it were an experimental first attempt. Like Sisyphus, the New Urbanist must begin at the bottom, pushing the project uphill against the inertia of the civil engineers, municipal officials, developers, building inspectors, elected officials, neighbors, environmentalists, marketing experts, loan officers, and all the rest. The difficulty encountered is astonishing. Even though the outcome—sprawl—has clearly been shown to be socially dysfunctional, choked in traffic, hideous, reviled by the public, and ecologically disastrous, there is resistance still! Sprawl continues to make up the vast majority of new development. Why?

Simple explanations are on offer: intellectual sluggishness, bureaucratic inertia, comfort with the status quo, aversion to risk. But there is something else at work, something fundamental and deeply embedded: this system is comprehensively organized by a unified theory.

Evidence is found in the coordinated activity of each disparate planning specialty. The analytical methodology of the traffic engineer is dependent on the precise functional segregation of single-use zoning. Absolutist environmental standards require geographic discontinuities that perpetuate the pod-like, single-use zoning diagrams. Environmental crossings are minimized by dendritic systems of thoroughfares that, as it happens, lend themselves to the traffic engineers' analysis. Lending institutions have standardized checklists that encourage the kind of large, homogeneous projects that can be minced and converted into "financial instruments," which, as it happens, translate perfectly into the stair-step densities of the zoning categories. Realtors are conditioned to place high values on the Standard Real Estate Products enabled by those selfsame homogeneous zones. There is underlying evidence that what has been presented as a neutral, market-oriented and technocratic system is, actually, heavily biased toward a certain model—suburban sprawl. Reform is resisted by a unified theory—nothing less.

Origins of the Theory of Suburban Sprawl

The dominant historiography of modern planning (which is to say, suburban sprawl) presents a sequence of empirically evolved, quasi-inevitable practices that have been professionally rationalized into a system based on "zoning." It is certainly true that a model based on the cellular categorization of zoning and its reconnection by a dendritic thoroughfare system is conceptually very elegant (dismal as the built results have been). But a different meaning of "rationalized" might be more applicable. The standardized protocols and pervasive statistics of planning may imply objectivity, which fits well with the American sense of equal treatment under the law, but more importantly, they allow bureaucrats and elected officials to use statistical analysis and numerical prescription as rationales for their decisions. This system is congealed around the undeniable advantage that it is easy to administer, lending itself to both the numerical prescription and the statistical analysis of potential outcomes that provide plausible rationales for the decisions of bureaucrats and elected officials.

There is, however, another possible history, one which posits that modern planning did not gradually evolve from empirical feedback, but rather arrived fully formed and hanging on the tail of the brilliant 30-year campaign to establish modernist architecture. Behind the current zoning system lie the theories promoted since the 1930s by Le Corbusier and his fellow polemicists of CIAM. This alternate genesis seems incredible to the planning profession, which "knows" that case law, protocodes, and empirical studies formed the fertile sediment.[1] It is evident, however, that this system proliferated worldwide over a firm theoretical foundation provided by Le Corbusier. Modernist/Corbusian/CIAM theory, in the immediate post-war period, cast aside both the Anglo-German empiricism of Unwin and Sitte and especially the Franco-American City Beautiful system that were its polemical nemeses. It left standing only the insipient City Healthy & City Efficient of the civil engineers, and the City Progressive of the reformers, all leading to a fusion of formidable technocratic credibility and ethical imperative.

This is not the place to detail this evolution, which hopefully will soon be only history. What is relevant to this volume is that there is a deeply embedded theory coordinating the current planning system, allowing it to persist despite its empirical failure. The weight of New Urbanist work, which is relatively uncoordinated, will not tip the scales of reform until there is an alternative comprehensive theory.

But before engaging in an attempt to provide such a theory, has there been no prior comprehensive attempt at reform? Only one: the environmental movement, specifically as translated into a design protocol by Ian McHarg. His *Design With Nature* sets forth environmental determinism as an alternate paradigm. Propelled by crisis no less than by hard science, McHarg's method is currently administered by environmental bureaucracies everywhere. It would be a contender to instigate reform if it were indeed comprehensive. The problem is that the protocol of *Design With Nature* stops where the green space ends. It does not include, nor does it make a proposition for, the human habitat. Because it offers no guidance for the design of urbanized areas, the many McHarg-influenced developments, such as the Woodlands in Texas, Hilton Head in South Carolina, Sea Ranch in California, and Amelia Plantation in Florida, offer only standard, single-use zoning, albeit in a "cluster" aesthetic. Outside of the preserved natural spaces, the developed areas of these projects remain, in their socioeconomic and environmental performance, indistinguishable from sprawl: everyone drives everywhere for everything.

Until very recently, the environmental movement neglected to create a proposition extending into the city. Hence the hidden failure of Portland's 20-year regional planning epic: most of what has been built within the achieved urban boundary has been suburban sprawl. And the recent green building movement has not been equipped to create urbanism—tending only to symbolize it.[2] Unfortunately, such greening does not create the most livable cities; it tends to create pretty sprawl. This brings us to the present impasse: today's pervasive "Landscape Urbanism" is propelled by an urban development system that is a combination of convenience and suburban sprawl. Despite its environmental credentials, it paradoxically reinforces the longevity of sprawl by aestheticizing it. What can be done? To be efficient, reform of the still-neglected urbanism within the urban boundary must be based on an extension of the embedded environmental ethos and methodology. This would have the advantage of familiarity within thousands of planning agencies, and it would be propelled by the tremendous political energy of the millions dedicated to an environment ethic.

What remains to be done is to extend the environmental protocol of McHarg into the city. This can be accomplished by deploying the Rural-to-Urban Transect.

Short History of the Transect

A transect is a scientific method for studying habitats, among other subjects. Following a fixed path through a given area, the observer notes the number, location, and distribution of various elements of interest. Its use in ecology inspired its adaptation for urban planning and design. The Rural-to-Urban Transect, known simply as "the Transect," allows for the identification and allocation of the various elements of urbanism, based on their suitability for given types of environments. Underlying the Transect is what used to be known as a natural law, which is defined as a principle derived from the observation of nature, and by right reason is thus ethically binding in human society.[3] The Transect's rural-to-urban declensions emerged organically in the natural/cultural evolution of human settlement, preceding its explicit conceptual formulation in the 18th century. That such a declension is timeless and cross-cultural can be easily experienced by walking from the center to the outskirts of Pompeii, or observed in the depiction of settlements in ancient Chinese scrolls. This pattern of development structured most towns and cities built before the advent of modern zoning, ca. 1930–1970. The Transect as a natural law is immanent, but its complete suppression by modernist planning protocols catalyzes the current need to re-present it as a theory toward an alternative, unified planning system.

The first explicit conceptual formulation of a scientific transect was created by Alexander von Humboldt in 1793 and illustrated by Joseph Meyer around 1860. It is thought to have been taken across the southern tip of South America, based on Humboldt's explorations from ocean to ocean, and includes taxonomic elements on and below the surface, as well as atmospheric conditions.

After Humboldt's transect, which analyzed only the natural aspects of habitat, the second appearance of a transect as an intellectual construct was a century later when the "Valley Section" was conceptualized by Sir Patrick Geddes. Geddes diagrammed a generic transect as a geographic section taken from upland to waterfront. It articulated a series of human (economic) societies ranging from hunters in the highlands to farmers in the foothills, to tradesmen along the shores. It was the first transect that included human activity corresponding with the declension of natural habitats. Humans were considered part of the habitat, if not yet "within nature," as the human symbiosis was framed exclusively in terms of nature's exploitation.

Why so questionable a proposition from an acknowledged multifaceted genius? It seems that Sir Patrick understood the ordering potential of a transect, but he could not transcend the limits of a time when nature was not conceived as a protagonist. Nature was there to be subjugated by humans. As stated in the previous introduction, both *On the Origin of Species* and the Old Testament provided support.

The next great proposition of the a transect appeared in *Design with Nature* in 1969—also by a Scotsman, Ian McHarg. A transect was immanent as a result of McHarg's analytical protocol. His transect was more scientifically sophisticated than Geddes', but less comprehensive, being entirely a progressive defense, by definition, of natural habitats, with the social habitats to be located in the low-value residue, and no further proposition regarding the areas to be inhabited by humans. McHarg's great contribution was that his transect was made operational by a series of transparent overlays designed to discover values of the land. The process progressively removed tiers of ecologically sensitive land from the realm of potential development. *Design With Nature* was the origin of legislated environmentalism, as it is a process objective enough to be defended in a court of law.[4]

Current environmental laws are based largely on the extension, technocratization, and legalization of this methodology. McHarg, however, did not make equivalent propositions for those residual areas to be urbanized. This omission confirmed the latent human/nature opposition that now pervades the environmental ethos: nature is sacred, and the city profane. The application of *Design With Nature* has led to four decades of community designs that are environmentally well-intentioned and aesthetically green, but otherwise identical to sprawl in their socioeconomic and carbon effects. This is the reality of Columbia in Maryland, Reston in Virginia, the Woodlands in Texas, and other "new towns" of that vintage—now found in full revival as "Landscape Urbanism." Though all include copies of New Urbanist town centers, the rest of the areas are extremely diagrammatic, with market-segmented housing pods, shopping centers, and office parks all duly buffered by the protocol-designated "environmental" preserve areas. The priority given to natural continuities cauterizes the thoroughfare network, which reduces walkability and the feasibility of transit, therefore increasing driving and making the few arterials that do connect quite congested given the typically low density of the residential areas. This model has failed because of an absence of a corresponding theory for the urbanized areas.

About two decades after *Design With Nature*, Christopher Alexander made a subsequent transect proposition in *A Pattern Language*. This is by no means as explicit as the prior ones. Rather, it is implied by the series of patterns, principally Nos. 2, 14, 29, and 36. Taken together these form a transect, but it is lost in the other 252 patterns. Alexander did not recognize it as the general theory capable of reconciling urbanism and environmentalism.

Re-Emergence of the Transect

The current manifestation of the Rural-to-Urban Transect is a result of the compilation of *The Lexicon of the New Urbanism* from 1994 to 1998.

In 1994, the Congress for the New Urbanism was organized around nine task forces, one of which was chartered to establish a common nomenclature. This group proposed to create a lexicon conceived as an alphabetized list of useful terms accompanied by their definitions.

This soon foundered, as it became apparent that most of the elements to be defined could be understood properly only in relationship to others. In authentic urbanism, the same as in true environmentalism, a tug on any one thing rustles something elsewhere. Rather than alphabetical order, urbanism called for its terminology to be grouped as taxonomies of related terms.

This established, it seemed natural to classify the terms within each taxonomy according to a declension convenient to each. For example, to array open spaces according to environmental performance, thoroughfares by relative traffic capacity, and building types according to the ratio of lot area occupied.

However, such disparate declensions did not support the organic conception displayed by authentic urbanism. They tended, instead, to reinforce the isolation of specialists—planners, traffic engineers, environmentalists, urban designers, landscapers, architects, land use attorneys, developers, bankers, and marketing experts—that has built the precarious Babel of current suburban-sprawl practice.

This characteristic of modern planning is the origin of its failure. Despite being implemented through a sequential protocol that engages all the specialists, the resulting plans are not properly integrated. Each profession is permitted to impose its perquisites, with the result typically being a collection of urban elements rather than urbanism itself. Thoroughfares are designed exclusively for the statistical traffic flow; the salvageable natural environment is scientifically circumscribed. Shopping centers, office parks, and residential enclaves are allocated in zoned isolation. Self-referential architecture ignores the thoroughfares while ornamental landscaping ignores the buildings. Such places, when they mature, are sometimes called "edge cities." They contain all the statistical elements of towns and cities, but they are really only cartoon versions of the real things.

The search for a theory to correlate the taxonomies yielded the chance re-discovery of the transect. A transect has heretofore been understood as an ordering system deploying a geographic gradient to arrange the sequence of natural habitats. This conception of the transect proves to be extensible to the human habitat, as every component of urbanism also finds a place within a continuous gradient of rural to urban. Combining aspects of the scientific method and the cultural analysis begun by Geddes, the transect proved extensible into the built environment, as all of the components of urbanism are suitable for certain environments along a gradient from the most rural to the most urban. For example, a street is more urban than a road, a raised curb more urban than a swale, a brick wall more urban than a shingled one, an allée of trees more urban than a cluster. And there is a declension in between: even the character of public lighting can vary from metropolitan to rustic according to fabrication of streetlights from sculptured cast iron, simple extruded pipe, rough wood posts, or providing nothing but the moon and the stars. In the Rural-to-Urban Transect, this declension has been systematized into six Transect Zones, each having a distinct character.

Beyond being a system of classification (of description), the Transect is an instrument of design (of prescription). The correlation of the various specialized components on a common rural-to-urban continuum provides the basis for a system of zoning that creates complex, contextually appropriate human environments.

There are benefits to such an integrated system of zoning. First, it eradicates the self-referential prescriptions of specialists. Second, each Transect Zone is an immersive environment, a place where all the component elements reinforce each other to create and intensify the character of a specific place. Several such immersive environments within a single neighborhood would attract social diversity, in contrast to the vast homogenous tracts guaranteed by conventional zoning.

The most important contribution of the Transect as an underlying theory may be to implementation. Experience shows that New Urbanist projects are technically difficult to permit. The codes and standards now in place of conventional suburban development, despite their appearance of objectivity, recognize only the conventional monocultures of zoning. Introducing a complex community into such a system is akin to running a new computer application on an incompatible operating system, requiring great effort to create an interface that is destined to never run optimally anyway.

The current dominant theory does not process authentic urbanism. An alternative, based on the Transect, would. The Transect should be neither imposed nor protected, but confirmed through empirical success. With time and the contributions of many representatives of the specialties, it could become as comprehensive as the current standard, as convenient to implement, and it would result in better places to live.

A note on the use of terms: Readers will find varying capitalization of the term "transect" throughout the book. The editors hoped to reduce confusion by using a convention that, when not capitalized, refers to the scientific tool or to a generic application to human habitat, to distinguish it from the specific theory of human settlement known as the Rural-to-Urban Transect. Capitalized as "Transect," the term should be understood as short for that theory.

1. Another reason for the planning profession's incredulity is its refusal to acknowledge the wizard behind the curtain, particularly when the wizard was an architect. This is implausible to them today, at a time when architecture is so trivial. But we all should remember that as late as the 1920s, before the other planning profession came into existence as such, architects were the primary lords of creation.

2. Sym Van Der Ryn, the Urban Ecology Group, and Anne Whiston Spirn are not immune to the old adage, "When the only tool you have is a hammer, every problem looks like a nail." Their propositions tend to the greening of what should be paved urbanism.

3. This, despite being from a current dictionary, is obviously an archaic 18th-century interpretation. Jefferson's, "We hold these truths to be self-evident," is an allusion to natural law. Today, I suppose one would call the Transect "a hypothesis."

4. The Rural-to-Urban Transect has been tested in a score of urban planning projects by the planning firms of DPZ; HOK; Torti Gallas; Dover, Kohl; Placemakers and many others, both in greenfield and infill sites at the scale of the region and the sector. The Transect-based SmartCode includes the integration of pubic works standards as well as a GIS compatibility protocol. The Transect is compatible with other analytical tools, such as William Hillier's Space Syntax. The Center for Applied Transect Studies is coordinating the work of the various specialists interested in building a comprehensive alternate system. It has also been harnessed as an organizing system by the U.S. plan service industry.

Part One:
IMAGES

EXPLAINING THE TRANSECT

This illustration helps explain how the ecological use of the transect was adapted for use in urban design and planning, following a line across a given area and documenting the various elements found in each point along the line. In the early years of the 20th century, the natural transect became the ethical basis of environmentalism, as the "natural law" that certain flora and fauna belonged symbiotically together and within a specific mineral and climactic environment became the legal basis for the protection of species within their habitats.

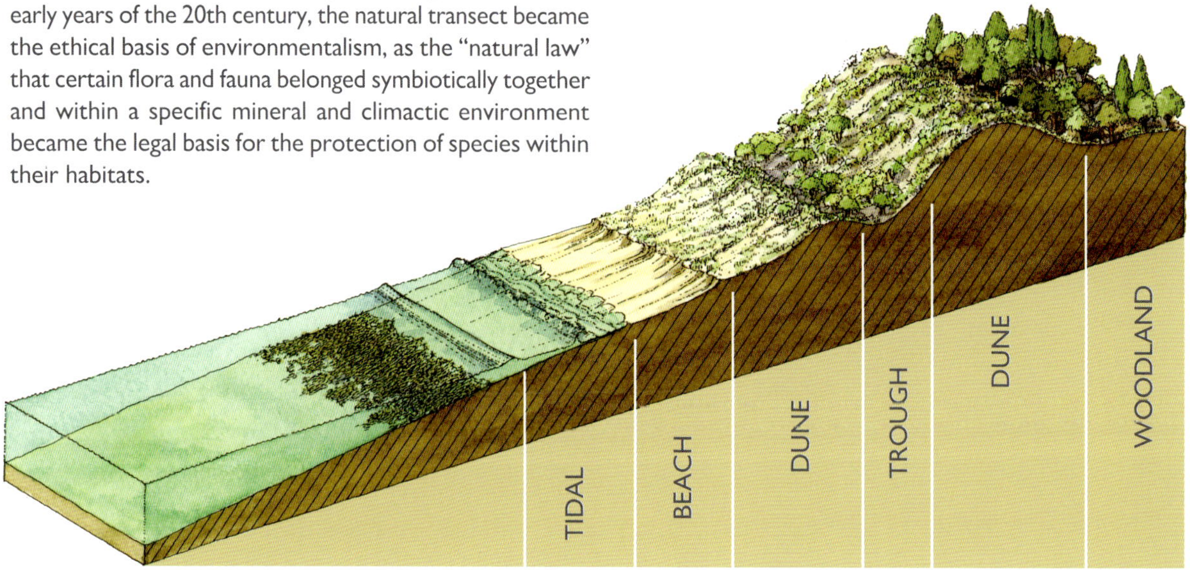

EUSEBIO AZCUÉ FOR DPZ CODESIGN

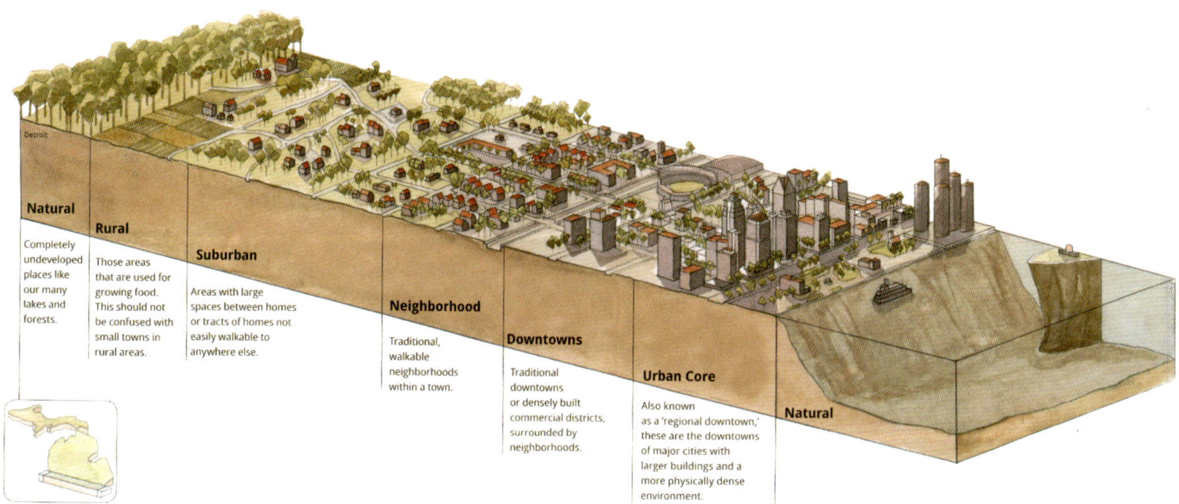

MIPLACE PARTNERSHIP

Similar in framing to the purely natural transect illustrated above, is a complete natural-urban declension representing Detroit. One can see nature at both ends—the gradual feathering to farm and woodland on one side and the abrupt juxtaposition to the river on another. Between them are the typical North American urban habitats. The descriptions for this transect don't correlate in scale to the Rural-to-Urban Transect, as they mix the community scale with the finer-grained T-Zone scale.

DPZ CODESIGN

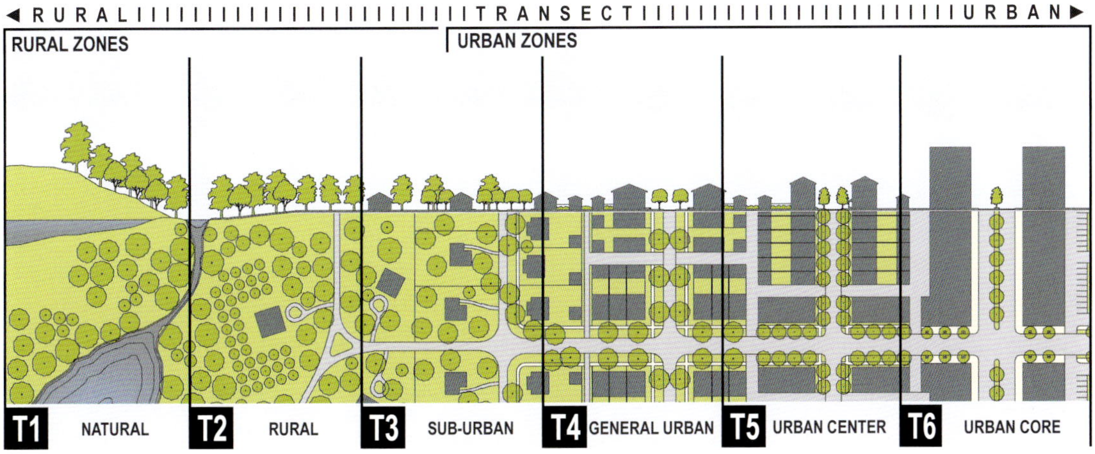

	◄ Rural	Urban ►
PRIVATE	LESS DENSITY	MORE DENSITY
	LARGER BLOCKS	SMALLER BLOCKS
	PRIMARILY RESIDENTIAL	PRIMARILY MIXED-USE
	SMALLER BUILDINGS	LARGER BUILDINGS
	MORE GREENSCAPE	MORE HARDSCAPE
	DETACHED BUILDINGS	ATTACHED BUILDINGS
	ROTATED FRONTAGES	ALIGNED FRONTAGES
	YARDS & PORCHES	STOOPS & SHOPFRONTS
	DEEP SETBACKS	SHALLOW SETBACKS
	ARTICULATED MASSING	SIMPLE MASSING
	WOODEN BUILDINGS	MASONRY BUILDINGS
	GENERALLY PITCHED ROOFS	GENERALLY FLAT ROOFS
	SMALL YARD SIGNS	BUILDING-MOUNTED SIGNAGE
	LIVESTOCK	DOMESTIC ANIMALS
PUBLIC	ROADS & LANES	STREETS & ALLEYS
	NARROW PATHS	WIDE SIDEWALKS
	HIGH L.O.S. STANDARDS	LOW L.O.S. STANDARDS
	OPPORTUNISTIC PARKING	DEDICATED PARKING
	LARGER CURB RADII	SMALLER CURB RADII
	OPEN SWALES	RAISED CURBS
	NIGHT SKY	BRIGHT LIGHTING
	MIXED TREE CLUSTERS	ALIGNED STREET TREES
	MORE SILENCE REQUIRED	MORE NOISE ALLOWED
CIVIC	LOCAL GATHERING PLACES	REGIONAL INSTITUTIONS
	PARKS & GREENS	PLAZAS & SQUARES

This diagram from a SmartCode shows how virtually every physical element that comprises the natural and the cultural environment may be put into parametric order by the Rural-to-Urban Transect. This is a summary of those elements that should be calibrated for code writing. The intention of the SmartCode set of municipal regulations is the avoidance of monocultures (especially functional ones). Virtually everything is allowed everywhere, but controlled by intensity, according to the T-Zone. The module on Agrarian Urbanism is an example of the expansion of a line of this table (see page 82). The descriptions for this Transect don't correlate in scale to the SmartCode Transect, as they mix the community scale with the finer-grain T-Zone scale.

ROBERT ELVES

This aerial photo shows a regional transect of Chicago. It should not be confused with the scale at which the normative Transect is applied, which is a much finer grain. Here we can see T-1 at both the top (lake) and bottom (prairie) of the image, but the vast area in between that looks from this distance to be all T-3 Sub-Urban might contain several Transect Zones per neighborhood when viewed at a lower altitude or from the ground. In fact, there are numerous T-5 Urban Centers scattered throughout the "low" area that cannot be perceived from this distance. Similarly, the downtown Loop area that looks entirely T-6 from a distance also contains T-4, T-5 when you zoom in.

GOOGLE EARTH 2010

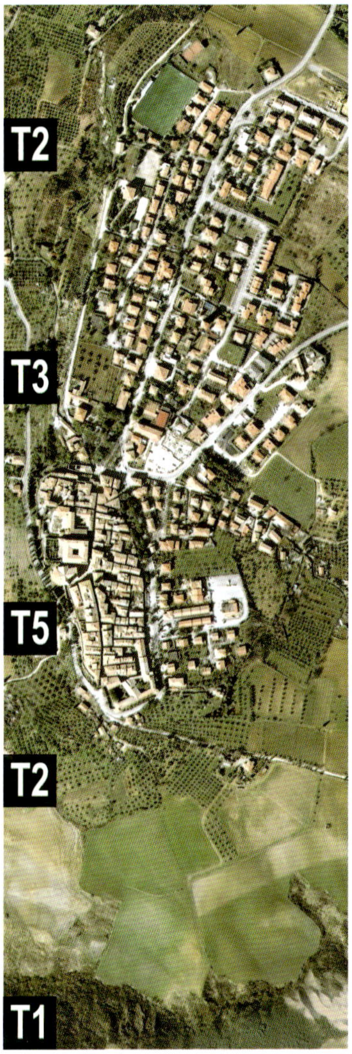

PIENZA

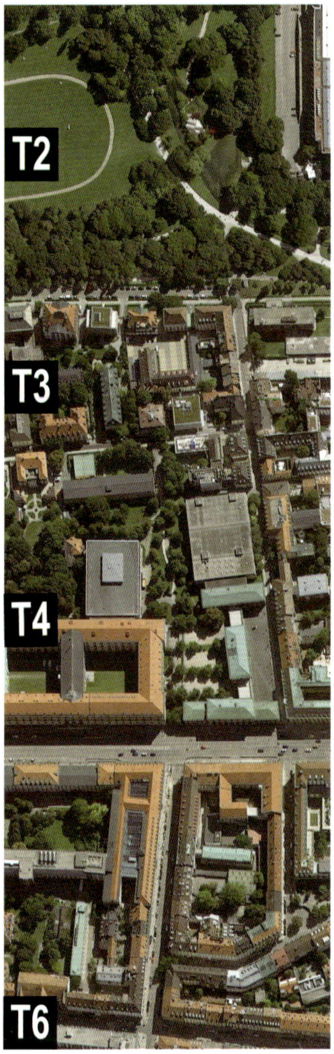

MUNICH

This set demonstrates the potential of aerial photography for the analysis of Transects and for calibration. It is a conventional aerial photograph. The Transect Zones are called out by scrutiny of the photo and synoptic survey on foot. These are extractions selected for their perfect Transects. Taking one street will often provide the classic Transect section, including all T-Zones. Forty blocks is vast enough that the sample strips for each would also include other Transect Zones in a traditional city like Portland. For example, the T-3 area undoubtedly includes some T-4 and T-5. The full Transect of Portland may be experienced in the length of forty blocks shown. Espanola Way on Miami Beach displays all the Transect Zones within a walk of eight blocks.

GOOGLE EARTH 2010

PORTLAND

MIAMI

POUNDBURY

WASHINGTON

GOOGLE EARTH 2010

NEW YORK

ATLANTA

BATH

ROME

These six urban patterns involve only two mosaics of T-Zones—in radical juxtaposition. Poundbury shows a neo-medieval hard edge to the rural—very much a European conception of urbanism within the landscape. New York City shows the obverse: Central Park places the landscape within the city—and has an equally hard edge. Washington, adjacent to Rock Creek Park, is like New York in that the intensity of the urban T-Zones increases approaching the landscape—reflecting the increase in real estate value of the long, green views. Peachtree Street in Atlanta is a declension from most- to least-dense. The intensity of the declension from T-6 to T-3 and T-2 within three blocks is remarkable! These six instances serve to correct a misunderstanding of the explanatory Transect diagram, which is drawn as a declension. The juxtaposition of non-contiguous Transect Zones exemplifies a "mosaic" or a set of "patches" that correspond with the actual urban fabric of most cities.

JORGE PLANAS DPZ CODESIGN

T-1 and T-2

T-2 and T-3

T-3 and T-4

T-4, T-5 and T-6

These fences provide a fine-tuned declension of the Transect discipline at the smallest operational scale. This is an example of just one architectural element, combining a concern for the material, its finish, and its form. They are from the 1920–1930 reconstruction of Williamsburg, Virginia. Since Williamsburg is a lineal "roadtown," the rural edge and the urban main street are within three blocks of each other. These fences thus are found within a very short distance. They provide a lesson in immersive character. Note the syntax: 1. rough-hewn cattle pickets, 2. rough-hewn zig-zag (without joinery), 3. same with joinery, 4. milled but unpainted boards, 5. painted and elaborated boards, 6. turned and dove-tailed lumber, 7. unpainted brick, and 8. painted brick surmounted by wrought iron. Each of these languages is appropriate to its Transect Zone techniques, and if allocated to the wrong one would instantly become kitsch. (Also see the diagrams on page 70.)

DPZ CODESIGN

As an omnivorous taxonomic engine, the Transect not only reconciles the elements of the natural and urban habitats, but it can process all sorts of items, even those as personal and varied as pop culture and clothing. The irreverent Senen Antonio, a partner at DPZ CoDESIGN, created the set above in the early 2000s, when Paris Hilton and Brad Pitt were iconic fashion plates, plotting their outfits according to the Transect Zones. The exercise seems humorous, but it depicts the concept of the Transect in such a way that non-professionals can grasp it. Take, for example, Paris in a bathing suit, appropriate as it is in a T-1 Natural Zone (such as a beach), and then imagine her wearing that in a T-5 Center. Such a wardrobe choice would be out of place. Her T-2 Rural outfit belongs on a farm, and her T-3 Sub-Urban attire might fit on a tennis court. Her translucent dress was surely photographed at a nightclub in T-6. That dress in T-2 would be as inappropriate as overalls and a pitchfork would be at the nightclub.

Even items as specific as footwear can be plotted along the Transect. In Sarasota, Florida, a middle-aged man was asked to pull the shoes out of his closet and place them in the rural-to-urban declension, to demonstrate the Transect's taxonomic power. In only a minute the shoes were placed in a row that everyone present agreed was a clear example. This demonstration was as convincing as a lecture to the skeptics present.

JONO MILLER'S SHOES

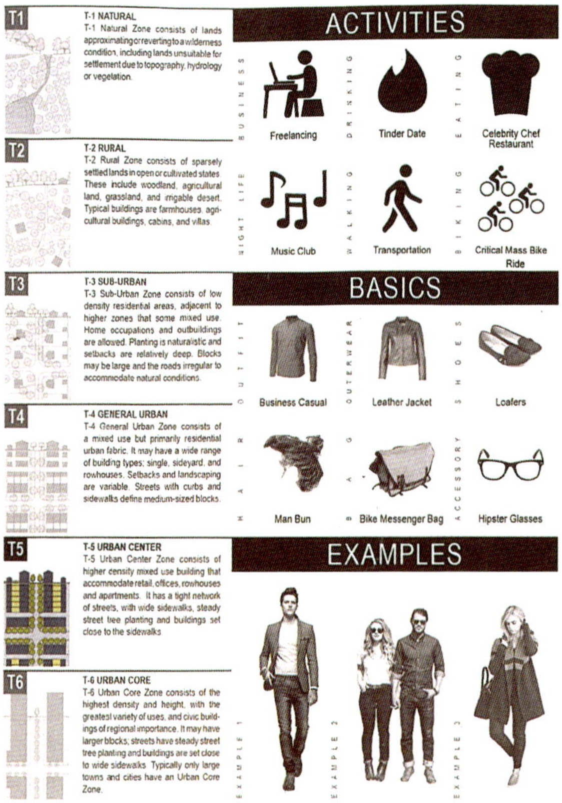

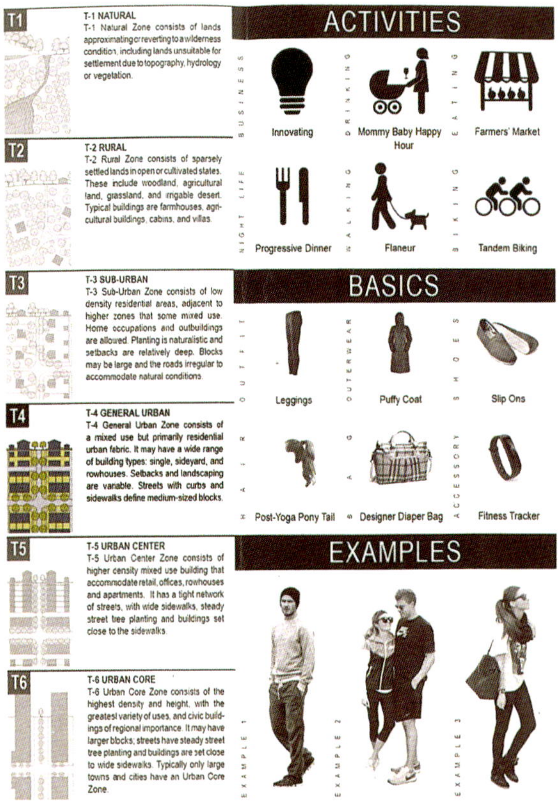

Continuing the use of cultural touchstones to explain the concept of the Transect, an unknown party took the normative Transect diagram, isolated each T-Zone, and added activities and fashion to explain how each immersive habitat compares to the others.

KEITH DUQUETTE, *THE HOUSE BOOK*

DPZ CODESIGN

Apart from the technical aspects that are described throughout these illustrations, there is something about the Transect that can be understood instinctively. The illustration above appears in *The House Book*, written for children by Keith DuQuette. Another children's story that explains the concept is Aesop's fable, "The Town Mouse and the Country Mouse."

To the left is a candid shot of Lyla Khoury, having just sketched a Transect. This is quite an advancement over the usual childhood drawing of a house with door, a window, and a pitched roof with a chimney. SmartCode pioneer Laura Hall once observed in a classroom that when boys were given toys to build a neighborhood, the boys built single towers and monsters, and the girls assembled houses, streets, and blocks.

EVOLUTION OF THE TRANSECT

A

B

C

This transect, taken from a typical countryside, through a village, and onto countryside again, is from a nearly 20-foot-long Chinese scroll. Variations of such illustrations date from as early as the tenth century. This particular version was completed in 1736 by Ch'ing court painters. The rich vernacular depicts scenes of daily life. The first vignette is rustic, evolving by the gradual increase in hu-

A

B

C

NATIONAL PALACE MUSEUM OF TAIPEI

man activity into an urbanism approximating the Transect Zones T-3, T-4, and T-5. A difference from North American urbanism is that the streetline is maintained by walls, with the intensification of density achieved within infill. This implied Rural-to-Uban Transect in Chinese culture supports the idea that the Transect is a cross-cultural and timeless phenomenon: a natural law.

FONDAZIONE MUSEI SENESI

This medieval transect from 1339 is purely binary, without a rural-to-urban declension. The hard edge of fortification forms a hard boundary to be negotiated. The typical medieval city would successionally develop the full set of Transect Zones as the boundary was gradually transcended by growth and safer times. The purity of both the urban and the natural as depicted might well have been the reference to *Good Government* that is the name of this fresco. A companion referring to *Bad Government* has been damaged, but one suspects that it showed ruins within the city and suburban sprawl over the countryside.

PETER H. RAVEN LIBRARY

The first known scientific transect is this illustration of 1860 following the conception of Alexander Von Humboldt of 1793. It is a transect taken across the Chimborazo volcano in Ecuador, based on Humboldt's explorations from the Atlantic to Pacific coasts of South America. This curiously expressionistic document, with its vertical exaggeration, smoke and snowcaps, labels taxonomies on the surface of the earth, beneath the surface (like current New Urbanist "Light Imprint" infrastructure sections), and also, apparently, the atmospheric conditions above. It records only natural phenomena—nothing of human activity appears. That combination will await Patrick Geddes.

PATRICK GEDDES

A century after Humboldt, the Scotsman Patrick Geddes drew the famous "Valley Section," a generic transect taken from a ridgeline to shoreline—what today would be called a "watershed." This is the first transect that associates natural conditions with human presence. In this case, the human relationship to nature is presented in terms exclusively of exploitation—a 19th-century conception. Geddes' transect was pervasive in the education of geographers until the 1970s, when the environmental ethos began to look askance on the human right to exploit nature—despite the agreement on this right uniquely of Darwin *and* the Old Testament, which permeated Geddes' time.

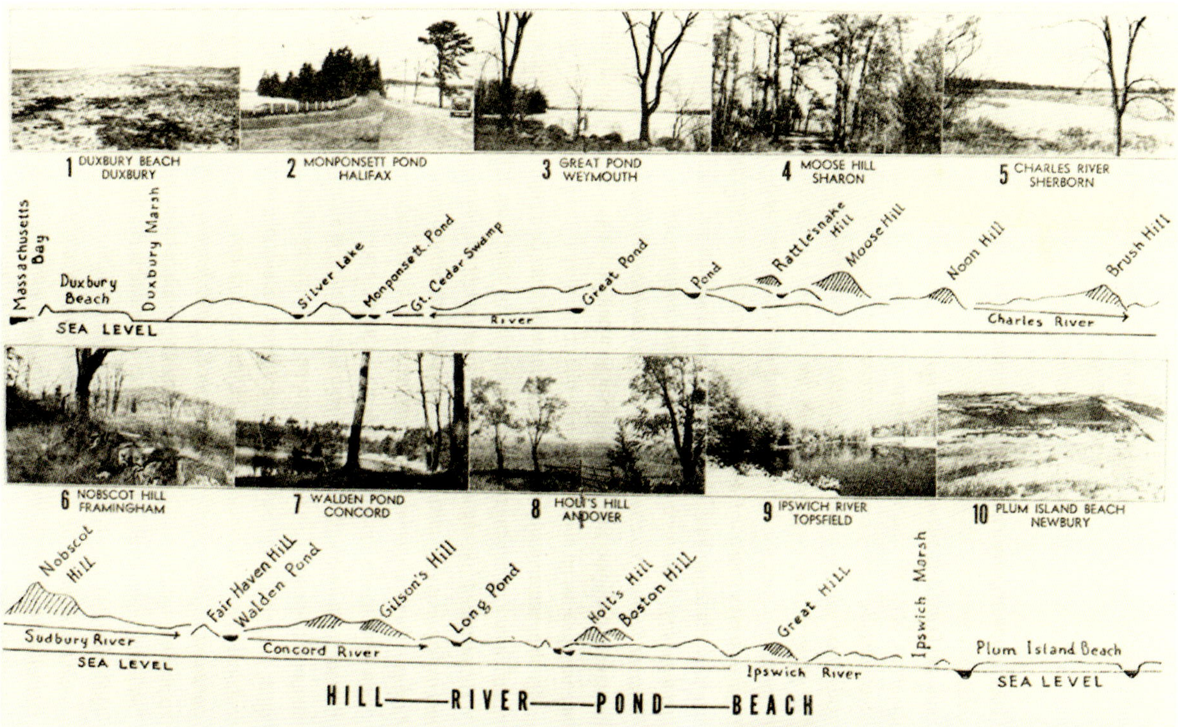

BENTON MACKAYE

This transect, by the American Benton MacKaye, is very typical of the "scientific" or "biological" transect that undertakes to sample exemplary conditions. This shows a series of typical locations in the vicinity of Boston. Prepared in order to establish a regional park system, probably to support Boston's famous Green Necklace. Benton MacKaye was the pioneering environmentalist who conceived and established the Appalachian Trail.

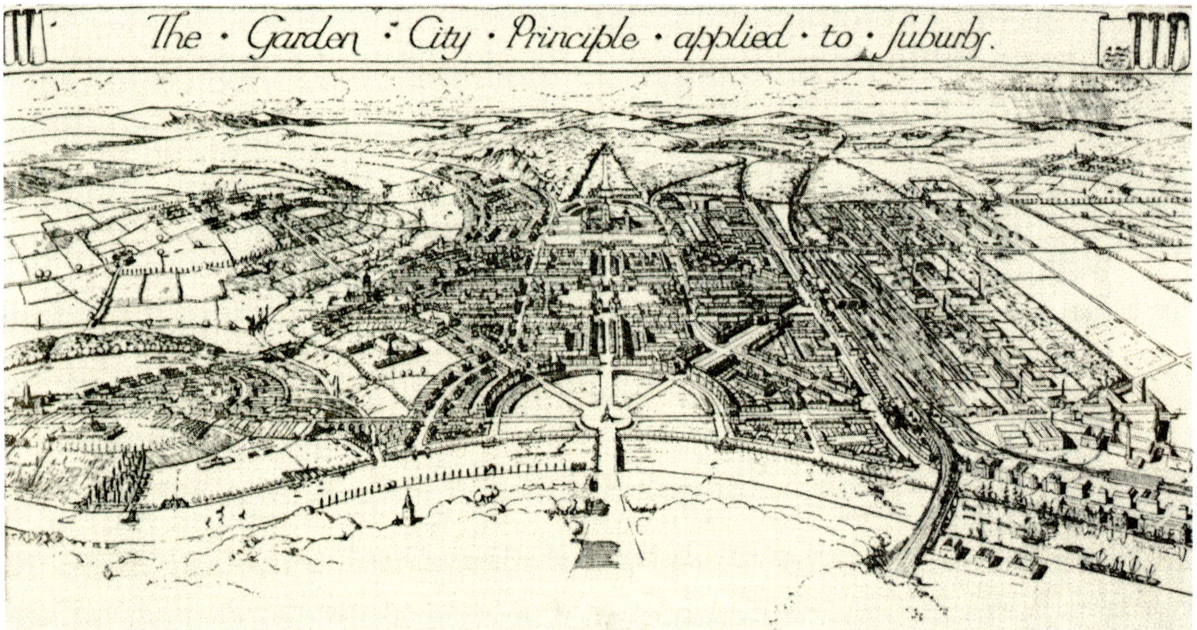

RAYMOND UNWIN

These illustrations of complete cities and towns predate the Transect, but the concept is embedded within them. Both are from the early 1900s. The one on the right is by the Canadian George Clinton Mackenzie, and the one above is by Raymond Unwin, the great designer of Garden Cities. The plan by Mackenzie diagrammatically illustrates the characteristics of a Transect-based urban fabric. The blocks at the bottom of the drawing are rectangular and defined by a continuous perimeter of buildings. This urbanism evolves toward increasingly free-standing buildings and progressively informal geometries of blocks—presumably in response to natural incidents. Such rural-to-urban declensions were commonplace until the disarray permitted by widespread car ownership. The variables of the Transect are illustrated with such clarity that no explanatory text was necessary. McKenzie's North American conception assumes a suburban hinterland in contrast with the hard-edge boundary of Unwin's version. It is one of the propositions of the Garden City model to have a hard edge, bounded by an agricultural greenbelt, and villages appearing beyond. Both have railways, which supply an industrial district: the manufacturing areas on the right of Unwin's drawings and the blocks at the bottom of Mackenzie's.

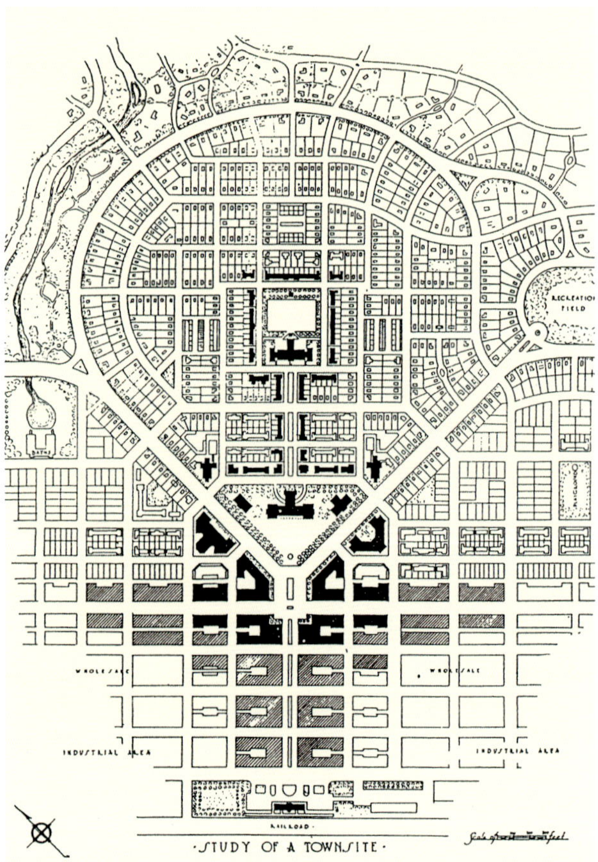

GEORGE CLINTON MACKENZIE, INDUSTRIAL HOUSING

ESSEX COUNTY COUNCIL

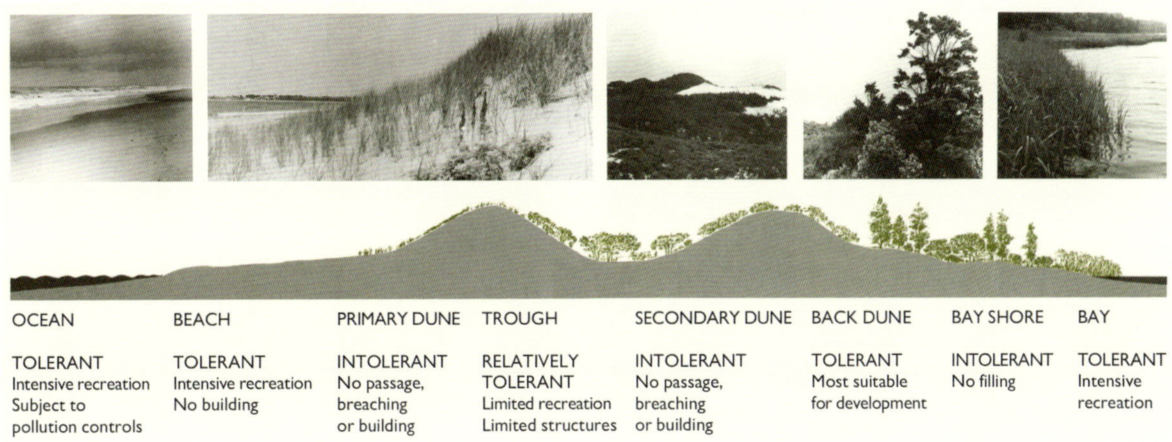

This transect appeared in Ian McHarg's *Design With Nature* of 1963. It is a clear exposition of natural ecological zones. McHarg's brilliant analytical/operational system did not integrate the human habitat. The built form was relegated to wherever nature was least valuable. No proposition for the human habitat was made, so in McHarg's designs, communities would be indistinguishable from suburban sprawl, except for the lush landscaping. In the sense of contempt for the human place in nature, McHarg is a step backward from his fellow Scotsman Geddes' transect a half-century earlier.

ESSEX DESIGN GUIDE

This drawing could be considered the first modern integrated transect of urbanism. It appeared in the *British Essex Design Guide* of the early 1970s. The terminology is rather unsystematic, but it does deploy six zones. This is a strong confirmation of the Rural-to-Urban Transect, which also has six zones, although it is not a precedent, as the New Urbanists did not become aware of its obscure existence until the research for this book was undertaken. An important difference is that the Rural-to-Urban Transect, reflecting normative conditions, does not include habitats that are "unsatisfactory"—instead, the T-3 Sub-Urban Zone is observed as supportive residential patches in compact communities.

METROPOLIS

TOWN

ARCADIA

PARK

INDUSTRY

ARABLE

WILD

GORDON CULLEN, TOWNSCAPE

"We are concerned with the intrinsic quality of the various subdivisions of the environment, and start with the great landscape categories of metropolis, town, arcadia, park, industrial, arable and wild nature. These are the traditional categories and there is no certainty that they will continue to exist in the way we know them. On the other hand whatever the future may hold, one thing appears to be certain and that is the principle of categorization; for without distinction between one thing and another all we get is a form of porridge which will maintain life only if one can refrain from vomiting it up... The critical category is at the bottom: wild nature or hinterland. If there is plenty of this, the old ingrained laissez-faire form of expansion and exploitation causes little concern since the overall balance is still held. But once the hinterland is itself consumed then suddenly a new situation is created. All is thrown back on itself and the expansion of one category can only be achieved at the expense of another. In other words, free action comes to an end, and we are forced to regard the environment as a related complex of activities; just as the universal franchise forced politicians to regard society as a balance of relationships and not a system in which the privileged exploited the unwashed multitude."

Gordon Cullen: The Concise Townscape (1961).

SMITHSON FAMILY COLLECTION

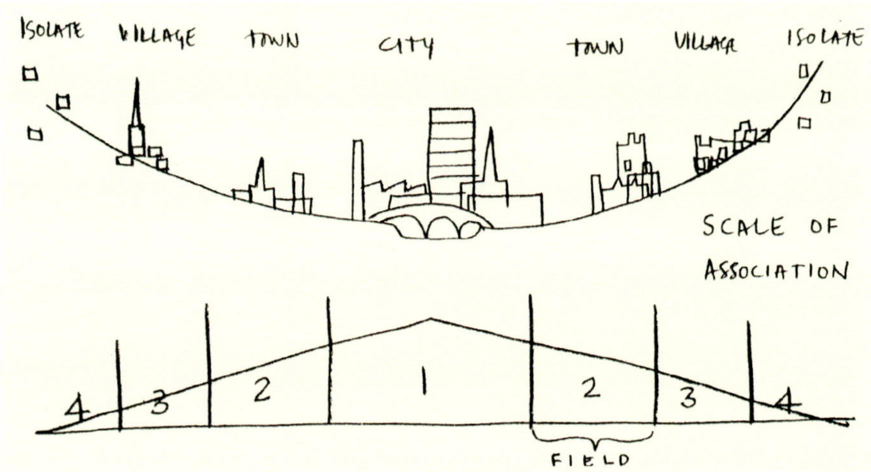

This transect (suffering from the bad graphics in which 1960s architects took perverse pride) is by Peter and Alison Smithson. It was one of the scattershot of diagrams deployed by Team 10 in the reform of Modernist planning by CIAM. CIAM had conceptualized the theoretical basis of zoning and hierarchical, dendritic automobile-based thoroughfares that degenerated into America's suburban sprawl. The fully developed Rural-to-Urban Transect may be considered to correct and complete the Team 10 reform.

CHISTOPHER ALEXANDER ET AL., A PATTERN LANGUAGE

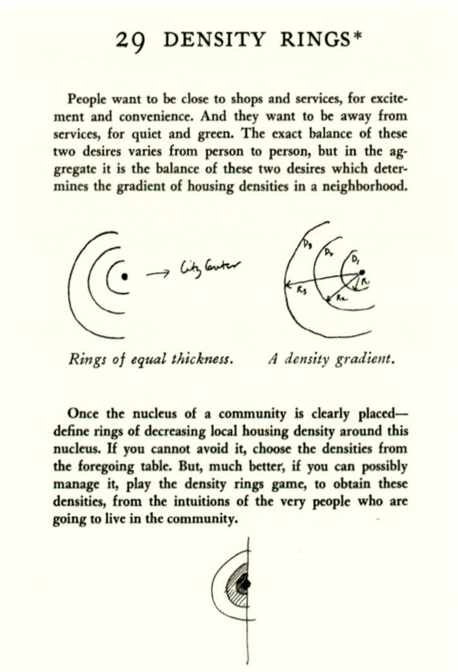

29 DENSITY RINGS*

People want to be close to shops and services, for excitement and convenience. And they want to be away from services, for quiet and green. The exact balance of these two desires varies from person to person, but in the aggregate it is the balance of these two desires which determines the gradient of housing densities in a neighborhood.

Rings of equal thickness. *A density gradient.*

Once the nucleus of a community is clearly placed—define rings of decreasing local housing density around this nucleus. If you cannot avoid it, choose the densities from the foregoing table. But, much better, if you can possibly manage it, play the density rings game, to obtain these densities, from the intuitions of the very people who are going to live in the community.

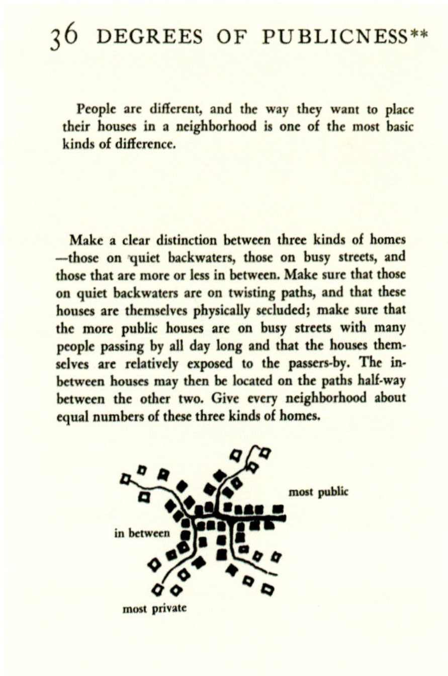

36 DEGREES OF PUBLICNESS**

People are different, and the way they want to place their houses in a neighborhood is one of the most basic kinds of difference.

Make a clear distinction between three kinds of homes—those on quiet backwaters, those on busy streets, and those that are more or less in between. Make sure that those on quiet backwaters are on twisting paths, and that these houses are themselves physically secluded; make sure that the more public houses are on busy streets with many people passing by all day long and that the houses themselves are relatively exposed to the passers-by. The in-between houses may then be located on the paths half-way between the other two. Give every neighborhood about equal numbers of these three kinds of homes.

Christopher Alexander's *A Pattern Language* predates the Rural-to-Urban Transect, so he did not recognize it as a general theory capable of reconciling urbanism and environmentalism. Transects do recur sporadically, however, if not specifically, where they are applicable. For example, they are behind some of the patterns, such as numbers 2, 14, 29, and 36.

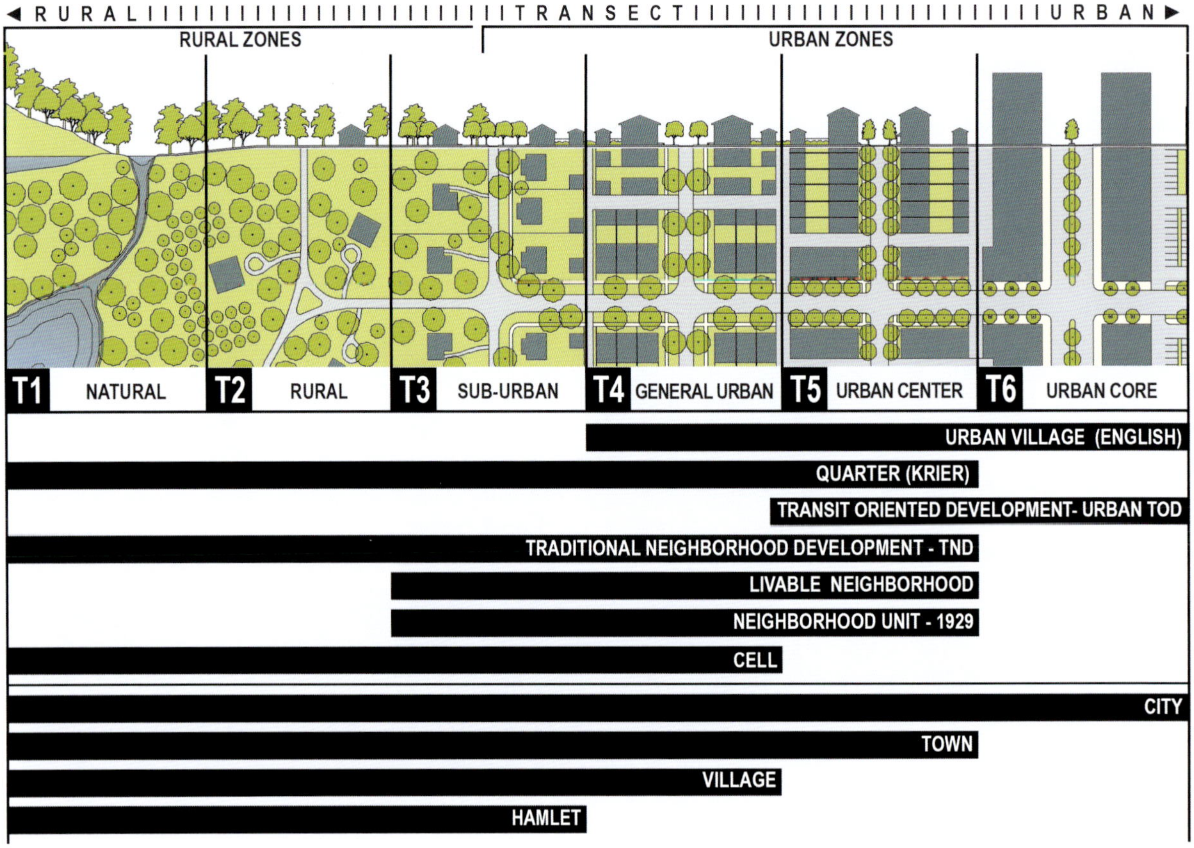

DPZ CODESIGN

Despite a great diversity of terminology, most planning concepts other than single-use zoning take the neighborhood as a model. They have in common being socially and functionally diverse communities that are walkable and manifest an urban gradient from urban center to rural edge. Variations are due to a particular emphasis on density, spatial definition, transportation, or implementation. The above diagram indicates the Transect Zones typically found within the various settlement types listed on the black bars. Neologisms: The Urban Village, formulated by Patrick Geddes early in the 20th century, is used both in the U.K. and Seattle. The Quarter, a transnational European term, was rationalized by Leon Krier. The Neighborhood Unit, the most influential U.S. proposal, was formulated by Clarence Perry in 1929 for the New York Regional Plan. The Cell proposal of Team 10 is influential in the British New Town movement and permeates the English-speaking colonies. Traditional Neighborhood Development (TND), Transit-Oriented Development (TOD)—the latter with its synonym Pedestrian Pocket—and the Australian Livable Neighborhood are New Urbanist models. Traditional Terms: A Hamlet is a neighborhood in the making, standing free in the countryside. By virtue of its location away from transportation, the Hamlet has a weak center. A Village is a complete neighborhood standing free in the countryside. The strong center of a Village can usually be attributed, not to the resident population, but to its location on a transportation corridor. A Town is an assemblage of several neighborhoods, sharing a substantial center. A City is similar to a town in its neighborhood structure but has a core supported by the surrounding region.

ILLUSTRATIVE TRANSECTS

DAN CARY, TREASURE COAST REGIONAL PLANNING COUNCIL

This bas-relief is installed in the office of the Treasure Coast Regional Planning Council in Stuart, Florida. It was carved by the former executive director of the agency, Dan Cary. An early adopter of the Transect, Cary was typical of those in the biological sciences who understood the Transect immediately—unlike the explicit planning professionals, who have more difficulty assimilating the Transect because it is more complex than the function-based zoning categories. The Transect reconciles all the disciplines that may play a part in the design and administration of urbanism—not just the planners.

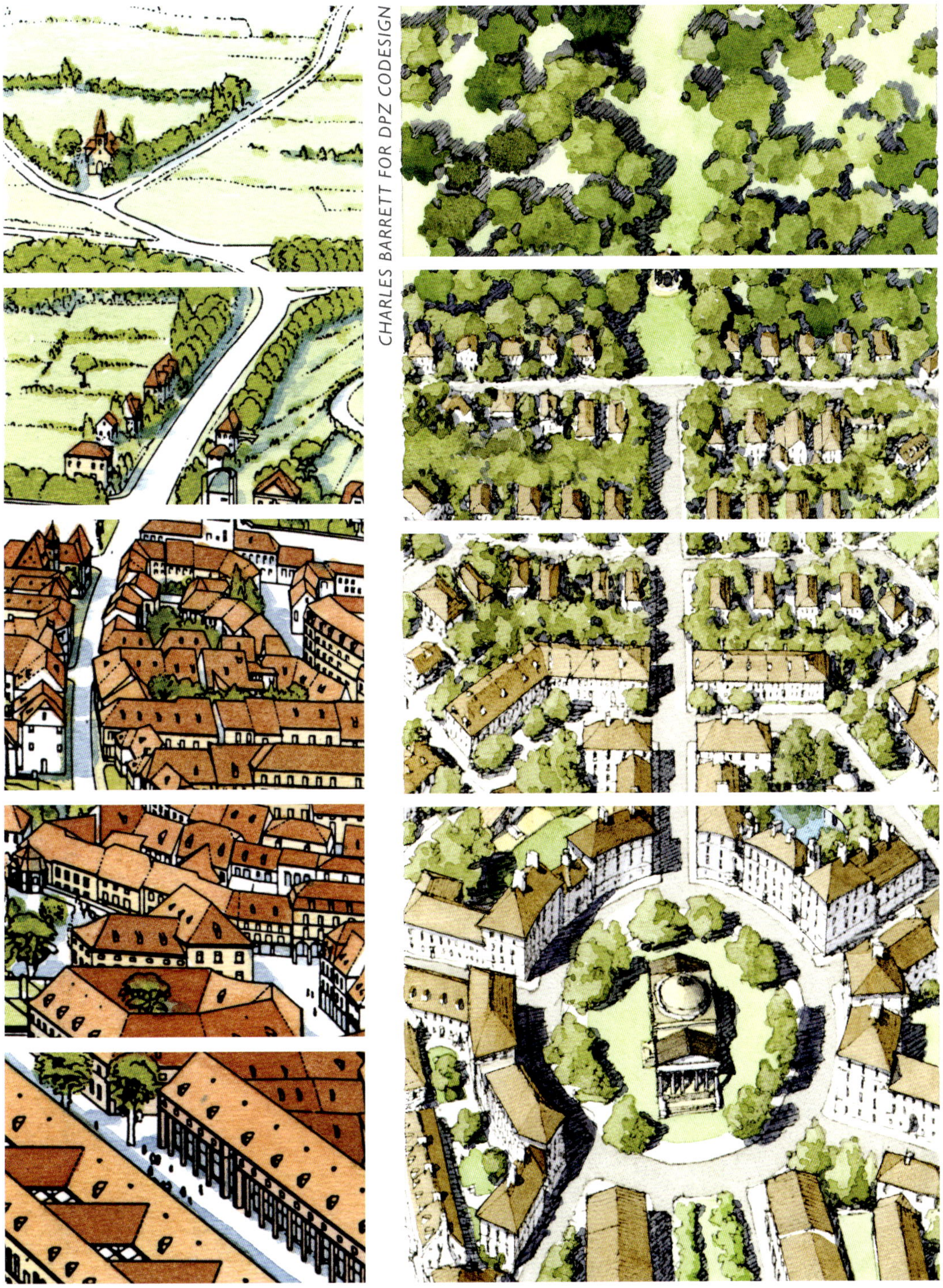

LÉON KRIER

CHARLES BARRETT FOR DPZ CODESIGN

These illustrations both predate the Rural-to-Urban Transect. The first, of Echternach, Luxembourg, is by Léon Krier, and the second, of a village in Annapolis, Maryland, was drawn by Charles Barrett. Each was extracted from a full town drawing to make the implied Transects obvious.

SETH HARRY FOR DPZ CODESIGN

In the 1990s, New Urbanists understood the importance of allocating differing elements of the built environment according to context, and began using the four designations of Neighborhood Edge (1), Neighborhood General (2), Neighborhood Center (3), and Town Center (4). This diagram was created to explain that concept to participants in the collaborative process of design. Unlike most diagrams, which present a continuous declension, this one focuses on typical intersections, giving the idea of "patches," or a mosaic, which is a more accurate reflection of a city. This conception had yet to integrate nature with the urban, which was accomplished when the Rural-to Urban Transect was created soon after.

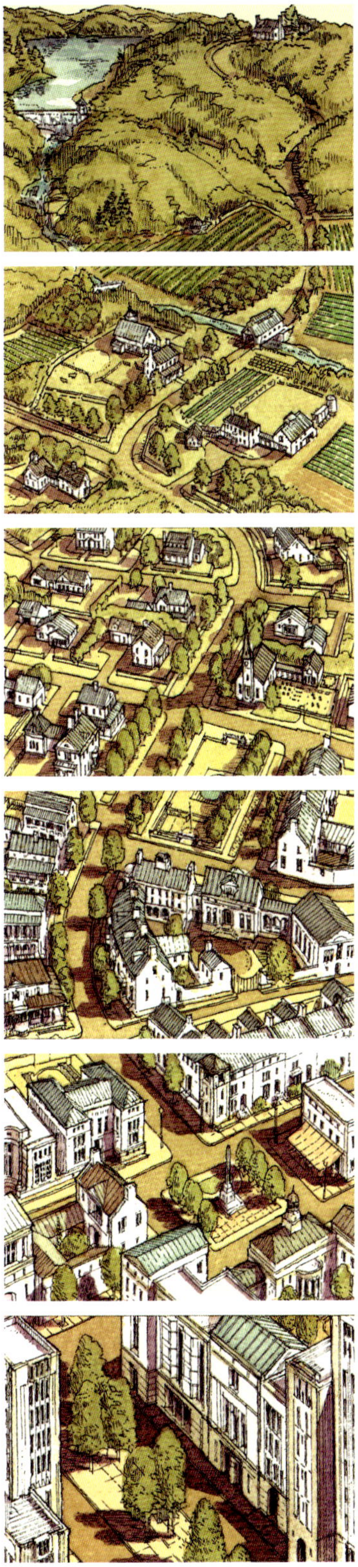

JAMES WASSELL FOR DPZ CODESIGN

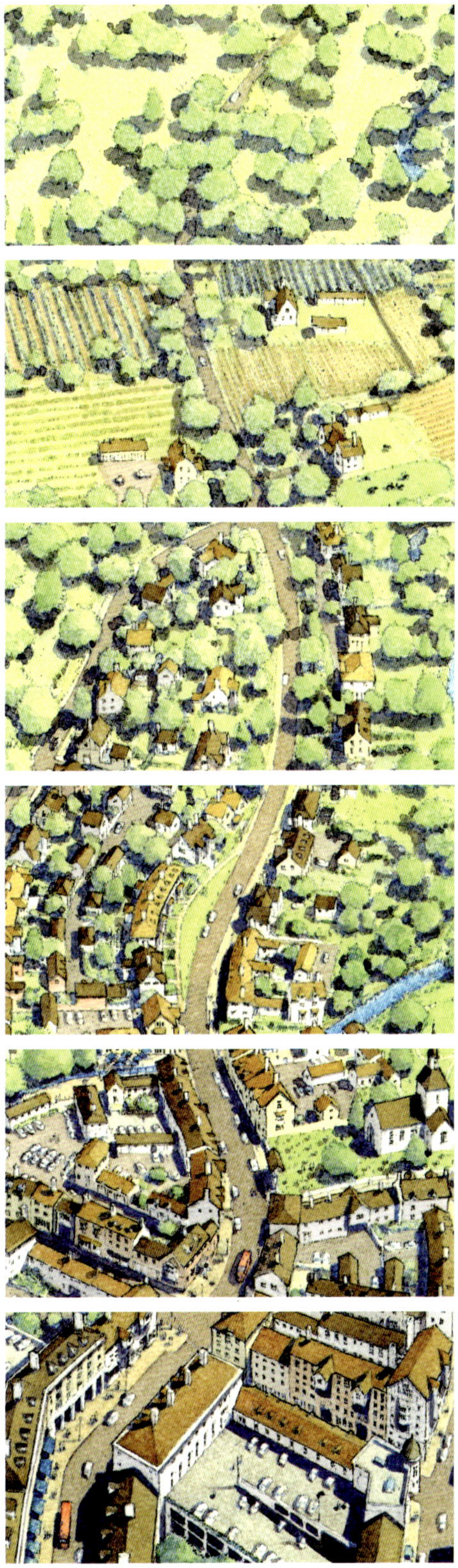

CHRIS RITTER FOR DPZ CODESIGN

Over the years, many hands have illustrated Transects of many places. Heavily inspired by the extract of Krier's Echternach illustration on page 39, they often show winding roads passing through intensifying contexts to represent localized versions of the Rural-to-Urban Transect. The first on the right is one of the earlier Transect illustrations, from the United States, and the second was produced for the county of Hertfordshire in southern England. Both were colored by Eusabio Ascué.

CITY OF BEAUFORT

BRIAN REEVES, ANDREW VON MAUR AND TROY HOMENCHUK FOR ANDREWS UNIVERSITY

The illustration on the left of this page represents the historic coastal city of Beaufort, South Carolina, and the other is for the Abaco Islands in the northern Bahamas. The drawings on the opposite page are episodic, and let slip the urban contiguity of drawings inspired by Krier's Echternacht. In this case, the point of view is not the bird's eye, but closer to the vantage point of the human eye, as was the drawing on page 40. As a result, they are more analytical of architectural and urban design variables rather than the regional scale. The one on the far right represents energy production along the Transect.

JAMES DOHERTY FOR DOVER, KOHL & PARTNERS

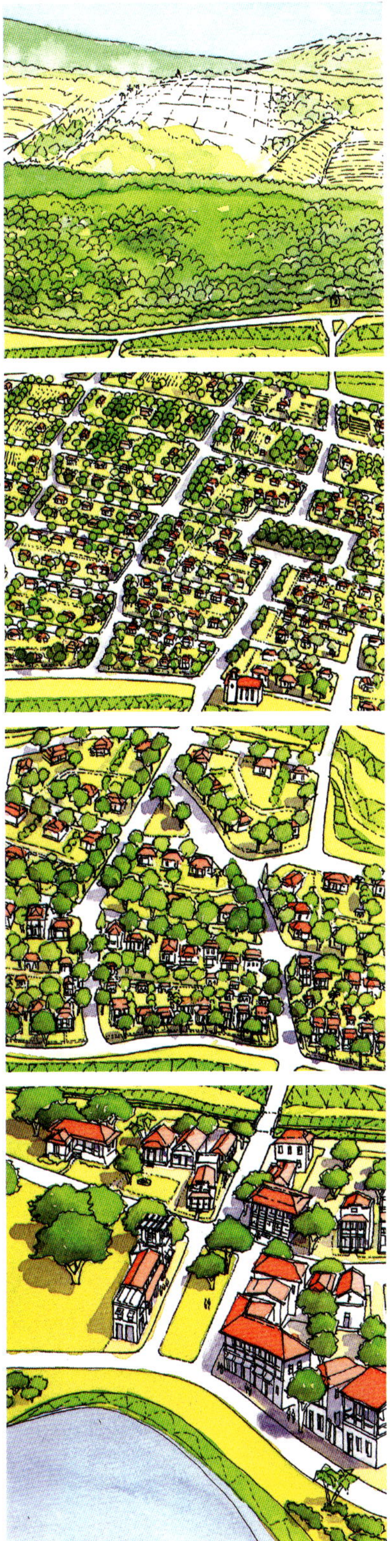

DEDE CHRISTOPHER FOR PLACEMAKERS

DHIRU THADANI

GEOFF DYER FOR PLACEMAKERS

GEOFF DYER FOR PLACEMAKERS

All the illustrations on these two pages were by Geoff Dyer for Placemakers, in the same format as the extract of Krier's Echternacht. They represent widely different places across the United States, but are braced by the constancy of the Transect Zones.

GEOFF DYER FOR PLACEMAKERS

GEOFF DYER FOR PLACEMAKERS

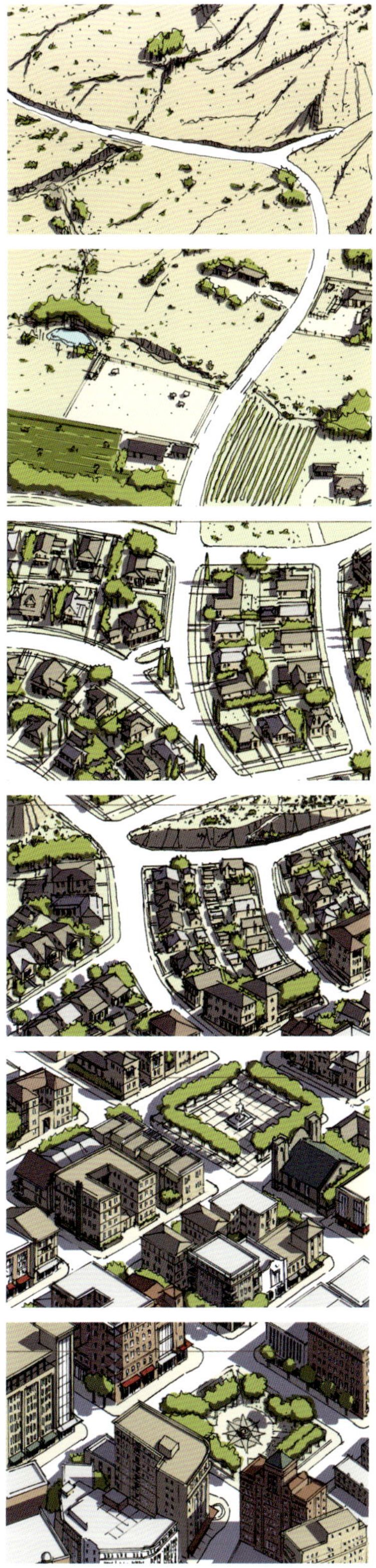

DOVER-KOHL & PARTNERS

MICHAEL MORRISSEY FOR DPZ CODESIGN

These Transect images of Richmond, Virginia, on the left and Sarasota, Florida, on the right are episodic, like those on page 42, one giving the viewer the sense of standing on the street and the other a more romanticized vision of what could be, but both portraying the specific of each distinct, immersive habitat.

ANDREW VON MAUR FOR PLACEMAKERS

This Transect for Thompson's Station, Tennessee, emphasizes the relative quantity of each Transect Zone. From a small T-6 core and progressively greater amount covered by other T-Zones to a very large amount of T-1 open space—which is as it should be.

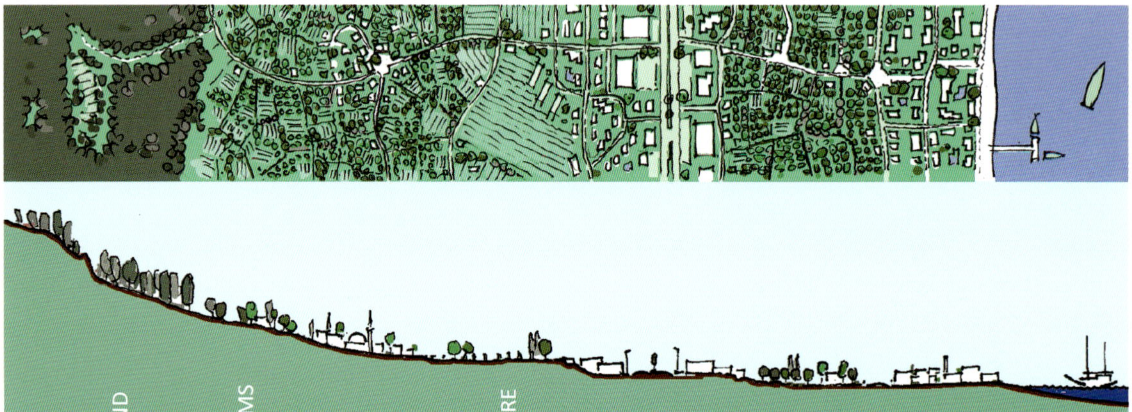

	FOREST LAND	FAMILY FARMS	VILLAGE	LARGER AGRICULTURE	STRIP	GARDENS	SHORE	SEA
CURRENT	• Bee keeping	• Diverse produce • Handcarfts	• Foodcraft (olive oil, wine) • Handcarfts	• Conventional mechanized monoculture	• Retail • Wholesale retail • Small industry	• Diverse organic produce	• Beach tourism • Second homes	• Blue voyage
POTENTIAL	• Passive low impact recreation • History hikes	• Foodcraft • Food and handcraft walks • Farm stays	• Food fairs • Art & craft coops • Color festival • Commissary		• Farm to beach restaurants • Foodcraft centers	• Garden restaurants • Garden shops • Garden hotels • Graden stands	• Food tourism • Food festivals	
MARKETING		• Farm to beach labels and flags • Food passports	• Farm to beach labels, shops and kiosks		• Businesses as CSA members • Farm to beach office, shops and kiosks	• Farm to beach labels and flags • Food passports	• Businesses and second homes as CSA members • Farm to beach shops and kiosks	• Boats as CSA members

KORKUT ONARAN

This Transect, which emphasizes agricultural production, is by Korkut Onaran, who is from both Turkey and Colorado. It is influenced by both mountain countries, as well as by Patrick Geddes' Valley Section. Although not specifically Turkish, the periodic religious towers (and not just the core fabric) indicate it might be in the spirit of the Middle East.

LOCAL TRANSECTS

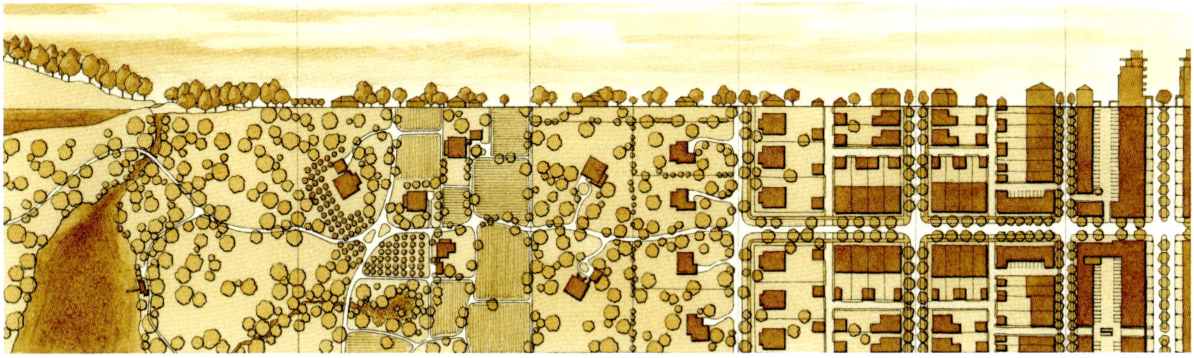

EUSEBIO AZCUÉ FOR DPZ CODESIGN

This Transect diagram is similar to the standard one, but colored in response to the southwestern United States. Most American cities of 1850–1940 are typologically similar, regardless of the region. What sometimes change are the natural setting and the architectural expression.

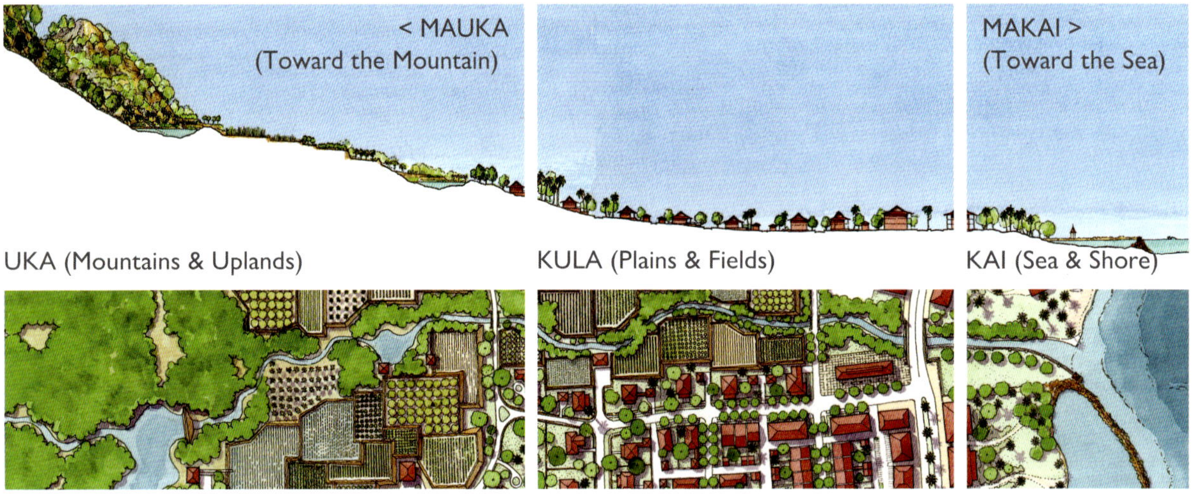

EUSEBIO AZCUÉ & JAMES WASSELL FOR DPZ CODESIGN

This Transect diagram was prepared specifically for Maui, Hawaii. It demonstrates the physical and cultural order for a new town designed by DPZ. The Mauka-Makai concept of orientation and habitation on the land is, in the case of the Hawaiian Islands, not a revival, but a survival. The terms used in this Transect are in current, daily use.

ATELIERS DE LA PENINSULE

A drawing of Luang Prabang, Laos, shows a village on an island within a river. This was conceived as a work to be sold to tourists, but also happens to be an accurate record of a local Transect. It is similar in conception to the scroll on pages 28 and 29, but documents a specific place. Perhaps the Transect is an idiographic code in Asian culture.

EUSEBIO AZCUÉ FOR DPZ CODESIGN

The photograph that underlies this illustration is of Nassau, Bahamas. It shows an immanent Transect before its undermining by modern technocratic systems such as zoning. The colored drawing completes the set, extending it hypothetically to include T-2 Rural. The added sea provides the constant of an island urbanized relative to a shoreline.

DHIRU THADANI

The standardized Transect diagram of the SmartCode is here modified by Dhiru Thadani to reflect the specific building and public spatial character of Washington, DC. Calibration is essential for SmartCodes to avoid stifling local culture—as do conventional zoning ordinances. The accompaniment of local photography is a simple, economical, and highly effective way to illustrate the concept to the public.

DON POWER FOR UNION STUDIO

This illustration of Providence, Rhode Island, is geographically compressed, but otherwise faithful to the natural and built elements at the mouth of the Providence River. It would be instantly recognizable to locals.

DOVER-KOHL & PARTNERS

The Transect above uses "patches" to provide more explicit examples of Fayetteville, Arkansas, and includes an additional T-5 subzone in the sixth position to reflect local conditions. The diagram below of Gabon, Africa, includes three types of views as well as descriptions of context, uses, and building types for each T-Zone.

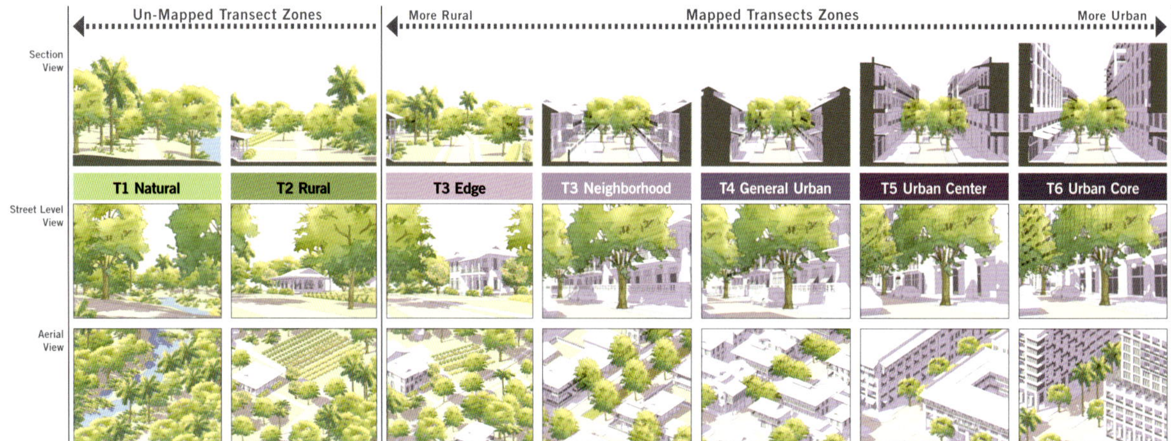

	T1 Natural	T2 Rural	T3 Edge	T3 Neighborhood	T4 General Urban	T5 Urban Center	T6 Urban Core
Description	The T1 Natural Zone consists of lands approximating or reverting to a wilderness condition, including lands unsuitable for settlement due to topography, hydrology or vegetation.	The T2 Rural Zone consists of sparsely settled lands in open or cultivated states. These include woodland, agricultural land, and grassland. Typical buildings are farmhouses and agricultural buildings, plus cabins and villas primarily for vacation homes and eco-tourists.	The T3 Edge Zone consists of large lot, detached buildings located near the edge of the community. Planting is naturalistic. Curbs and sidewalks may be present, but are not required. The street and block layout is non-rectilinear to accommodate topography and natural features.	The T3 Neighborhood Zone consists of small to medium lot, detached buildings. The lots are surrounded by a wall that clearly defines private space and creates a defined edge along the street. Shared streets, or streets with curbs and sidewalks define medium sized-bocks. Planting is more formal. The street and block layout can be rectilinear or non-rectilinear to accommodate topography and natural features.	The T4 General Zone consists of small to medium lot, attached and detached buildings, with little or no front or side setbacks that combine horizontal and vertical mixed uses within this form. The lots are surrounded by a wall that clearly defines private space and creates a defined edge along the street. Shared streets or streets with curbs and sidewalks define small to medium sized walkable blocks. Thoroughfare layout is typically regular, except when addressing topography or natural features.	The T5 Urban Center Zone consists of medium to large lots, primarily attached buildings, with no front setbacks and little or no side setbacks with a vertical mixed uses within this form. The buildings provide a fairly continuous edge along the street with walls defining edges not defined by the building. Streets with wide sidewalks and regular street tree planting define small to medium sized walkable blocks.	The T6 Urban Core consists of large lots, tall, attached buildings, typically with no front or side setbacks with a high intensity of vertical mixed uses within this form. The buildings provide a continuous edge along the street with walls defining edges not defined by the building. Streets with wide sidewalks and regular street tree planting define small to medium sized walkable blocks.
Uses	None	Residential, Agricultural, and Eco-tourism	Residential only; Agricultural permitted as a secondary use on a Residential lot	Residential by Right; Non-Residential by Review	Open	Ground Floor Commercial by Right; Ground Floor Non-Commercial by Review; Upper Floors Open	Ground Floor Commercial by Right; Ground Floor Non-Commercial by Review; Upper Floors Open
Building Types	NA	NA	Cottage Home; Villa Home	Cottage Home, Village Home; Sideyard Home	Flex Building; Sideyard Building; Courtyard Building	Courtyard Building; Mid-Rise Building	Mid-Rise Building; High-Rise Building
Typical Scale	NA	1-2 Stories	1-2 Stories	1-2 Stories	1-3 Stories	2-5 Stories	2-5+ Stories

OPTICOS DESIGN FOR THE PRINCE'S FOUNDATION

OPTICOS DESIGN

Carefully localized Transect images from Kingsburg, California, Flagstaff, Arizona, and Richmond, California, further demonstrate that Transects are political tools as well as technical. People will trust you more to understand their situation if you can draw their place recognizably. For the public process, this provides *the mystique of technique.*

To some extent all Transect drawings are instructive. They edit reality by means of visual abstraction or compression. The three on this page demonstrate different degrees of instructiveness. The first is a section through Pienza that explains everything necessary. It was done quickly and from memory. The second, a laborious diagram of the Transect in Sitges, Spain, illustrates exact instances of the urban fabric, even to the extent that some may identify their own type of house. This, too, is a kind of clarification. The third is an example that clear Transects exist in reality.

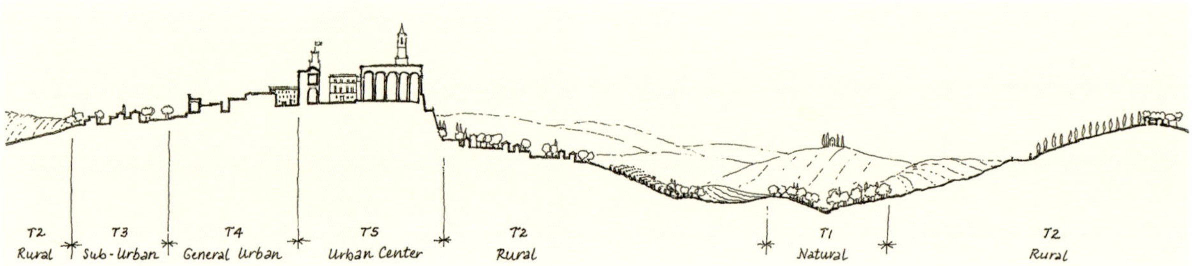

ELIZABETH PLATER-ZYBERK

This quick sketch to explain Pienza to students is by Elizabeth Plater-Zyberk. Note that to the left, the drawing shows smooth transitions from T-2 through to T-5. The right shows the city wall as a radical juxtaposition of T-5 and T-2. Such juxtapositions occur around Central Park in New York City (see page 22).

DHIRU THADANI

T-1 ZONA NATURAL | T-2 ZONA RURAL | T-3 ZONA SUB-URBANA | T-4 ZONA URBANA CENTRAL | T-5 ZONA DE CENTRO URBANO | T-6 ZONA DE CORAZON URBANO

DPZ CODESIGN

Certain towns display such a pronounced clarity of the Transect that a single wide-angle photograph will reveal it. This one is from the large town of Ronda, Spain. Unlike the photographic Transect of Nassau, this one included the natural and rustic zones and therefore did not require a supplementary drawing to complete it.

T-3 PROVIDENCE, RI

T-4 PROVIDENCE, RI

SANDY SORLIEN

T-5 PROVIDENCE, RI

T-6 PROVIDENCE, RI

These photographs comprise a pedestrian's-eye view of the Transect in Providence, Rhode Island, with the original T-4 image flipped horizontally to provide easier comparisons among the T-zones.

SANDY SORLIEN

T-3 NAVADA CITY, CA

T-4 NAVADA CITY, CA

T-5 NAVADA CITY, CA

This pedestrian's-eye view of the Transect was photographed in Nevada City, California. It is a true transect line that can be walked in five minutes, rather than spot-sampling as many Rural-to-Urban Transects are done.

REGIONAL SCALE TRANSECTS

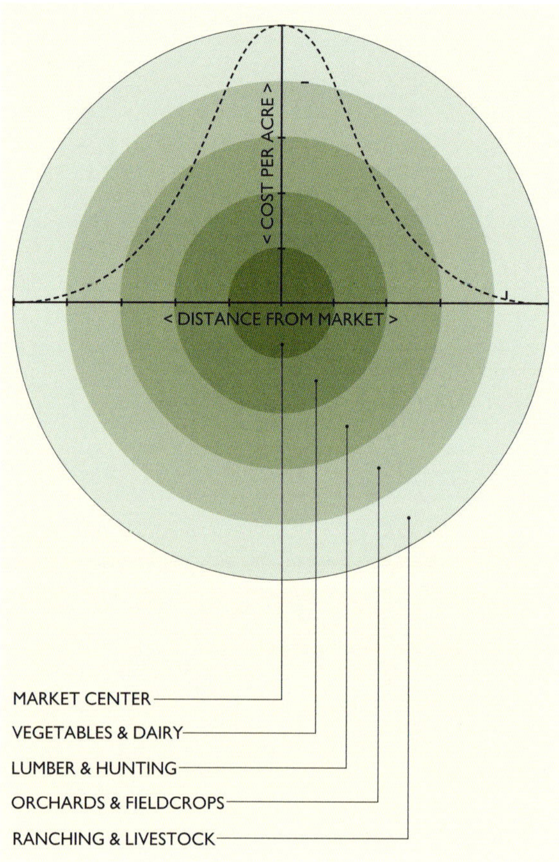

(Left) Johann Heinrich von Thünen was a prominent 19th-century German economist. In *The Isolated State*, he developed the first serious treatment of regional economies. To analyze agricultural land value, von Thünen developed an abstract model of a regional sector with a city market located centrally, surrounded by uninhabited land. Factors such as topography, climate, soil conditions, production costs, and mode of transport were assumed to be constant. The model deployed four concentric rings of agricultural activity. As vegetables and dairy products needed to get to market quickly, they would be produced closest to the city, in the first agricultural ring. Lumber for building and burning, being heavy and difficult to transport, was also grown close to the city, in the second ring. The third ring was reserved for orchards and grain crops, requiring more land to cultivate while being less perishable than vegetables and easier to transport. As livestock could walk to the market, it was assigned to the fourth, farthest ring, and land beyond the fourth ring was wilderness. The entire concept was undermined by the advent of refrigerated transportation. The arguments for maintaining a greenbelt have recently been reformulated to reflect the ascendancy of environmental and social requirements for the retention of open space and to reflect adaptation to the travails of climate change, requiring a dependable agricultural hinterland, assuming that transportation will become less dependable and more expensive, as it was in Von Thünen's time.

The diagram on the right, from *The City* by Robert Park and Ernest Burgess, 1925, depicts a concentric regional transect of Chicago. It is an apparently similar transect—at the metropolitan scale, also physical—but is graded by building type rather than by function or purpose. The urbanity is one great fried egg (or stadtkröne) of a city. This single-point centrality is so rare as to be non-existent. The theory has held up no better than von Thünen's, as it negates the multinodal neighborhood structure.

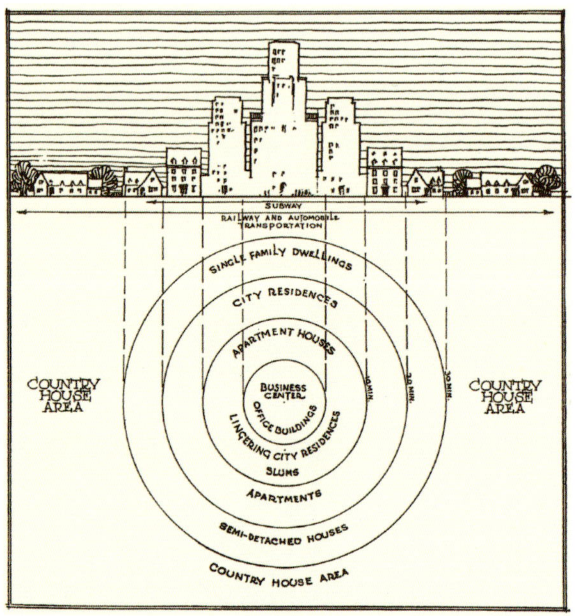

ROBERT PARK & ERNEST BURGESS, THE CITY

ANDREW VON MAUR FOR ANDREWS UNIVERSITY

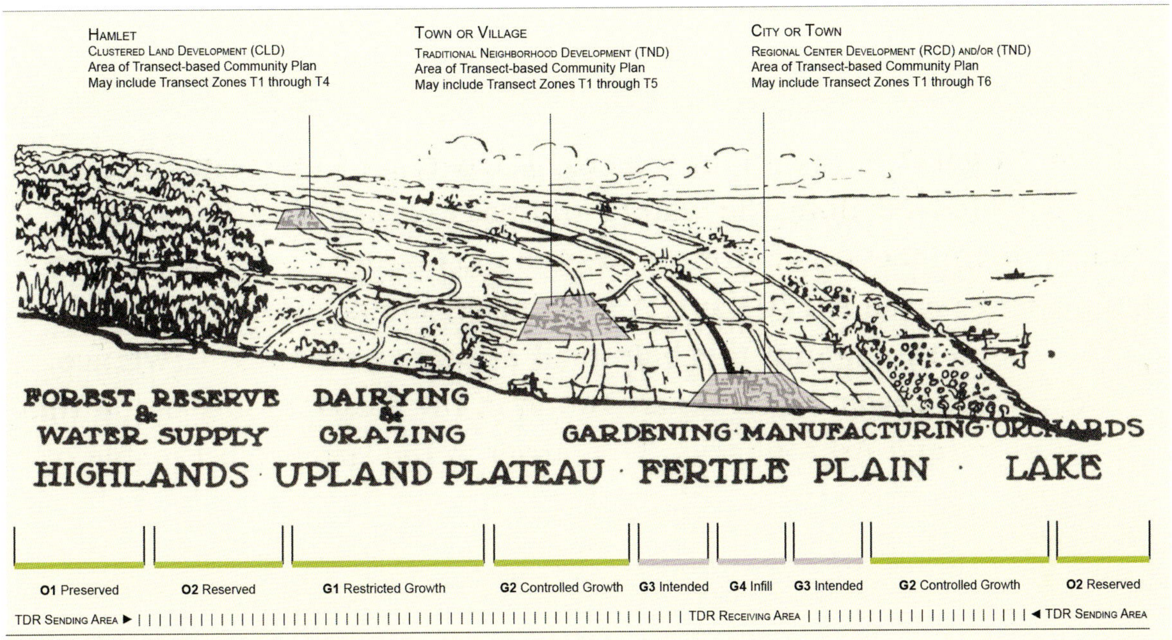

ILLUSTRATIVE DIAGRAM OF A SECTOR-BASED REGIONAL PLAN
APPLIED TO A REGIONAL PLAN FOR WESTERN NEW YORK

Large-scale regional transects may be highly abstract, as shown by the previous two with their concentric circles, but they can also be as detailed as these. The top regional Transect is consistent with the nesting relationship of sectors and community units in the SmartCode. At first glance it looks like the Hawaii Transect on page 50, but the scale is much larger here, as the purple areas represent entire settlements. Only within those settlements would the more urban Transect Zones be observed or applied.

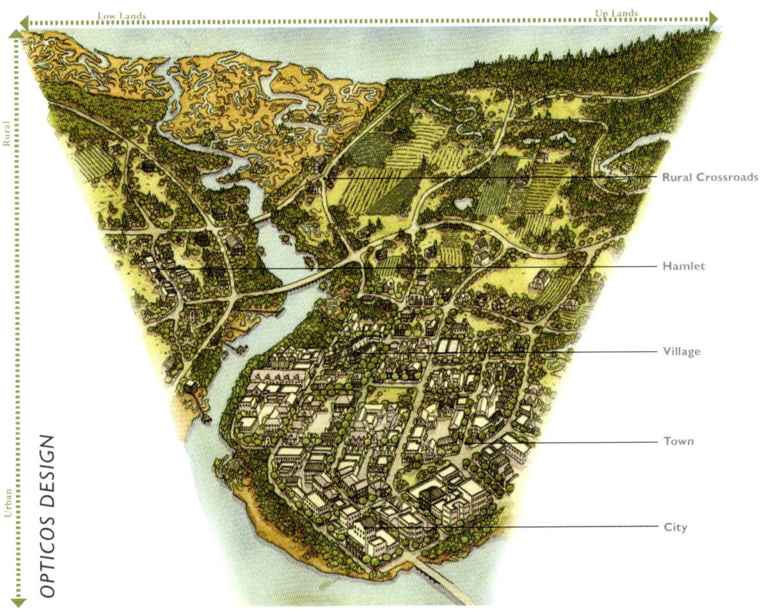

OPTICOS DESIGN

The graphically balanced presence of T-2 and T-1 in some illustrations (including the model Transect diagram) can create the erroneous impression that the urban T-Zones also extend over miles. Rather, as established in the labels for this Beaufort, SC, watershed-scale transect, there would be numerous community types, each containing Transect Zones. The wedge format is instructive to indicate relative land area consumed by different densities of settlement.

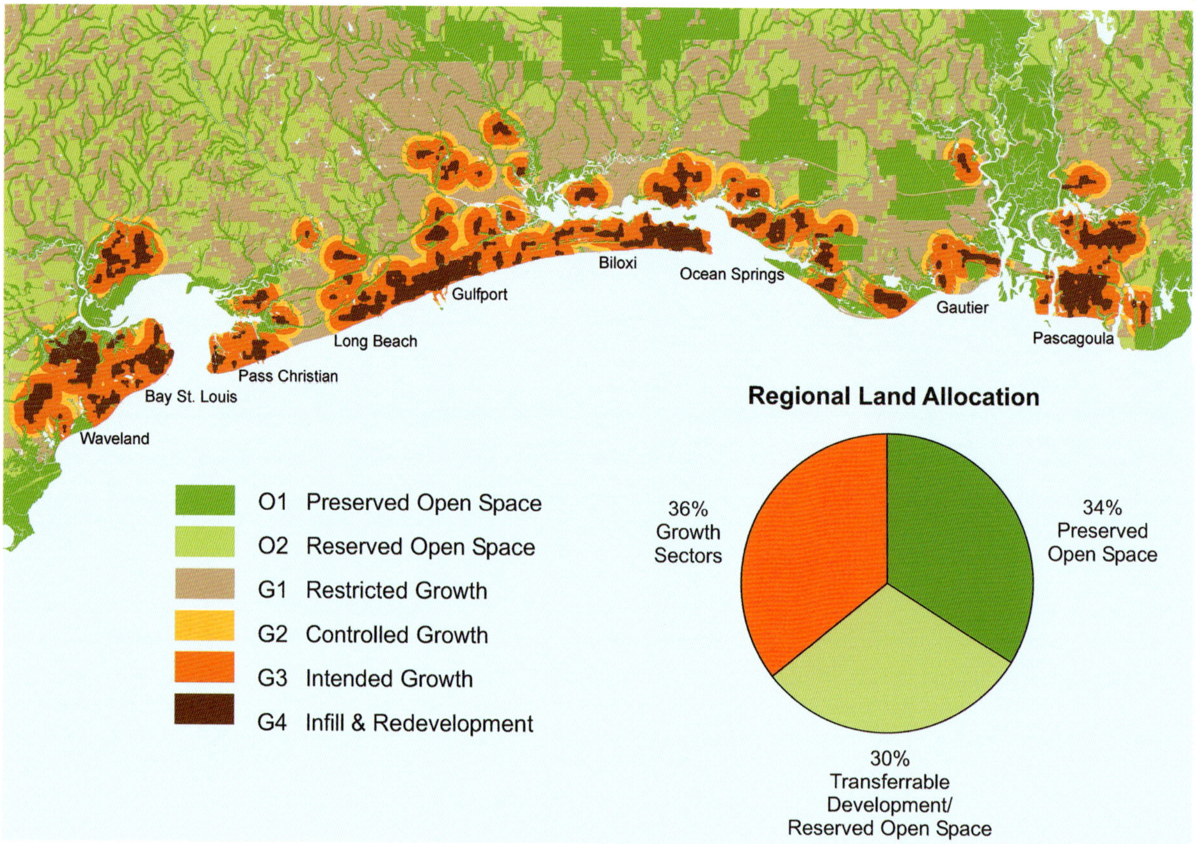

ELIOT ALLEN FOR CRITERION

The Transect may be described as fractal or, perhaps, as nested. It can operate at the scale of architecture (see the fences of Williamsburg); at the most commonly illustrated scale of urban design; and also at the regional scale. Devised by Eliot Allen, the Criterion system of regional analysis is a protocol based on GIS information. It factors the dozens of metrics to determine six regional sectors. This map of the Mississippi coast was prepared in just a few days on an emergency basis for the Katrina charrettes conducted by the CNU. It connected with the Mississippi SmartCode's nested scales: Each of the four Growth Sectors allows certain community types, and each of those communities is made up of different mixes of Transect Zones. Community plans can plug right in.

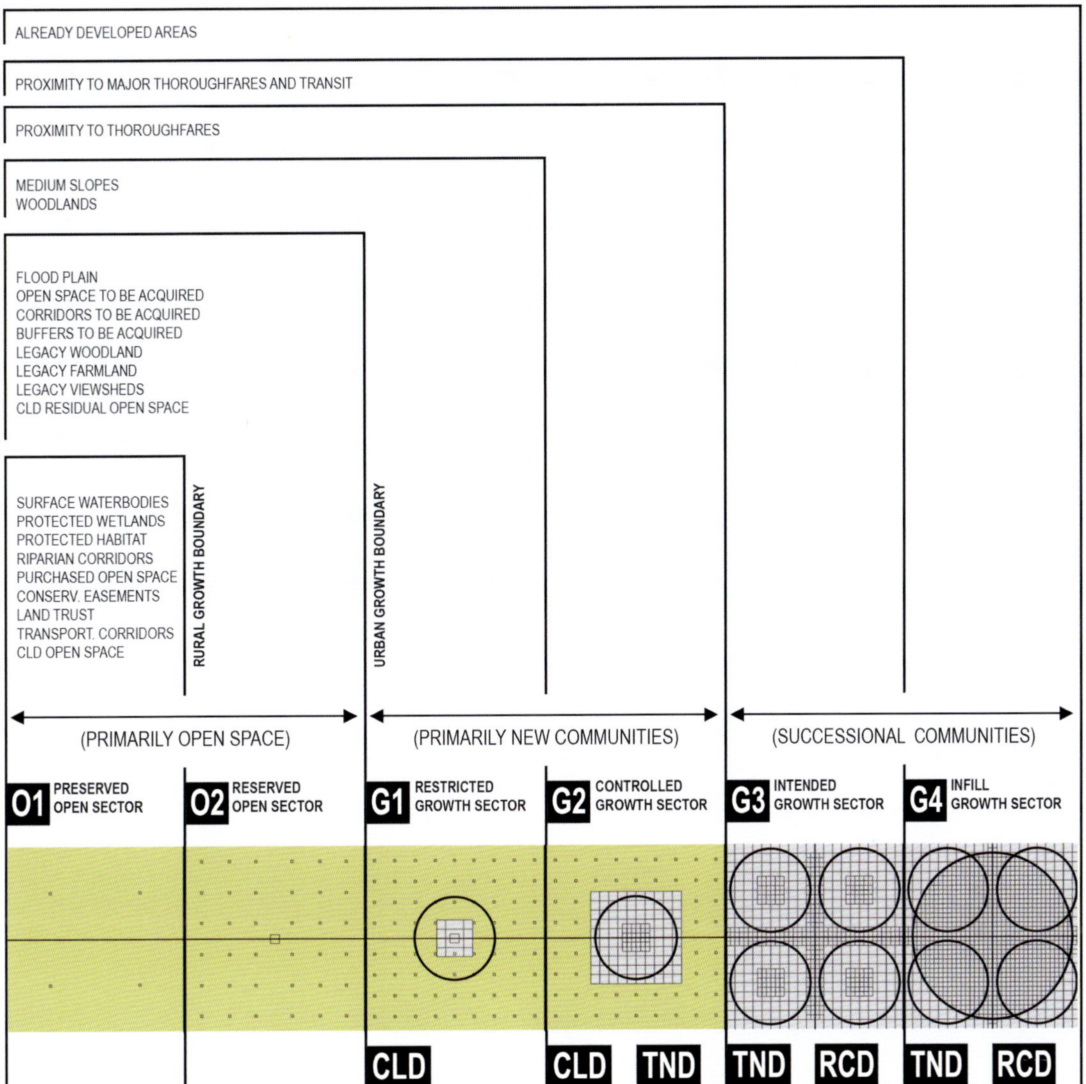

	O1	O2	G1 CLD	G2 CLD	G2 TND	G3 TND	G3 RCD	G4 TND	G4 RCD
T1	NO MINIMUM	NO MINIMUM	50% MIN	50% MIN					
T2	NO MINIMUM	NO MINIMUM			NO MIN	NO MIN			
T3			10 - 30%	10 - 30%	10 - 30%	10 - 30%		VARIABLE	
T4			20 - 40%	20 - 40%	30 - 60%	30 - 60%	10 - 30%	VARIABLE	VARIABLE
T5					10 - 30%	10 - 30%	10 - 30%	VARIABLE	VARIABLE
T6							40 - 80%		VARIABLE

DPZ CODESIGN

This table from the SmartCode parallels the mapping by Eliot Allen on the previous page. The upper half processes G.I.S. criteria to determine future land use (FLU) sectors suitable for preservation, reservation, or development (growth). The lower half allocates appropriate community types for each sector. The communities themselves are constituted from a parametric range of locally calibrated Transect Zones. This flexible protocol is made operational by the legal language in the SmartCode. Municipalities, regional governments, and private developers can each plug into the scale that applies to their situation. For example, if a satisfactory FLU plan already exists, community scale plans can plug in.

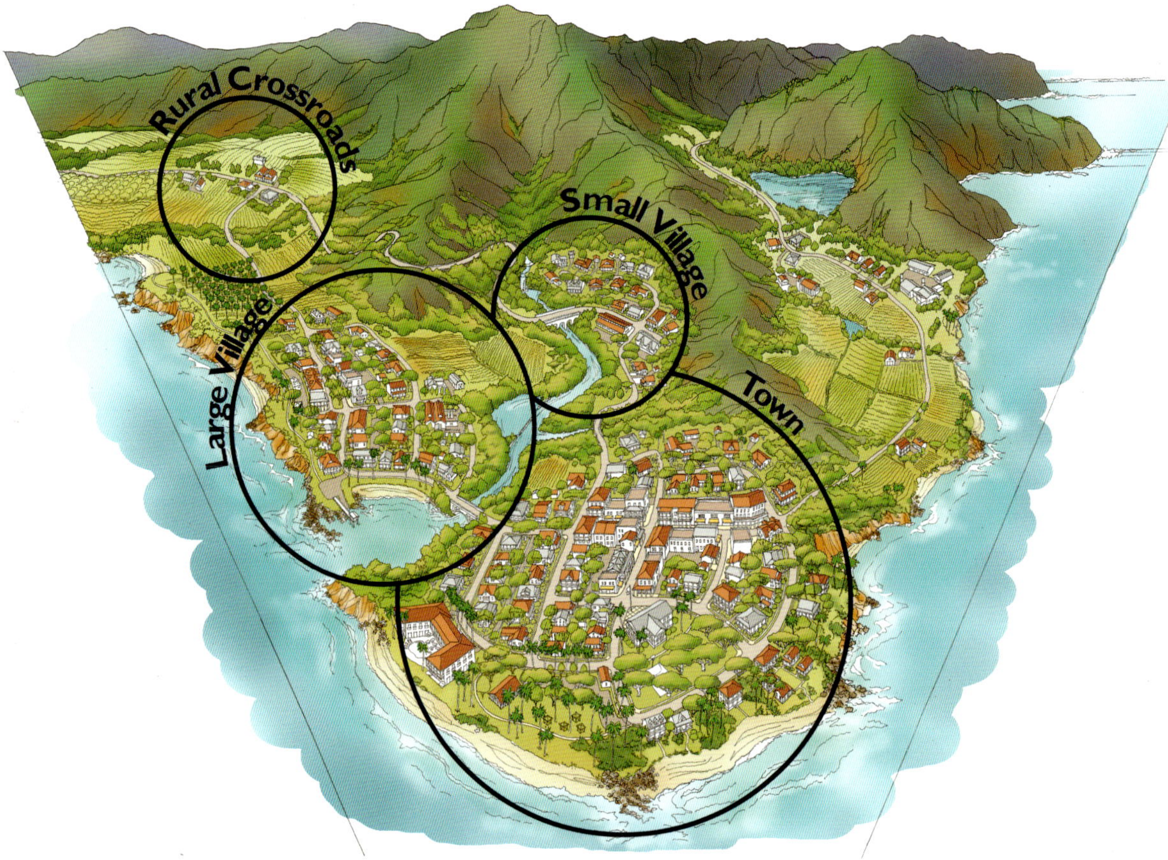

OPTICOS DESIGN

A regional depiction, depending on scale and topography, often creates a range of community types with a declension from urban to rural, as seen here from right to left. This approach is also useful as a political instrument to provide different community types for different types of people. Not only are Transect Zones within the communities providing habitat choice, but the communities themselves provide habitat choice. It shows the different types of thoroughfares, maintaining the constant of the pedestrian shed, and playing off the intensity of the T-Zones.

PETER RICHARDS

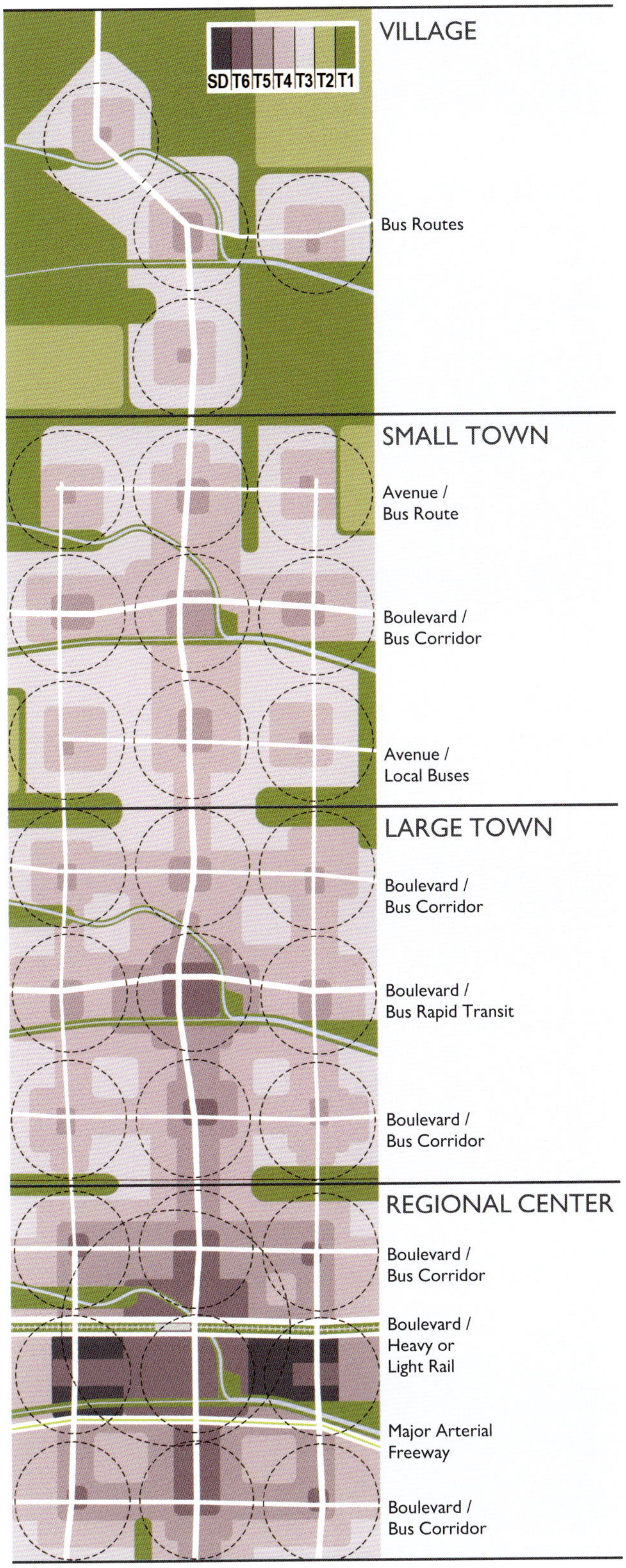

TOM LOW FOR DPZ CODESIGN

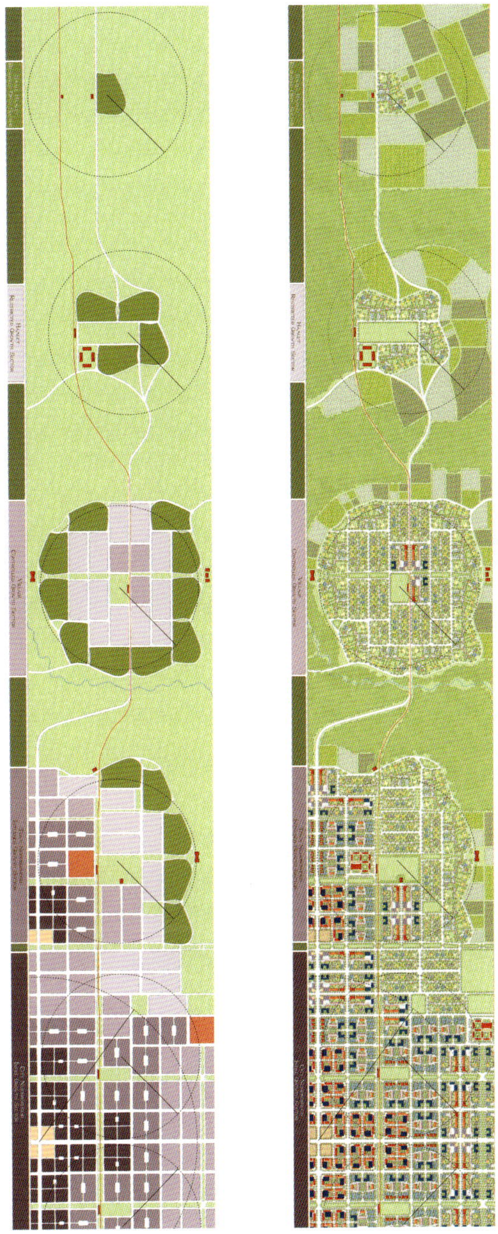

The diagram on the left, by Peter Richards, is a hypothetical model of the SmartCode regional protocol applied to Australia. It assembles community types along a regional transect, increasing by the intensity of the settlement. The circles are ¼-mile-radius pedestrian sheds. The colors are keyed to the six Transect Zones that make up the communities or serve them. Also shown is the connecting transportation infrastructure. The Tom Low diagrams on the right are similar in scale and concern, with more open space.

URBAN DESIGN TRANSECTS

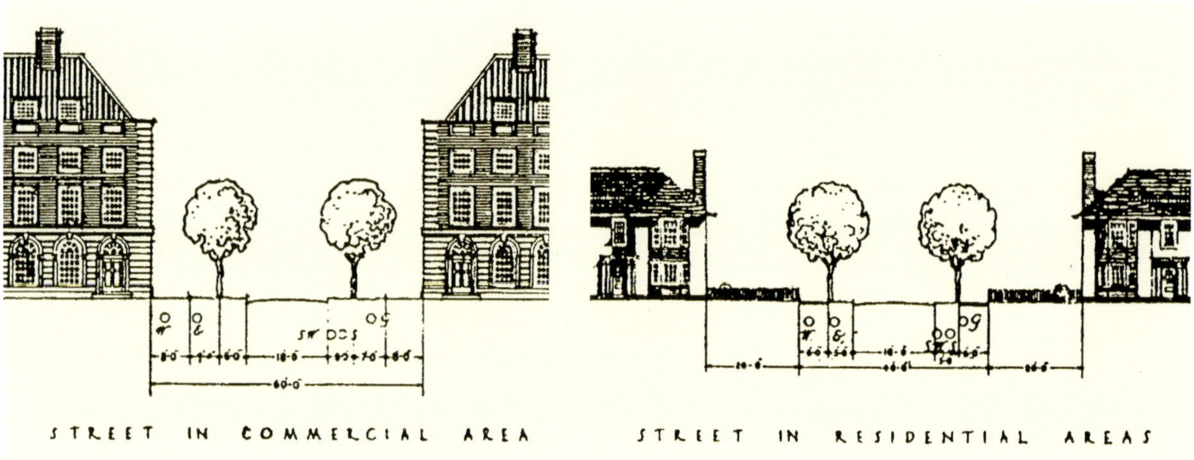

JM DENT & SONS LTD

At the architectural scale, an overlap of transect technique may exist between building *syntax* (style) and building *type* as it occupies its allotment of land. The two above are street sections from British Garden City practice—in this case Welwyn. The public and the private realm are drawn simultaneously, as was standard practice. There is more than a hint of the intended commercial and residential architectural syntax

The drawing below is from one of the excellent Stalin-era manuals on urbanism. In this case there is no architectural syntax, only evidence of a declension of building spacing, building setback, and building frontage width. The location of the trees remains unaccountably diagrammatic—but their heights are correlated along with the building height—the reverse of standard Western practice, where the trees are usually larger toward the rural end, the lost American Elm main streets notwithstanding.

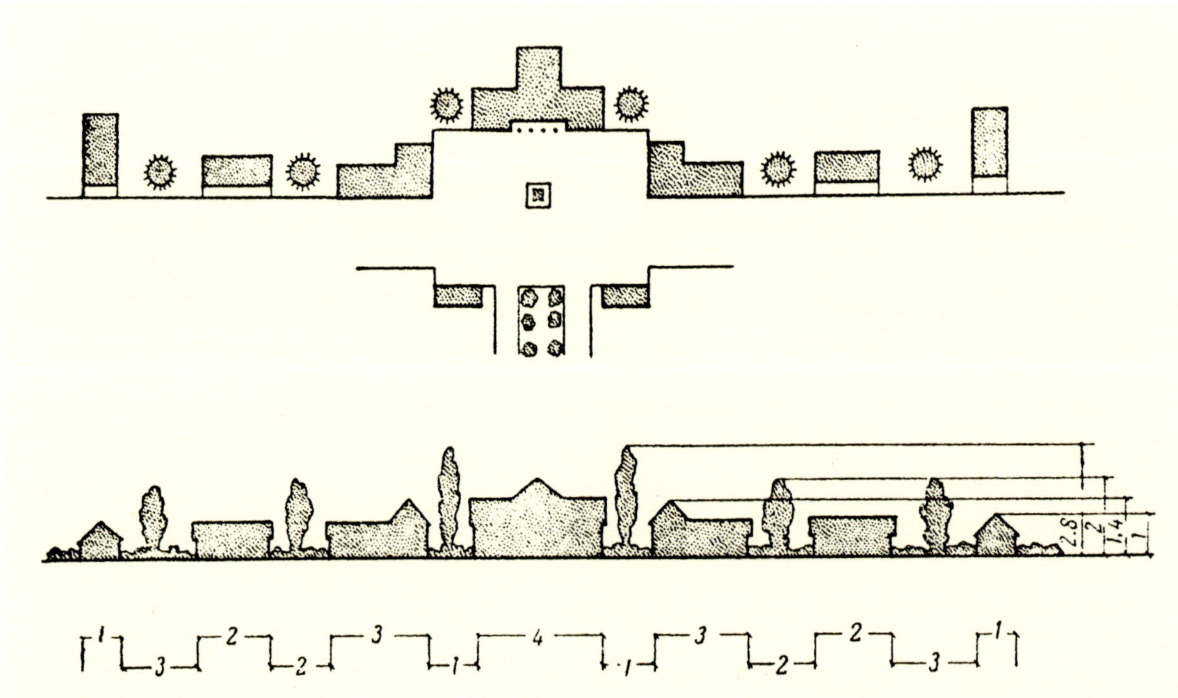

SELHOZGIZ, THE PLANNING OF RURAL SETTLEMENTS

GIBSON WORSHAM

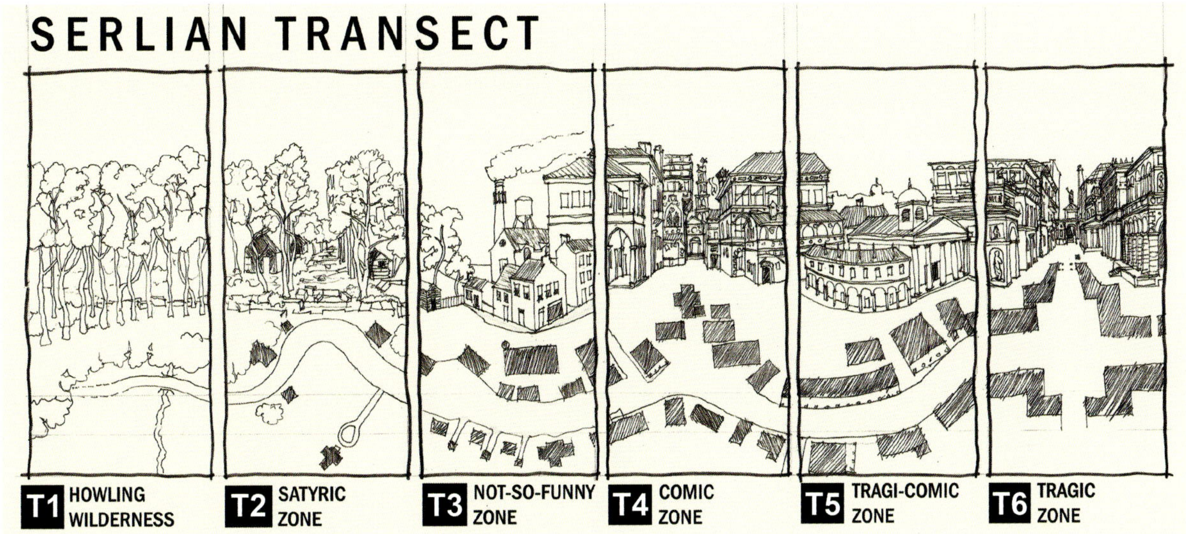

This skillful and tongue-in-cheek sketch adapts the Vitruvian and Serlian theatrical scenes (see page 70) to place them on a comedic and rural-to-urban gradient.

PORPHYRIOS ASSOCIATES

Note the declension of architectural character in these three pavilions. The one on the right, while appropriately rustic, is less so than the two on the left. Even within the narrow range of the rural, it is remarkably rich. In search of a reason to decide on design syntax, a transect sampling can provide a basis that is more intelligible to the uninitiated in architectural theory than is the designer's personal preference.

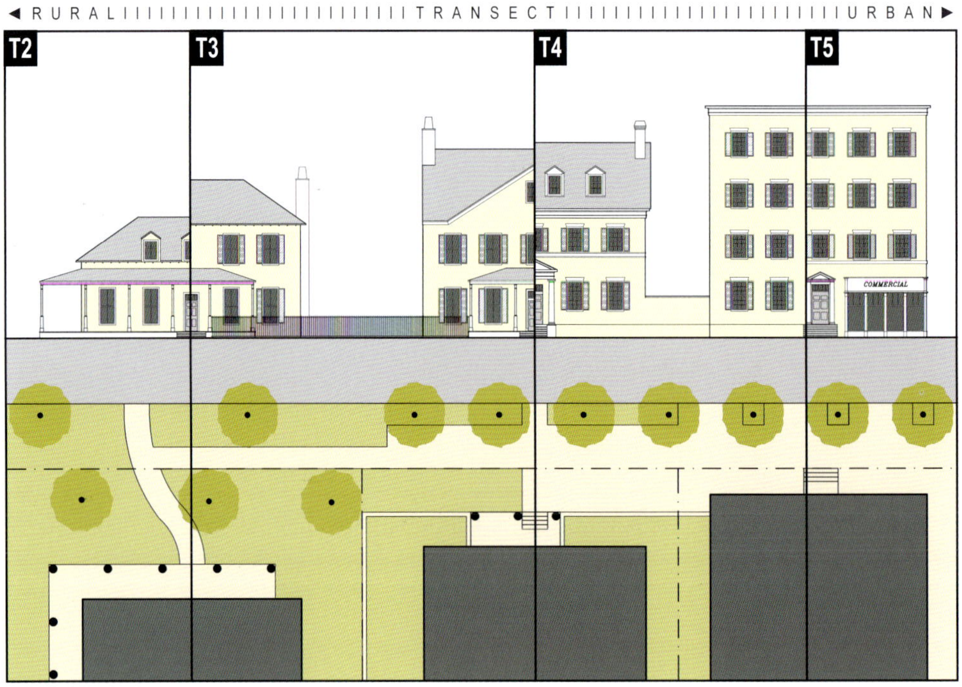

DPZ CODESIGN

The illustrative Transect above combines public and private frontages, particularly refinements of architectural articulation. Among the more obvious variables of height and setback are the variations of floor elevation and elements such as shopfronts, stoops, porches, and roof type. The drawing below by Charles Barrett predates the Rural-to-Urban Transect, but illustrates how the same elements contribute to an immersive habitat.

CHARLES BARRETT FOR DPZ CODESIGN

EUSEBIO AZCUÉ FOR DPZ CODESIGN

This binary illustration of a river setting shows its rural T-1 and T-2 context and its urban T-5 and T-6 variant. This is an educational drawing prepared to convince the public that a waterway should alter in section—from riparian corridor to embankment—according to its context. This is in contradiction to Landscape Urbanist theory, which maintains the ideology that the natural trumps all else in hydrology. For an extended discusson of this phenomenal misapprehension, see *Landscape Urbanism and its Discontents* by Duany and Talen, 2013. While localized basement flooding or combined sewer overflows may call for more natural filtration and retention in urban zones, walkable cities like Philadelphia have installed green stormwater infrastructure (GSI) that respects context by not clipping pedestrian connections or deepening setbacks. For sprawl repair, GSI can help calm traffic if designed as stormwater bumpouts or median swales where thoroughfares are too wide. (See page 95.)

SEBASTIANO SERLIO, *LIBRO PRIMO DI ACHITETTURA*

RURAL

URBAN

CIVIC

These well known "theatrical" scenes were drawn in the Renaissance treatise of Sebastiano Serlio, as illustrations of a Roman text by Vitruvius. They have received over the centuries a variety of interpretations. "There are three levels in the language of architecture; one may be called Civic, the second, Urban, and the third, Rural. Their variation of syntax and vocabulary express differences in character. The character of the civic core is achieved by means of columns, pediments, ornament, and elements aspiring to institutions. Urban character expresses private dwellings, with ordinary balconies, fenestration, and such elements. Sub-Urban character is a vernacular derived from unrefined, natural, rustic elements of landscape."
– Re-translated by Andrés Duany in 2013 as a prescription for a Transect-based architectural language.

KARL FRIEDRICH SCHINKEL, *LEBENSWERK*

LEON KRIER, *THE ARCHITECTURE OF COMMUNITY*

The Classical language for bearing and spanning known as "The Orders" also falls along a rural-to-urban gradient. These were explored under a transect discipline by Karl Friedrick Schinkel in his unpublished treatise (*Das Architektonische Lehrbuch*, circa 1840). From upper left to lower right, the stone order progressively changes from the most rustic to the most refined condition. It evolved much more than the Vitruvius/Serlio. The drawing to the right is Léon Krier's architectural lesson for the Transect: primitive to cultured, rural to urban, vernacular to classical, wood to stone, etc. The language is differentiated in all these regards. This expression is achieved within the lineage of the Ionic Order.

SPECIALIZED TRANSECTS

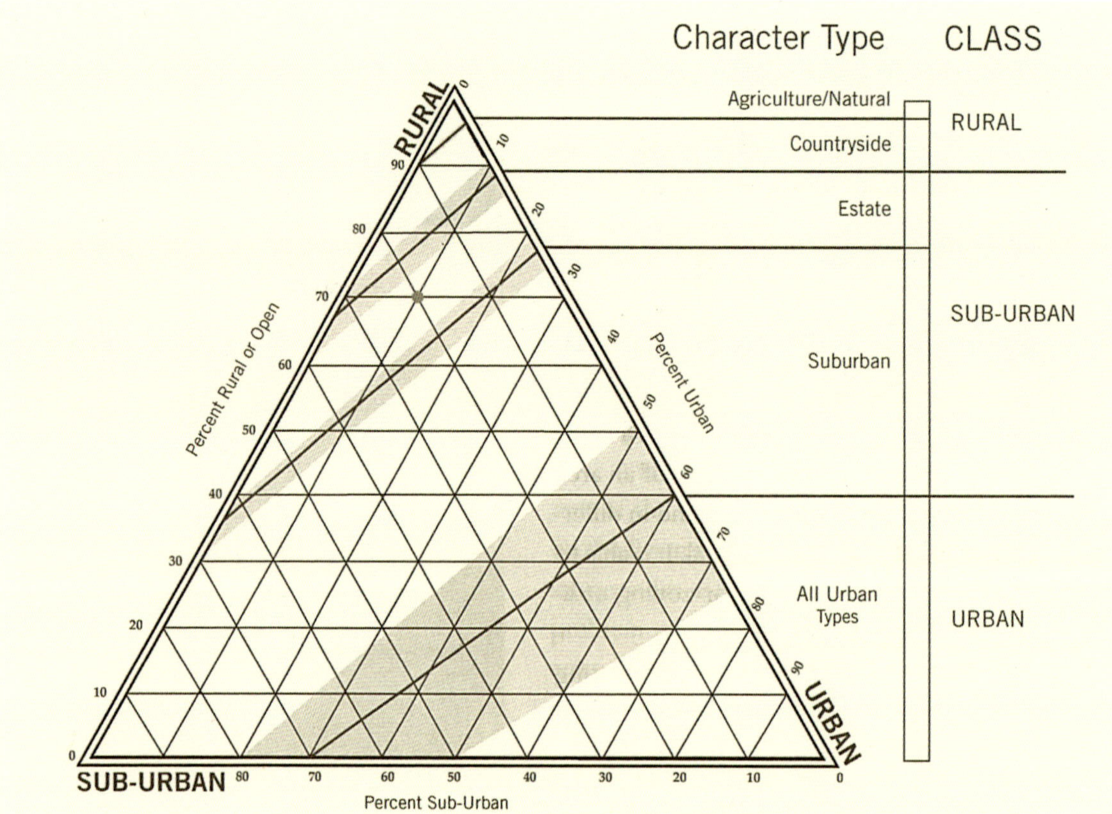

Community character diagram. Dot shows an area 70% rural, 20% sub-urban, and 10% urban.

Lane Kendig became influential in the 1970s with his "Performance Zoning," the general concept of which was sound if in distinct contrast to the precision of the form-based code. Its failure to take hold was possibly due to the excessive discretion it required of regulators, without providing a principle on which to base decisions. In his recent work, he has provided the principle in the form of "Character Types," which is similar to the Transect. It is perhaps not that the Transect influenced Kendig as much as the immanent logic of a rural-to-urban declension.

Before

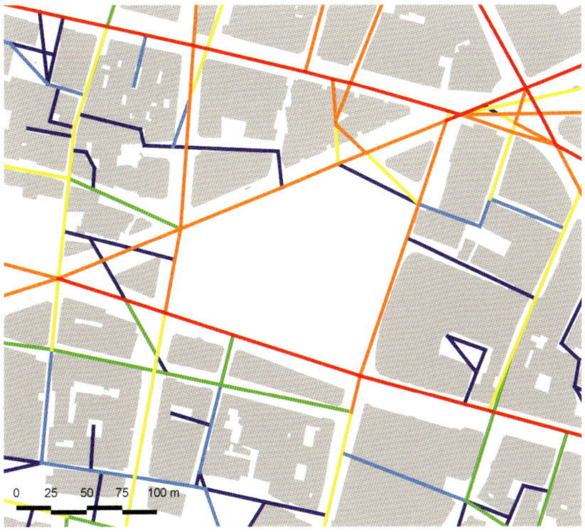

After

SPACE SYNTAX LIMITED

The Space Syntax analysis, which examines connectivity and the commercial intensity of thoroughfares in the images above, may also serve as an analytical tool for evidence of existing Transects. The higher the T-Zone, for example, the higher the degree of connectivity. The grid "glows" red where there is high connectivity and is blue where there is less. This happens to coincide with the networks found in most urban transects—even with the dendritic thoroughfare system of suburban sprawl. This can be verified by looking at an aerial photograph of Nantucket (below) that shows small blocks toward the town center (T-5) on the right and larger blocks eventually becoming the sparse network of country roads (T-3, T-2). The Space Syntax analysis, which is computerized, can be a fast first step in the calibration of Transect Zones, and later verified by synoptic survey.

GOOGLE EARTH 2019

	T2	T3	T4	T5	T6	SD
TREE 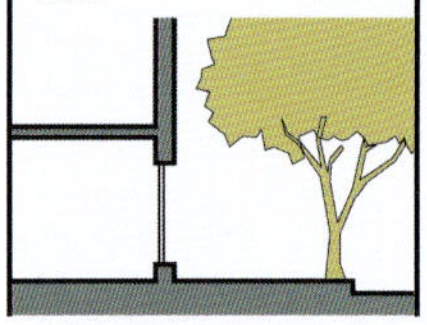	▪	▪	▪			▪
AWNING 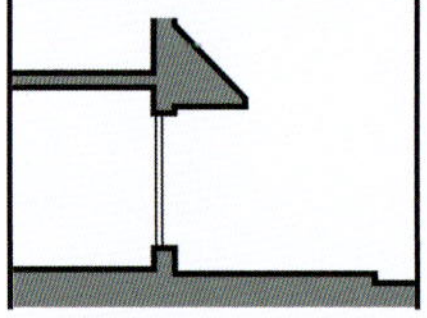			▪	▪	▪	▪
PORCH 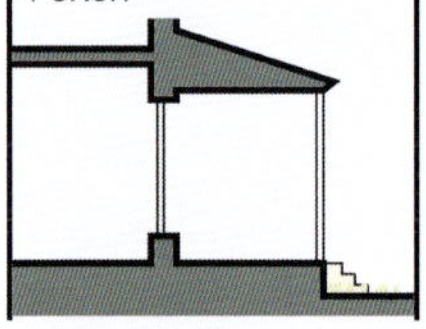	▪	▪	▪			▪
ROOF OVERHANG 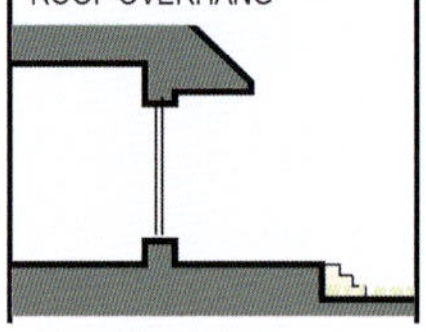	▪	▪	▪	▪		▪
EXTERIOR SHADE 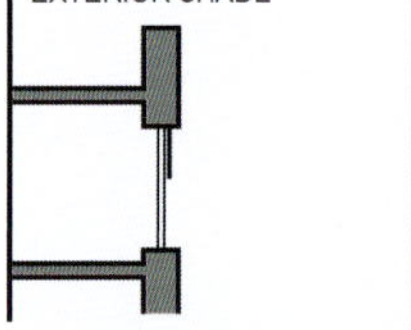			▪	▪	▪	▪
LIGHT SHELF 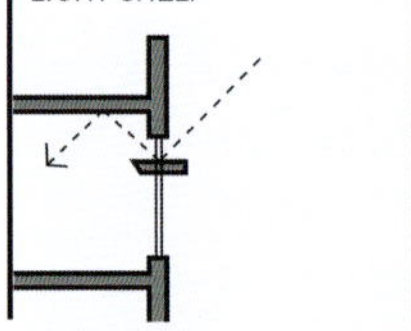			▪	▪	▪	▪
DEEP WINDOWS 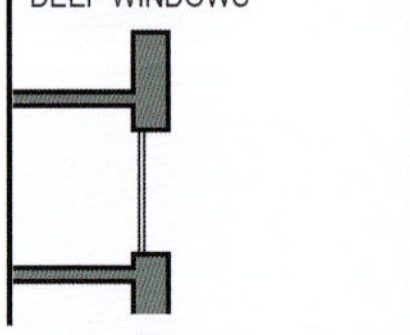	▪	▪	▪	▪	▪	▪
DOUBLE SKIN 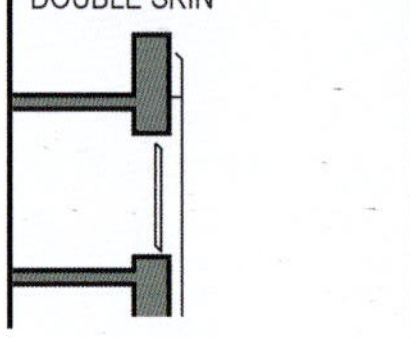				▪	▪	▪

FARR ASSOCIATES FOR THE SMARTCODE

This table, from the Sustainable Urbanism module of the SmartCode, illustrates methods to achieve levels of shading on fenestration within the Transect Zones. Note that each device is applicable to multiple Transect Zones, as the SmartCode is parametric, with no one-to-one allocations.

Public lighting varies in intensity and also in the specifics of the fixture—according to the Transect. The table shows four common types and dark sky. Specifications for the streetlights corresponding to these types would be approved by the utility company and listed in the SmartCode Module.

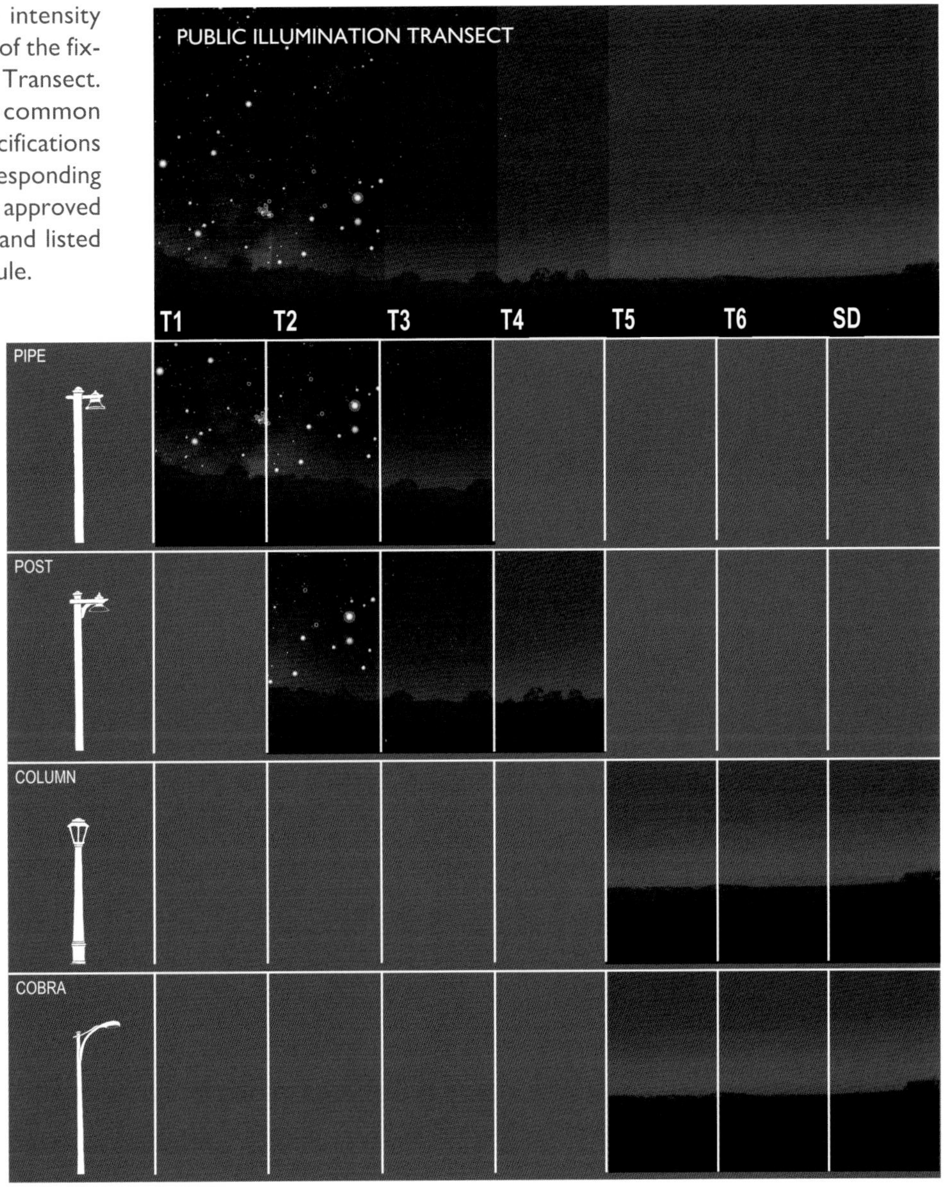

AARON PARKER FOR THE SMARTCODE

Some confusing criteria is simplified and resolved by the diagram below (not yet having received the T-Zone allocation). It is equally destructive to the complex functions of the public realm to require bike lanes everywhere as it is to have them nowhere.

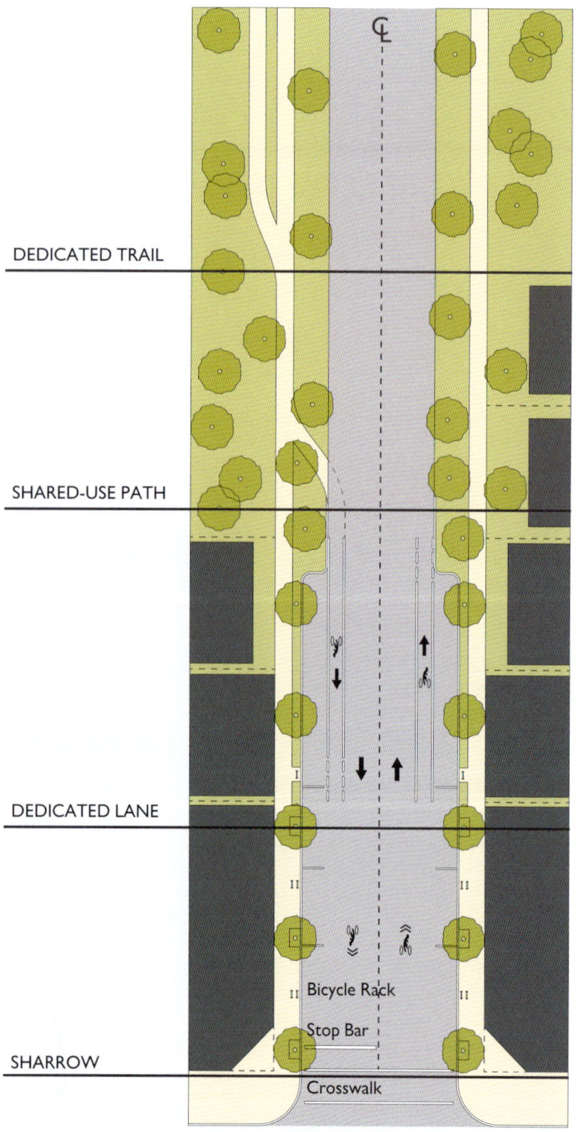

MIKE LYDON FOR THE SMARTCODE

	T1	T2	T3	T4	T5	T6	SD
POLE 	·	·	·	·	·	·	
OVAL 	·	·	·	·	·	·	
BALL 	·	·	·	·	·	·	
PYRAMID 	·	·	·	·			
UMBRELLA 	·	·	·	·			
VASE 	·	·	·	·			

DPZ CODESIGN FOR THE SMARTCODE

The table above shows six common types of street tree canopies and their allocation appropriate to T-Zones. The local planning office selects species suitable for the bioregion.

SETH HARRY FOR THE SMARTCODE

As a taxonomic engine, the Transect provides both analytical and projective capability, as shown by this complex projective construct for retail along the Transect. It includes five variables: 1. the retail categories as defined in *The Lexicon of the New Urbanism* (correlated to the ULI categories); 2. the Transect Zone; 3. the community type as composed of Transect Zones; and 4. the geographic frequency of the retail type. It is also useful to project and to guide successional evolution over time.

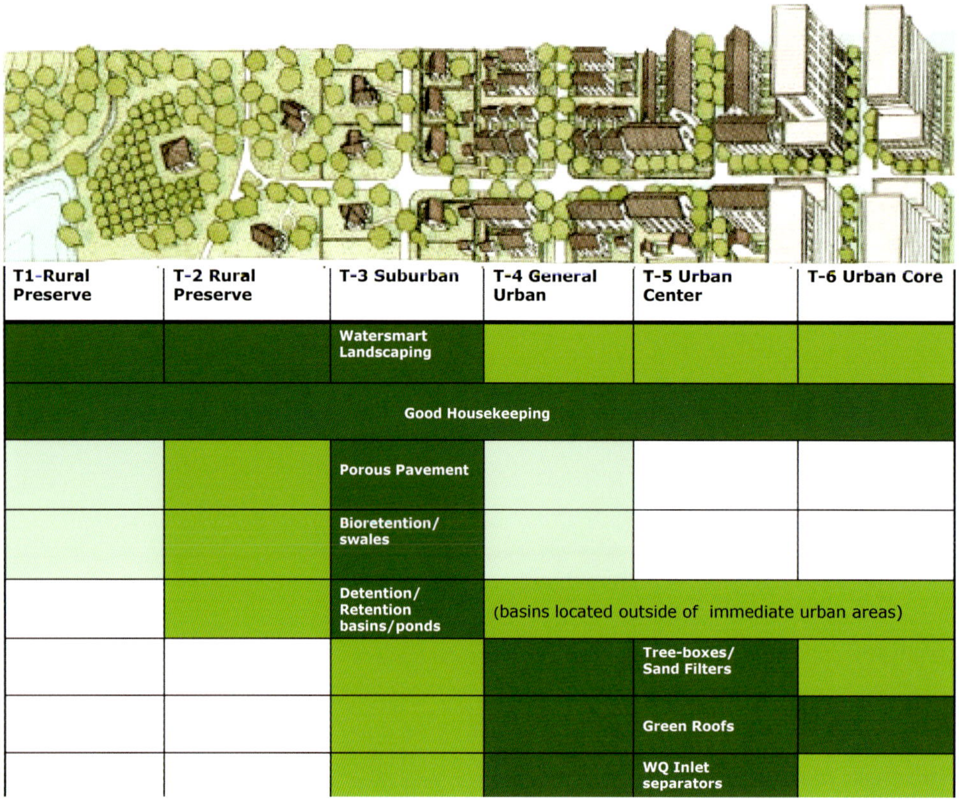

PROFESSOR JOHN JACOB, CHOICES FOR GROWTH

This diagram was one of the first specialized Transects, created by a professor at Texas A & M University. This one, like those opposite, engages the ever more important issue of hydrology. These are the basis for the absent theory of landscape urbanism proposed by Chalres Waldheim at the Harvard School of Design.

These charts—and many others—are integrated into *The Light Imprint Handbook* by Tom Low. This is one of several major freestanding texts that support the SmartCode and its modules. The Transect is a taxonomic engine that can place both cultural and technical variables in geographic order, for allocation such that they are mutually supportive—immersive—as would be the symbiotic elements of a natural habitat. In these plates, various elements of hydrology—pavement, channeling, storage, and infiltration—are assigned parametrically (across several T-Zones). The misallocation of such technology would result in the universal rustication typical of landscape urbanist practice: density without urbanism.

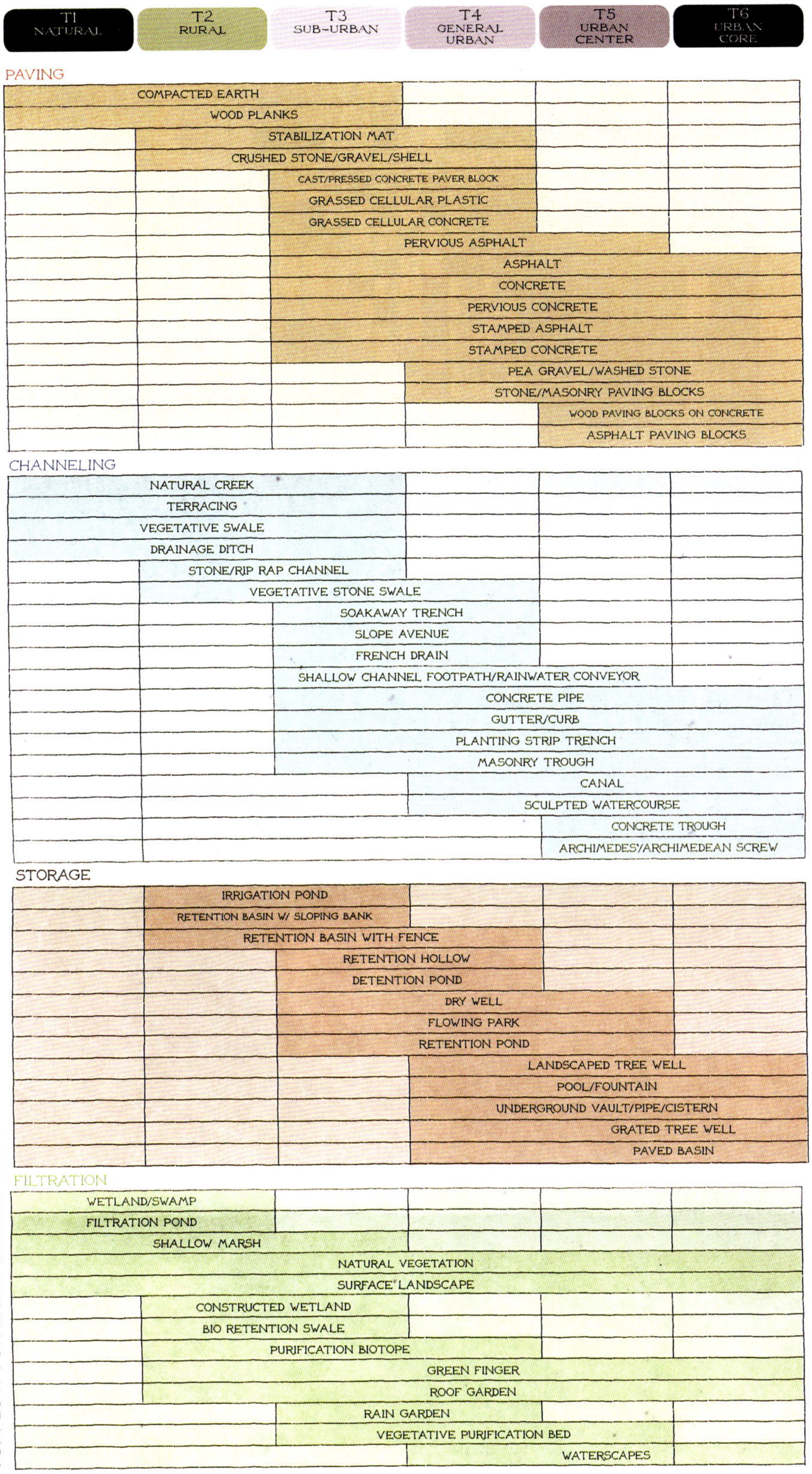

TOM LOW FOR LIGHT IMPRINT DPZ CODESIGN

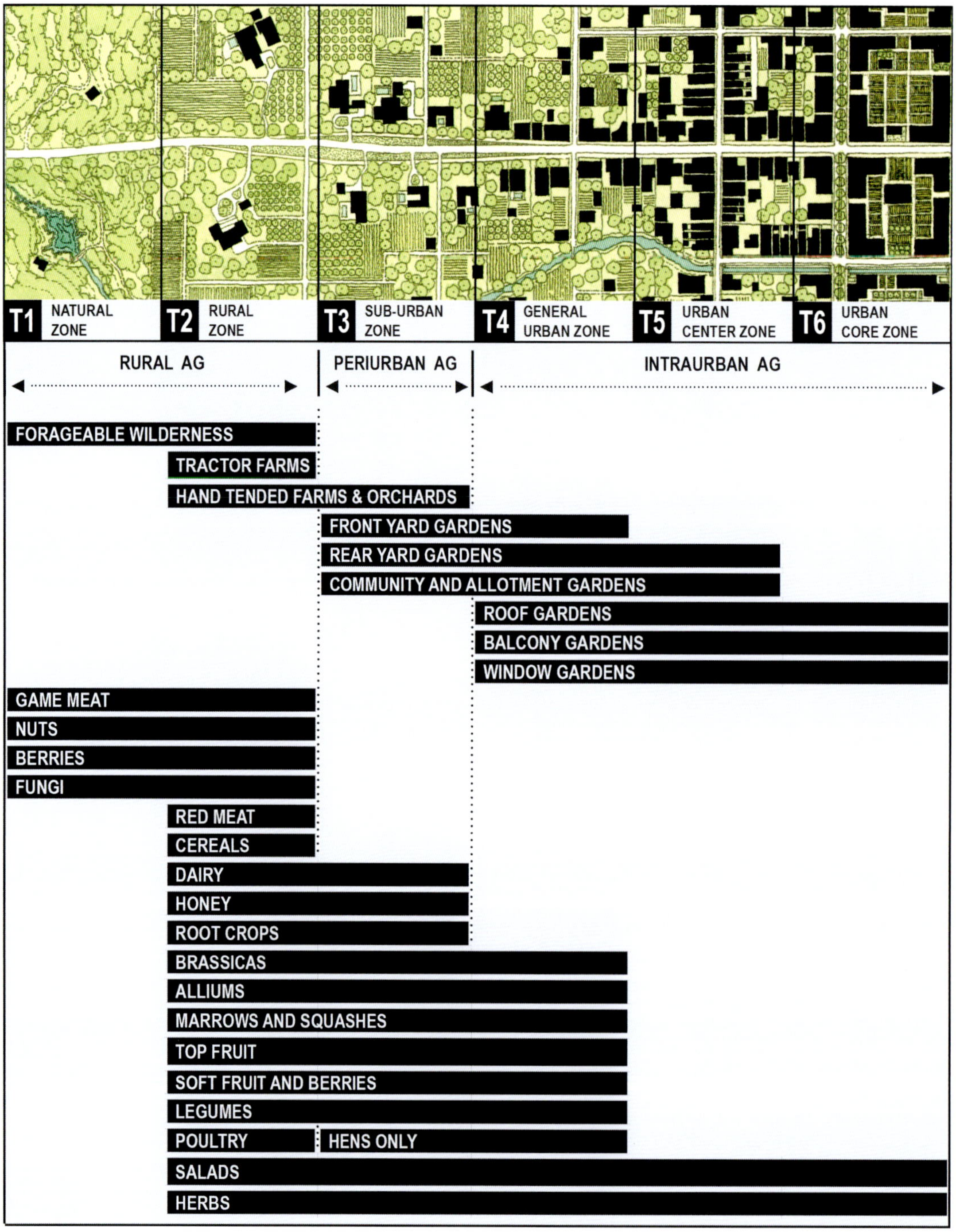

CHRIS RITTER FOR DPZ CODESIGN

This diagram may recall von Thünen's effort to analyze agricultural land value (see page 58), but instead shows how the Transect can be applied to human processes as well as to the natural. This example of a hypothetical English village shows the location and variety of agricultural activity (above) and the produce associated with each (below). The diagram incorporates research by the Prince of Wales School. Note that the standard Transect diagram was adapted to show agriculture in its varying relation to urbanism.

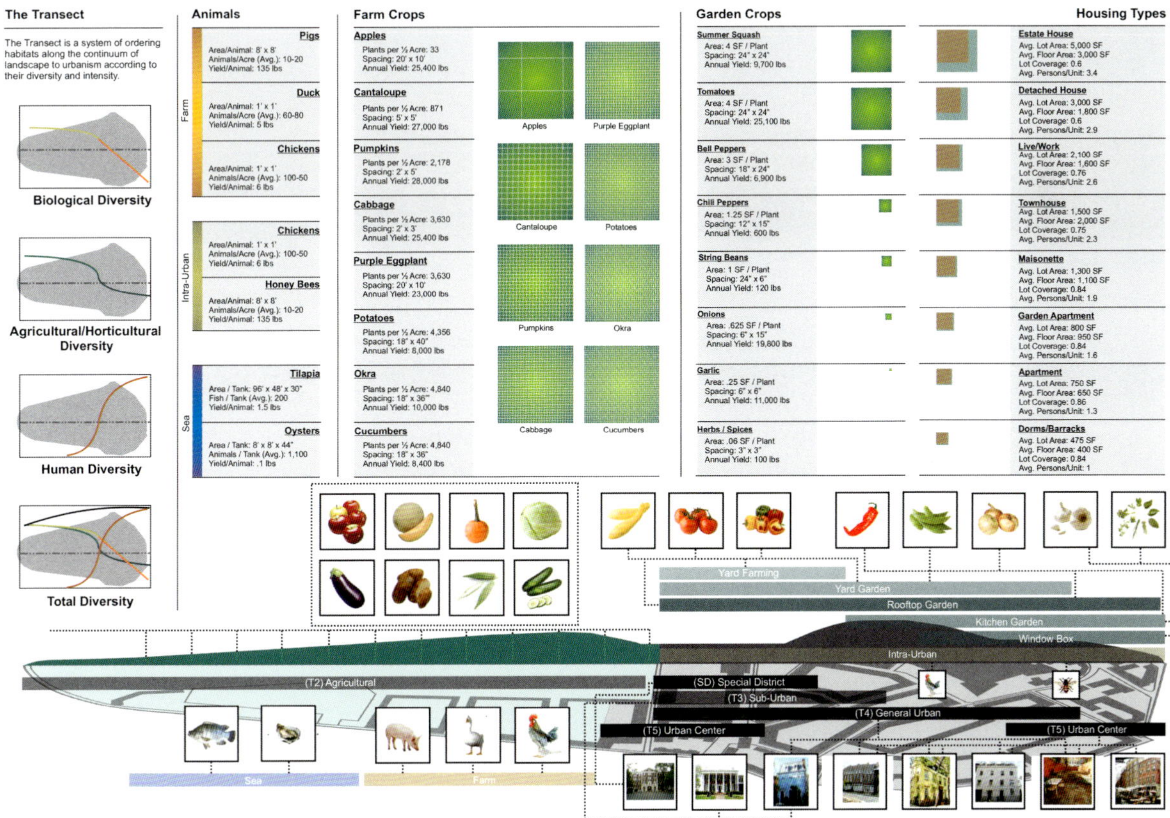

This is an American version of the diagram opposite, but incorporating additional concern for diversity. It provides spatial allocation of animals and crops as well as human dwellings. It is from a counter proposal for Governor's Island in New York City.

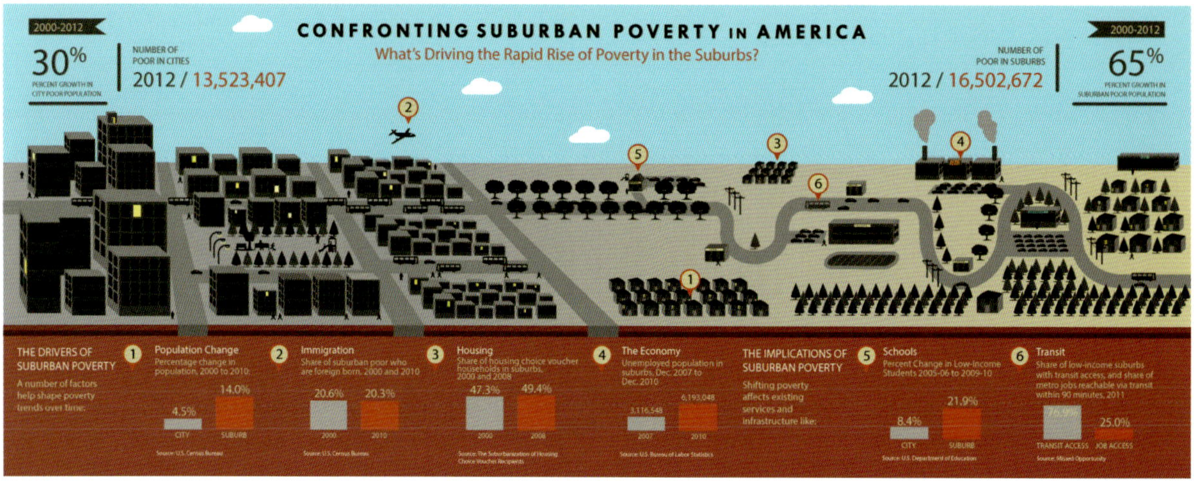

ELIZABETH KNEEBONE, ALAN BERUBE

These two images show the social phenomena of poverty, above, and health care, below. Each can be spatially overlapped in mapping, despite dealing with different concerns, as shown by the disparity of the graphics. The diagram above uses a generic rural-to-urban frame of reference, while the one below employs the Rural-to-Urban Transect as a tool, which allows correlation across specialties.

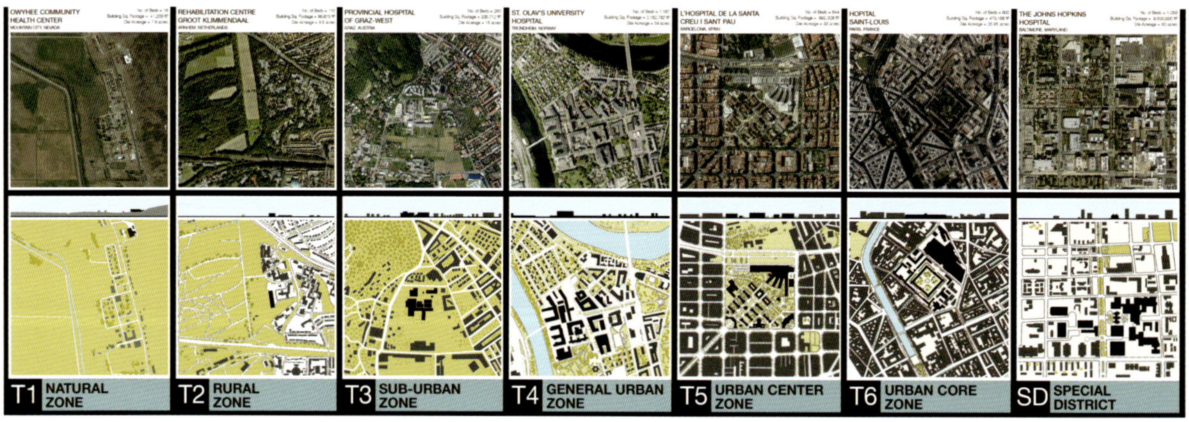

SHALINIE PERSAUD UNIVERSITY OF MIAMI

This graphic for a Phoenix transit-oriented development is intended to summarize the parameters that organize the regulatory elements in form-based codes, public works manuals, and other standards and regulatory documents. The graphic focuses on T-4, T-5, and T-6 because they have sufficient density to support transit.

EUSEBIO AZCUÉ FOR DPZ CODESIGN

The upper drawing clarifies the declension of open space types, from park to green, to square and to plaza, detailing the size and formality of landscaping pavement and spatial enclosure. The lower diagram displays a sprawl-to-urban, rather than rural-to-urban, transect of the relationship of parking to building. There is an increase of surface parking with suburban-sprawl typologies so that those place types to the left have no possibility of hiding the parking from the pedestrian. Suburban-sprawl typologies begin to become inevitable at that point. The SmartCode allocates each to a symbiotic relationship of the urban elements. The ones on the left of the diagram, if inserted within those on the right, would be destructive, just as the ones on the right would be entirely wasted in the absence of a similar allocation and relationship on the other side of the thoroughfare. Note the increase of unassigned space to the left. This coincides with lower real estate value and tax base, as Charles Marohn and Robert Orr have demonstrated. Not only does it show different frontage conditions from car-dependent sprawl to walkable town, but also how, with deliberate coding, the condition on the left could evolve to that on the right, i.e., placeless to place. (See page 207.) Note this does not represent the normative T-3 Sub-Urban Zone, which is a limited residential patch in a complete community and does not include surface-parking frontages.

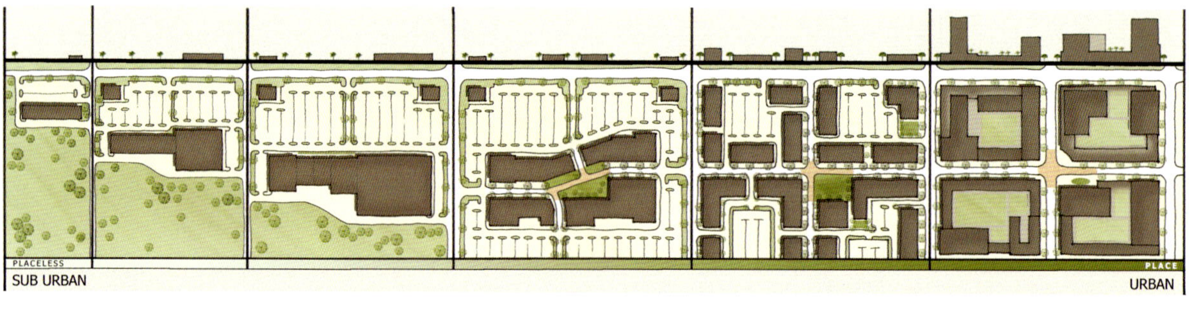

BILL LADITKA, WIGHTMAN & ASSOC.

SUCCESSIONAL TRANSECTS

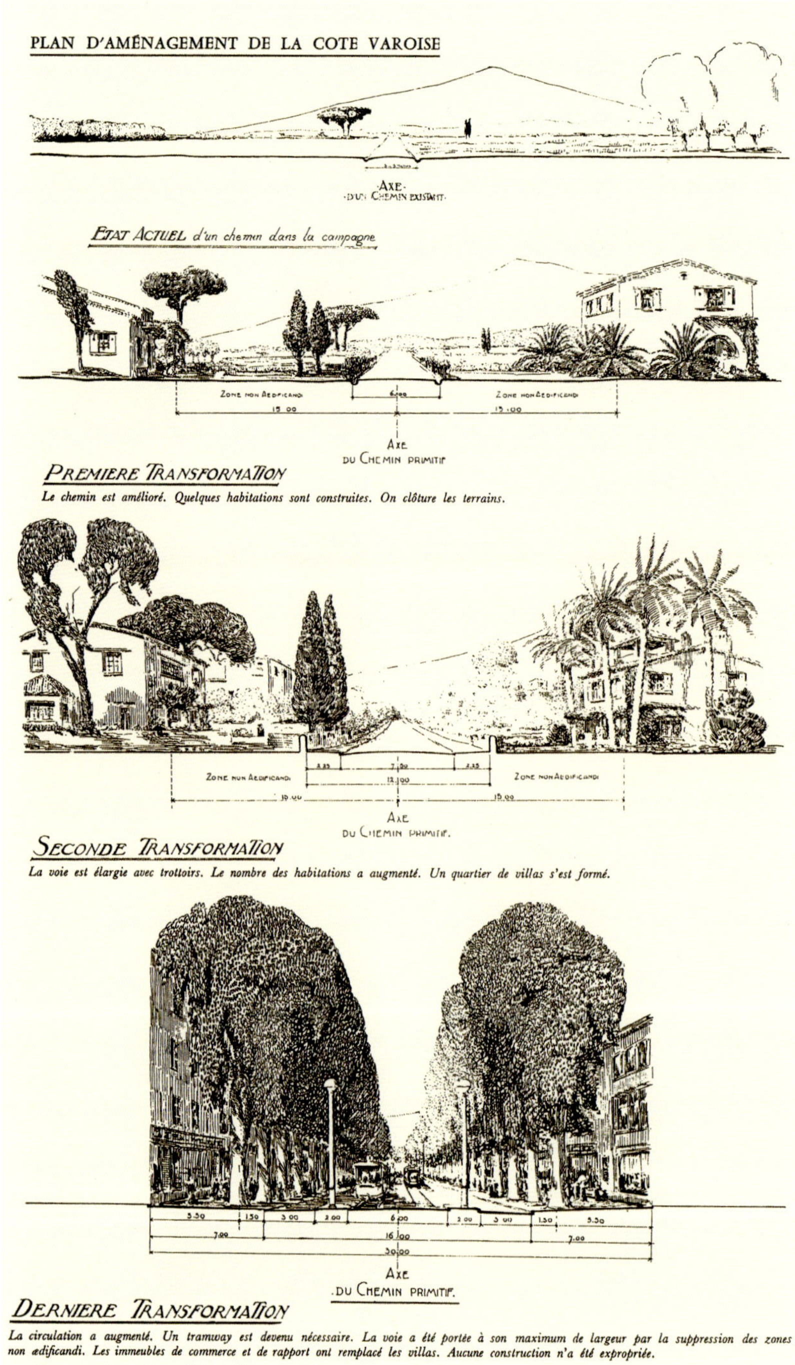

A marvelously evocative transect for the South of France was prepared in the 1920s by the great Mediterranean urbanist Henri Prost. Successional as well as spatial, it posits a "climax condition" as the "derniere transformation." This was translated into the six Transect Zones by DPZ in order to illustrate the successional urbanism of the SmartCode (opposite).

EUSEBIO AZCUÉ FOR DPZ CODESIGN

The declension of the Transect Zones provides a spatial and a geographic progression from rural to urban, as can be seen from this sequence, which can be read as that of entering a city. It also has a temporal or successional manifestation, as the series can also be understood as instances of a city maturing by becoming more urban over time. This is analogous to the "successional" concept in nature in which grassland prairie gradually evolves to woodland, and then to a climax forest. In urbanism the climax would be the equivalent of an area designated for historic preservation.

STEVE PRICE FOR DPZ CODESIGN

These images show the successional results of sprawl repair. First the existing 1980s-vintage office building is converted into a loft building, and then the parking lot is converted into a pedestrian-friendly street with buildings on both sides, parallel parking, and wide sidewalks. This is perfectly achievable if incorporated into a successional protocol such as the SmartCode. Suburban zoning does not allow buildings to evolve. It is regrettable that conventional suburban place types must utterly collapse before they can be subjected to sprawl repair.

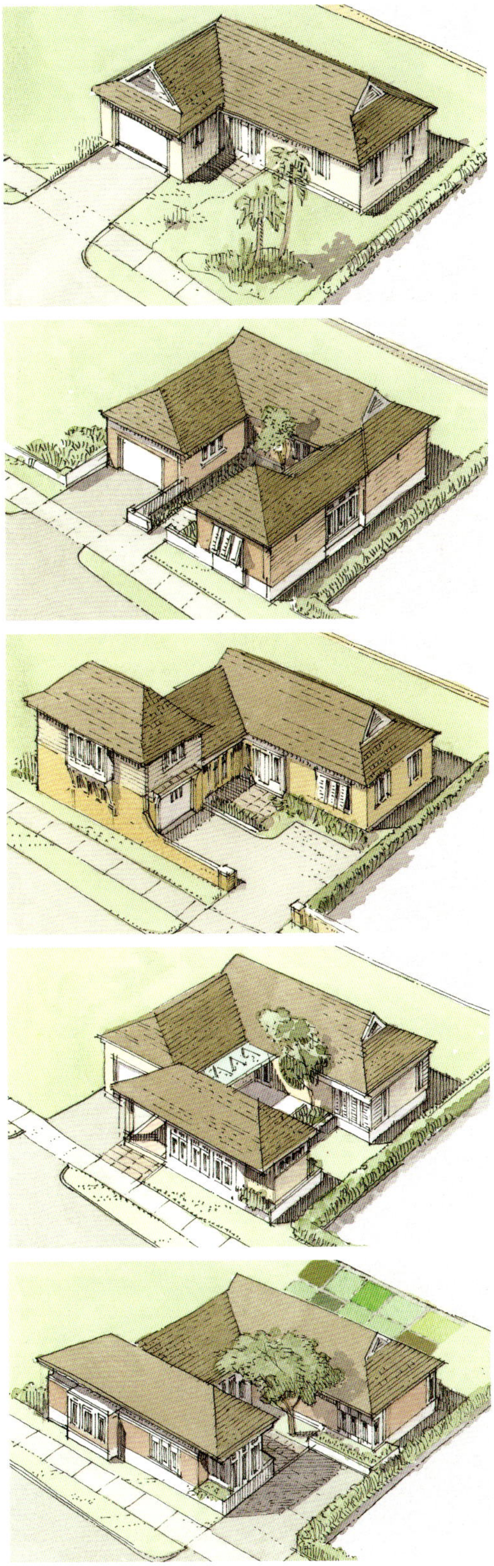

JAMES WASSELL FOR DPZ CODESIGN

The suburban residential condition is typically a 25-foot front setback dominated by a driveway and a garage door. In the first of these sprawl repair alternatives, a new wing is added, creating an entry courtyard and preventing the garage and driveway from dominating the street view. In the second, the existing garage footprint is converted to additional living space as a two-story structure. In the third, a detached outbuilding is built in the front yard, creating a private interior courtyard and again preventing the garage and driveway from dominating the street view. The final alternative removes the garage. In its place sits a one-story addition delineating the street. The garden in the backyard remains intact in each version. As the façade comes closer to the sidewalk, the habitat begins to evolve from conventional suburbia to a more urban, walkable condition, either T-3 or T-4 depending on surrounding patterns.

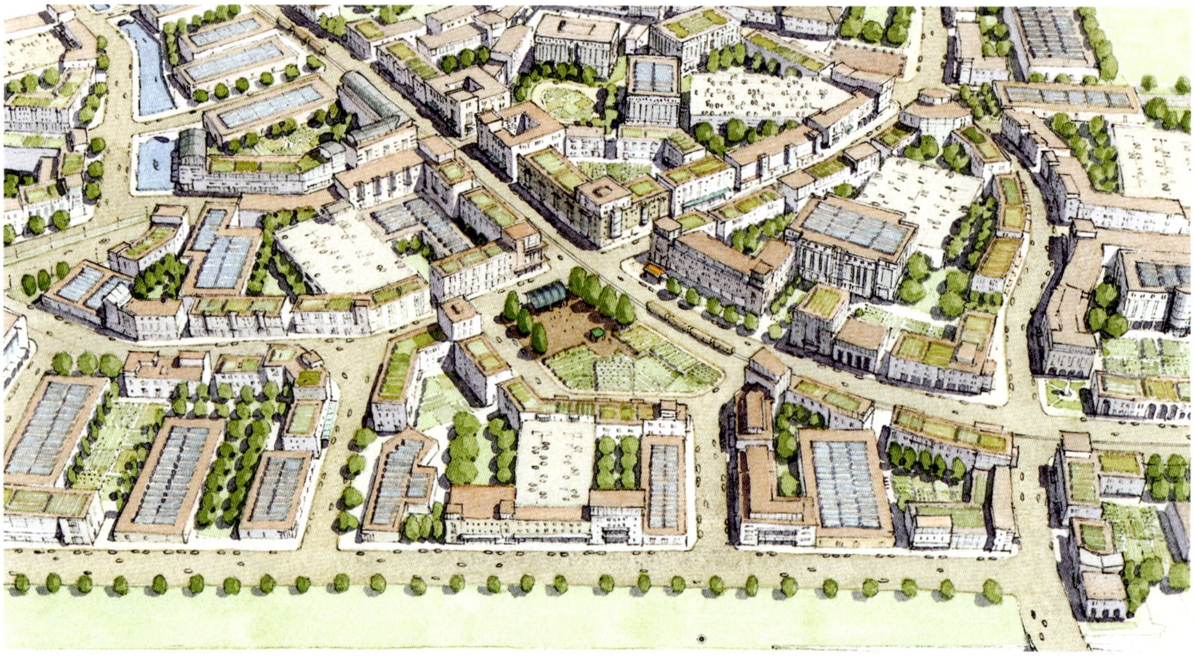

CHRIS RITTER FOR DPZ CODESIGN

These drawings are among many by Chris Ritter that illustrate the transformation of the conventional sprawl building types in Galina Tachieva's *Sprawl Repair Manual*. This transformation is also a kind of successional urbanism. Léon Krier has said that the campaign to retrofit and repair suburban sprawl is the mission of the century. This may be coded in a SmartCode as the successional transformation of, first, CSD to walkable urbanism, and then potentially of lower T-Zones (T-3, T-4) to higher (T-4, T-5, T-6).

COMPARATIVE TRANSECTS

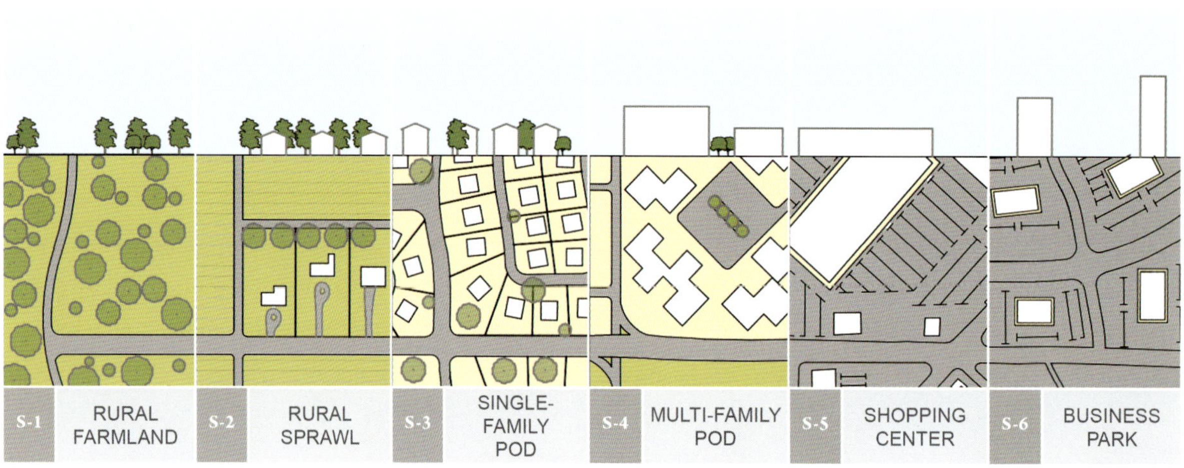

DPZ CODESIGN

These diagrams are similar in substance to those on page 92, but technical rather than illustrative. The one above was created for the *Public Works Manual*, and the one below for the *Sprawl Repair Manual.* They demonstrate, among other things, the color palette that would symbolize on regulating plans the Transect-based zones and the ones corresponding to the single-use zoning of Conventional Suburban Development (CSD). Since CSD pre-exists and persists, the color schemes for mapping must be different, even in a committed Transect-based regulatory environment. The yellow-orange-red range is that of the existing zoning system. The red-blue range was derived from an extinct system used before the First World War.

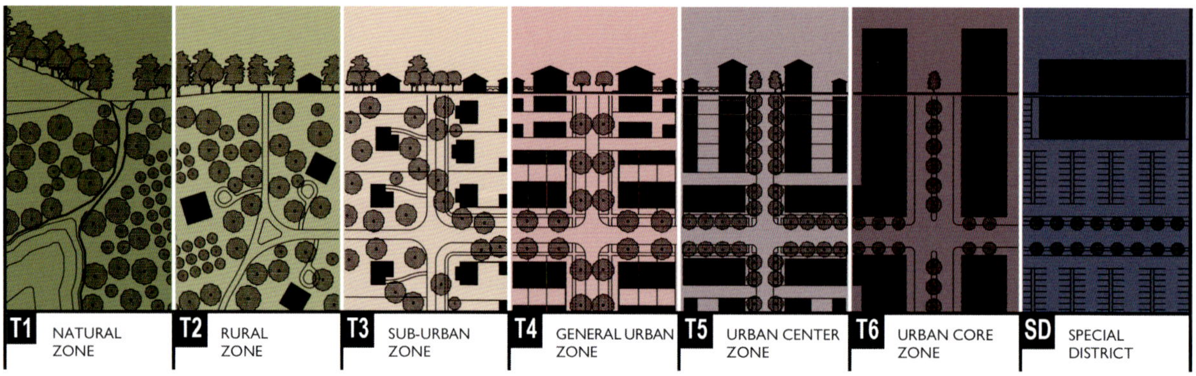

DPZ CODESIGN

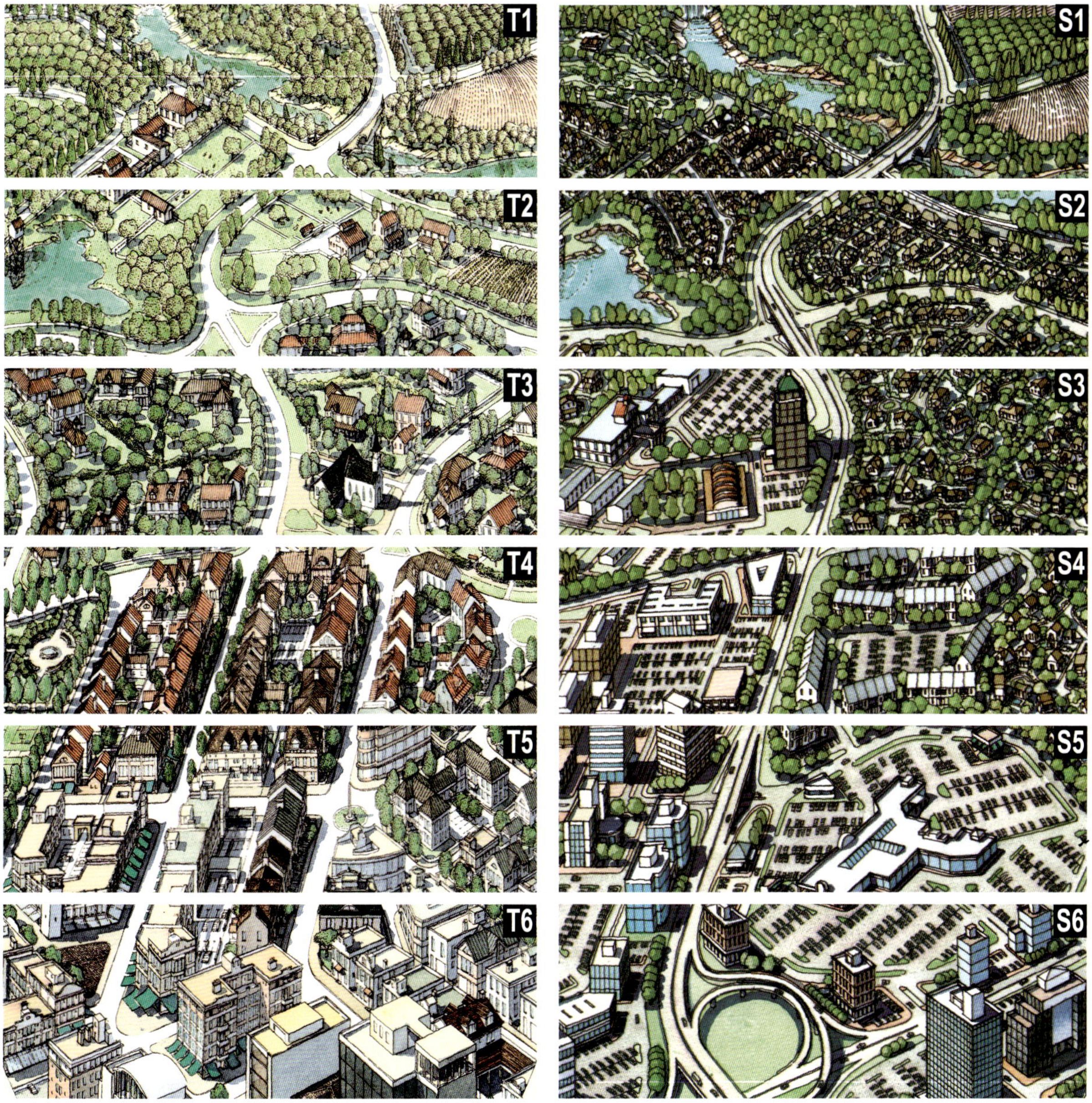

EUSEBIO AZCUÉ FOR DPZ CODESIGN

In a sustainable human habitat, natural and cultural elements are mutually supporting, as evidenced by its health and perhaps even its beauty. Traditional urbanism manifests such durable and beneficent characteristics of habitat. The Rural-to-Urban Transect assumes this premise of symbiosis in each human habitat zone, and the SmartCode is deployed to achieve it. The sprawl transect illustration on the right serves as contrast. While conventional suburban development consists of 19 "real estate products" or "place types," it manifests characteristics that can also be rationalized (S-1 to S-6) in a manner similar to the Transect on the left. This pairing argues that the place types on the right can be repaired, by means of the SmartCode's Sprawl Repair Module, to resemble the sustainable urbanism on the left. Like all such Transect drawings, this has a political or "illustrative" purpose, rather than a technical or operational one, like the diagrams and tables in the SmartCode.

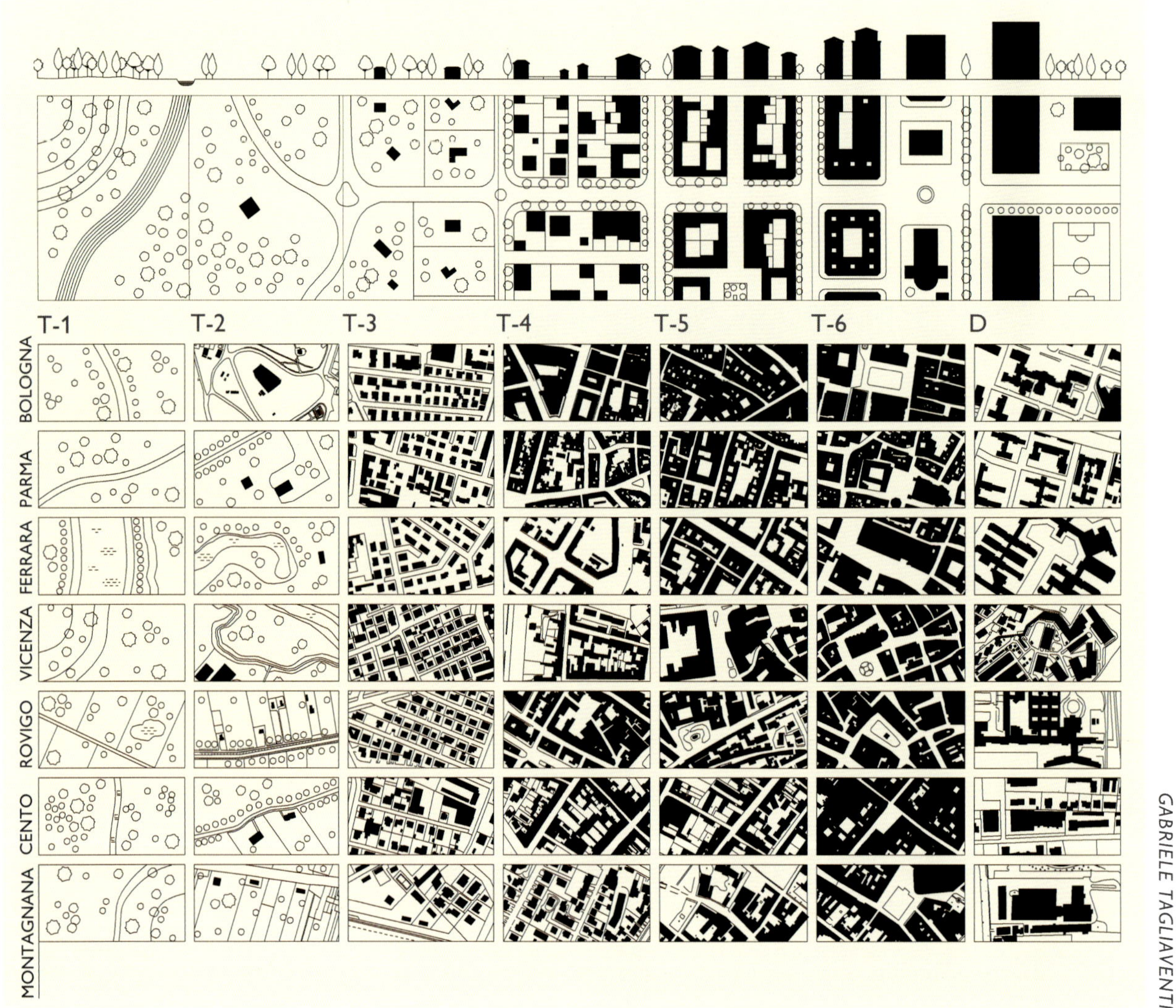

Similar in graphic layout to the Stockholm Transect on page 112, this diagram is for Italian cities. They are similar in that neither is an abstraction. Each T-Zone is extracted as a quadrat from the existing urban fabric.

ALEX MACLEAN

All pre-modernist urbanism manifests a variation of the Transect. Comparison by quadrat can demonstrate general differences between cities (read horizontally) as well as precise comparisons between their T-Zones (read vertically). For example, this set would allow a comparison of the typologies of two Caribbean cities, Key West and New Orleans. Depending on the height of the aerial and the mix of ground conditions, some of these squares contain more than one Transect Zone, but the dominant one is labeled. These images form part of a major work of analytical aerial photography by Alex MacLean.

THE TNU TREE

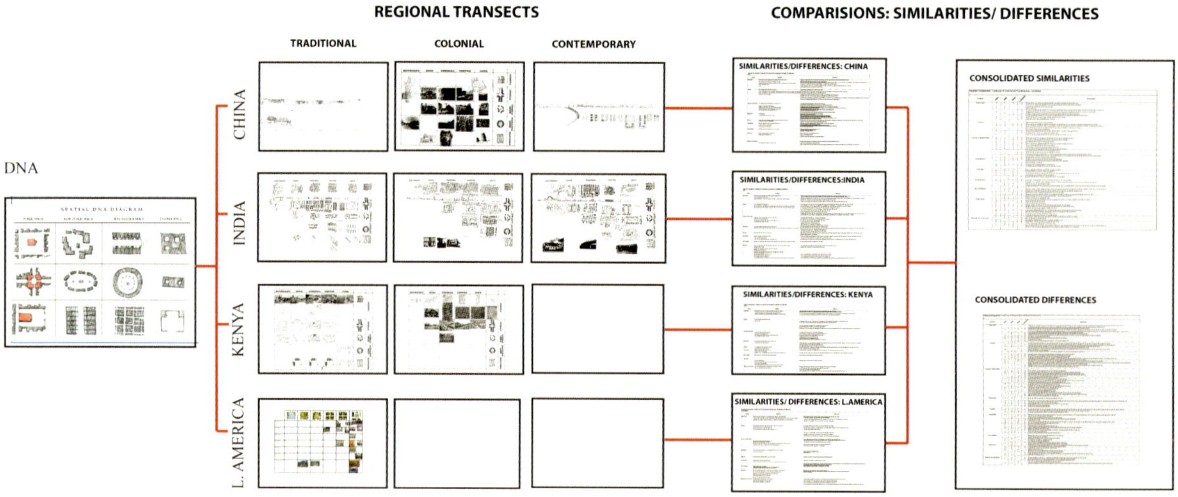

These diagrams are from a study of urban patterns in several countries prepared by the office of Torti Gallas and Partners. The top diagram shows the countries analyzed. The following diagrams pertain to India, analyzing similarities and differences between the traditional, colonial, and contemporary periods of India. Different kinds of urbanism display different cultural, social, political, and economic regimes. It is possible, for example, to extract and analyze the three T-5 Zones for comparative analysis.

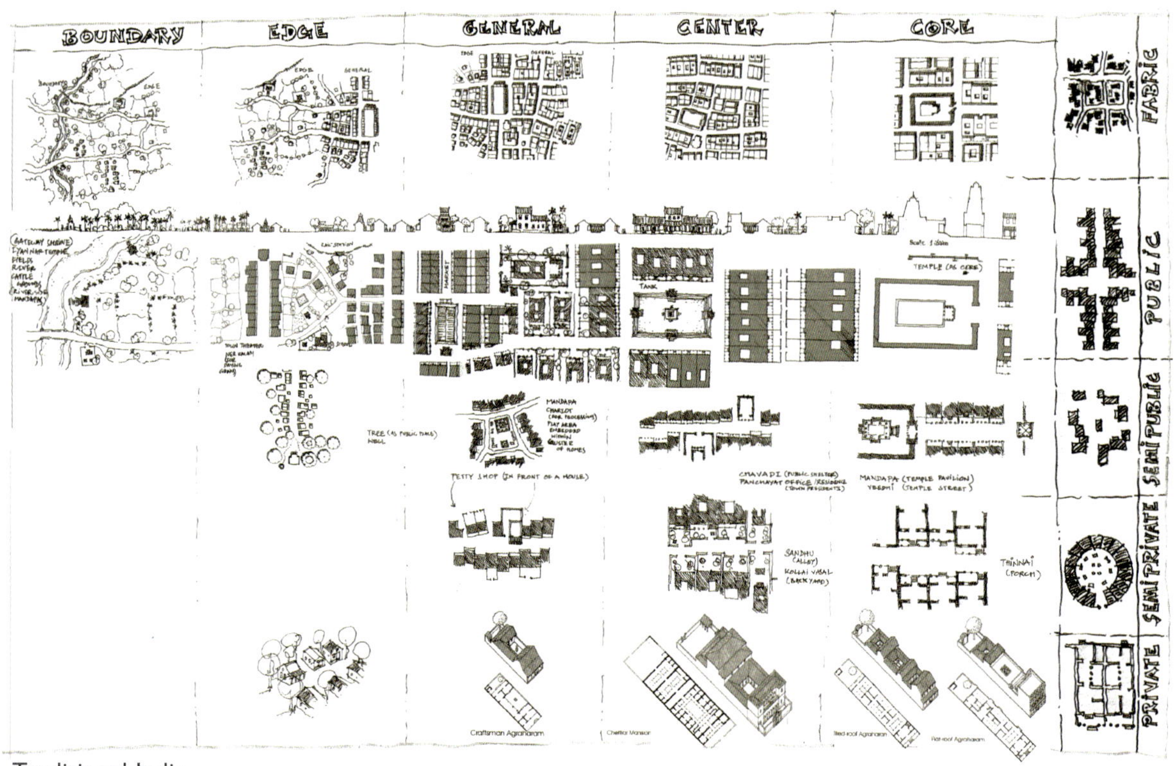

TORTI-GALLAS

Traditional India

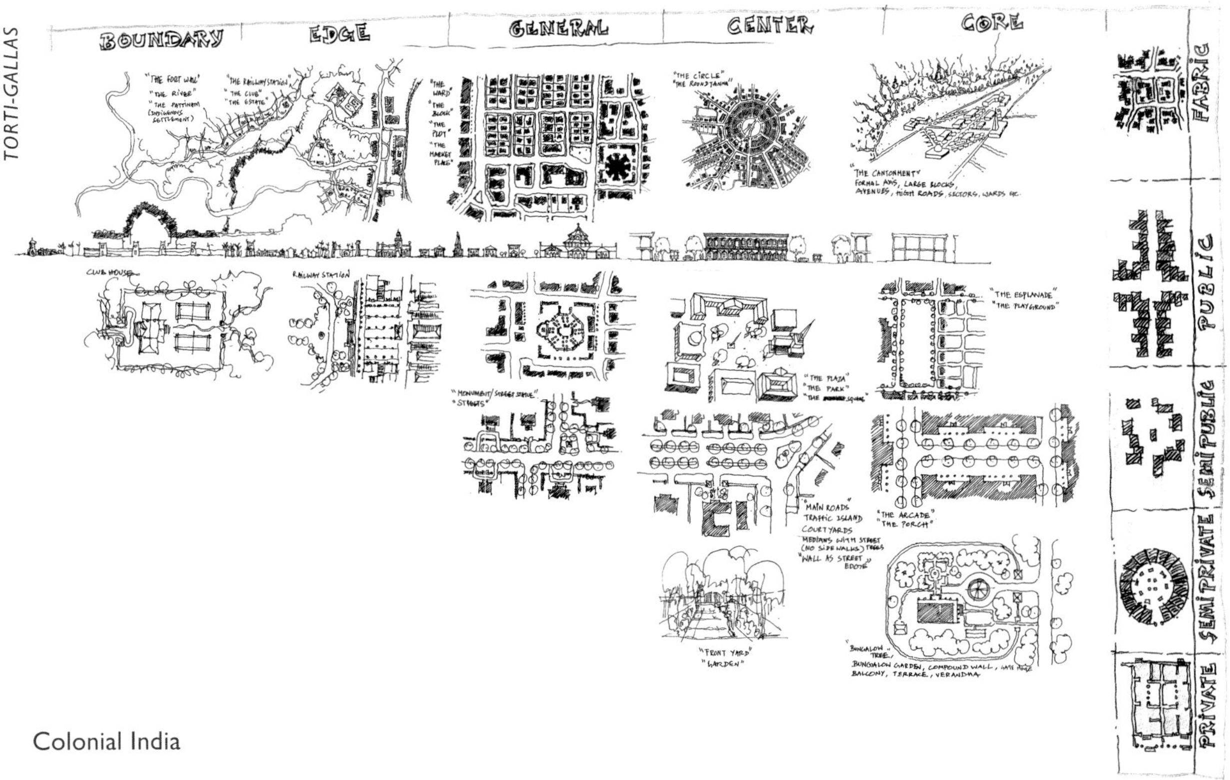

Colonial India

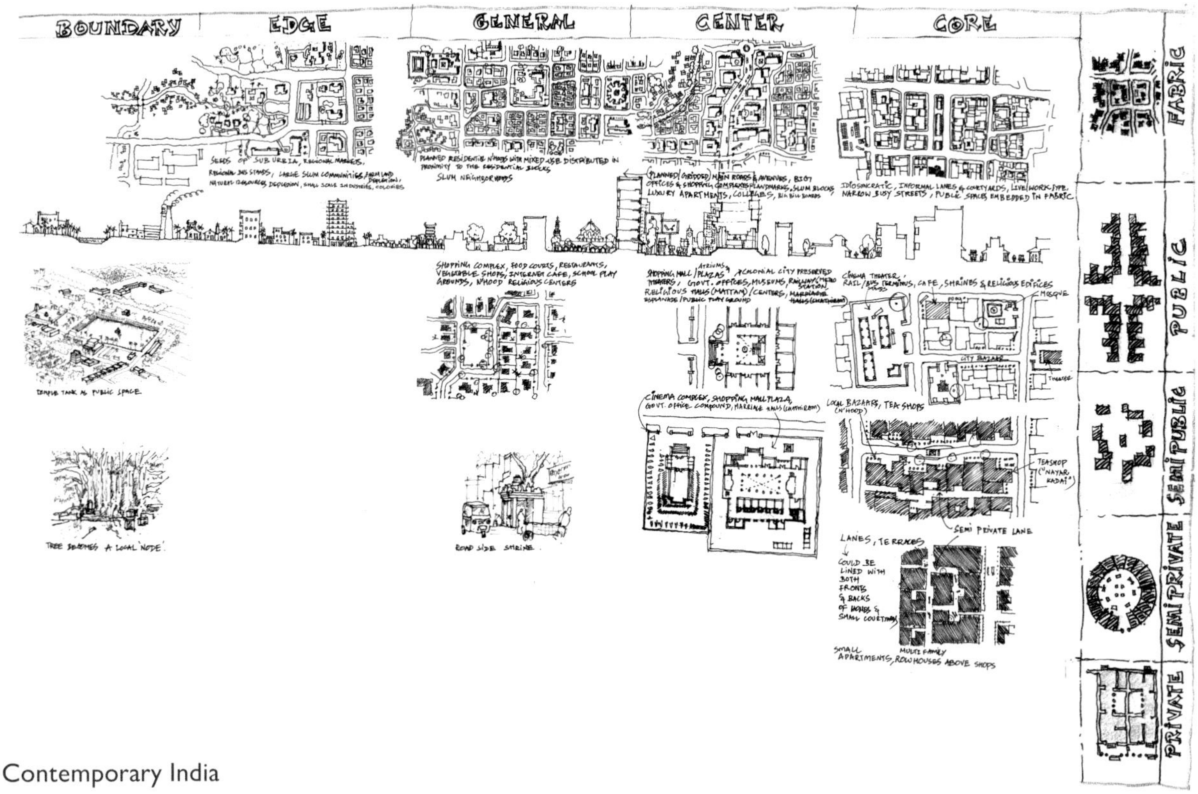

Contemporary India

PROJECTING THE TRANSECT

T1 	**T-1 NATURAL** consists of lands approximating or reverting to a wilderness condition, including lands unsuitable for settlement due to topography, hydrology or vegetation.	**Building Type:** **Building Placement:** **Frontage Types:** **Building Height:** **Open Space:**	Natural landscape with some agricultural use Not applicable Not applicable Not applicable Farms, parks, greenways
T2 	**T-2 RURAL** consists of sparsely settled lands in open or cultivated states. These include woodland, agricultural land, grassland, and irrigable desert. Typical buildings are farmhouses, agricultural buildings, cabins, and villas.	**Building Type:** **Building Placement:** **Frontage Types:** **Building Height:** **Open Space:**	Primarily agricultural with woodland & wetland and scattered buildings Variable setbacks Not applicable 1- to 2-story Parks, greenways
T3 	**T-3 SUB-URBAN** consists of low-density residential areas, adjacent to higher zones with some mixed-use. Home occupations and outbuildings are allowed. Planting is naturalistic and setbacks are relatively deep. Blocks may be large and the roads irregular to accommodate natural conditions.	**Building Type:** **Building Placement:** **Frontage Types:** **Building Height:** **Open Space:**	Lawns, and landscaped yards surrounding detached single-family houses; pedestrians occasionally Large and variable front and sideyard setbacks Porches, fences, naturalistic tree planting 1- to 2-story with some 3-story Parks, greenways
T4 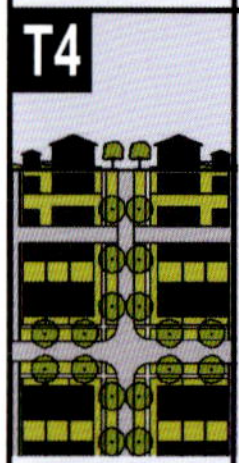	**T-4 GENERAL URBAN** consists of a mixed-use but primarily residential urban fabric. It may have a wide range of building types: single, sideyard, and rowhouses. Setbacks and landscaping are variable. Streets with curbs and sidewalks define medium-sized blocks.	**Building Type:** **Building Placement:** **Frontage Types:** **Building Height:** **Open Space:**	Mix of houses, townhouses & small apartment buildings, with scattered commercial activity; balance between landscape and buildings; presence of pedestrians Shallow to medium front and sideyard setbacks Porches, fences, dooryards 2- to 3-story with a few taller mixed-use buildings Squares, greens
T5 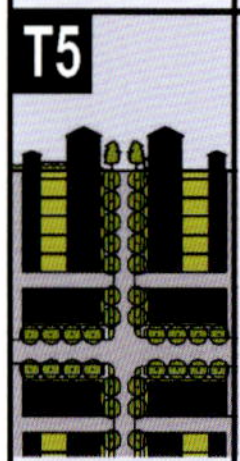	**T-5 URBAN CENTER** consists of higher-density mixed-use buildings that accommodate retail, offices, rowhouses and apartments. It has a tight network of streets, with wide sidewalks, steady street-tree planting and buildings set close to the sidewalks.	**Building Type:** **Building Placement:** **Frontage Types:** **Building Height:** **Open Space:**	Shops mixed with townhouses, larger apartment houses, offices, workplace, and civic buildings; predominantly attached buildings; trees within the public right-of-way; substantial pedestrian activity Shallow setbacks or none; buildings oriented to street defining a street wall Stoops, shopfronts, galleries 3- to 5-story with some variation Parks, plazas and squares, median landscaping
T6 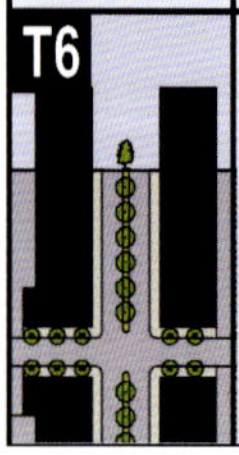	**T-6 URBAN CORE** consists of the highest density and height, with the greatest variety of uses, and civic buildings of regional importance. It may have larger blocks; streets have steady street-tree planting and buildings are set close to wide sidewalks. Typically only large towns and cities have an Urban Core.	**Building Type:** **Building Placement:** **Frontage Types:** **Building Height:** **Open Space:**	Medium- to high-density mixed-use buildings, entertainment, civic and cultural uses. Attached buildings forming a continuous street wall; trees within the public right-of-way; highest pedestrian and transit activity Shallow setbacks or none; buildings oriented to street, defining a street wall Stoops, dooryards, forecourts, shopfronts, galleries, and arcades 4-plus story with a few shorter buildings Parks, plazas and squares; median landscaping

Although the SmartCode technically induces the habitats (or "immersive environments") that constitute the Transect Zones, the community process often calls for an extended verbal explanation. This table provides this in two formats. The column on the left is running prose, while the other is more technical. This table is not literally followed in a zoning code, but acts to guide "Purpose" or "Intent" statements used for variances and administrative waivers. It should be customized for each municipality or HOA.

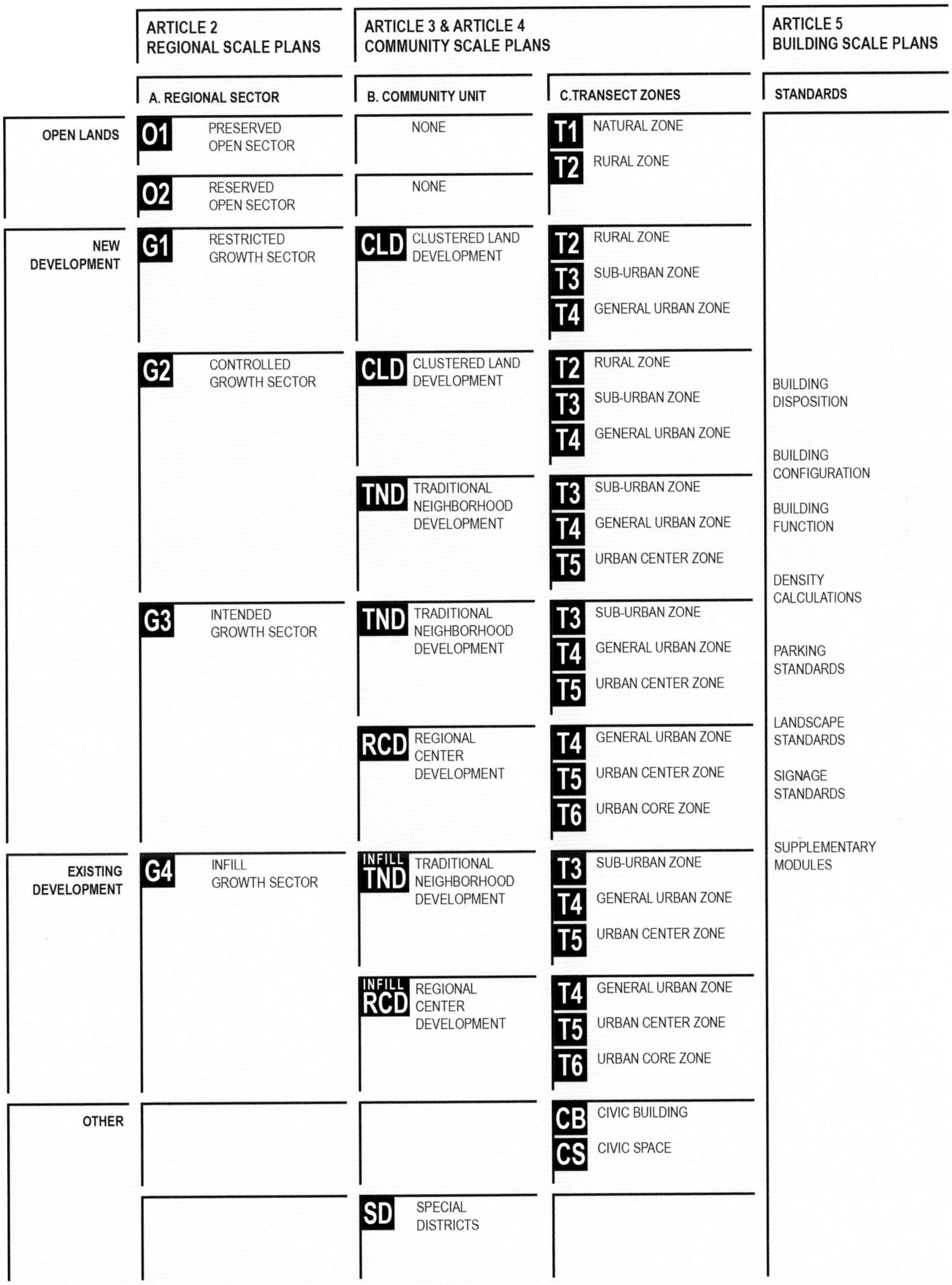

DPZ CODESIGN

This outline of the SmartCode presents the operational level of the Rural-to-Urban Transect shown opposite. Transect Zones are nested within Communities, and Communities are in turn nested within Sectors. On the far right, each T-Zone contains the elements appropriate to it, the standards for which are provided in a brief form-based zoning code, Article 5.

A. COMMON YARD: a planted Frontage wherein the Facade is set back substantially from the Frontage Line. The front yard created remains unfenced and is visually continuous with adjacent yards, supporting a common landscape. The deep Setback provides a buffer from the higher speed Thoroughfares.

B. PORCH & FENCE: a planted Frontage wherein the Facade is set back from the Frontage Line with an attached porch permitted to Encroach. A fence at the Frontage Line maintains street spatial definition. Porches shall be no less than 8 feet deep.

C. TERRACE OR LIGHTWELL: a Frontage wherein the Facade is set back from the Frontage line by an elevated terrace or a sunken Lightwell. This type buffers Residential use from urban Sidewalks and removes the private yard from public Encroachment. Terraces are suitable for conversion to outdoor cafes. Syn: Dooryard.

D. FORECOURT: a Frontage wherein a portion of the Facade is close to the Frontage Line and the central portion is set back. The Forecourt created is suitable for vehicular drop-offs. This type should be allocated in conjunction with other Frontage types. Large trees within the Forecourts may overhang the Sidewalks.

E. STOOP: a Frontage wherein the Facade is aligned close to the Frontage Line with the first Story elevated from the Sidewalk sufficiently to secure privacy for the windows. The entrance is usually an exterior stair and landing. This type is recommended for ground-floor Residential use.

F. SHOPFRONT: a Frontage wherein the Facade is aligned close to the Frontage Line with the building entrance at Sidewalk grade. This type is conventional for Retail use. It has a substantial glazing on the Sidewalk level and an awning that may overlap the Sidewalk to within 2 feet of the Curb. Syn: Retail Frontage.

G. GALLERY: a Frontage wherein the Facade is aligned close to the Frontage line with an attached cantilevered shed or a lightweight colonnade overlapping the Sidewalk. This type is conventional for Retail use. The Gallery shall be no less than 10 feet wide and should overlap the Sidewalk to within 2 feet of the Curb.

H. ARCADE: a colonnade supporting habitable space that overlaps the Sidewalk, while the Facade at Sidewalk level remains at or behind the Frontage Line. This type is conventional for Retail use. The Arcade shall be no less than 12 feet wide and should overlap the Sidewalk to within 2 feet of the Curb. See Table 8.

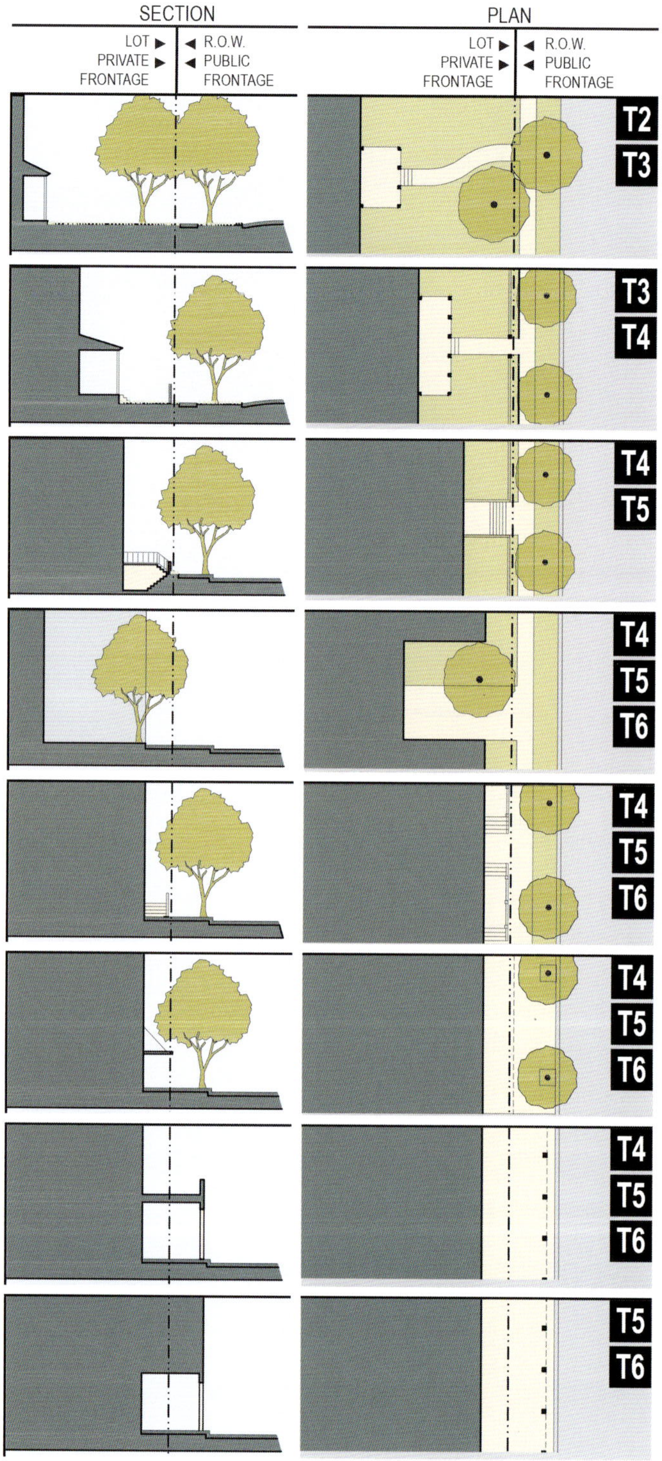

DPZ CODESIGN

The private frontage is the area between the building facades and the lot lines. Here a visual illustration is provided in addition to the legalistic standards. In this version of the SmartCode, the capitalization of some terms alerts users that the terms are defined in the glossary.

R U R A L | | | | | | | | | | | | | | | | | | | | T R A N S E C T | | | | | | | | | | | | | | | | U R B A N

	T1 T2 T3 HW & RD	T1 T2 T3 RD & ST	T3 T4 ST-DR-AV	T4 T5 ST-DR-AV-BV	T5 T6 CS-DR-AV-BV	T5 T6 CS-DR-AV-BV
A. ASSEMBLY: The principal variables are the type and dimension of Curbs, walkways, Planters and landscape.	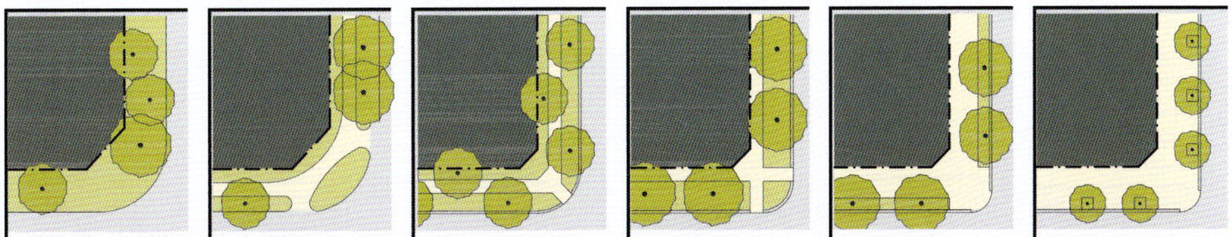					
Total Width	16-24 feet	12-24 feet	12-18 feet	12-18 feet	18-24 feet	18-30 feet
B. CURB: The detailing of the edge of the vehicular pavement, incorporating drainage.	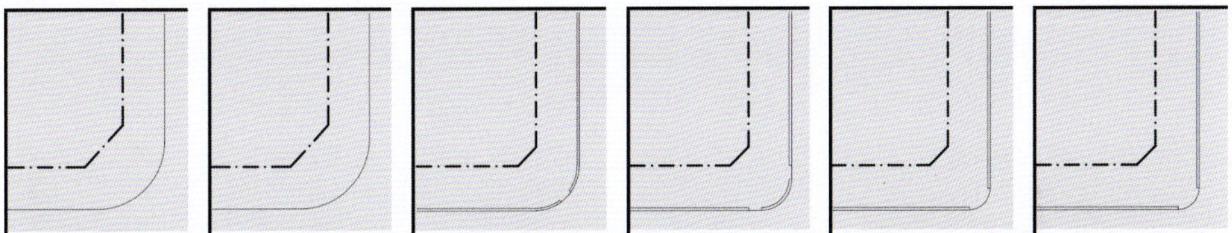					
Type	Open Swale	Open Swale	Raised Curb	Raised Curb	Raised Curb	Raised Curb
Radius	10-30 feet	10-30 feet	5-20 feet	5-20 feet	5-20 feet	5-20 feet
C. WALKWAY: The pavement dedicated exclusively to pedestrian activity.	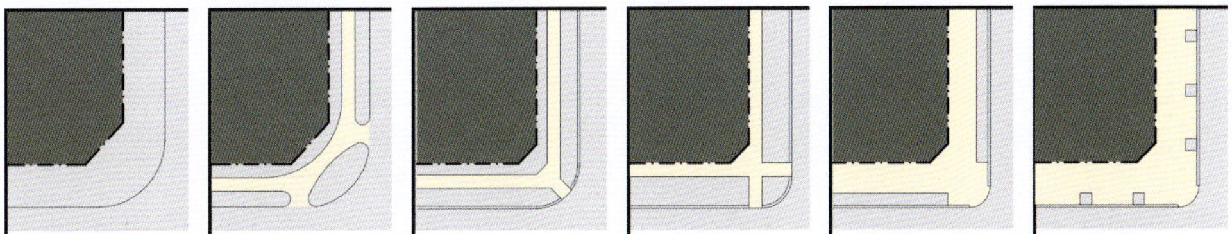					
Type	Path Optional	Path	Sidewalk	Sidewalk	Sidewalk	Sidewalk
Width	n/a	4-8 feet	4-8 feet	4-8 feet	12-20 feet	12-30 feet
D. PLANTER: The layer which accommodates street trees and other landscape.	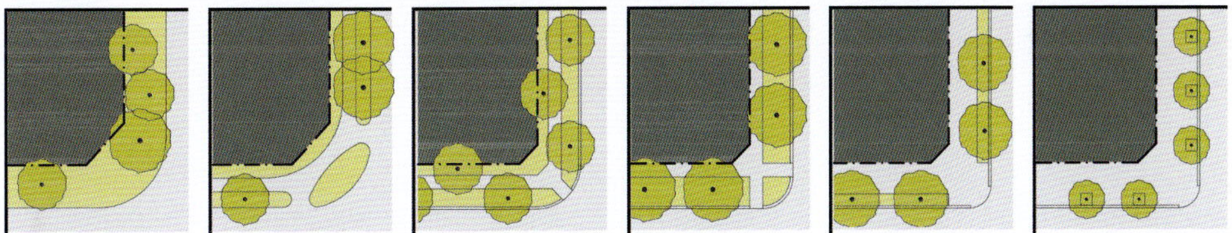					
Arrangement	Clustered	Clustered	Regular	Regular	Regular	Opportunistic
Species	Multiple	Multiple	Alternating	Single	Single	Single
Planter Type	Continuous Swale	Continuous Swale	Continuous Planter	Continuous Planter	Continuous Planter	Tree Well
Planter Width	8 feet-16 feet	8 feet-16 feet	8 feet-12 feet	8 feet-12 feet	4 feet-6 feet	4 feet-6 feet

The public frontage is the collection of elements—curbs, walkways, and planters—allocated to specific thoroughfare types within Transect Zones. Lighting and locally appropriate planting species appear on pages 77 and 78.

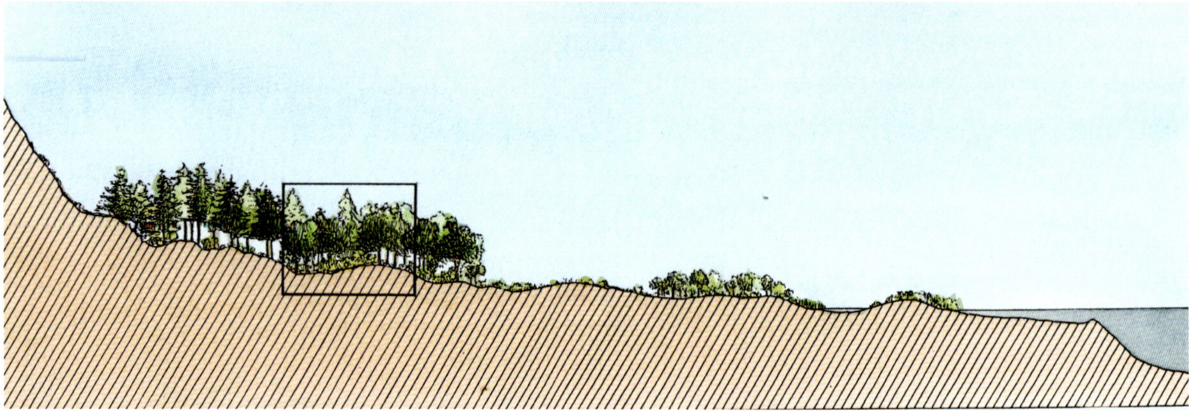

EUSEBIO AZCUÉ FOR DPZ CODESIGN

The environmental assessment of a site requires the identification of typical habitat zones by means of a synoptic survey. This involves a first determination from aerial photography, followed by visual field verification. The entire site is not studied in detail, as this would be exceedingly inefficient and costly. Only the typical habitat zones are subject to the two analytical protocols: the *dissect* and the *quadrat*. The dissect (on the left) is a sectional cut that includes what is on the surface of the ground, above the ground (including the microclimate) and what is underground (the humidity and water table). See the Humboldt transect on page 30 for an example. For the quadrat (on the right), a normative square is delineated within which all flora and fauna are quantified. From the results of these two analyses of typical eco-zones, the characteristics of the other similar zones can be assumed.

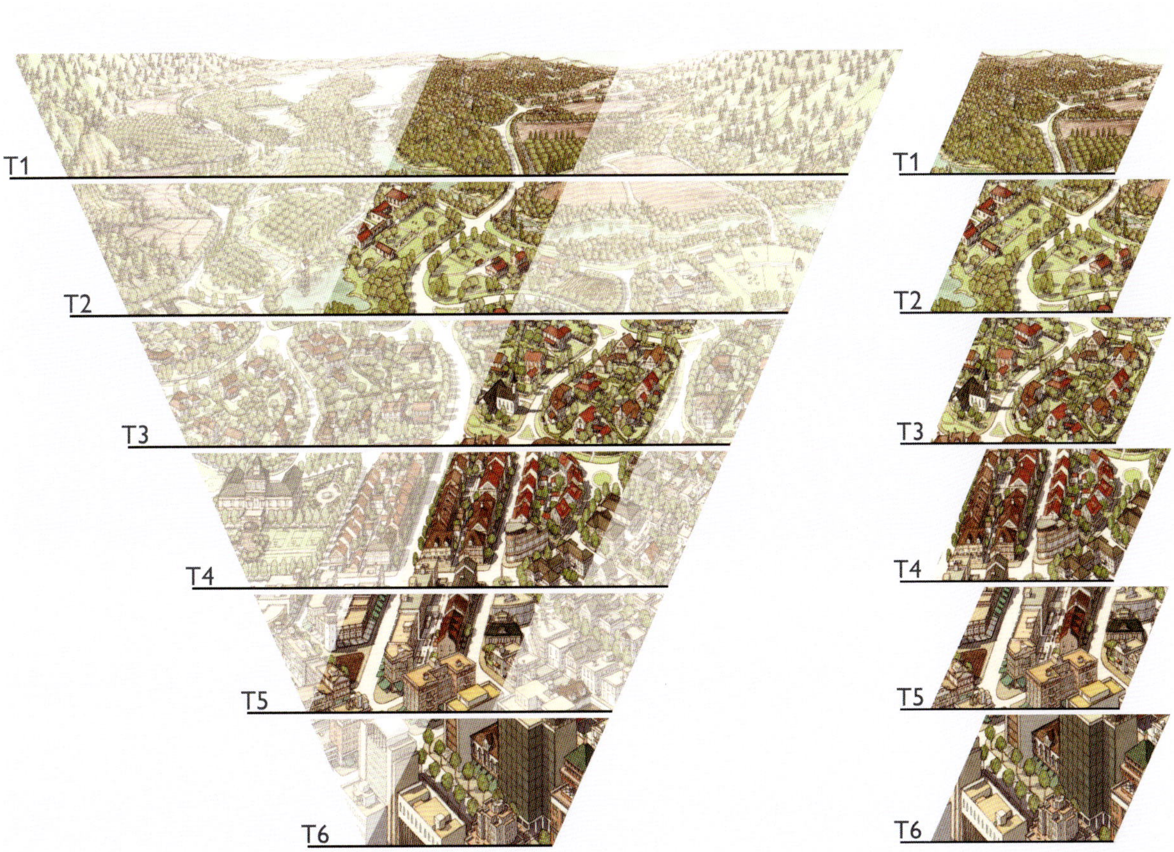

EUSEBIO AZCUÉ FOR DPZ CODESIGN

Urban areas can be analyzed by a method similar to the environmental assessment protocol described opposite, and with the same efficiency. A synoptic survey from an aerial photograph first identifies the most desirable of the typical place types of a city. These selections would be field verified, with public participation. The analysis involves the equivalent of a *dissect*, which in this case is a section taken through both public and private realm, including the street, its landscape and sidewalk, yard and frontage, the building size, backyard, and alley. The equivalent of a *quadrat* would take a block of lots on both sides of the selected street for quantity takeoffs of unit density and built area, pavement, pervious surface, lot coverage, on- and off-street parking, planting, etc. From the results of this dissect and quadrat, a code for each Transect Zone could be easily derived.

ANALYSIS FOR TRANSECT ZONE T3 - SUB-URBAN **GENTILLY TERRACE**

QUADRAT

1. ST. ROCH AVENUE @ LOMBARD STREET

Average Block Dimension	250' x 600'
Average Units per Acre	6.8 units
Average Lot Size	50' x 115'
Average Lot Coverage	36%
Average Parked Cars per Acre	13.7 cars
Average Trees per Acre	4 trees

DISSECT

2. PUBLIC FRONTAGE

Public Frontage Type	Avenue
Spatial Width	186'
Posted Design Speed	TBD MPH
R.O.W. Width	100'
Moving Lanes	1 @ 10' Two ways
Parking Lanes	8' both sides
Pavement Width	36'
Curb Type	Raised
Curb Radius	10'
Neutral Ground	22'
Sidewalk	12'
Planter Type	Continuous
Planter Width	4'
Planting Pattern	Allee 60' o.c.
Tree Type	Live Oak
Bike Way Type	N/A
Bike Way Width	N/A

3. PRIVATE FRONTAGE

Private Frontage Type	Common Lawn / Porch & Fence
Principal building height	2 stories max.
Outbuilding height	1 Story
First floor above grade	36" min. avg
Watermark Level	TBD
Building disposition	Edgeyard
Lot Size	72' x 120'
Lot coverage	40%
Buildout percentage at Setback	20% of lot width min.
Front Setback	48' min.
Side Setback	TBD min.
Rear Setback	TBD min.
Outbuilding Setback	TBD min.
Front Encroachment	10' max.
Side Encroachment	2' max.
Ground Level Function	Residential
Upper Level Function	Residential

SANDY SORLIEN

This card summarizes the metrics of the *quadrat* and *dissect*, in this case for the Gentilly neighborhood of New Orleans. It can be directly transferred to the summary table opposite. From there it is activated by the regulatory language of the SmartCode, within which the table is embedded.

	T1 NATURAL ZONE	T2 RURAL ZONE	T3 SUB-URBAN ZONE	T4 GENERAL URBAN ZONE	T5 URBAN CENTER ZONE	T6 URBAN CORE ZONE	SD SPECIAL DISTRICT	
a. ALLOCATION OF ZONES per Pedestrian Shed (applicable to Article 3 only)							(see Table 16)	
CLD requires	no minimum	50% min	10 - 30%	20 - 40%	not permitted	not permitted		
TND requires	no minimum	no minimum	10 - 30%	30 - 60 %	10 - 30%	not permitted		
RCD requires	no minimum	no minimum	not permitted	10 - 30%	10 - 30%	40 - 80%		
b. BASE RESIDENTIAL DENSITY (see Section 3.4)								
By Right	not applicable	1 unit / 20 ac avg.	2 units / ac. gross	4 units / ac. gross	6 units / ac. gross	12 units / ac. gross		
By TDR	by Variance	by Variance	6 units / ac. gross	12 units / ac. gross	24 units / ac. gross	96 units / ac. gross		
Other Functions	by Variance	by Variance	10 - 20%	20 - 30%	30 - 50%	50 - 70%		
c. BLOCK SIZE								
Block Perimeter	no maximum	no maximum	3000 ft. max	2400 ft. max	2000 ft. max	2000 ft. max*		
d. THOROUGHFARES (see Table 3 and Table 4)						* 3000 ft. max with parking structures		
HW	permitted	permitted	permitted	not permitted	not permitted	not permitted		
BV	not permitted	not permitted	permitted	permitted	permitted	permitted		
AV	not permitted	not permitted	permitted	permitted	permitted	permitted		
CS	not permitted	not permitted	not permitted	not permitted	permitted	permitted		
DR	not permitted	not permitted	permitted	permitted	permitted	permitted		
ST	not permitted	not permitted	permitted	permitted	permitted	not permitted		
RD	permitted	permitted	permitted	not permitted	not permitted	not permitted		
Rear Lane	permitted	permitted	permitted	permitted	not permitted	not permitted		
Rear Alley	not permitted	not permitted	permitted	required	required	required		
Path	permitted	permitted	permitted	permitted	not permitted	not permitted		
Passage	not permitted	not permitted	permitted	permitted	permitted	permitted		
Bicycle Trail	permitted	permitted	permitted	not permitted*	not permitted	not permitted		
Bicycle Lane	permitted	permitted	permitted	permitted	not permitted	not permitted		
Bicycle Route	permitted	permitted	permitted	permitted	permitted	permitted		
e. CIVIC SPACES (see Table 13)						* permitted within Open Spaces		
Park	permitted	permitted	permitted	by Warrant	by Warrant	by Warrant		
Green	not permitted	not permitted	permitted	permitted	permitted	not permitted		
Square	not permitted	not permitted	not permitted	permitted	permitted	permitted		
Plaza	not permitted	not permitted	not permitted	not permitted	permitted	permitted		
Playground	permitted	permitted	permitted	permitted	permitted	permitted		
f. LOT OCCUPATION								DISPOSITION
Lot Width	not applicable	by Warrant	72 ft. min 120 ft. max	18 ft. min 96 ft. max	18 ft. min 180 ft. max	18 ft. min 700 ft. max		
Lot Coverage	not applicable	by Warrant	60% max	70% max	80% max	90% max		
g. SETBACKS - PRINCIPAL BUILDING (see Table 15)								
(g.1) Front Setback (Principal)	not applicable	48 ft. min	24 ft. min	6 ft. min 18 ft. max	2 ft. min 12 ft. max	2 ft. min 12 ft. max		
(g.2) Front Setback (Secondary)	not applicable	48 ft. min	12 ft. min	6 ft. min 18 ft. max	2 ft. min 12 ft. max	2 ft. min 12 ft. max		
(g.3) Side Setback	not applicable	96 ft. min	12 ft. min	0 ft. min	0 ft. min 24 ft. max	0 ft. min 24 ft. max		
(g.4) Rear Setback	not applicable	96 ft. min	12 ft. min	3 ft. min*	3 ft. min*	0 ft. min		
Frontage Buildout	not applicable	not applicable	40% min	60% min	80% min	80% min		
h. SETBACKS - OUTBUILDING (see Table 15)								
(h.1) Front Setback	not applicable	20 ft. min +bldg setback	20 ft. min +bldg setback	20 ft. min +bldg setback	40 ft. max from rear prop	not applicable		
(h.2) Side Setback	not applicable	3 ft. or 6 ft.	3 ft. or 6 ft.	0 ft. min or 3 ft.	0 ft min	not applicable		
(h.3) Rear Setback	not applicable	3 ft. min	3 ft. min	3 ft.	3 ft. max	not applicable		
i. BUILDING DISPOSITION (see Table 9)						* or 15 ft. from center line of Rear Alley		
Edgeyard	permitted	permitted	permitted	permitted	not permitted	not permitted		
Sideyard	not permitted	not permitted	not permitted	permitted	permitted	not permitted		
Rearyard	not permitted	not permitted	not permitted	permitted	permitted	permitted		
Courtyard	not permitted	not permitted	not permitted	not permitted	permitted	permitted		
j. PRIVATE FRONTAGES (see Table 7)								CONFIGURATION
Common Yard	not applicable	permitted	permitted	not permitted	not permitted	not permitted		
Porch & Fence	not applicable	not permitted	permitted	permitted	not permitted	not permitted		
Terrace or Dooryard	not applicable	not permitted	not permitted	permitted	permitted	not permitted		
Forecourt	not applicable	not permitted	not permitted	permitted	permitted	permitted		
Stoop	not applicable	not permitted	not permitted	permitted	permitted	permitted		
Shopfront & Awning	not applicable	not permitted	not permitted	permitted	permitted	permitted		
Gallery	not applicable	not permitted	not permitted	permitted	permitted	permitted		
Arcade	not applicable	not permitted	not permitted	not permitted	permitted	permitted		
k. BUILDING CONFIGURATION (see Table 8)								
Principal Building	not applicable	2 Stories max	2 Stories max	3 Stories max, 2 min	5 Stories max, 2 min	8 Stories max, 2 min		
Outbuilding	not applicable	2 Stories max	2 Stories max	2 Stories max	2 Stories max	not applicable		
l. BUILDING FUNCTION (see Table 10 & Table 12)								FUNCTION
Residential	not applicable	restricted use	restricted use	limited use	open use	open use		
Lodging	not applicable	restricted use	restricted use	limited use	open use	open use		
Office	not applicable	restricted use	restricted use	limited use	open use	open use		
Retail	not applicable	restricted use	restricted use	limited use	open use	open use		

ARTICLE 5

ARTICLE 2, 3, 4

DPZ CODESIGN

This is a technical summary of the metrics in a typical SmartCode. It is used as a checklist. It requires legal language, which makes up the bulk of the final code, to activate it as regulation. It is the expression of the metrics that appear in the SmartCode to be locally calibrated by *dissect* and *quadrat* as described opposite.

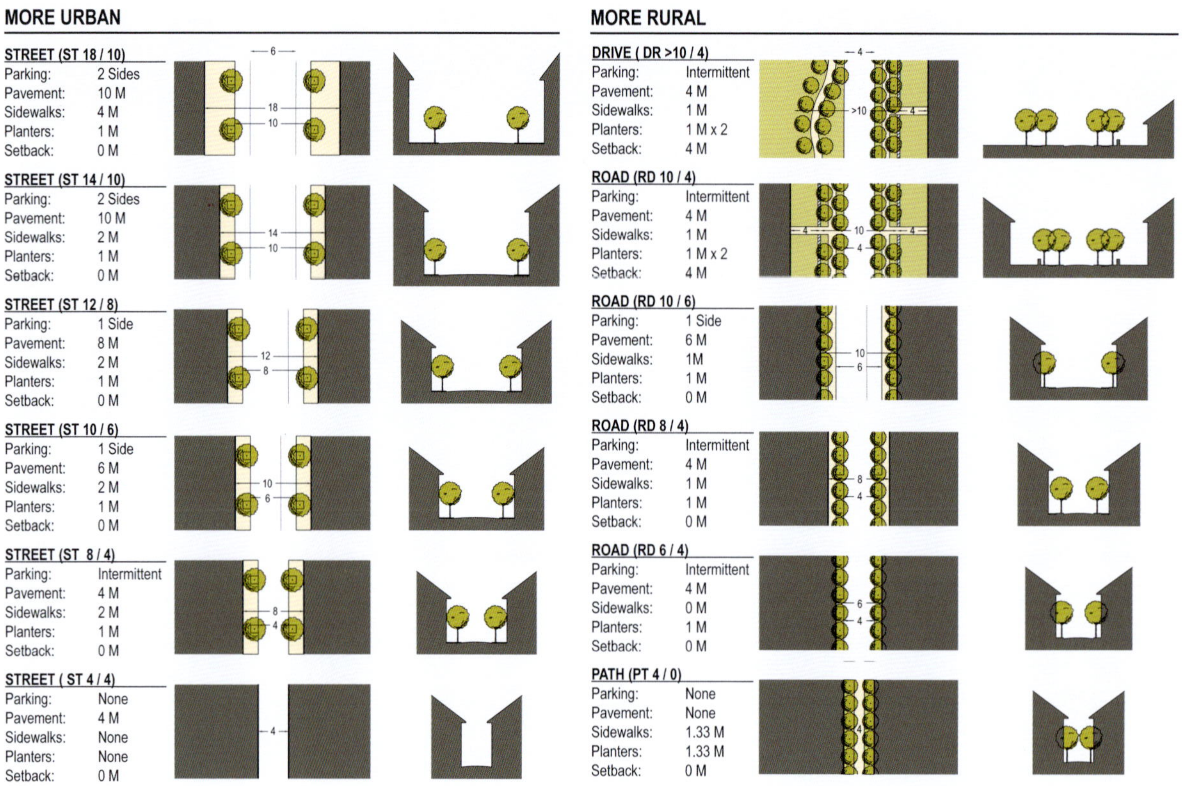

This declension of thoroughfare types was created for the new town of Heulebrug in the Netherlands.

OPTICOS DESIGN

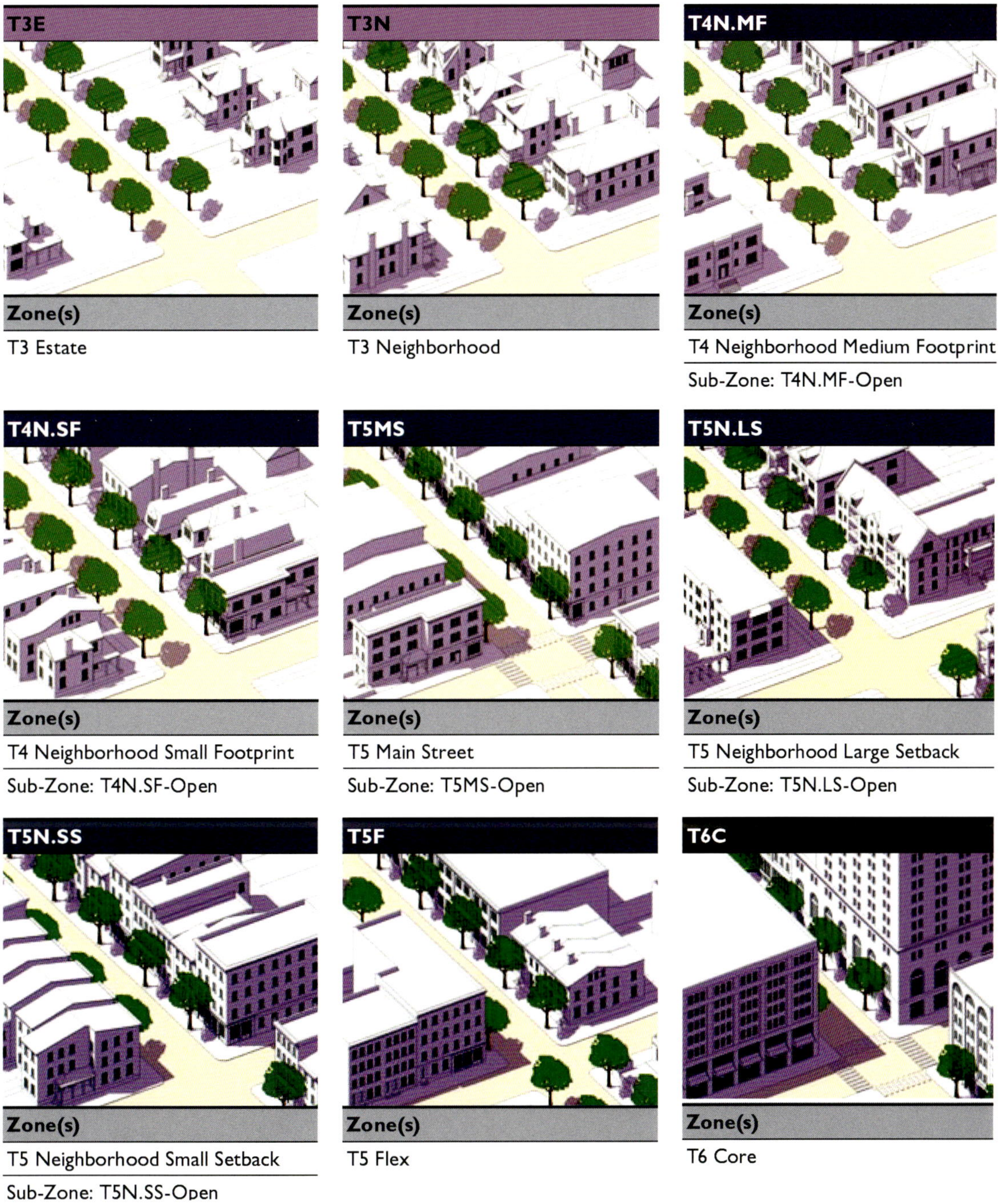

Cincinnati's Transect-based code, like all form-based codes, includes abstracted illustrations of permitted types. The bird's-eye, or axonometric, view is typical to reveal essential relationships between buildings and between a building and the street. The illustrations correspond to legally activating text and specific standards, as with conventional zoning codes. However, it is possible to create an ideographic code, like the Chinese scroll seen on pages 28 and 29, predominantly or entirely from visual information. It would be appropriate for an illiterate or post-literate culture, and in any case supplies the regulator with a didactic instrument to communicate the concept.

These illustrations are taken from the new code of the city of Stockholm (1997). Being context-based, the code proposes that construction in each zone be in the character of the existing urbanism and architecture. Given the marked urban-to-rural mosaic of Stockholm, it is very similar to a Transect-based code. This code controls for an architecture of *place* rather than *time*. An architecture of its time was threatening to homogenize the diversity of Stockholm's immersive zones and to make Stockholm indistinguishable from modern cities everywhere. This code is accompanied by a poster-sized chart illustrating colors, textures, and even window types. Opposite are the pages of four of the zones. The diagram below uses a single image to summarize each of the 12 zones.

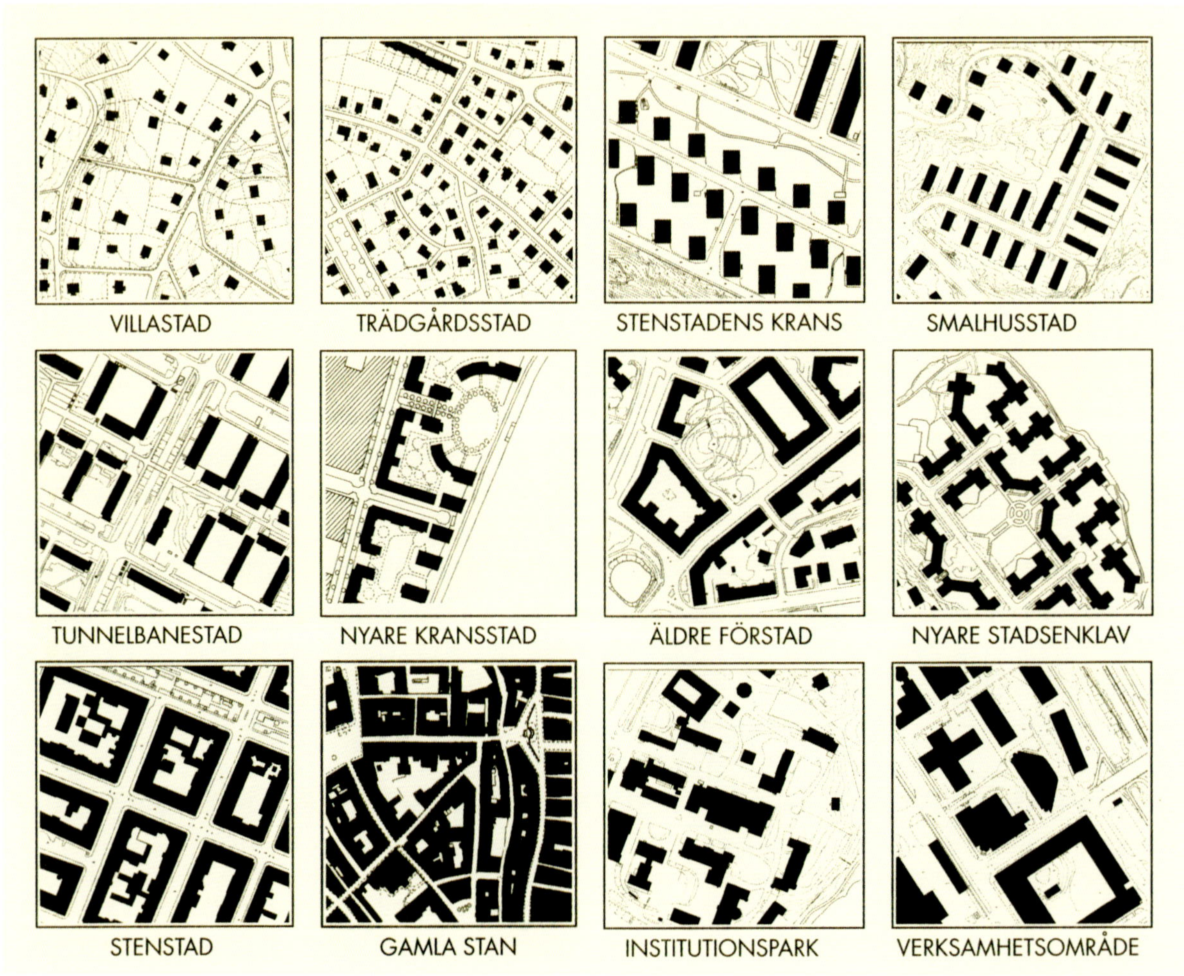

STOCKHOLM CITY PLANNING DEPARTMENT

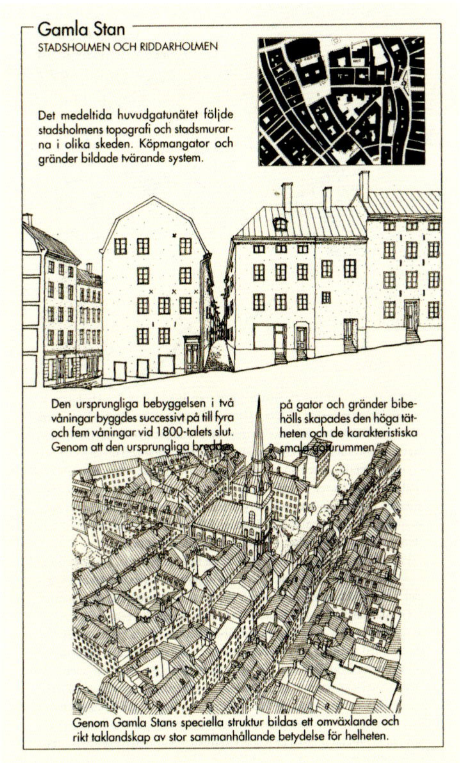

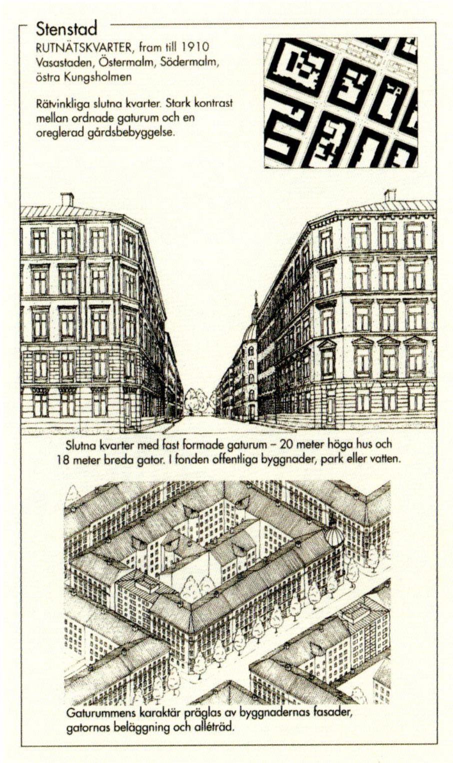

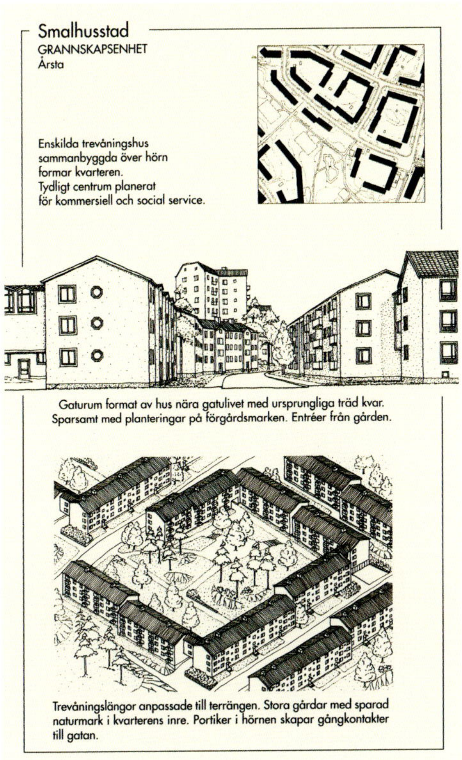

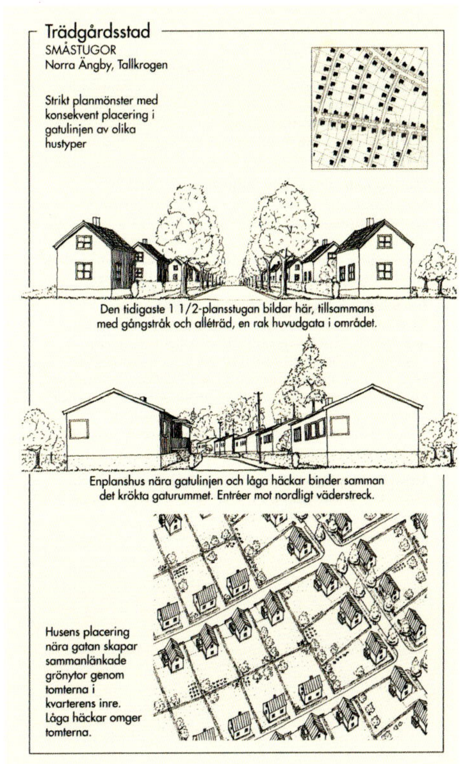

STOCKHOLM CITY PLANNING DEPARTMENT

Part Two:
TEXTS

COMMUNITY ACROSS THE TRANSECT

ELIZABETH PLATER-ZYBERK & CHARLES C. BOHL

Eighty percent of everything ever built in America has been built in the last 50 years, and most of it is depressing, brutal, ugly, unhealthy and spiritually degrading.

– James Howard Kunstler, *The Geography of Nowhere*[1]

In 2030, about half of the buildings in which Americans live, work and shop will have been built after 2000. While these projections may seem overwhelming, they also demonstrate that nearly half of what will be the built environment in 2030 doesn't even exist yet, giving the current generation a vital opportunity to reshape future development.

– Arthur C. Nelson, "Toward a New Metropolis: The Opportunity to Rebuild America"[2]

The 80 percent of the American built environment described by Jim Kunstler as the "Geography of Nowhere" has appeared incrementally over the last half century under the influence of land-use regulations and a web of codes, standards, and business practices that now represent a national system for the mass-production of sprawl. The placeless character of what passes for community building today is the product of an ad hoc framework that governs making and remaking the physical form of neighborhoods, cities, rural areas—and entire regions.

This "hidden" regulation of place has been the subject of increasing scrutiny. As Andrés Duany has observed, "what is assumed to be a neutral, market-responsive and technocratic system is actually heavily biased."[3] Empirical studies have now confirmed a regulatory bias favoring conventional suburban development at the expense of more varied local and urban forms.[4] Nevertheless, the power of sprawl as a business strategy and wealth generator has remained largely unchallenged. As a result, there is today a crucial need for a more explicit understanding of how hidden instruments such as engineering standards, building codes, zoning ordinances, lenders' guidelines, and other professional tools shape the possibilities for place making and community building long before any designer ever picks up a pencil.[5]

Among those studying American development trends, real estate analyst Christopher Leinberger has written that the development industry is now focused on building the same 19 real estate product types in every community in America.[6] These generally represent single-use, stand-alone properties with floor-area ratios from 0.1 to 0.4 (i.e., where buildings cover only between 10-40 percent of a total site area, and the rest is devoted primarily to parking).[7] These standardized product types have been refined by the industry over many decades, making them relatively easy to finance, build, lease, and sell. In recent years the growth of real estate investment trusts (REITs) have transformed these real estate properties into commodities that can be bundled and traded as investment portfolios.

Together with a lowering of interest rates, such commoditization has provided much of the basis for the building boom that lasted until 2007, and such development now pervades the fabric of our metropolitan areas. Yet, the staunch opposition to growth in communities nationwide also reveals how satisfying basic functional needs is not enough. While the real estate industry has become very good at building these single-use, automobile-oriented projects, the projects themselves are not very good at building communities. Ad hoc aggregations of single-use projects have proven to be ill suited for building communities that are socially diverse, environmentally sensitive, and economically sustainable. The result is a widespread dissatisfaction with growth and sprawl, and the clamoring for new methods of building communities that are more distinct, memorable, livable, and worth caring about.

Contemporary ways of envisioning, planning, and building communities—based on planning for land-use zones, traffic flows, and the production of real estate products—stand in stark contrast to earlier ways that Americans planned towns and cities. Here is Benton MacKaye, writing in the late 1960s, about the rationales that informed the community builders of his hometown, Shirley Center, Massachusetts, when it was founded in 1753:

> The committee made its report and recommendations (their "town plan"). The cornerstone would be the Meetinghouse (the "sacred tree" that went with the moot-hill). On one side would be the Churchyard, dedicated to eternity. On the other side the Common, devoted to posterity. Around this would be "clustered," besides the homesteads and the Town Hall, the Meetinghouse, Schoolhouse and Country Store. They would make the "*five senses*" that constitute a complete rural community: home, government, religion, education, and commerce each represented by its appropriate structure.[8]

The above passage shows how much knowledge of true community building has been lost in recent times. The good news, however, is there will be a great opportunity in coming years to go beyond current hypercommercial practice to build healthier, more fulfilling environments. As the Brookings Institution study cited at the beginning of this article estimates, nearly *half* the built environment in the United States will be built or rebuilt over the next 25 years.[9] The question is, will the same system—the same types of codes, policies, business models and practices—continue to mass-produce sprawl and cookie-cutter places? Or can the current and succeeding generations make the most of their "opportunity to rebuild America" to enable a greater variety and quality of places to be built that will meet a greater variety of needs?

We believe the positive resolution of this question cannot be based simply on zoning reform within the current framework. In recent decades many attempts to create better regulatory tools—through planned-unit development, flexible zoning, performance zoning, overlay districts, design guidelines, and the like—have produced little or no gain. Today, communities with weak or nonexistent zoning, such as Houston, simply offer different arrangements of the same sprawl-inducing types as more regulated communities. As long as the basis of regulation and development remains divorced from holistic concepts of environment and society, of the region and community character, the results will be the same.

A Normative Theory and Framework for Place Making

The contemporary American landscape has evolved from a tapestry of vast natural areas and agricultural lands dotted with small hamlets, villages, towns, and cities into a world composed largely of segregated zones, into which are placed mass-produced real estate products linked by an expansive automobile-oriented infrastructure. As Dolores Hayden observed in *A Field Guide to Sprawl,* "Words such as city, suburb and countryside no longer capture the reality of real estate development in the United States."[10]

Through the years, there has been no shortage of theories, concepts, and studies examining the American landscape for what it is. The literature ranges from the perceptive work of William Whyte, who first coined the term "sprawl" in the 1950s; to Robert Venturi and Denise Scott-Brown's embrace of the common commercial strip in *Learning from Las Vegas*; to J.B. Jackson's writings on "vernacular landscapes"; to all manner of research attempting to define the "costs of sprawl."[11] However, Kevin Lynch once referred to such work as "status quo" theory, because it merely described the world as it is (or was). By contrast, "normative" theories have the power to describe the world as it ought to be.[12]

What has been lacking is a more holistic, regional framework for a normative theory based on *character of place*. Such a theory would transcend and guide more technocratically defined land-use zones, floor area ratios, open-space standards, environmental regulations and roadway carrying capacities. The problem hasn't simply been the lack of distinctive rural and urban (normative) models, but the relentless and often insidious grafting of suburban types—building-lot configurations, frontages, street types, landscaping, public works, open space—onto urban and rural settings. This has fueled the destruction of the city and the countryside as well as frustrated the construction of new urban places. A normative theory based on character of place could offer people a vision they can better understand and invest themselves emotionally in. The Rural-to-Urban Transect proposes one such theory.

The Transect is a way of locating and understanding a variety of different types of human settlement within a comprehensive web of natural and human habitats. As a historical concept, its origins have been noted in work by Patrick Geddes, Ian McHarg, and Christopher Alexander.[13] Douglas Duany, the landscape architect credited with introducing the idea to the New Urbanist movement, has traced a "Transect sensibility" even further back to such 18th-century geographers and naturalists as Alexander von Humbolt. *The SmartCode Manual* describes the Transect in these terms:

> A transect, in its origins (Von Humboldt, 1790), is a geographical cross-section of a region used to reveal a sequence of environments. Originally, it was used to analyze natural ecologies, showing varying characteristics through different zones such as shores, wetlands, plains, and uplands. For human environments, such a cross-section can be used to identify a set of habitats that vary by their level and intensity of urban character, a continuum that ranges from rural to urban. In Transect planning, this range of environments is the basis for organizing the components of urbanization: building, lot, land use, street, and all of the other physical elements of the human habitat.[14]

The Transect is important within the New Urbanism movement because it provides, when applied in codes such as the SmartCode, a regional framework for planning that encompasses a fuller spectrum of rural, sub-urban (which the Transect distinguishes from conventional suburban development) and urban environments. Although the Charter for the New Urbanism includes regional principles, the primary focus of New Urbanist practice has been at the scale of traditional neighborhood developments (TNDs) and transit-oriented developments (TODs). Early regional planning by New Urbanists was generally organized according to environmental and transportation systems that essentially allowed the mapping of locations for new urban nodes. The Transect encompasses a more complete range of human settlement types, addressing relationships between urban, sub-urban and rural areas, and attempting to define the basic physical characteristics that differentiate them.

The Transect reflects the recognition that a sustainable future must embody an interrelated continuum of natural and human habitats—natural, rural, sub-urban, and urban—with differing settlement densities and opportunities for social encounter and human activity. In particular, it attempts to distill general physical characteristics of urbanism that have existed for 5,000 years—the hamlet, village, urban neighborhood, town, and city—in relation to each other and the natural world.

It is important to distinguish the theory of the Transect from its practical applications. It should also be emphasized that the Rural-to-Urban Transect is a normative model that should be locally observed and calibrated when creating a code. The Transect of a given place will be determined by its culture, geographic region, settlement patterns, and local examples of what constitutes natural, rural, sub-urban, and urban character.

Within New Urbanism, the use and view of the Transect continues to evolve—as does the degree to which individual New Urbanists incorporate it into their thought and work. The most detailed application of the Transect can be found in the SmartCode. This "form-based" model zoning code originated as a proprietary alternative to "use-based" zoning practice. It is now distributed as "freeware" via the Internet. Where the Transect is an overall theory of human settlement, the SmartCode represents one application of it that is intended to guide the building of cities and towns.

Apart from the SmartCode, a wide variety of planners, urban designers, transportation planners, and architects—including many who do not identify themselves as New Urbanists—now use the ideas of the Transect on either an informal basis or as a formal framework to facilitate community planning, design regulating plans, or organize typologies of streets, buildings, open spaces, and other aspects of the physical environment. In transportation, for example, the Transect is being applied to establish a more context-based framework for the design of urban thoroughfares.[15] And in land-use planning, where there is now widespread interest in the potential of form-based coding as an alternative to use-based zoning, there are now dozens of firms creating their own model codes that reference the Transect but are distinct from the SmartCode.[16]

Of Places, Theories of Places, and the Practice of Place Making

The Transect has been proposed as a prism for analyzing the degree of urbanity of everything from building frontage, lampposts, street trees, and stores, and has even been applied to create humorous Rural-to-Urban Transects of hair styles and shoes. The theory has been represented graphically through a simplified typology of "Transect Zones."

The Transect most widely used by New Urbanists divides the human environment into six such zones, from very rural, to sub-urban, to urban. The capital letter T (for "Transect Zone") and a sequence of numbers provide a shorthand for referring to these areas: T-1 Natural Zone, T-2 Rural Zone, T-3 Sub-Urban Zone, etc.[17] What distinguishes the physical character of each of these "immersive" settings is the manner in which everything—e.g., building types, heights, and setbacks; open spaces; the character of streets, alleys, and passages; and the design of street lighting, landscaping, trees, and street furniture—reinforces a certain overall physical character of place.[18]

For proponents, the attractiveness of the Transect lies in its ability to present a simple and concise continuum of settlement types that can be employed to sort out rural, suburban, and urban characteristics. Yet this simplicity has also been singled out as one of its principal weaknesses. For example, critics typically object to the implication there must always be a smooth gradient of settlement patterns from rural to urban, from low, to mid-, to high densities. But this is not, in fact, a tenet of Transect theory. The theory specifically allows for the juxtaposition of different zones. Adjacencies such as between the residential neighborhoods of Coral Gables, Florida, and that city's downtown do not violate Transect principles. Neither would the presence of a large natural area adjacent to a downtown. Indeed, such dramatic juxtapositions do occur with Manhattan's Central Park, Philadelphia's Fairmont Park, and Washington, D.C.'s Rock Creek Park. Generally speaking, in terms of developing a plan for a region, juxtapositions of Transect Zones will create fewer problems than lack of consistency within a zone or an overall lack of variety of zones.

Another common criticism of the Transect involves the relatively small number of zones into which it attempts to order a complete range of settlement types. In fact, its six conceptual Transect Zones were actually conceived as a way to expand the range of settlement types and satisfy a broader range of residential preferences than are available today in a climate of finance, zoning, and building regulation that can produce only bland homogeneity.

As a typology of generalized conditions, the Transect parallels Sidney Brower's research on residential preferences. Brower has distilled some 33 qualities associated with broad concepts of ambience, engagement, and choicefulness into four residential neighborhood types.[19] The four types are "centers," identified as denser neighborhoods associated with city living; "residential partnerships," similar in quality to conventional suburban subdivisions, and representing exclusive, homogeneous, family-directed neighborhoods; "small towns," closest in character to traditional towns and villages; and "retreats," including rural retreats, but also encompassing gated communities and condominium/apartment complexes.

Ironically, a third concern with the Transect—quite opposite to the first two—is that its zones are ***too*** fine-grained and specific. In fact, early versions of the Transect focused primarily on three general conditions: the urban edge, the general (as in "general urban neighborhood condition"), and the center. Those who prefer this typology believe it provides a looser framework that could be applied within a single block. They argue that the more detailed the Transect Zone definitions become, the more problematic they will be for describing the complexity of actual cities.

While many of these criticisms contain elements of truth, they obscure one of the real strengths of the theory. Transect theory aims to establish a dialogue between an overall regional framework for planning that encompasses a fuller spectrum of rural, sub-urban, and urban environments and the use of locally derived design forms. *The SmartCode*, for example, employs a nesting relationship in which regions contain community units such as villages, traditional neighborhoods, and metropolitan centers, and the community units contain mixes of Transect Zones. Regardless of the number of zones delineated, the Transect theory calls for calibration to reflect specific local and regional differences. A "General Urban Zone" in Louisville is not expected to resemble the same zone in Chicago or Miami. The extent to which mixed uses are present, the combination of building types, variations in setbacks, landscaping, and architecture are all anticipated in applying the Transect. Thus, unlike conventional use-based zoning, the Transect model requires research into regional architectural and urban forms, which can then be incorporated into more place-based regulations.

The Transect has also been criticized for its failure to account for the complexity of places, particularly the complexity of historic villages, towns, and cities. One cannot disagree with this point, that Transect theory cannot prescribe or predict the complete variety and complexity of historic cities, developed over centuries. However, it is also true that recognizable, common, underlying structures may exist among places in such a city, and between the more rural, sub-urban and urban places of a particular region and culture. And the desire to understand the formal basis of such similarities and differences is not unique to the Transect. Indeed, throughout history, from Aristotle to A.E.J. Morris, there have been many attempts to propose general principles of built form, and theorists have tried to describe the qualities of different types of places.[20]

Unlike many of these purely descriptive efforts, however, what some critics find most troublesome is the use of such descriptive typologies to guide the shaping of actual new communities and regions. They argue that, in this role, the Transect would "replace the inefficiencies of one system with the promises of another with similar consequences."

This would be a common concern with any proposed system, but this critique fails to engage the system that is presently doing so much harm. Place making and community building, at least in the United States, are currently regulated by coding mechanisms. Bringing about positive change and reforming the current system will require the creation of effective alternatives. Further, to be legally defensible, an effort must be made to coordinate specific proposals for change with an underlying theory.

Transect theory clearly attempts to occupy a difficult position. As a new normative theory, it is variously criticized as too complex or not complex enough; too much like conventional zoning or not similar enough to underpin a legally defensible system. Others have embraced the Transect as a theoretical framework, but maintained that the same results can be achieved using a more transparent terminology that does not resort to "T-Zones." Such simplicity and transparency, however, have never been the hallmark of planning codes and regulations.

One has only to examine the 227 pages of code, manual, and appendices in version 9.2 of the SmartCode to see how difficult it is to move from the simplicity of the Transect theory to actual code writing. As the Transect is extrapolated into model codes, and as these are adapted for use at the urban and regional levels, it is natural that complexity will increase. For example, the SmartCode already distinguishes between three "plan types," six "sector types," and four "community types"—in addition to the six Transect Zones, specialized districts, and separate guidelines for civic spaces and buildings. A close look at the simplified drawings of the six primary zones themselves will also reveal that these have continued to evolve so that two alternate conditions can now be seen within each zone except the T1 Natural Zone. These were developed, in part, to illustrate conceptual transitions from one zone to the next.

As a variety of form-based codes have been created by other community-building professions, debate has also ensued over which element (e.g., Transect Zones, street types, frontage types, lot types, etc.) should control the others. Similar debate has emerged concerning the significant differences encountered in applying Transect-based approaches to new neighborhoods and towns versus existing cities.

Differences of opinion also exist within Transect-based planning circles concerning the treatment of single-use areas. The Transect typology does explicitly provide for single-use, special purpose areas ("districts") such as institutional campuses, airports, and heavy industrial zones. However, New Urbanists have long debated whether single-use residential subdivisions, office parks, and shopping centers should be included in the T-3 Sub-Urban Zone, considered the "bread-and-butter of American urbanism." As currently defined, the Transect excludes these forms.[21] In contrast to large-lot, single-use, automobile-oriented subdivisions with very little connectivity, the Transect defines the T-3 zone as walkable, relatively compact, primarily residential, single-family neighborhoods where other uses are also allowed. Thus, even though conventional single-use areas may be recognized where they exist, the implication is they will evolve over time into walkable neighborhoods that incorporate a mix of housing types and uses.

Toward a Culture of Good Place Making

The question remains whether any systematic approach to regulating place making and community building is capable of producing something close to "the good city." The excessive legal, technical, and administrative constraints on place making and community building present a challenge, if not a crisis, for our generation's capability to build more livable, beautiful, and enduring communities.

The ideal has perhaps been articulated in Christopher Alexander's opus, *The Nature of Order*. This four-volume study, which extends his work on pattern languages, proposes a generative model of place making that will "allow anyone, and any group of people, to create beautiful, functional, meaningful places."[22] Perhaps the Transect is just one step along this much longer path away from the technocratic regulation of community design toward what Alexander envisions as a bottom-up model in which a culture of good place making is reborn, and where citizens directly participate in the shaping of the places they live, work, and go about their daily lives.

The theory and application of the Transect is a work in progress, and is currently the subject of far more extensive discussion and debate than the sampling included here. Ongoing research and debate concerns everything from the establishment of environmental performance measures for Transect Zones, to the definitions of the zones themselves, to potential connections between Transect theory and diverse philosophical traditions such as pragmatism and natural law.

Future research and discussion could include an extrapolation of David Enwicht's "exchange opportunities," where a city's value might be measured by the number and magnitude of potential exchanges, as explored through a Transect of places for social encounter.[23] Eliot Allen's propositions for a more fine-grained Transect of natural settings, which are currently reduced to T1 Natural and T2 Rural zones, also represents a rich topic for further study. A more explicit exposition on architecture and the Transect would also be extremely useful.[24] The nuances of the Transect in high-density cities for the purposes of form-based coding is also in need of further study. And an in-depth piece might consider how the Transect might further resolve urbanist and environmentalist perspectives, allow reconsideration of relationships between built and natural environments, and reintegrate cities and towns within larger ecosystems. (See essays on pages 127 and 167.)

According to the demographers, we have been presented with the opportunity to rebuild America. Unfortunately, if we continue to use the existing web of codes, standards, and regulations that govern the development and redevelopment of our communities, we are doomed to continue building in unsustainable ways. If change is to come, alternative regulatory tools will need to be developed based on an entirely different set of desired outcomes. In particular, a new framework must emerge that will enable a greater variety and quality of places to be preserved and built. The Rural-to-Urban Transect represents one alternative framework to guide such change.

This essay was orginally published in Places Journal, *March 2006.*

1. James Howard Kunstler, *The Geography of Nowhere* (New York: Simon & Schuster, 1993).

2. Arthur C. Nelson, "Toward a New Metropolis: The Opportunity to Rebuild America" (Washington, D.C.: *The Brookings Institution Metropolitan Policy Program, 2004*).

3. Andrés Duany, "Introduction to the Special Issue: The Transect," *Journal of Urban Design, Vol. 7, No. 3* (2002), pp. 251–60.

4. Rolf Pendall found clear links between bias in existing land-use controls favoring conventional patterns and the development of sprawl: Pendall, "Do Land Use Controls Cause Sprawl?" *Environment and Planning B: Planning and Design, Vol. 26, No. 4* (1999), pp. 555–71. Emily Talen and Gerit Knapp's study of planning regulations in Illinois found de facto prohibitions against more compact, mixed-use, walkable neighborhood design: Talen and Knaap, "The implementation of Smart Growth Principles: An Empirical Study of Land Use Regulation in Illinois," *Annual Conference of the Association of Collegiate Schools of Planning* (Atlanta, GA, 2000).

5. See Eran Ben-Joseph, *The Code of the City: Standards and the Hidden Language of Place Making* (Cambridge, MA: MIT Press, 2005); Eran Ben-Joseph and Terry S. Szold, eds., *Regulating Place: Standards and the Shaping of Urban America* (New York: Routledge, 2005); and Paula M. Craighead, ed., *The Hidden Design in Land Use Ordinances* (Maine Arts Commission and the University of Southern Maine Design Arts Project, 1991).

6. Christopher B. Leinberger, "Retrofitting Real Estate Finance: Alternatives to the Nineteen Standard Product Types." *Places*, 2005, 17, No (2005), pp. 24–29.

7. Leinberger, "Retrofitting Real Estate Finance."

8. Benton Mackaye, *Expedition Nine: A Return to a Region* (Washington, D.C.: The Wilderness Society, 1969). Emphasis added.

9. Nelson, "Toward a New Metropolis."

10. Dolores Hayden, *A Field Guide to Sprawl* (New York: W.W. Norton & Co., 2004).

11. See William H. Whyte, ed., *The Exploding Metropolis* (Garden City, NY: Doubleday, 1958); Robert Venturi et al., Learning from *Las Vegas: The Forgotten Symbolism of Architectural Form* (Cambridge, MA: MIT Press, 1977); and John Brinckerhoff Jackson, *Discovering the Vernacular Landscape* (New Haven, CN: Yale University Press, 1984).

12. Kevin Lynch, *Good City Form* (Cambridge, MA: MIT Press, 1981).

13. Duany, "Introduction to the Special Issue: The Transect"; Andrés Duany and Emily Talen, "Transect Planning," *Journal of the American Planning Association, Vol. 68, No. 3* (2002), pp. 245–66; and Emily Talen, "Help for Urban Planning: The Transect Strategy," *Journal of Urban Design, Vol. 7, No. 3* (2002), pp. 293–312.

14. Andrés Duany et al., *SmartCode & Manual* (Miami: New Urban Publications, Inc., 2005).

15. The Transect provides the basis for the four context zones in a 221-page report published by the Institute of Transportation Engineers. See James M. Daisa et al., "Context Sensitive Solutions in Designing Major Thoroughfares for Walkable Communities" (Washington, D.C.: *Institute of Transportation Engineers*, 2006).

16. Examples of form-based codes can be found on the Web site for the Form-Based Codes Institute (FBCI) at www.formbasedcodes.org.

17. Early on, a conscious choice was made to choose a designation system that would allow transect-based codes to resemble more conventional ones.

18. As noted by one reviewer of this article, "there are many more ways in which the character of habitat varies than 'from rural to urban' and that the character of place is fundamentally determined by the quality of experience, including social experience that it affords and while these are qualified by the physical they are not determined by it." The authors concur. Potential relationships between physical character and quality of experience are a core subject of environment and behavior research. In contrast to those who would diminish the importance of the physical environment as "physical determinism," however, the authors maintain the essential role that the physical environment plays in through which different configurations and qualities of the physical environment variously enhance or constrain opportunities for different types of activities and meanings.

19. See Sidney N. Brower, *Good Neighborhoods: A Study of In-town and Suburban Residential Environments* (Westport, CT: Praeger Publishers, 1996); and Sidney N. Brower, "The Sectors of the Transect," *Journal of Urban Design, Vol. 7, No. 3* (2002), pp. 313–20.

20. A.E.J. Morris, *A History of Urban Form: Before the Industrial Revolutions* (New York: John Wiley & Sons, Inc., 1994).

21. Subdivisions, office parks, shopping centers, and other conventional suburban formats are identified within the SmartCode as a list of single-use categories for the purposes of mapping existing conditions, but not for the purposes of plan-making.

22. Christopher Alexander, *The Nature of Order. Book One: The Phenomenon of Life* (New York: Oxford University Press, 2002); *Book Two: The Process of Creating Life* (New York: Oxford University Press, 2002); *Book Three: A Vision of a Living World* (New York: Oxford University Press, 2005); *Book Four: The Luminous Ground* (New York: Oxford University Press, 2004).

23. David Engwicht, *Reclaiming our Cities and Towns: Better Living with Less Traffic* (Gabriola Island: New Society Publishers, 1993).

24. For one example, see Michael Lykoudis and Philip Bess, eds., *Acroterion: The Work of the University of Notre Dame School of Architecture 2004/2005* (Notre Dame, IN: University of Notre Dame School of Architecture, 2005). This presents an entire year of student and faculty work as organized by the Rural-to-Urban Transect.

POSTSUBURBAN PLANNING:

ANDRÉS DUANY & DAVID BRAIN

The United States has been experiencing a phenomenon without precedent. While our cities have maintained their fiscal and political reliance on continued economic growth, the very idea of urban growth has acquired strong negative connotations in the popular imagination. Americans have come to fear the growth of their communities, and this fear has become a powerful political force. Citizens who may not take the time to vote for the next president will nevertheless turn out in large numbers to oppose a real estate development. How did it come to be that a people who built the constellations of villages, towns, and cities that span the continent should have so radically changed its ethos?

Such fear of growth is not unfounded. Whereas once growth represented an increase in the wealth of the community and the possibility of continuous improvement in the quality of life, there are reasons why citizens might now see it only as an increase in traffic, an influx of social problems, higher taxation, and the loss of open space. Neither is it surprising that there is a lack of faith in regulatory efforts to mitigate such problems. The proliferation of technically complex regulation and the unpredictable results of an elaborate public process have undermined popular trust in the government's ability to act as steward of our common interests and private developers' ability to act as agents of civic improvement.

The common outcome is not only sprawl itself, but also a political incapacity to support either systematic alternatives to sprawl or substantively rational planning. Planners often observe that there are only two things about which they can count on finding a consensus in the public process: the criticism of sprawl and the equally passionate rejection of density. In the popular imagination, sprawl is bad, but density seems worse; growth is bad, but regulations infringe on freedom, and they are ineffective at preventing bad outcomes anyway. When the negative consequences of development are combined with the breakdown of trust, civility, and respect for democratic process, it becomes difficult for many to imagine a pattern of growth that could be capable of improving both human and nonhuman environments.

Over the last 30 years, this impasse has both fueled and been fueled by the environmental movement. The effects of the environmental movement have been indirect, through the shaping of popular attitudes against growth, and direct, through the influence of environmental concerns on planning and land use regulation.[1] Although there is no question that there has been measurable improvement in certain environmental indices of conventional real estate development, this campaign has also produced deeply counterproductive outcomes. An unintended consequence of the way environmental concerns have been incorporated into the regulatory regime governing development has been a reinforcement of certain tendencies that produce low-density suburbia.

Environmentalism vs. Urbanism

These unintended effects of the environmental movement are clearly apparent in the tensions that have emerged between environmentalists and New Urbanists in recent years. New Urbanism emerged in the 1980s as a response to the broken promises of suburbia and an effort to improve the quality and diversity of the human habitat. Where the environmentalists had focused primarily on protecting nature from further incursions by humans, the New Urbanists focused on the problem of accommodating humans in ways that serve their needs and, incidentally, produce environmentally responsible patterns. Where the environmental response was to attack sprawl but avoid the necessary issues of density and mixed uses, the New Urbanist response to the social and environmental damage associated with even closely regulated suburban growth has been to provide the practical and social amenities of pedestrian-oriented, compact, diverse, and transit-ready neighborhood patterns.[2]

Many on both sides find the conflict between environmentalism and urbanism puzzling. How could it be that two sets of values so fundamentally well intentioned—a concern for the natural environment and a concern for building healthier human communities—often find themselves on opposing sides?

There is no reason why environmentalism and urbanism cannot be reconciled, and every reason that this reconciliation is necessary. In practice, however, contradictions emerge from both the techniques and the politics of planning.

Some of the tension between environmentalists and urbanists is the result of underlying philosophical differences. The environmental movement, responding to the sense of crisis that shaped its formation, has focused on limiting growth and protecting natural systems from human despoliation. The fundamental orientation of environmentalism is now supported by a scientific understanding of natural ecosystems as the very basis of the continued existence of human life on the planet. In the context of the American environmental movement, however, the science of environmentalism has been tied to a romantic ideal of wilderness that envisions a pristine natural world as if it were not inhabited at all by humans. This vision provides the baseline that runs through the diversity of the environmental movement, from John Muir and the early conservationists of the nineteenth century to the biocentrism and "deep ecology" of today.[3] Although some would say that the core belief of modern environmentalism is reflected in Aldo Leopold's notion that all life is integrated into a single "biotic community," the health of the biotic community is typically measured in terms that do not include the health and literal sustainability of human communities.

William Cronon has argued for the need to rethink the idea of the wilderness as representative of the core values of American environmentalism. He writes:

> To the extent that we celebrate wilderness as the measure with which we judge civilization, we reproduce the dualism that sets humanity and nature at opposite poles. We thereby leave ourselves little hope of discovering what an ethical, sustainable, honorable human place in nature might actually look like...By imagining that our true home is in the wilderness, we forgive ourselves the homes we actually inhabit. In its flight from history, in its siren song of escape, in its reproduction of the dangerous dualism that sets human beings outside of nature—in all of these ways, wilderness poses a serious threat to responsible environmentalism at the end of the twentieth century.[4]

Cronon's call to rethink wilderness has been echoed by some scientists, who have recognized the need for a more balanced scientific study of the world's ecosystems, given that human impact is pervasive and that we need to understand the ecological functioning of the human habitat itself, and not just its impacts on a pre-existing nature.[5] The current ecological paradigm privileges a pristine nature and regards the presence of humans as a disturbance in a system that is understood in terms of its condition prior to any human influence. As a result, in practice as well as in theory, a good human community can be "green" only by being invisible—so interspersed into conserved and supplemented nature that it disappears from sight. This is the ideal that has helped to give credibility to the hyper-landscaped suburban sprawl since Hilton Head, and that is held up as a "best practice" in some circles. Measured against such an ideal, urbanism can appear only as a negative condition, never as an organization of positive choices for the improvement of human communities.

Even so, there are grounds for common cause between environmentalists and urbanists. The two movements have common roots in reaction to the destructive effects of conventional suburban development, and there has been a proliferation of alliances between the two movements. Yet many of those who are struggling to build better urban habitats for humans are finding that those who would seem to be their natural allies in the environmentalist camp are turning up at public meetings as opponents to New Urbanist solutions to sprawl. In spite of explicit efforts among national environmental organizations such as the Sierra Club to mobilize anti-sprawl initiatives, urban projects that recognize the link between urbanity and land conservation often run up against environmental opposition at the local and regional level.

This contradiction is partly the result of the way the environmental movement produced a "quiet revolution in land use regulation" focused on open space and the definition of where not to build.[6] This logic has guided the integration of environmentalism into a technical and regulatory system that tends inadvertently to enforce suburbanization. We can see evidence of this in the requirements for "greening" urbanism in the form of maximum lot coverages, ubiquitous landscaping, and on-site stormwater detention requirements.[7]

Even those who have argued for "sustainable development" have had to struggle against a persistent suspicion that sustainability can be a kind of "green wash" for the growth orientation that got us into trouble in the first place. Indeed, this accusation is often warranted. It is easy for the practical application of the ideal of "sustainable development" to remain superficial when the primary measures of environmental performance imply simply increasing the naturalistic quotient of conventional projects. Consider flagship projects based on this measure: Hilton Head in South Carolina or the Woodlands in Texas. What resulted from these reforms was a greener, more attractive suburban sprawl. Sensitive environmental land was preserved and the rest was given over to low-density, highly landscaped single-use zones, connected by well-buffered arterials. As conventional subdivisions and strip shopping centers are hidden behind berms, the economic segregation of suburbia is exacerbated, and it is impossible to walk to any useful destination. The outcome of this environmental model is that the better parts of nature are preserved while traffic-generating and socially dysfunctional development is camouflaged with a naturalistic aesthetic.

Techniques for measuring the "ecological footprint" of human settlement have inadvertently supported a misanthropic attitude.[8] Cities are assessed in terms of quantitative measurments of their brute consumption of raw materials and energy, and as producers of waste, heat, and even light.[9] By such measures, the environmental performance of the great cities of the world (London, New York, etc.) looks dismal, whereas the best measures seem to be found in low-density suburbs. Although there is political value in quantifying the effects of human settlement in this way, there are fundamental theoretical and methodological problems inherent in drawing generalizations from data aggregated without attention to the functional differences between urban contexts. Assessments are taken from the outside, with complete indifference to the inner workings of the city as human habitat.[10] The city appears as a black box, into which resources flow and from which waste emerges. By such measures, the austerities of widespread poverty might lead to the best performance. It is assumed that the city's impact is to be accounted in terms of a cost imposed on nature, rather than regarding the city and the natural region as part of a common history in which resources are generated as well as exploited.[11] One cannot make sensible assessments of an optimal "energy budget" unless there is an understanding of the human values for which one is budgeting and an analysis of the form and qualities of the human places that are to be sustained by the budget.

A regulatory apparatus that is focused on the protection of nature rather than on a positive vision of human places reinforces a tendency toward a politics of obstruction. When Paul Murrain spoke at the Ninth Congress for the New Urbanism (New York, 2001), he created a furor by pointing out contradictions that have emerged between environmentalism and urbanism. He was careful to preface his comments by noting that he sees no contradiction between defending things "natural" and being passionate about urban places, commenting that he believes "contiguous, sizeable urban tracts are as vital to the sustainable agenda as pristine ones are to environmentalists." According to Murrain: "However, far too often many environmentalists measure their success as stopping things from happening. Often it makes no difference whether it is sprawl or urbanism. If they green, fracture, or de-densify the urbanism, that is 'making something better.'"[12]

High-density urbanism is regarded in terms of its negative impact on nature, quantified as an "ecological footprint" that is always too large to be defensible. Clearly it makes sense to argue that "sustainable communities should be conscious of their resource needs and waste streams, ensure that they do not destroy and exhaust the bioregion in which they are situated, and seek to minimize the environmental pressures placed on other regions and countries."[13] However, an emphasis on the design of cities in terms of resource flows and waste streams has to be balanced by an adequate theory of urbanism in its own terms, representing the functionality of the human habitat to be sustained and not just the natural ecosystems it can only be seen as destroying.[14]

The Results of Specialization

The consequences of this environmental perspective are amplified by the way it has been ingrained in the protocols of specialized experts who are trained to focus only on their particular piece of the process. Those concerned with natural systems are insistent that the concerns they represent be given priority, and those who focus on road construction, say, or urban design, do the same for theirs, with no way to resolve contradictions. The adjudication of conflicts involves disaggregating the elements of concern so that they can be handled in isolation by each specialist. The components are treated as abstract problems defined within each discipline, rather than as the interconnected task of creating places that, precisely because they are put together in a certain way, meet social, economic, and ecological objectives. Environmentalism in professional planning has not yet evolved the technical capacity to assess authentic urbanism, nor to articulate the tradeoffs between conservation and intense development in terms that allow for the reliable and effective (not to mention efficient) political resolution of conflicts.

Many problems derive from the fixations of different kinds of environmental specialists. For example, in Hillsborough County, Florida, the regulated minimum size of a tree planter is 120 square feet. That means that you need about 10 feet by 12 feet in order to plant a street tree—even in a downtown. The specialist is biologically correct: a tree in Florida does indeed need 120 square feet of unpaved surface to truly flourish, but that is considering only the tree, not any of the other aspects of designing a street, where the tree must participate in concert with building, sidewalk, and curb toward the creation of a pedestrian-oriented public place. The technical specification is based on the expert's knowledge of contented trees. In urban settings, however, trees have always been asked to compromise, to live in planters that are four feet square and even smaller. In a regulatory regime where the specialists each contribute in isolation, it is the community as a whole that is always compromised.[15] The cumulative effect of meeting standards defined separately for each component leads to decidedly suboptimal outcomes, but there is no technical framework within which to make precise and defensible assessments of the cumulative effects of allowing particular compromises between the requirements of nature and the needs of humans.

Downtowns in southwest Florida have great locational and cultural assets, and are ripe for redevelopment. It is initially a puzzle as to why renovation or infill is slow to happen. As it turns out, one of the primary obstacles is the requirement that to renovate a building or redevelop a lot, the developer is required to manage the stormwater entirely on the property. There may be perfectly good drainage in the street on which the property sits, but the requirement is to detain the rainwater on-site.

The authors of such rules may have been imagining a pond where the water can be allowed to infiltrate slowly into the aquifer, or simply held so that added impervious surface doesn't flood the adjacent properties. This is a perfectly reasonable standard for a greenfield site, but it makes redevelopment and infill difficult, especially as whatever space is available on a small lot is required to meet parking requirements as well. As a result, the only places that redevelop naturally in southwest Florida are places so valuable that it is feasible to agglomerate land sufficient to build structured parking or a cistern. In downtown Fort Myers, for example, a developer was prepared to build a mixed-use town center on the site of a completely paved, dead shopping center—a classic infill project of the type that mitigates sprawl. The local environmentalists were in favor of it, but the regulations at the Southwest Florida Water Management District allowed for no flexibility in adjusting the regulations to respond to the specific conditions. In cases where there is controversy, there is likely to be even less flexibility, as the opponents press for enforcement to the precise letter of the law.

There is a certain logic to this regulatory system. The idea is to manage the environmental consequences of development by making each site take responsibility for its share of the overall impact of growth. The advantage of internalizing environmental solutions within each project is that the public burden is reduced, at least in the short run. The indicators of ecological performance tend to be defined as discrete measures for purposes of clarity and fairness, and the expectation that projects be subject to the same regulations means that the application of standards has to ignore significant differences of urban context. This situation has three unfortunate consequences: developers are driven away from infill settings to greenfield sites, where it is easier and more cost-effective to meet such standards; redevelopment is only possible if the market supports relatively up-market and high-profit projects, limiting economic diversity in the outcomes; and designers are pushed to naturalistic solutions that tend to disrupt the functionality and character of pedestrian-oriented urbanism.

Some problems are exacerbated when the idea of "greening" the city is simply being taken too literally. At a meeting of the Congress for the New Urbanism in Portland (1997), for example, one of the local members announced, "We (in Portland) will not stop, until there is a forest in every square and a stream beside every street." One might accept this simply as rhetorical overstatement, but it also can be seen as a symptom of an attitude toward nature that regards social space as blight, to be mitigated by plant material and naturalistic water features. There are good arguments for greening, but it cannot be a matter of imposing blanket rules; the goal cannot be simply to squeeze in as much nature as possible.

Other examples result from absolutism in efforts to provide protection for wetlands, greenways, and wildlife corridors. Again, it isn't that such protections are unnecessary or unimportant. However, a regulatory approach that gives ultimate privilege only to natural features, with no adjustment to the specifics of context, tends to favor conventional suburban development patterns at the expense of either the urban or the rural character of places. Developers often find themselves constrained to preserve isolated wetlands that can retain no real ecological value, while being completely free (or even compelled by the fact that it is all they have left) to destroy wooded upland that might be significant for human recreational use. A demand for intact greenways often disrupts connectivity of urban street networks, thus favoring the "dendritic" street system characteristic of conventional suburbia. As a result, the creatures may have easier access to their food sources or their mates, but the humans end up spending their time polluting the atmosphere on gridlocked arterials.

A New Urban Environmentalism

Many of the recent campaigns of the environmental movement have taken up a concern for the conservation of open space of any type, not just of ecologically sensitive areas. This became a fixation on the idea of an "urban growth boundary" as the predominant strategy for the regional scale of planning. One symptom has been the uncritical apotheosis of Portland. The problem is not that putting geographic controls on the outward expansion of urbanized areas is a bad idea, but that this technique is regarded by many as "solving sprawl," with a consequent lack of attention to the importance of the community pattern within the boundary.

As an actual presence on the land, the Portland urban boundary is a negligible physical artifact. The principal difference it creates is that outside the boundary the farmer is a farmer, whereas inside the farmer has become wealthy by selling or subdividing. The value differential is so extreme that the line is inherently unstable, and so the boundary surreptitiously or overtly moves—and will continue to do so. In a capitalist system, there is too much at stake economically to establish a defensible line when there is no environmental determinant on the ground. But that is not the most immediate problem.

The real problem is apparent in the area between the excellent historic neighborhoods and the boundary—most everything that has been newly developed is identical to sprawl anywhere else: strip shopping centers, unwalkable arterials, and automobile-dependent residential subdivisions. As a result, it is not only of regrettably low quality, but it suffers from the chronic inability of suburban patterns to accommodate increasing density, adding a final determinant to the inherent instability of the growth boundary.[16]

The urban growth boundary, which was heralded as a great victory for the environment, was also a tremendous boon to developers. Elsewhere environmentalist groups contest every project, often forcing developers to do a better job. In Portland, the developers were essentially given free range within the urban boundary, effectively neutralizing the possible influence of reform-minded groups on the character of development that was taking place inside.[17] The environmental effects of growth depend on the specific urban pattern within the boundaries of growth, but environmental groups were not equipped to assess this, so it slipped their attention until too late for much of the area within the boundary.

At its core, the underlying principle of the urban growth boundary is essentially a defensive strategy. It is similar in logic, although at a regional scale, to the idea of "clustering." The best we can hope for, it would seem, is to contain humans within geographic limits that keep them from unduly encroaching on nature. The need to do a better job with the land that is to be developed as human habitat has not been of direct environmental concern. This approach reduces the effectiveness of an environmental proposition precisely to the extent that it focuses only on the limits of growth. If the environment is defined as the landscape devoid of human action, then we have given up on the ability to manage nuances of the interaction between the social and natural aspects of the world. Fortunately, conceptions of "sustainability" and "sustainable development" have substantially moved the discourse (and practice) of environmentalism beyond simplistic notions of an imagined Nature that simply needs to be protected from humans.

We can see a similar limitation in some recently evolved manifestations of the Smart Growth movement, although it has been allied with New Urbanism from its very beginnings. Smart Growth advocates tend to concentrate on policy at the regional scale, largely oriented toward the maintenance of congruent urban growth areas. From the scale of the region, discussions of Smart Growth tend to skip down in their attention to the level of green building standards. These are valid practices in themselves, but no less so than the issues of community design—that middle scale that links architecture with regional issues. Smart Growth explicitly recognizes the community scale in principle, but there has been less than adequate political emphasis on the provision of social diversity, mixed uses, and walkability. The unintended consequence of this uneven commitment is that often no distinctions are made in practice between New Urbanist development and conventional suburban development, so long as the project is within the designated growth areas. Lack of rigor at the scale of urban design has allowed NIMBYism ("Not in my back yard"), under the banner of Smart Growth, to attack good New Urbanist greenfield development as sprawl.[18]

In Sarasota County, for example, the local chapter of the Sierra Club and local environmental interests sided with no-growth organizations in opposing a new comprehensive plan that was intended to discourage the existing pattern of low-density sprawl, encourage compact mixed-use villages, and sustain the diversity of landscapes. The opposition focused on the fact that the new plan would allow more development beyond the current urban services boundary, although it is plainly evident that the line drawn on the map has little relationship to what appears on the ground. There has been a consistent leakage of large-lot subdivisions and other development outside the boundary. Many of the local environmentalists explicitly preferred that the county be built out with an even spread of five-acre "ranchettes" (according to current zoning) rather than by clustering development into villages and requiring developers to make planned allotments of land to connected systems of open space. The aim of the opposition was simply to allow as few people as possible to settle beyond the mythical urban boundary, ignoring the persistence of the socially as well as ecologically problematic form of purely residential, exclusively upscale automobile-dependent subdivisions.

Although many environmentalists prefer to think of themselves as embattled outsiders struggling against the establishment, the fact is that environmentalism has been thoroughly institutionalized into the rigid bureaucratic process against which New Urbanists often find themselves struggling. The problem is not only with specialized environmental regulation, but also with the way specialized expertise has become interlocked in both government and the market, such that it cannot be overcome by tackling simply one locus of the problem. Stefanos Polyzoides has described this as "operating on autopilot," an image that captures the reality of a system that builds places in ways dictated more by prior programming than by humane or rational response to immediate conditions.

One of the most striking things about this system is the extent to which its components contribute to self-reinforcing patterns of sprawl. Even when it is possible to arrive at a consensus regarding the general desire for patterns other than conventional suburbia, there is resistance from the system itself. Advocates for a project may succeed at convincing the individuals involved—the fire marshal, the transportation department engineer, the planning commissioners, and others—of the reasonableness or desirability of a proposal, only to run up against impersonal standards or routines in another part of the system. The local fire marshal might come to agree as to the desirability of a proposed variation from conventional practice, for example, but the insurance companies or the mortgage lenders might then present obstacles for the proposal. What makes current protocols so difficult to countermand or adjust is that they have over the years concatenated into a comprehensive and tightly interlocking system with its own internal rationality. This is one of the reasons why, as Chris Leinberger has shown, there are only 19 types of real estate product in the market. The pervasive protocols reinforce the sprawl pattern that is easily recognizable by the system.[19]

Central to this system is conventional zoning, which has certain features that make it conceptually elegant and efficient to administer. By separating everything into defined categories based on use, it becomes easy to control and assess outcomes using precise quantitative measures. Traffic is one particularly important area where measurement is facilitated by conventional zoning. The traffic engineers can, with apparent precision, predict that a particular type of project will generate a certain number of car trips per day. Their job is facilitated by the zoning categories as well as their own design standards. When the separation of land into single-use zones is coupled with a system of thoroughfares based on a dendritic pattern (cul-de-sac, local, collector, arterial, highway), it becomes easy to construct models that predict "level of service" for traffic. The ability to interrupt the street network also happens to support the effort to maintain the connectivity of the environmental systems (greenways, wetlands, etc.).[20] In the new town of Abacoa, for example, the traffic network was originally designed to have three routes through each neighborhood, so that no street would be overloaded and all would be pedestrian-friendly. The integrity of the greenways,[21] however, required the elimination of what were regarded as redundant connections, reducing the number from three to one for each neighborhood, and thereby undermining the human permeability and functionality of public space. The assumption among the specialists is that the "green" considerations—the functionality of the animal habitats—trump the social requisites of human habitats, even on land exceptionally well-located to be urbanized.

Over time there has been a translation of parking requirements into building types (such as walk-up apartments, townhouses, etc.) that correspond to zoning categories. These also correspond to recognized market segments. Such standardization is the reason why there are so few building types with normative standing in current development practice. The demands created by the car, and supported by the categories of zoning code, create a repertoire of routine building products that are market-tested and so recognized by the loan officers who provide the financing. The incentives for sticking to the standard products are increased by the extent to which loan officers are likely to resell the loan in the secondary financial market—the Real Estate Investment Trusts (REITs) and pension funds with billions per year to invest in such mortgages. Efficient decisions are a requisite of massive investment protocols and so they must be guided by checklists controlling the acceptable attributes of the property, and these, of course, happen to correspond to building types that correspond to zoning and ultimately to parking. Adherence to standard products minimizes transaction costs and reduces procedural friction as one moves through the development process.

Many of the problems emerge because the system focuses attention on discrete measures, but lacks the capacity for adjustment based on the interactions of the measured conditions as they are assembled into whole places. There is no capacity for the kind of responsiveness to context that is necessary when designing and planning for the complexity of human communities, especially as they change over the course of their history. The current system is compelling from the standpoint of institutions operating on the supply side of land and capital, and from the standpoint of bureaucratic administration, but not because it is an optimal way in which urban elements might be organized to produce beneficial social and ecological outcomes. That is surely evident from observing the last decades of development under this system.

A Reconciliation of Environmentalism and Urbanism

Although there is in principle no reason for a conflict between environmental concerns and a commitment to urbanism, there are significant conflicts in practice as a result of the way discrete issues are coordinated within the regulatory regime and within the conventional practices that have hardened into the professional division of labor. There is a conflict between the quantitative measures associated with a system of specialized expertise and the challenge of creating suitably complex places to meet the changing needs of society and economy. Finally, there is a conflict between politics that encourages simplistic tactics and the nuanced understanding necessary to enable a declension of compact, diverse, walkable communities.

The environmental movement has carved out a stronghold on the moral high ground. Within American culture, dominated as it is by individualism, it is very difficult to give legal and political standing to substantive notions of the public interest or the common good. Nonetheless, environmentalism has succeeded in establishing concern for the natural environment as a definition of the public interest that can even—at least in certain cases—override concern for the rights of private property. This is not to say that such invocations of the public interest are always uncontested or that they don't sometimes fail, but the achievement is really quite extraordinary.

Second, the environmental movement has been successful in having environmental requisites written into state and federal law, and into the local regulatory regimes that are the most immediate context of land use decisions. If one can find at least one "listed" species[22] on any specific parcel of land, one has immediate legal means to cause even powerful economic interests to make substantial concessions. On what other grounds is it possible to stop a highway, for example—long an unquestioned symbol of progress? Whole communities of humans have been pushed aside for highway construction, but certain fish and fowl have caused even the most single-minded transportation department officials to reconsider their designs.

This regulatory regime has given rise to specialized professionals charged with representing the interests of nature. Their authority is technocratic, their language precise and standardized, their operations dependent on specific statistical measures of performance that tend to single out ecological conditions understood to be indicative of the acceptable limits of human interference. This expertise has standing equal to any of the others in the division of labor among specialists—traffic engineers, market analysts, zoning administrators. All are given mutually recognized prerogatives in the regulatory process by their ability to represent their concerns in technical and quantitative terms.

Finally, along with the advantages of growing moral authority and the legitimacy provided by claims to scientific expertise, the environmental movement has not forgotten its tradition of morally energized activism, now institutionalized in a great number of organizations. Some of these organizations assign their impressive resources to the expression of the pervasive fear of growth, becoming ready allies for any local interests motivated to oppose projects for any reason.

The powerful combination of a capacity to mobilize collective action with the moral leverage of claims to represent a legitimate public interest, and a regulatory regime that gives its concerns legal standing, enables (and even makes routine) effective protest, and tends to discourage the kind of intricate and informed discourse necessary to produce significant solutions to complex problems. Although the intervention of environmental activists can and does result in making some projects better, their power to cause friction is much greater than their capacity for encouraging creative solutions, thus tending to delay, dilute, or simply stop development—good or bad—from happening.

In cases where environmental regulation has been an obstruction to good work, the defensive response is "But that's not environmentalism! Those are NIMBY reactionaries, masquerading as environmentalists." That may be so, but the point is that the environmental movement has succeeded in having its concerns institutionalized as a significant part of the system that helps to perpetuate sprawl. Good intentions have been translated into a procedural regime—with its particular politics—that too often causes activists to undermine even their own stated goals.

Clearly environmental concerns are critically important as a component of the way we plan and design human settlements. However, the tendency has been to focus too exclusively on the protection of what is understood to be nature and not to give sufficient attention to the relationship of human economy, values, and the opportunities afforded by natural systems.

Recent environmental thinking has made great progress in correcting this imbalance. For example, William Shutkin has also pointed out that traditional environmentalism has been narrowly concerned with a romantic ideal of protecting the wilderness and has relied too much on legal and policy tools that "disparage economic growth without proposing legitimate alternatives, thus decoupling economic challenges from environmental problem solving."[23] Shutkin offers one among several recent articulations of the idea of "civic environmentalism."[24] According to Shutkin: "Civic environmentalism confronts the irony that most Americans seem to care more about protecting remote natural areas than the very places they inhabit, and posits the notion that we would have to spend less time worrying about protecting remote areas if we ensured that the places where people actually live are environmentally and socially healthy."[25]

Although this kind of thinking is finding growing currency, and has affected practice in some exemplary cases, for the most part it has yet to penetrate the front lines where environmental ideas are rendered operational: the way environmental protection is written into regulation, the ways environmental science is used to inform the political process, and, of course, the way environmental concerns and rhetoric are used to mobilize popular interests. Counteracting sprawl is possible only if one has a clearly articulated and technically elaborated proposition concerning the alternative. Environmentalism needs a theory of urban form as much as New Urbanists need a theory that enables them to understand the ecological impact of urban development.

The challenge is to forge a technical reconciliation between environmentalism and urbanism that is simultaneously responsive to political requirements. There is an urgent need for a technical framework that strikes a better balance between the protection of natural ecosystems and matters of urban design concerned with meeting human needs and realizing human values. This framework must be capable of operating effectively in the context of a modern legal and regulatory system, and also simple enough to allow a productive role for citizens to participate.

The key to a solution is to dissolve the tendency to see economy and culture as outside nature, and to let the needs of humans back into environmental discourse and practice. Humans must have standing in a system encompassing choices that reflect both urban and natural values. Among significant human needs, we should include a need for diverse types of communities capable of accommodating a range of individual lifestyle choices, some that are intensely urban and others that are progressively more rural. The framework must specify with technical precision the varied integration of appropriate natural elements into human settlements of different types and at different scales, and the way these settlements should integrate into varied natural settings as part of regional systems.

New Urbanists have been struggling for years to create patches and work-arounds that allow urbanism to interface with the operating system that was designed to support conventional suburban patterns of development. In the early phases of the New Urbanist movement, practitioners tried to address the obstacles piecemeal, responding to the objections of the zoning administrator, traffic engineer, loan officer, environmentalist, marketing expert, and so on, as they came up. But this has been found to be far too time consuming, given the rate of growth in the United States, and it requires well-intended and extraordinarily patient developers who are more willing to weather greater difficulty than those building sprawl. It is now necessary to move from the mentality of designing interfaces (that are always less than optimal) to the design of an alternative operating system, one that is as comprehensive and as elegant as the one it is intended to replace, simple in the ways that it needs to be, yet capable of generating the complexity required by human communities. In order to complement the asymmetry of the environmental perspective, a theory is necessary that encompasses both the social and natural variables, balancing them to achieve quality human habitats as an integral tool in the pursuit of sustainable environmental outcomes. This theory can be based on the Rural-to-Urban Transect.

The Rural-to-Urban Transect

A transect is simply a kind of cross-section, a line traced across geography. In ecology and environmental science, it is a sampling technique. One draws a line along some observable gradient—wetland to upland, valley floor to mountain top—and then takes samples at intervals, systematically analyzing the characteristics of the minerals, plant communities, and animal habitats along the way, including soils, flora, fauna, humidity, and microclimate. It is a technique that allows the scientist to make sense of the elements and patterns that make each habitat distinguishable, and also to understand their succession as part of a larger system.

Michael Barbour has described the "holistic" ideas of Frederic Edward Clements, a principal proponent of this kind of ecological thinking in the United States, beginning in the 1920s: "Clements had argued that natural vegetation tended over time to become organized into discrete units separated by narrow or broad ecotones. These units, which he named formations or associations (and which others have come to call communities), are uniform over large areas."[26]

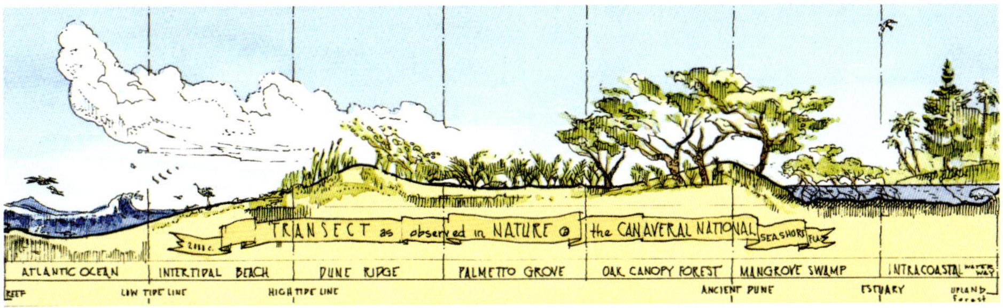

JAMES WASSELL DPZ CODESIGN

An analysis that moves along a transect between taxonomically distinguished communities provides an opportunity to capture both the associational attributes of those elements that make a single habitat or community identifiable and the relative intensity of distribution of certain elements across a gradient. The idea of a transect that includes the full range of environments shaped by human intervention, as a way to make sense of the relation between social and natural systems, has a lineage back to Patrick Geddes, with his 1910 illustration of the "Valley Section."[27] (See page 31.) One can identify the transect (or what Emily Talen has called a "transect sensibility") in a wide range of sources. It is essentially an understanding of context and a sense that not everything can be put anywhere and still function appropriately. There is an understanding that the allocation of elements and attributes corresponds to the distinctive character of different kinds of places, from the most natural and least affected by human intervention to the most cultural and most intentional—reflecting a range of human needs and desires, a range of social patterns, and a range of ways in which humans and nature interact. Once sensitized to this idea of a Rural-to-Urban Transect, one begins to perceive it everywhere and recognize its logic in the cultural coding of nearly every kind of artifact, from clothing to cuisine, from music to buildings.[28]

Conventional zoning—the current operating system—is primarily about distribution of functions. Originally guided according to a principle of avoidance of noxious adjacencies, it has become an instrument of statistical control, acceptable because its simplifications create some predictability in the development process, not because it produces livable neighborhoods or beautiful towns. In contrast, an approach to urban form guided by the continuum of the Rural-to-Urban Transect would focus attention on the complexity of different kinds of habitats, each of which responds to human needs both because of its distinctiveness and because of its place in a larger system of differences.[29] The Transect's extension of ecological theory to urbanism recognizes that there is a similar need to understand the character of distinctive communities sustained as part of a regional system. On the one hand, there is the view that much of what happens in cities is the result of elements that distribute themselves in space according to some specific logic (e.g., the logic of the markets for land, labor, and capital or perhaps the logic of intergroup competition).[30] On the other hand, a Transect-oriented perspective emphasizes that the various components of the built environment—building types, frontages, street sections, landscaping, and so on—interact to produce types of places, each of which can be seen as evolving toward a kind of "climax" condition. The analogy to plant communities is not exact, of course. Obviously the components of urban form are not adapting through their own efforts or reproductive processes like a plant or animal species, but adapted by humans (often shaping as well as reacting to surrounding conditions). However, the survival of certain urban and building typologies depends on the emergent properties of their association, and the coherence of these associations and the related differentiation of typologically distinct places is important for maintaining the diversity of human habitats. Two examples of this kind of association are the association of the density of the transportation grid with sustaining retail of a certain size, and the importance of on-street parking for pedestrian-oriented building frontage.

The Social Gradient of Places

The desirability of maintaining a diversity of human habitats along a Rural-to-Urban Transect has been supported by a variety of research findings. Although his typological declension was not originally intended to be regarded as an elaboration of the Transect theory, Sidney Brower's study of residential neighborhoods provides a good example of the connections between social values and choices in physical design.[31] (See page 217.) Brower set out to address what might seem to be a few simple questions: how do people choose residential areas when they have a choice? What qualities do people value? By examining the various dimensions of such choices, he was able to create a typology of residential communities that is based "in residential life-style rather than geographic location."[32] It is a typology that is not only descriptive, but captures the normative character of different kinds of places that manifest a particular experience of social order.

The typology focuses on three qualities, culled from 33 characteristics found in a range of satisfaction surveys, each having to do with ways that lifestyle and place are linked: ambience, engagement, and choicefulness. The first has most directly to do with physical qualities: the mix and pattern of land use, the "look and feel." The second has to do with "the way that residents engage and avoid engagement with one another and the extent to which they are facilitated or obstructed in this by the physical and social features." The last one has to do with the extent to which individuals are able to choose "where, how, and with whom they will live and the range of different types of living environments from which they may choose."[33] For example, it turns out that choicefulness is manifested in the sense that a particular place might represent a choice that one could willingly make and justify (whether or not one actually had a choice and whether or not this was actually the basis on which choices were made).

Brower identified four types of neighborhoods that emerge from a synthesis of empirical findings: center, small town, residential partnership, and retreat. A center community is bustling, varied, and changing, inhabited by diverse kinds of people and characterized by active public spaces that connect uses rather than separate them. It provides choices among many competing facilities and includes notable monuments and institutions. A small town community is less open and cosmopolitan than a center, has a strong sense of continuity and more parochial institutions and public places that cater to locals, but is still a vital public realm that provides connections between residents and welcomes strangers. A residential partnership is typically a bedroom community, associated with a single set of tastes or lifestyle, providing some shared amenities catering exclusively to residents, and a "cocoon of tranquility around the housing units of its members." A retreat emphasizes privacy and has no connecting facilities or shared amenities. It allows no outsiders and expects no connections between neighbors.

This typology implies not only physical variation, but also variations in qualities (such as expectations regarding the intimacy or frequency of neighborly engagement) relevant to the social character and experience of place. Many of the normative implications can be understood in terms of the way we organize relations along a gradient from the personal and intimate to the communal and parochial and, finally, to the impersonal and public. The key dimension of variation has to do with the balance in intensity between private and public space, with the more urban neighborhoods being characterized by connection to a more diverse and vital public realm. Brower found what might be a surprising distribution of preferences for different kinds of communities. Twenty-seven percent of Brower's sample stated a preference for the small town type. Only 22 percent stated a preference for a residential partnership, and three percent preferred to live in a retreat.

Brower's work points indirectly to the failures of conventional market research to identify the full range of American housing preferences. Conventional studies usually indicate a preference for the single-family enclaves of suburbia. A more complicated understanding of housing preferences, more in line with Brower's analysis, is supported by other analyses, such as studies using Zimmerman and Volk's "target market" methodology.[34] Brower clearly shows the functioning of the Transect in the way people think about communities, indicating both preferences and needs associated with a diversity of places, each of which depends on its internal characteristics and its geographical position relative to other places for its desirable qualities. A key dimension of the differences is the extent to which a neighborhood offers engagement with a social context (e.g., urbanism with its value in emphasis on the public realm as opposed to solitude and engagement with a more natural environment).

Volk and Zimmerman observed that the apparent uniformity of housing preferences revealed in conventional surveys is contradicted by the willingness of buyers to bid up the value of housing in Transect-based developments when the option is there.[35] They linked this confusion "to both the undifferentiated environments in which most Americans find themselves living, and, correspondingly, an inability on the part of surveyors and researchers to differentiate clearly the complexities of housing preferences."[36] In contrast with the usual supply-and-demand analysis, their methodology uses a mix of demographic and economic data, along with credit-card-based consumer preferences, to distinguish types of households, associate them with lifestyle preferences, and to determine the depth and breadth of the market for housing options arrayed along the Transect. One of their most striking findings is that there are definite patterns of movement along the Transect by households as they change in age, composition, or economic status. They also predict that as the baby boomers age, they are much more likely to prefer the kind of diverse communities characteristic of more traditional urbanism over the automobile dependence of the suburbs or the functional specificity of age-qualified subdivisions. Where Brower's study suggested a robust need for neighborhoods and communities that vary in the intensity of their urbanity, Volk and Zimmerman suggested that many of the failures of the market to deliver a satisfying range of residential choices can be traced to the failure to understand that statistically similar housing programs are differentiated by their location along the Transect. For example, a two-bedroom, two-bath unit is an utterly different lifestyle option when it is a cottage in a Sub-Urban Transect Zone and a loft in an Urban Center. Both Brower and Volk and Zimmerman noted that people commonly choose different kinds of communities at different stages in their lives, and Volk and Zimmerman suggested that movement along the Transect in favor of increased urbanity will increase steadily with the aging of the baby boomers.

Understanding Places Using Transect Zones

As a basis for understanding places and building a regulatory system, the Transect provides a common operating system for all specialized regulatory standards. Land use, building types, thoroughfare streetscape standards, signage guidelines, and environmental standards can all refer to the common platform. All those who are specialists can coordinate their work virtually without even knowing of each other's efforts. Each of the professions can begin to rewrite their standards (as the Institute of Traffic Engineers did, describing the effort as being "context sensitive"). For purposes of clarity and ease of administration, the diagram represents the gradient of the Transect in terms of six zones, from wilderness to urban core. These are called Transect Zones or T-Zones.

The six T-Zones are the unapologetically artificial calibration of a continuum in order to create a clear and cognitively manageable set of definitions, akin to the current planning standard of normative "zones," albeit each managing a desired complexity rather than an intended monoculture. The motivation for standardizing six zones is not only that it has worked well in empirical application in many analytical and design projects,[37] but that this number of variables approaches the threshold that most lay participants in the public process are able to handle without too much confusion. (For a longer exposition, see "Why Six Transect Zones" on page 175.)

DPZ CODESIGN

The first zone, designated Natural (T-1), is the most pristine natural condition, areas closest to the wilderness ideal and in which human intervention is oriented toward ecological stewardship rather than to accommodating human uses. This is not to deny that it often takes a great deal of human expertise to maintain the functioning of what appears to us as wilderness.[38] But in T-1, human use has to be restricted and categorically disciplined by the prerogatives of the natural systems.

The second zone is designated Rural (T-2). This zone comprises open space where there is some human intervention and habitation, usually associated with recreational and agricultural activity. In this zone, some preservation efforts might be oriented by particular kinds of cultural traditions such as hunting, but in ways closely related to justifying the retention of the place free of any but the lowest-density development.

The third zone is Sub-Urban (T-3), similar in some ways to, but not to be confused with, what is commonly called "suburban." This is a zone of human habitation where house and lot patterns are relatively low in density. The key difference from the conventional suburban pattern is that these are not monocultural residential zones, and that they are to be limited in extent by proximity to other T-Zones. This zone includes some mix of uses, including recognition of the reality of home occupations. Although this zoning category supports the market for conventional suburban lifestyles, it would serve the purpose (in the context of a Transect-based regulating plan) not to segregate but to weave these residential patterns together with the other components of human settlement.

The fourth zone is General Urban (T-4). In the American context, this is the middle landscape that is most complex. Whereas the ends of the Transect tend to be very distinctive in either urban or rural character, the T-4 standards are set with relatively wide margins, allowing for a great variety of building types, setbacks, and uses. Many urban areas are in the midst of some kind of transition, usually reflected in a patchwork of spot zoning and variances. T-4 brings some institutional acknowledgement of these transitions, and it also acknowledges an identifiable place for the messy vitality preferred by some.

The fifth zone is designated as Urban Center (T-5). This can be the commercial "corner" area of a neighborhood or the "Main Street" of a town. In this zone, the alignment of buildings form a continuous frontage wall, clearly defining the space of the street as a locus for commercial activity, while still accommodating residential uses in appropriate forms. This zone can be applied to protect or project an intensely pedestrian-friendly urban fabric and as a way of enabling the provision of ordinary daily needs within walking distance of T-3 and T-4 zones.

The sixth zone, Urban Core (T-6), is reserved for the most intensely urban areas with the highest density of jobs and the locus of civic institutions of regional importance. It supports a typical downtown of a medium-sized or large American city. T-6 rigorously maintains the integrity of urbanity and is the zone that most clearly needs and supports forms of transit.

A seventh zone is the Special District, an exceptional category for those places that need to be allocated to a single use in some way: Hospitals, university campuses, large-scale industrial facilities, or anything else that cannot be accommodated within the intrinsically complex Transect Zones. By retaining a place for such circumstances within the system, it becomes unnecessary to compromise the mandatory diversity of the other zones. Note that the single-use District is the exception and not the norm, as is the case with conventional zoning.

Transect-Based Codes

Transect-based coding approaches the problem of control over urban development in a manner that is fundamentally different in both its goal and functioning from conventional zoning. The Transect focuses on the conditions that maintain character and diversity within a series of typologically distinct places. The main focus of a Transect-based code is calibration of the mixture of component elements in order to turn what might be problematic adjacencies into symbiotic relationships that give variously urban and rural areas their value.[39] This is in sharp contrast with the way that currently conventional zoning puts emphasis on keeping things simplified and separated so that unfortunate adjacencies can be avoided or mitigated, and so that the aggregate impact of different uses can be measured. For this reason, Transect-based codes tend to be generative rather than simply a list of prohibitions. Both systems keep the political and administrative protocols of control and predictable outcomes in place.

There is efficiency and comfort in having a consistent set of categories. Architects can refine a new set of building typologies; traffic engineers can extend the available repertoire of thoroughfares and develop level-of-service measures for normative mixed uses; environmentalists can set criteria for a gradient of permissible impacts on nature. In the end, each specialist can retain the prerogatives of their professional disciplines, yet by adhering to the mandatory declension of six standards (rather than the current single standard), they can contribute to the efficient production of complex places. The separate handbooks of the specialists can be reformulated to defined settings—neither the frightening free-for-all of the existing rules, as often results from "planned unit development" ordinances, nor the rigidity of the existing system, which requires endless variances and exceptions in a way that ultimately undermines both control and predictability of outcomes.

A Transect-based code constructs a coordinated set of specifications for the component elements of the natural and human habitat, each part potentially delegated to the specialists who design or regulate them but on a common platform integrating the whole. As in conventional zoning, a Transect-based code includes the concept of land use, but as one element among others and always subject to the discipline of the urban and architectural configurations appropriate to the place. Each T-Zone would allow all of the functions (residential, lodging, office, retail, manufacturing), but each in different degrees of mix or intensity. For example, lodging might take the form of a convention hotel in T-6 and a bed and breakfast inn in T-4, whereas T-3 might allow an ancillary apartment for rent. More subtle distinctions can also be made (e.g., one might be allowed to refinish furniture but not cars as a business in T-3).

For example, the frontages—the way the buildings meet the street—should be arrayed from the most rural to the most urban. The arcade over the sidewalk is the most urban, defining the most pronounced spatial enclosure, then, progressively, the shop front, the stoop, the forecourt, the dooryard, the porch and fence, and the common lawn. (See page 104.) The specific types might vary regionally, but the point is that there is a full declension of frontages corresponding to the level of urbanity. By way of contrast, conventional suburban codes effectively allow only two frontages: the 25-foot front yard and the parking lot.

The coding of the streetscape is another example of the Transect in action. At the most urban end of the Transect, one might see a single species of tree in regularly spaced planters. At the more rural end, the sidewalk has become a path, and the trees become clusters of multiple species in a naturalistic arrangement. This simple gradient controls one of the most common Transect abuses: the impulse to green urban centers with berms, naturalistic landscaping, and wandering paths. While such landscaping may be visually attractive, it undermines commerce and the informal social life associated with it.

The example of downtown Fort Myers demonstrates the need for the gradient of responses associated with the Transect. The downtown boasts a quarter mile of embankment on the river, but the mangroves have become so thick that one can no longer see the river. It was suggested that the mangroves might be trimmed down to eye level, but this was declared impossible under regulations that do not differentiate contextually between the Everglades and a downtown waterfront. In this way one more reason for living downtown instead of the suburban fringe has been inadvertently eliminated by a standard concerned only with defending the natural condition. This case exemplifies the tendency to homogenize the human habitat toward a common greening that results in a degenerate urbanism that is neither urban nor rural.

For every environmental condition (and every element of the built environment), there should be at least six standards generated. To take the preservation of wetlands as an example: For the set-back from a river running through T-1, a mile or two is a reasonable expectation. When the river comes into T-3, however, it becomes a "riparian corridor" and the set-back requirement could be decreased to 50 feet of intact nature. As the river passes through a T-6 urban core, it makes no sense to keep to a standard that prevents humans the reward of access to the water as a feature that enhances the urbanism. At the most urban end of the Transect, an embankment—as in Paris, London, Chicago, Amsterdam, Rome, or Charleston—should be permitted. (See image on page 69.)

Once one has defined the Transect Zones, forms of human settlement can be understood in terms of a combination of zones. Each type is defined to include at least three different zones. A hamlet consists of T-2 and T-3, with a small amount of T-4 to accommodate a corner store. A village has some rural T-2, but ranges from mostly T-3 to the T-5 of a main street area. A town may have T-4, T-5, and T-6. Precluded would be the unrelieved expanses of a single zone that is typical of suburban sprawl. Sprawl is manifested at least as much by its socioeconomic monoculture as by its extent, dependency on the automobile, and consumption of land area at a high rate. By requiring a structured mix of uses within each T-Zone, as well as a range of T-Zones within each community, Transect-based planning catalyzes the requisite social and functional diversity, the absence of which creates the environmental impact of automobile-dependent sprawl.

Radical Adjacencies and Successional Planning

Because the Transect is represented as a continuum, the diagrams sometimes lead to the erroneous assumption that a community ought to be zoned so that it builds up centroidally, as in a medieval village. Although it is possible to build in such a pattern, most places simply do not work that way. There are always discontinuities and even radical juxtapositions. Take, for example, a Transect analysis of a historic neighborhood near downtown Syracuse, New York. The avenue consists of tall buildings and is a fully developed example of T-6. Nearby there is a patchwork of T-4, T-3, and even a T-2 area that is a surviving rural enclave. This radical adjacency between a T-2 and a T-6 zone may be regarded as a positive asset, as in the more famous case of New York City between Fifth Avenue and Central Park. The Transect helps to make sense of this kind of idiosyncratic urban fabric and to help decide to maintain it or to allow portions of it to evolve into the next (successional) Transect Zone. It is most certainly not intended to be a technique for ironing out urban complexity into a consistent set of concentric rings. The gradient of the Transect is an analytical convention not intended to be transcribed onto the landscape. The Transect operates like a color wheel, with six primaries that enable a command of the chroma and saturation of a palette while providing the guidance to avoid producing murky colors.

The parametric approach to the standards of a code can provide for reasonable flexibility within each T-Zone while also minimizing harsh transitions between them. For example, building heights overlap between zones. If one zone is one to four stories, the next zone might be set to three to six stories, and the next to four to ten stories. The areas of overlap are potentially the richest in diversity, allowing for the urban equivalent of what are called "ecotones" in ecology.

This approach also allows the possibility of the urban equivalent of what ecologists call "succession" in natural growth. Succession is analogous to what we would ordinarily consider "history" or the patterns of organic growth associated with traditional cities. The Transect-based approach offers this crucial difference from conventional zoning, which is written so that allocations are permanently fixed and as if change in the built landscape were an extraordinary and always problematic event. Changes in density or use require either variances or categorical re-zoning. As these adjustments accumulate over time in extended series of disconnected and poorly coordinated decisions, the result is unlikely to be orderly growth, cumulatively positive outcomes, or political contentment. Both the inflexibility and the disorderly patterns of change are reinforced by the rigidity and over-simplification of conventional zoning. The Transect establishes parameters of order while allowing the adaptability that communities require over time. Systematic political consideration of succession in Transect Zones would avoid "spot zoning," allowing villages to become towns and towns to become cities in the course of time. Only when the urban equivalent of the natural "climax" condition is achieved would a preservationist regime be justified.

The point of planning, it would seem, is to manage the process of change so that it leads to continual improvement while avoiding undesirable outcomes along the way. A Transect-based code offers a way to institutionalize the process of adaptation to changing circumstances, ensuring that component elements can evolve in a coherent manner and avoiding the aberrations and destructive unpredictability that gave rise to zoning in the first place. (See Successional Transects, page 87.)

Analytical Techniques

It is useful to realize that the Transect is not only a synthetic, but also an analytical, technique. It is a tool for understanding the urbanism that already exists, as well as for planning for its continued improvement. This is important because the standards of a Transect-based code should be derived from an empirical survey of a specific community. The Transect of New Haven is not the same as the Transect of Santa Fe. The parametric ranges that define each zone are different, and the elements must be locally calibrated. What is constant, however, is that there are always ranges of rural-to-urban zones. Even across local differences, the consistency of the analytical framework enables comparison that both illuminate variations specific to places and enable planners and designers to learn generalizable lessons that can be skillfully applied in other contexts. (See page 97.)

As an analytical technique, the Transect is unusually efficient. The current method of surveying a community begins by assessing all streets and buildings, then taking the collected information and boiling it down to a manageable number of elements, such that a code can be written. This is an enormously time-consuming and expensive process. Armed with the Transect, a planner can study a place in the same way environmental scientists and engineers study a site. They don't scrape off all the layers of earth and rock, analyze them, then put them back. They take core samples of typical areas on the site. They perform a synoptic survey to establish representative places (referents) to be studied thoroughly, and from these are drawn technical data that lead to specific recommendations. These analytical techniques include the *dissect* and the *quadrat*. The *dissect* is a section that cuts both above and below the ground to determine flora, fauna, and microclimate, as well as subsurface composition of the soil, humidity, and root structure. The *quadrat* sets the boundaries of a normative area—for example, an ecologist might mark off a 100-foot square and then assemble a comprehensive quantitative inventory of the plants and animals found within the sampled area. (See page 106.) In a similar way, the planner can first identify certain locations that are typical "referents" of each Transect Zone and then study those examples intensely. The planner can then use the inherently distilled results to develop normative standards that reflect a community's recognition of its best and/or most typical places.

In a 2002 architectural studio at Yale, the Transect was used in this way. Students analyzed 10 American cities, each one in three days, collecting only the necessary information to write a code. They were told to go to cities like Santa Barbara, Charleston, Santa Fe, or Boston and to spend a couple of days walking around with an eye to identifying the most paradigmatic urban location (for T-6), then the most satisfying sub-urban location (for T-3), and then to identify two evenly graded ones between (for T-4 and T-5). On the third day, they were to perform a *dissect* and a *quadrat* at each one of their selected locations. The *dissect* involved photographing, measuring, and quantifying the characteristics of public space and its elements: species of street tree, type of planter, set-back, building height, etc. The *quadrat* was formed from the lots encompassed by opposing block faces, and the students counted the areas of commercial use, the number of residential units, trees on private and public land, on- and off-street parking, and so on. The result was a quick proto-code, locally calibrated to the distinctive urbanism of the place. (This process has been refined, and is explained in "The Synoptic Survey" on page 185.)

There is a need to develop such techniques for the sake of economy. American planning has become too elaborate and hence expensive, often putting the necessary skills out of reach of many ordinary communities that need it most. The simplified Transect system can be accessible to places with little in the way of budget for planning, perhaps only able to afford to purchase (or copy) standard boiler plate codes. At the same time, the system can be developed to a level of technocratic mystique equal to that of any other of the quantitative specialists in the political process: the traffic engineer, the environmentalist, and the developer. Armed with the conceptual precision of a Transect-based analysis, the planner (often the sole generalist) can put forward propositions responsive to the broad range of human concern, with clarity and authority no less founded in data than the specialists who look after the interests of cars, trees, stormwater, or various animal species.

The Promise of Post-Suburban Planning

If one takes a square mile of conventional suburban development, an assessment will often find most of the elements of a town, with "some assembly required." The growth of the last decades has provided everything necessary for towns, but the individual has to drive around all day to put it together. As a result there are none of the benefits of urbanism—neither the convenience nor the quality of human experience, neither the public realm nor the opportunities for civility. Many of the problems in the modern development industry result from the way planning practices reinforce the homogenizing protocols involved in managing large aggregations of capital; the simplifications associated with technocratic administration; and the legal practices that have been shaped by responding to and reinforcing the tendencies of an impersonal regulatory system. The solution is not as simple as just getting rid of regulation, as these practices are now thoroughly institutionalized in the supply side of the market and reflected in attitudes and expectations on the demand side.

The prospect of what may be called post-suburban planning is likely to depend on our ability to install a comprehensive theory of urbanism in a form that is compatible with the existing legal frameworks and to harness this theory to the politically powerful ethos of environmentalism.

The Transect provides a theoretical basis for integrating a science of both natural systems and human settlements into planning and policy. It enables an understanding of the broad ecological picture that doesn't fetishize nature or make it impossible (as some environmentalism tends to do) to organize environmentally acceptable choices into politically sustainable patterns, or to respond systematically and intelligently to the challenge of creating human habitat that is dense, compact, and connected.

Conventional assessment techniques currently measure ecological impact in a way that tends to favor low-density suburban development. Ecological performance shows steady decline from the moment a human steps foot on the scene, and becomes almost completely degraded in the urban core. Such conclusions are drawn from the fact, for example, that water filters through to the aquifer more easily when the density is lower and pavement therefore less. However, such a measure makes no sense at the regional scale, when maintaining low densities in order to address water quality issues has the ultimate result of spreading human impact more widely, disrupting more of the natural systems and multiplying secondary impacts such as atmospheric pollution through increased traffic. The specialized science of environmental assessment tends inadvertently to encourage the position that the "solution to pollution is dilution," the idea that spread out, humans won't do as much damage. This view is persistent, in spite of the evidence that spreading humans more thinly on the ground has been shown to be as damaging to social, economic, and political health as it is to the natural environment. And the result is that policies driven by this kind of thinking exacerbate the political difficulties, as accumulations of well-intended actions lacking overarching vision lead to consequences that are plainly socially, economically, and ecologically damaging.

When the appraisal of environmental impact is reconsidered from the standpoint of an integrated, Transect-based theory, ecological performance drops instead in the middle ground (T-3), where the efficiency in the human consumption of land is not enough to balance its hidden and secondary impact on natural systems. This is particularly true insofar as the naturalistic appearance of the suburban landscape actually masks deeply disrupted natural systems (e.g., the effects of soils compacted, plantings that require irrigation and chemical treatment, and atmospheric pollution that results from extended travel distances). Measures of ecological performance must take into account the efficiencies as well as the impacts associated with the variety of urban settlement patterns. To the extent that humans are attracted by the social values embedded in urbanism, they feel less compelled to use nature as a buffer between themselves and their fellow humans, and hence less likely to insist on large lots and monocultural residential areas. Ecologically, the most efficient pattern of human settlement is dense, compact urbanism, traded off symmetrically against carefully preserved areas and certain lower-density sub-urban settlement areas. In contrast with a settlement pattern reflecting the mix and diversity of Transect-based development, conventional suburban development produces a consistently low level of both social and ecological value across the whole Transect.

The Transect system measures the exchanges required by growth in a systemic way, integrating the measurement of environmental and social performance. As a regulatory technique, it offers opportunities for sophisticated transactions, not just the painful downward tradeoffs that have given growth its uniformly bad reputation. A properly systematic assessment could encourage efforts to achieve the higher scores at the ends of the Transect, as the more rigorously urban zones (T-4, T-5, and T-6) sustain economic and social values. Residents of such zones may not so readily want to leave them for large-lot subdivisions if the absence of a yard large enough for private amenities were compensated by the attractions of a truly lively street life and the resources of an urban public realm. Overall, Transect-based planning could optimize the curves defined by the whole system of tradeoffs between maintaining natural ecological conditions and producing forms of habitation that meet the full range of human needs and values. In this way, we are most likely to make substantial progress toward sustainability in the widest sense.

In contrast, the environmentally driven regulatory impulse to green the city ends up suburbanizing even the urban core and undermining the advantages and amenities of urbanism, reducing it to a poor substitute for real suburbia and creating an uncompetitive component within the overall market. Not many are interested in trading in the large yards and easy parking that provide the comforts and convenience of suburbia without the compensation of the pedestrian interest and convenience of dense urbanism. Transect-based urbanism would keep humans contained not by the proscription of an urban boundary, but by desire and choice. There is ample evidence of this: Substantial numbers of people willingly select (and pay a premium for) an urban lifestyle wherever authentic urbanism is still to be found.

As a technical matter, the Transect makes it possible to think in precise terms about an environmental science that is geared to a comprehensive ecological solution—one that achieves the kind of specificity required to create regulations that can be administered by existing technocratically oriented administrative protocols. As a matter of politics, the Transect makes it possible to bring clarity to the choices that citizens need to make in the political discussions that attend (and should attend) growth. The conceptualizations and analytical representations enabled by the Transect system can help citizens understand the forms and nature of urbanism in a way that enables them to make informed and rational choices about the future of their communities.

Perhaps the most important asset of Transect-based planning is that it is inherently oriented toward the market, toward providing an array of places that are desirable for those who have a choice of where to live. This includes the American middle class, whose lifestyle will otherwise continue to be a root cause of some of the most destructive environmental problems we face. It also implies the possibility of integrating places for people who have historically been faced with little choice, precisely because of the way a Transect-based system helps to expand the range of choices in building mixed-use and mixed-income communities. Thus it holds promise to reconcile the environmental ethos and the concerns with social equity that have typically been represented by the political left with the expansion of "choice" as exercised through the free market that is the central conviction of the political right. The problems that confront us do not otherwise hold even a glimmer of the promise of resolution, short of the agonies of a long economic emergency that might render some of these discussions moot, but that none of us should wish upon the nation.

This essay was orginally published in Regulating Place: Standards and the Shaping of Urban America*, 2005, Routledge.*

1. See Adam Rome, *The Bulldozer in the Countryside: Suburban Sprawl and the Rise of American Environmentalism* (Cambridge: Cambridge University Press, 2001).

2. See the *Charter of the New Urbanism*, reprinted with detailed commentary in *The Charter of the New Urbanism, eds.* Michael Leccese and Kathleen McCormick (New York: McGraw Hill, 2000).

3. See Roderick Nash, *The Rights of Nature: The History of Environmental Ethics* (Madison: University of Wisconsin Press, 1989) for an illuminating discussion of the ideological roots of this perspective.

4. William Cronon, "The Trouble with Wilderness; or, Getting Back to the Wrong Nature: Rethinking the Human Place in Nature," in *Uncommon Ground, ed.* William Cronon (New York: Norton & Co, 1996): 81.

5. See James Collins et al., "The New Urban Ecology," *American Scientist 88, no. 5* (September 2000).

6. Rome, 221.

7. Ironically, some of these standards also enforce an inappropriate urbanization in rural areas, requiring a highly engineered stormwater infrastructure that forces developers to be more destructive of the land than they would otherwise need to be.

8. See discussion of William Rees's concept in Timothy Beatley, *Green Urbanism* (Washington, D.C.: Island Press, 2000): 19–20, and Timothy Beatley and Kristy Manning, *The Ecology of Place: Planning for Environment, Economy, and Community* (Washington, D.C.: Island Press, 1997).

9. Not per capita consumption, where they are more efficient than suburbia, but absolute measures that are then translated into open space consumed in the city's support. This is the very recipe of anti-urbanism. Properly applied, the technique of analyzing an ecological footprint can be a useful measure. However, it tends to be used only to reinforce the sense of environmental destruction wrought by urbanism.

10. For example, as Michael Mehaffy has pointed out to us in discussions of London, measures of the ecological footprint of the city of London have not taken into account the fact that the city supports a tourist population as well as residents.

11. William Cronon provides an important alternative view of the relationship of the city to the reshaping of its region in *Nature's Metropolis: Chicago and the Great West* (New York: W. W. Norton, 1991). Cronon's account of the wide-ranging impact of Chicago's development on the development of the whole region raises questions regarding the status of nature in relation to the city, as well as the appropriate boundaries for analysis of the relevant ecocycles that make up a city.

12. Paul Murrain, "The Urban vs. the Green Imperative; An Unholy Alliance," *New Urban Post III* (Gaithersburg, MD, March 2002).

13. Beatley and Manning, 88.

14. There have been many influential books about urban nature and ecosystems, from Ian Mcharg's *Design with Nature* (New York: John Wiley & Sons, 1992), to Anne Whiston Spirn, *The Granite Garden: Urban Nature and Human Design* (New York: Basic Books, 1984), to John T. Lyle, *Design for Human Ecosystems: Landscape, Land Use, and Natural Resources* (Washington, D.C.: Island Press, 1999). In each case, these discussions are strong on the analysis of natural ecosystems and weak on the form and substance of the qualities of the human settlements that might warrant any sacrifice of nature as anything other than unfortunate and unavoidable.

15. In the case of a project that Duany Plater-Zyberk & Company has worked on in Hillsborough County, Florida, the requirement for a certain number of trees was met by making a reservation on one side of the project, planting great numbers of trees in it, and taking the trees out of the urbanized area. As a result, the whole project is lined with trees on the edge, just to get the mandatory number of trees because they each needed 120 square feet and there was no way to accommodate them within the street section.

16. Later, we discuss the idea of the successional tendencies of healthy urbanism, and the way conventional zoning and suburban patterns interfere with the ability of communities to change (or improve) over time.

17. To be sure, those mistakes are now being corrected with more attention to the issues of transit and the patterns of urban development. One recent scholarly paper attempted to measure the success of Portland's efforts, and the measures indicate substantial success in the war against sprawl at the neighborhood level, whereas there has been less measurable success at the regional level. Yan Song and Gerrit Knaap, "Measuring Urban Form: Is Portland Winning the War on Sprawl?" *Journal of the American Planning Association, Volume 70, Issue 2* (2004).

18. Kentlands, among others, has been criticized in this way.

19. As Leinberger observed: "Thus, the real estate development industry now has 19 standardized building types – a cookie-cutter array of office, industrial, retail, hotel, apartment, residential, and miscellaneous building types. These projects are easy and cheap to finance, build, trade, and manage. To take one example, a 'neighborhood center' will always be built on a 12 to 15 acre site, with 20% of the space set aside for building and the remaining 80% dedicated to parking. The center will invariably be anchored by a 50,000 to 70,000-square-foot grocery store, a 20,000–30,000 square foot drugstore, and in-line shops occupied by national chain retailers. It will draw its customers from 15,000 households in the 'neighborhood' in a 3 to 5 mile radius."

20. You can see the effects of this logic very clearly in the illustrations of the method of designing "conservation subdivisions." First, you identify the areas on the site that are to be preserved (wetlands, slopes, greenway connections, etc.). Then you lay out the roads to provide access to the pieces left over. See, for example, Randall Arendt, *Conservation Design for Subdivisions: A Practical Guide to Creating Open Space Networks* (Washington, D.C.: Island Press, 1996).

21. The greenways were entirely artificially constructed to simulate wetlands eliminated by farming in the 1940s.

22. As noted, not only "rare" or "designated" but even "listed"–a lesser standard–is now considered sufficient cause for concern.

23. William Shutkin, *The Land that Could Be: Environmentalism and Democracy in the Twenty-First Century* (Cambridge: MIT Press, 2000): 18–19.

24. See also Carmen Siriani and Lewis Friedland, *Civic Innovation in America: Community Empowerment, Public Policy, and the Movement for Civic Renewal* (Berkeley: University of California Press, 2001).

25. Shutkin, 14.

26. Malcom Barbour, "Ecological Fragmentation in the Fifties," in *Uncommon Ground: Rethinking the Human Place in Nature, ed.* William Cronon (New York: W. W. Norton, 1996): 234.

27. Ibid., 237.

28. As an aside, one might observe that a political limitation of modernist architecture has been a reflection of the refusal on the part of many modernists to elaborate conventional means to express this kind of sensitivity to context or to cooperate in this kind of encoding of meaning in built form.

29. See Emily Talen, "Help for Urban Planning: The Transect Strategy." *Journal of Urban Design 7, no. 3* (2002): 293–312.

30. The urban sociology of the early twentieth century and the so-called urban ecology models operate according to this kind of logic.

31. Sidney Brower, *Good Neighborhoods: A Study of In-Town and Suburban Residential Neighborhoods* (Westport: Praeger, 1996).

32. Ibid., xiv.

33. Ibid., xiii.

34. Laurie Volk and Todd Zimmerman, "American Households on (and off) the Urban-to-Rural Transect," *Journal of Urban Design 7, no. 3* (2002): 341–352.

35. Ibid., 343.

36. Ibid., 344.

37. The Transect as a basis for coding has been used by the firms of Moule & Polyzoides, Dover/Kohl, Torti-Gallas, Mouzon & Associates, and Duany Plater-Zyberk & Company. There are more, but these are most familiar to the authors.

38. For a discussion of the problem of "wilderness," see William Cronon, "The Trouble with Wilderness; or, Getting Back to the Wrong Nature: Rethinking the Human Place in Nature," in *Uncommon Ground, ed.* William Cronon (New York: Norton & Co, 1996): 69–90.

39. See Emily Talen, *Urbanism in America, Ideals, Connections and Conflicts* (New York: Routledge, 2005).

THE TRANSECT STRATEGY

EMILY TALEN

There exist a seemingly infinite number of proposals for organizing, developing, and rectifying the problems of urban environments. From an urban planning point of view, these proposals vary by scale—from lot configuration to regional planning—as well as by ideological orientation—where one proposal seeks to celebrate local vernacular traditions, another seeks wholesale redevelopment of economically defined "blight." In the midst of this range of proposals, and somewhat tangential to them, it is often the cold face of zoning regulation that actually determines the form, pattern, and design of the urban environment.

This paper seeks to support Transect-based planning by exploring the ways in which Transect strategies resolve the tensions, or conflicts, that exist in contemporary urban planning practice.

Planning Tensions and Transect Resolution

The Transect approach has intuitive appeal, and more than 100 communities have adopted Transect principles explicitly in their new land use plans and regulations.[1] But the concern in the remainder of this paper is with identifying and explaining a different kind of positive effect that results under Transect planning. Specifically, the Transect may offer a way to resolve some of the deep-rooted tensions that currently (and historically) plague the practice of urban planning in capitalist countries. I have succinctly organized these tensions into three interrelated groups: the tension between three-dimensional form and two-dimensional pattern; the tension between planning for order vs. planning for diversity; and finally, the tension between "town" and "country" and the problems that have resulted from our failure to find the proper relationship between the two. All of these tensions are characteristic of current, western capitalist approaches to urban planning, but they are not necessarily intrinsic qualities of urban planning per se—in the sense that they are beyond resolution.

It is possible to see these tensions operating simultaneously, often pulling planners in opposite directions. Long-range comprehensive plans compete with short-range zoning codes; the need for orderly neighborhood units and streetscapes conflicts with the desire to maintain "everyday urbanism"; and the need for compact development competes with an apparent preference for "wide open spaces." In a sense, the dilemma of contemporary planning practice can be seen as an inability to resolve these ongoing conflicts.

The problem is that these conflicts are not usually part of a natural dialectical process in which the resolution of two opposite trends leads to a progression of ideas. For example, the problem of rectifying long-range comprehensive planning that is two-dimensional and long-term with short-term three-dimensional implementing codes like zoning may be linked to a failure to conceptualize them in similar terms. They are seen as polarizing rather than as part of a healthy, ultimately resolvable planning approach. Similarly, the quest for some kind of urban order is pitted against the need to respect local diversity in such a way that the two are seen as opposite and tension-ridden, and therefore not likely to be integrated.

These tensions and the way in which they are perpetuated rather than resolved can be viewed historically, but they have a very contemporary context as well, played out in the debate over the legitimacy of New Urbanism. In fact it is the failure to resolve the tension between form and pattern and between order and diversity that lies at the root of the critique of New Urbanism. For example, much criticism focuses on what is perceived to be a rigid spatial ordering that does not allow for a plurality of viewpoints.[2] There are critiques that New Urbanism is either too compact for most people's preferences (too much "town") or too much like current suburban patterns of development (too much "country"). It may be possible, however, to see order and diversity, town and country, as interconnected parts.

Either historically or contemporaneously, the tensions do not constitute a healthy debate between two sides. Nor are they about changing needs. While it is recognized that multi-sided problems can be constructive and do not always have to be neutralized, planning tensions tend to be chronic and debilitating, often rendering planning ineffective. Harland Bartholomew, an early leader in American city planning, lamented the failure of comprehensive planning in this same context already in 1943, stating that the fundamental objectives of city plans were not being appreciated. Instead, such plans were being dismissed as too visionary or impractical.[3]

In the paragraphs that follow, it is argued that the Transect approach helps to resolve these planning tensions through its ability to build a durable system of organization. In a sense, the Transect offers one approach to integrating these tensions in such a way that they become two sides of the same coin rather than different coins altogether. This integration is based largely on nature—a system that is not culturally derived or relativistic, but durable in its ability to interconnect diverse elements.

Form vs. Pattern

One of the most long-lasting tensions of 20th century urban planning practice is the seemingly intractable problem of positioning architectural, three-dimensional design in relation to pattern-oriented, two-dimensional planning. Generally, the former is physically specific, short-term, and covers a small area, single project or planned community. The latter, conversely, tends to be physically vague, long range, and covers a large area in a comprehensive manner. The difficulty of bringing the two approaches into a shared framework is reflected in the difference between the urban designer's "master plan" and the urban planner's "comprehensive plan."

The differences can be enormous. One requires design skill and the ability to communicate notions of beauty and urban space, while the other requires analytical skill and the ability to evaluate socio-economic forecasts. One is seeking the tangible qualities of urban form while the other is trying to account for an entire metropolitan area at once, including the interrelationships among the elements of various urban systems. The short-term and immediate is usually viewed as irrelevant or perhaps even antithetical to the long-term projections of community growth. This situation has a long history in American urban planning, and is in some ways exemplified by the competing ideologies of Frederick Law Olmsted, Sr., and his son Frederick Law Olmsted, Jr., the former promoting visionary plans, the latter focused on administrative process.[4]

Most planners and designers would agree that there is a need to consider both form, as a specific, short-range quality, as well as pattern and its longer-term, more generalized focus. It seems obvious that the two endeavors would benefit enormously from a healthier, more productive integration. Urban designers are acutely aware of this need—in particular, that it is necessary to find the right linkage between two- and three-dimensional views of the built environment. Certainly there has been no lack of effort in the search for a meaningful vocabulary. Edmund Bacon used the art of Paul Klee to communicate the interrelation between planning and architecture. Bacon described the gray rectangles of Klee's "Polyphonic Architecture" as suggesting "usual planning procedures," while the architecture shown sets up "a harmony which reverberates through all the spaces, showing that it is not necessary to design in detail every square foot of an area to achieve a great and unified work."[5]

Realistically, this approach to unifying planning and architecture—pattern and form—is too abstract for most planners seeking implementable solutions. What has emerged instead is a partial resolution in which zoning, which is supposed to be based on long-range planning, has assumed much greater practical effect than planning. Zoning does have an effect on pattern as well as form, but its concern is neither geographically broad nor temporally long-range. It works one lot and one building at a time. Long range comprehensive planning, on the other hand, quite apart from conventional zoning, seeks to guide the overall urban pattern in a much more abstract way, and in a manner that is rarely backed by legally enforced codes.

It is interesting that this somewhat classic planning tension is highly visible in the history of urban planning in the U.S. The tension is rooted in the beginnings of the profession, which had its first national conference in 1909 and was formally organized as the American City Planning Institute in 1917. One of the longest running stories in urban planning history is the tale of Alfred Bettman, the lawyer from Cincinnati who failed to adequately distinguish the difference between planning and zoning and therefore caused "20 years of confusion," according to renowned planner T.J. Kent.[6] The damage done by Bettman's inclusion of zoning as one of the five elements of planning in his highly influential Standard City Planning Enabling Act of 1928 is by now a standard entry in most renditions of U.S. planning history.[7]

On the surface of it, the basic argument separating planning (long-range pattern) and zoning (short-range form) makes sense. Planning is supposed to be about the future visions and long-term aspirations of a community. Zoning, on the other hand, is narrowly focused and piecemeal, dealing directly with immediate building issues that cannot adequately reflect on long-term community goals. Zoning, in other words, does not really care about pattern in a meaningful way, nor about spatial relationships or comprehensive thinking in which interrelationships between parts of the urban system are causally linked. But in terms of numbers and legal enforceability, zoning has always had the upper hand. As early as 1927 in the U.S., there were three times as many zoning ordinances as plans, and by 1941 the ratio had increased to 10 to 1.[8] Our current system is one of "good plans, bad zoning," and implementation regulations continue to defy the most well-intentioned plans.[9]

The underlying assumption fueling the notion that zoning and planning must be kept separate is at least partly flawed. It states that if planners are dealing with short-range, physical problems of urban three-dimensional form, they can therefore not be thinking simultaneously in terms of long-range, "big-picture" goals. Or, such long-range goals are first set by an all-encompassing plan, only later to be worked out in terms of implementation through zoning. A tangible issue, however, is that this institutionalized division between zoning and planning, reflective of the division between form and pattern, has had very negative effects. It has meant, for one thing, that American cities lack an appropriate definition of space, resulting in an American spatial pattern that is disorganized and often illegible. The narrow application of zoning codes, resulting in some of the worst sprawl and most explicit social segregation, has reached legendary status.

The relevance of the Rural-to-Urban Transect can now be brought in, for it is possible to reason that there has not been a successful linkage between form and pattern—short-term zoning and long-term planning—because the theoretical infrastructure necessary to do it has been underdeveloped. In light of the fact that zoning lacks long-range vision and long-range planning lacks implementable specificity, one remedy is to seek a solid theoretical basis for linking the two. This is precisely where the Transect may be of use. It is both a geographic spatial patterning system in which long-range objectives about the integration of urban and natural systems are given relevance, and it is also a very specific view of urban form grounded in the coding of urban elements. The Transect accomplishes comprehensive long-range visioning not by trying to simulate every complex human interaction, but by tying discrete elements into a larger system.

Transect planning thus offers a different approach to the usual separation of planning and zoning by incorporating planning goals directly into the devices of implementation. Rather than "forcing" zoning and subdivision regulations to conform to well-conceived plans (often an unsuccessful endeavor), the plan and zoning code are conceived as being inseparable from the outset. This is one way to imbue an aspiration document, often hopelessly vague and ambiguous in terms of implementation, with legal enforceability. It serves to enjoin urban form and urban pattern.

The SmartCode is an example of how the integration of planning and zoning can occur. The SmartCode integrates procedures for the preparation of plans directly into the code and uses these procedures as the main organizing structure of the code. These are not plans in the sense of long-range, comprehensive plans that are often vaguely defined and difficult to translate into code. The plans that make up the SmartCode are specific guiding principles of good urban form that are used to provide a framework for the various Transect Zones.

Ultimately, resolving the tension between form and pattern is a matter of finding the right way to foster interdependency. The Transect as a conceptual framework relies on interdependencies in order to work. One zone is defined by its relation to others—it is either more or less urban, more or less rural, identified by way of its position along the rural to urban continuum. Another interdependency, already discussed, is that Transect Zones combine to form different types of communities. In this way, no section along the Transect exists in isolation: Transect Zone definition depends on its interrelation with other immersive Transect environments. Importantly, this represents a conceptual link to other current strains of thinking that call for urban integration on a number of levels: the plea for regionalism, cities without suburbs, and cities that are not autonomous and self-centered but thrive on metropolitan interdependencies.[10]

Order vs. Diversity

Diversity does not mean chaos. The individuality of experience found in the Las Vegas commercial strip, immortalized in Venturi, Brown, and Izenour's *Learning from Las Vegas*, and more recently celebrated in "Everyday Urbanism," are not necessarily the best examples of what is meant by diversity as a defining characteristic of urbanism.[11]

Order in urbanism has to be reconciled with diversity, and this was a key contribution made by Jane Jacobs, who argued that order is not the opposite of diversity. Yet order has not been well regarded as a concept in urbanism in the latter half of the century, since it has often been equated with the attempt to deny social conflict and control the unexpected. This is why M. Christine Boyer critiqued planning as an imposer of "disciplinary order and ceremonial harmony" where humans are organized, but alienated.[12]

The critique of order is rooted in the fact that almost all ideas about the spatial planning of cities have been linked to some form of social planning and reform.[13] The transparency of social intent has differed—more overt in Haussmann's grand planning, perhaps less authoritarian in the planning of neighborhood "units"—but the issue of social manipulation has always been a source of disapproval. Ironically, however, the social damage caused by planning policies can not be blamed on spatial planning ideals in their purest form, but instead on their incomplete and inappropriate application.[14] A strident example is the insidious zoning separation schemes—that had, and continue to have, profound social effects—that evolved out of Progressive Era spatial planning models.

Social order can be viewed as both cause and effect of the second notion of order in planning—the idea of separation. This phenomenon of planning exists on a much more applied level, where planning implementation has translated into the notion of separating uses into functional classes. This is the legacy of conventional zoning, the outcome of which has been homogeneous, rigidly segregated suburban housing developments that are ordered in the extreme.

Despite these significant problems with the idea of order in planning, lack of order is equally problematic. When planners are diffident and cautious about order, the result can be haphazard growth or chaotic urban form. This results when, on the one hand, there is an elevation of the importance of the "mythic aspect of the ordinary and ugly,"[15] and on the other, there is a promotion of the view that strip malls merely represent a new, as yet underappreciated, aesthetic ideal.[16] This is the extreme of planning relativism, akin to a philosophy that separates facts from values, regards all human nature as relative, and believes that virtues cannot be identified or ranked. It has ideological similarities to what philosopher Susan Haack has called "preposterism"—that "finding out how things really are" is viewed as nothing more than a "smokescreen hiding the operations of power, politics, social negotiation [and] rhetoric."[17]

By tying its system of order to nature, not social processes, the Transect resolves both issues simultaneously. The key is that it focuses on the diversity of elements that make up a system of order—the same type of structure found in nature,[18] but here applied to a system of city building. As in nature, order does not mean a lack of complexity. On the contrary, complexity is an intrinsic, inseparable part of order. The Transect emulates this natural, ordered system of complexity. It therefore eludes the criticism that the organization of spatial form must be a search for control over moral and political order.[19]

It is critical to understand the link between natural ordering systems and natural diversity. The Transect is successful as a system of order because it appeals to natural order, connecting to the idea that intricately complex environments are nevertheless part of an ordered system. The idea of diversity within an underlying system of ecological order may at first seem elusive, but it actually works to replace abstract modernist notions of infinite and uniform space with "immediate, concrete [and] particular" notions of place.[20] A few prominent planners have adeptly recognized this link, stressing the need for urban diversity that mirrors and integrates with the complexity of natural ecologies. Ian McHarg applied this to the regional scale, believing that the fundamental problem with conventional suburban sprawl was the imposition of a destructive simplicity on a complex system. Jane Jacobs emphasized the intra-urban situation, pointing out that the diversity of a healthy city is analogous to the diversity of a natural ecosystem.[21]

Outside of planning, the link between natural and urban environments has been gaining recognition. The current "new urban ecology," focused on developing the link between urban and natural ecologies, is finding renewed attention.[22] The Transect approach extends this thinking to a logical, applied integration at the scale of building. Using this system, the elements of the city are arranged in such a way that, rather than a randomly occurring collection of urban elements, they make up part of a whole. This kind of "organicism," where individual parts belong to an urban whole, has been criticized by Kevin Lynch, but others have viewed it as an essential basis of holistic (rather than piecemeal) approaches to planning.[23] In some sense, the connection between parts and the whole is analogous to the relationship between diversity and order.

Most importantly, basing urban order on an ecological connection frees planners from having to rely on notions of social order. In this conceptualization, social agreement is not particularly relevant. There is no need to connect spatial pattern and moral order in the way that planning idealists like Ebenezer Howard or urban sociologists like Robert Park did. The notion of an organized spatial form that seeks to similarly organize human beings becomes irrelevant. If planners seek some way to strengthen the ecological bond between the human world and the natural world, the focus can be about linking humans and nature, not about creating social utopias.

There are some interesting connections to be made between this view and the view of "radical center" theorists, discussed by cultural historian Frederick Turner.[24] In this theoretical view, the universe is not deterministic but is self-renewing and infinitely creative, as demonstrated in phenomena like fractals. This way of thinking ultimately leads to the promotion of classical ideals in architecture, poetic meter in the arts, or even notions of ideal urban form in urban planning. But, because a sense of order is rooted in diversity at all levels, the problematic notion of rigid, deterministic order is avoided.

The Transect's sense of environmental order is based on maintaining proper interconnections among urban elements—a balanced mix of landscape, building type, and streetscape, for example—to create a series of immersive environments. But how does this notion of order relate to social systems? Since social order is rejected, what are the social goals of the Transect? The answer is, quite simply, that the Transect tries to accommodate a diversity of people. It does this by creating a diversity of living environments. And while it is true that, since this is a normative proposal, not every type of environment is envisaged by the Transect (explicitly excluding, in fact, most forms of single-use environments), there is nevertheless a strong emphasis on accommodating a variety of different types of human habitats. This goes some way toward promoting a plurality of viewpoints, creating a diversity of physical frameworks within which a diversity of people may flourish.

It is also relevant that Transect systems are locally generated, each determined in large part by local, vernacular traditions. Each zone of these local Transects can be said to be better or worse at satisfying the needs of a particular individual or family. This provides a useful framework for accommodating a diverse population.

Town vs. Country

Finding the proper integration of town (or city) and country (or nature) is a compelling subject that has engaged scholars in various disciplines for centuries. While it is possible to view the "man-made world" as "natural,"[25] it is more likely to be viewed in striking contrast to the natural world. We continually labor to create our "second world" in the world of nature, to use Cicero's phrase,[26] but whether this can be a harmonious integration is puzzling. What we do know is that our source for city building, and in particular our notions of beauty in the built environment, are derived from the systems of order and disorder found in nature.[27]

In the context of modern, particularly 20th century, planning practice, the issue is less metaphysical, and instead revolves very pragmatically around the issue of the growth or spread of cities into their surrounding hinterlands. And while the physical ramifications of "town" encroaching on "country" and the problems that are likely to occur is a main pre-occupation of modern planning, there is little evidence that the relationship has been adequately planned. The resulting "sprawl" has become a household term, and while the pros, cons, costs, measurement and effects are endlessly debated, in one sense the issue simply boils down to defining a proper relationship between town and country—city and nature.

One of the common reactions to resolving the tension between town and country is to surround the town with an impenetrable green belt. This idea goes back well before Ebenezer Howard's *Garden Cities*: "Ledoux, Owen, Pemberton, Buckingham and Kropotkin all had towns of limited populations with surrounding agriculture green belts."[28] There are varying opinions about the success of such approaches. A major limitation is that greenbelts are difficult and expensive to put into place. But another problem is that they do not necessarily have any bearing on development occurring within the greenbelt, which can still be sprawl. Further, development that occurs outside of the greenbelt can be just as objectionable as any of the worst sprawl the greenbelt was designed to eliminate. Greenbelts, in most instances, offer a temporary spatial stay of sprawl, but the effect is usually localized.

Another solution to resolving the tension between town and country in a planning context is opposite of Howard's garden city approach—the Corbusian proposal of extreme centralization, or "towers in a park." The vertical garden city of Le Corbusier houses the masses in high-rise apartments that clearly demarcate town from country, all in an effort to avoid what Thomas Sharp viewed in 1932 as the essential problem of "debased" town development, where "Rural influences neutralize the town. Urban influences neutralize the country. In a few years all will be neutrality."[29]

The extreme, Corbusian solution to reversing town and country neutralization stands in marked contrast to the traditional, prewar American city. One of its defining qualities, so foreign to our current manner of urbanization, was the gradual intensity of land use from periphery to center. The current metropolis, on the other hand, urbanizes rural environments haphazardly. The urban pattern plunges abruptly from edge-city high-rise to single-use residential development, creating a city that, instead of an organized system of greater or lesser intensity, is extended using "easily reproducible units pulled from the box of urban tinkertoys."[30]

This is not to say that an attempt to find the right balance and level of integration between town and country has not taken place. But there is no easy resolution. A large part of the issue, as far as physical planning is concerned, is how abrupt the change from one to the other should be. Should the city end steadfastly, like walled medieval towns or greenbelted cities? Neither approach has been successful in the American context. The walling of towns lacks practical expression in contemporary times (or, results, perversely, in the form of gated communities), and the political and ethical difficulties of greenbelting are notorious.

The Transect offers an alternative approach to finding the correct balance. It ties into a tradition of ecological planning that is more integrative than boundary-driven. Rather than stopping urban growth with physical barriers that underscore urban-vs-rural division, the Transect takes a different approach: it seeks to connect and integrate the two worlds along a continuum.

The idea of uniting rather than separating town and country has strong parallels to the regional planning approach advocated by Geddes, Stein, Mumford, and other members of the Regional Planning Association of America. These planners, in particular Patrick Geddes and Benton MacKaye, even made use of transects in their analysis of regions as a way of demonstrating ecological balance and the interconnection between people and their ecological region. (See page 31.) They spoke of the need to view "people, industry and the land as a single unit," emphasizing "human values hand in hand with natural resources," part of a lineage that leads directly to Ian McHarg.[31]

By now, the need to consider these relationships is a familiar dictum of planners, notably through the work of sustainability planners.[32] But there is a need to put maximal effort into translating environmental ideals into urban design specifics. Toward this objective, the Transect can be thought of as an environmentally conceived approach to urban design. Whereas traditional urban design is usually thought of as having nothing to do with environmental health,[33] the Transect situates urban design within an environmental framework.

The Transect's approach to the integration of town and country is an update on the idea of regionally dispersed garden cities, a concept advocated by the Regional Planning Association. The SmartCode, to use one example, identifies various types of community units within and outside of urbanized areas, and the mixes of Transect Zones they should contain. The modification accommodates a more diverse range of development types, paying greater attention to the interconnections of various urban elements at multiple points along the rural-to-urban gradient. This has the benefit of accommodating a greater range of development choices, thereby infusing a greater sense of realism in the land-development process. It also focuses on the need to work through existing development patterns. Rather than placing garden cities in a regional framework, the Transect seeks to position a more complex pattern of development types—i.e., immersive environments—in a regional framework. What is retained, however, is a clear focus on making sure that the integration between town and country does not neutralize either one in the process.

Conclusion

The three planning tensions discussed in this paper are endemic to a profession that has become mired in a culture of separation. This exists on multiple levels—professional specialization that separates economic development planners from transportation planners or environmental planners, a planning regulatory system that encourages land-use separation, and even a concomitant development industry that specializes in building or financing only certain, specific types of developments. Each of these separations create problems for planning practice by splintering efforts, pitting specializations against each other, and thwarting attempts to implement a more consolidated approach.

Similarly, the way in which the crisis of urban form has been characterized reflects a sense of separation, since urban problems are often viewed in terms of polarities. A classic example is the way in which the crisis of cities is seen as one of too-high density (the East End of London a century ago), or too-low density (Atlanta-style sprawl). These two extremes have come to be viewed in strikingly similar parallels,[34] but in either instance the resolution should not be—but often is—focused on obtaining the opposite. For the resolution of urban problems, planners tend to argue in terms of "opposites, antagonisms, old versus new, traditional versus modern, progressive versus reactionary."[35] The irony, of course, is that the failure to establish links between opposites can have disastrous effects. Ungers and Vieth, in *The Dialectic City*, point out that the failure to establish a connection between dialectic views of the city has produced a profound urban malady, where the modern ideology of a tidy, well ordered city has in fact produced the opposite—chaotic urban sprawl.

The Transect, as an integrative system, defies these opposites and antagonisms. It defines urban possibilities in terms of a continuum, using complementary elements. The result could be a significant move forward: the Transect connects the urban and the rural in a continuum, it seeks to combine the ability to have both order and diversity in the urban environment, and it better connects the goals of urban three-dimensional form and two-dimensional pattern. The Transect embodies the view that the crisis of metropolitan form is not one of too-high density or too-low density, but is an inappropriate mixing of elements, elements that need to be reintegrated in a more suitable way. This has the effect of resolving some of the most enduring "tensions" of urban planning.

The end result of the Transect system of integration, used to resolve planning tensions and separations, is a system that seeks beauty and "sense of place" in urban environments. These notions have been elusive in contemporary planning practice, and American planning policy in particular is reluctant to incorporate notions of beauty or "good urban form" in its approach. The Transect system of organization provides a practical means to accomplish such otherwise elusive objectives. As Witold Rybczynski, in *The Look of Architecture*, wrote: "To create a strong sense of place, the surroundings must be all of a piece: space, mass, shapes, and materials must reflect the same sensibility."[36]

This essay was orginally published in The Journal of Urban Design, *October 2002.*

1. The *SmartCode* has been implemented in several places in the U.S., such as Belmont, North Carolina and Hillsborough County, Florida.

2. See, for example, Harvey, David. 2000. *Spaces of Hope*. Berkeley: University of California Press.

3. Wilson, W. 1989. *The City Beautiful Movement*. Baltimore: Johns Hopkins University Press.

4. See Peterson, Jon. 1996. Frederick Law Olmsted Sr. and Frederick Law Olmsted Jr. *The visionary and the professional. In Planning the Twentieth-Century American City*, Mary Corbin Sies and Christopher Silver, eds., Baltimore: Johns Hopkins University Press. p. 37–54.

5. Bacon, Edmund N. 1967. *Design of Cities*. New York: Penguin Books, p. 319.

6. Kent, T. J., Jr. (1964), 1990. *The Urban General Plan*. Chicago: American Planning Association.

7. See Gerckens, Laurence C. 1994. "American zoning and the physical isolation of uses." *Planning Commissioners Journal 15:* p. 9.

8. Burgess, Patricia. 1996. *"Of swimming pools and 'slums'". In Planning the Twentieth-Century American City*, Mary Corbin Sies and Christopher Silver, Eds. p. 213–239.

9. Russell, Joel. 2000. "The secret life of a land-planning professional." *Bulletin of Science, Technology, and Society 20*, 4: 318–320, p. 319.

10. On regionalism, see Calthorpe, Peter, and William Fulton. 2001. *The Regional City: Planning for the End of Sprawl*. Washington D.C.: Island Press; on cities without suburbs, see Rusk, David. 1993. *Cities Without Suburbs*. Washington, D.C.: Woodrow Wilson Press; on metropolitan interdependencies, see Frug, Gerald E. 1999. *City Making: Building Communities without Building Walls*. Princeton, NJ: Princeton University Press.

11. Venturi, R., D.S. Brown, and S. Izenour. 1972. *Learning from Las Vegas*. Cambridge, MA: MIT Press; Chase, John, Margaret Crawford, and John Kaliski. 1999. Everyday Urbanism. New York: Monacelli Press.

12. Boyer, M. Christine. 1983. *Dreaming the Rational City: The Myth of American City Planning*. Cambridge, MA: MIT Press, p. 7.

13. Kostof, Spiro. 1991. *The City Shaped: Urban Patterns and Meanings Through History. Boston*: Little, Brown and Co.

14. See especially Hall, Peter. 1998. *Cities of Tomorrow*. Oxford: Basil Blackwell.

15. Kelbaugh, Douglas. 2000. "Three paradigms: New Urbanism, everyday urbanism, post urbanism—An excerpt from The Essential Common Place." *Bulletin of Science, Technology & Society 20, Issue 4*: 285–289, p. 287.

16. Kolb, David. 2000. *The age of the list. In Urban Space and Urban Conservation as an Aesthetic Problem*, Gregers Algreen-Ussing, Lise Bek, Steen Bo Frandsen and Jens Schjerup Hansen, Eds. Rome: L'Erma Di Bretschneider. p. 27–35.

17. Haack, Susan. 1998. *Manifesto of a Passionate Moderate: Unfashionable Essays*, Chicago: University of Chicago Press, p. 1.

18. See Gleick, James. 1988. *Chaos: Making a New Science*. New York: Penguin Books.

19. See Harvey, David. 2000. *Spaces of Hope*. Berkeley: University of California Press.

20. Walter, Eugene Victor. 1988. *Placeways: A Theory of the Human Environment*. Chapel Hill: University of North Carolina Press.

21. On McHarg, see Fishman, Robert. 2000. *"The American planning tradition: An introduction and interpretation."* In *The American Planning Tradition: Culture and Policy*. Robert Fishman, ed. Baltimore, MD: The Johns Hopkins University Press. p. 1–29; Jacobs, Jane. 1961. *The Death and Life of Great American Cities*. New York: Random House.

22. See Collins, James P., Ann Kinzig, Nancy B. Grimm, William F. Fagan, Diane Hope, Jianguo Wu and Elizabeth T. Borer. 2000. "A new urban ecology." *American Scientist 88, Issue 5*: 416–425.

23. Lynch, Kevin. 1981. *Good City Form*. Cambridge, MA: MIT Press.

24. Turner, Frederick. 1995. *Culture of Hope: A New Birth of the Classical Spirit*. New York: Free Press.

25. The Hegelian view; see Crowe, Norman. 1997. *Nature and the Idea of a Man-Made World*. Cambridge, MA: The MIT Press.

26. From De Natura Deorum, 1st century B.C.

27. See Turner, 1995.

28. Hall, Peter. 1998. *Cities of Tomorrow*. Oxford: Basil Blackwell, p. 91.

29. Sharp, T. 1932. *Town and Countryside: Some Aspects of Urban and Rural Development*. London: Oxford UP, p. 11.

30. Abbott, Carl. 1993. *The Metropolitan Frontier: Cities in the Modern American West*. Tucson, AZ: University of Arizona Press, p. 138.

31. Geddes, Patrick. 1915 (1949). *Cities in Evolution*. London: Williams & Norgate; MacKaye, Benton. 1925. "The new exploration." *Survey 54*: 153–7 and 192; Mumford, Lewis. 1925. "Regions—to live in." *Survey 54*: 151–2, p. 151.

32. See Beatley, Timothy and Kristy Manning. 1997. *The Ecology of Place*. Washington, D.C: Island Press.

33. Frey, Hildebrand. 1999. *Designing the City: Towards a More Sustainable Urban Form*. New York: Routledge.

34. Peel, M. 1995. *"The urban debate: From 'Los Angeles' to the urban village."* In P. Troy, Ed., *Australian Cities: Issues, Strategies and Policies for Urban Australia in the 1990s*. London: Cambridge University Press. p. 39–64.

35. Ungers, Oswald Mathias and Stefan Vieths. 1997. *The Dialectic City*. Milan: Skira, p. 14.

36. Rybczynski, Witold. 2001. *The Look of Architecture*. New York: Oxford University Press, p. 97.

A THEORY OF SUSTAINABLE URBANISM

ANDRÉS DUANY

The Crises

There are three great crises upon us, and they are of such magnitude that they may be considered permanent. These are climate change, peak oil, and the evaporation of national wealth, otherwise known as the real estate bust. Because the crises are all downtrends, there is a general feeling that they are related, and there is in fact an objective lynch pin: the lifestyle of the American middle class—the way we drive around for ordinary daily needs, dwell large on the land and in commoditized real estate products, and how we secure our food. It is that lifestyle, and now the worldwide export version, which is the cause of all the crises. If this lifestyle can be summarized, it is surely what we call "suburban sprawl."

Designers have become engaged in the reform, and while the first generation of responses has been restricted to buildings (LEED), the urban scale is now being deployed (LEED-ND). The name has been agreed to—it is to be "Sustainable Urbanism"—but confusion remains, as there are several paradigms that are serious contenders to that title. Among these are the Old Urbanism, the now-mature New Urbanism, and the nascent Landscape Urbanism. There is another, but given the seriousness of the situation, Irresponsible Urbanism might finally be dismissed from the planning discourse.

The Contenders

The term Irresponsible Urbanism was derived from Rem Koolhaas' piece, "Atlanta," which concludes, "The city is out of control, let us be irresponsible." From its origins in Broadacre City, this paradigm has been gradually dumbed down through decades of inbreeding at the ULI, to a vegetative state in the care of today's libertarian fringe. But it is not yet dead. One of the tasks of Sustainable Urbanism is to retain what the Irresponsible Urbanism did well: being marketable, relatively inexpensive, and easy to administer. If this is not achieved, it may rise again. Remember that suburban sprawl is the idiot savant of urban planning, able to sucker the sympathy of Herbert Gans, Robert Venturi, and Denise Scott Brown—and quite recently the apologists of "unprecedented typologies," as if its problem were the absence of a suitable aesthetic.

The Old Urbanism was informally named by Alex Krieger when he asked, "But isn't the New Urbanism just the Old Urbanism?" It is not too flattering, but the term seems to be more acceptable than "Traditional Urbanism." The Old Urbanism is in resurgence as more people notice that living densely, walking, and taking transit is an environmentally responsible lifestyle. The word is that a Manhattanite has half the ecological footprint of the average American. Its predicament is that it is technically at odds with current environmental standards. The Manhattan we know is an unattainable ideal that could not be built today for a multitude of reasons—the first being the hundreds of streams buried in pipes that its urban pattern requires. While it is an environmental success in its secondary consequences, it is an environmental disaster in its technical premises. The Old Urbanism values nature not at all—and those days are over.

Despite Alex Krieger's question, the New Urbanism differs from the Old Urbanism in many ways—one being that in the past, cities used to compete with other cities on a level playing field, but today, cities compete with their own suburbs—which have a greater range of typological resources. It is technically pitted against Irresponsible Urbanism's polymorphic agility, which is enabled by cheap land and cheap oil. The New Urbanism mitigates the enormous physical impact of the car, but does not eliminate it. Its predicament as a hybrid is that it is capable of combining the best as well as the worst aspects of both city and suburb.

Landscape Urbanism is also a hybrid. Having its origins in the formal conceits of garden design, it is now updated with the "green" touchstones of native plant species, naturalistic hydrological systems, and corridor topology. This design innovation is now offering its services as a setting for buildings—and not just as their ornamental appendage—thereby reaching for the mantle of urbanism. But that is more than it can bear; with tools limited to the imitation of nature, Landscape Urbanism cannot avoid the ruralization of even high-density schemes (the other side of New Urbanism's urbanizing of low density). With rabid bias against spatial definition, there is no such thing in its repertoire as a "corridor street" or a "square." The public realm is primarily therapeutic: rustic walking, rooting about with edible planting, and communing with nature are surrogates for the social activity fostered by Old Urban places. Even Landscape Urbanism's vaunted engagement with "infrastructure" amounts to buffering arterials, improving the design of stormwater apparatus, and the decorating of parking lots with porous paving. But an urban paradigm cannot be based on the implantation of natural vignettes in the residual places between buildings. Besides, Landscape Urbanism is too adept at being compromised by providing a green camouflage for the so-called "unprecedented typologies" of big-box retailers and junkspace office parks.

The Challenge

How to assess these three contenders for Sustainable Urbanism, when there is not yet any kind of consensus within this new discourse? One way is to establish an abstract theory that can provide the test while it is itself being qualified by the integrity and usefulness of its testing process. This protocol must manifest that mystique of technique that underpins credibility in the modern political forum. And its metrics must be based on recognizable forms of natural processes so that environmentalists may be conscripted among the informed assessors rather than remain intransigent NIMBYs. Moreover, the theory must be simple enough to be administered by a bureaucracy that is accustomed to the robotic protocols of Euclidean zoning.

The Theory

Would the Rural-to-Urban Transect serve this rather abstract challenge as it has so many utilitarian ones?[1]

The Transect is an environmental theory based on geography that ranges from wilderness to urban core. By integrating environmental methodology for habitat management with zoning methodology for urban design, the Transect breaks down the customary specialized assessment, enabling environmentalists to consider the design of the cultural habitats, and urbanists to protect the natural ones. It can analyze and project the mix of human and natural elements that symbiotically create functional habitats. Today it is a freeware operating system available for zoning codes and other technical standards intended to replace the current system of zoning. It has proven to be a powerful taxonomic engine for the wildly disparate elements that must comprise a Sustainable Urbanism.

As the proposed General Theory of Sustainable Urbanism must mediate between worlds, it proposes as a common currency the concept of diversity, which both the natural sciences and the social sciences employ as an index. Both biological and economic activity is based on transaction (of chemicals, of heat, of goods or services). A currency is designed to clarify the evaluation of what is given in exchange for what is gained. A transaction is physically, economically, or politically sustainable so long as it is a fair trade. For instance, the NIMBY regime arose with the consciousness that suburban sprawl was not a fair trade; that a housing subdivision or shopping center was an exchange downward for the loss of a field or woodland. Before suburban sprawl, development was generally considered an upward trade: a woodland or farm might be lost, but what the village or town gained was considered good value. For example, the wetlands of the Charles Town Peninsula were lost, but the City of Charleston was considered to be a fair gain. It would not have been acceptable if what had replaced them was a suburban resort like nearby Hilton Head.

The Transect could elucidate a General Theory of Sustainable Urbanism with an equation:

> At any point on the Rural-to-Urban Transect, the aggregate density of the social and natural diversity after urbanization must be approximately equal to or greater than the density of the natural diversity prior to urbanization.[2]
>
> **N: Σ [Ds +Dn]post ≈ > N: [DN]pre**
>
> N = a constant number
>
> Ds = the diverse socioeconomic activities per unit of land, after urbanization
>
> Dn = the diverse natural habitats per unit of land, after urbanization
>
> DN = the diverse natural habitats per unit of land before urbanization

The graphs on the following page show the paradigms contending for Sustainable Urbanism in terms of this equation as an illustration of the General Theory.

Figure A: With the Old Urbanism, the social diversity of the T-6 Urban Core correctly rates higher than T-3 Sub-Urban. But there is a conceptual problem, as this lopsided measure assigns an even lesser value to T-2 Rural—and T-1 Natural has no value at all. The Old Urbanism created value by creating jobs, housing, shops, and entertainment. The diversity was achieved by their organic proximity in pedestrian sheds when cars were rare. The positive environmental consequences of the Old Urbanism are compactness, complexity, walkability and transit viability. The negative is that land must be denatured by network continuity into a commodity suitable for compact building. The Old Urbanism manifests an excellent environmental performance, but it cannot be inaugurated or extended without the elimination of nature.

Figure B: Landscape Urbanism's problem is that the T-3 Sub-Urban rates higher than the T-6 Urban Core, which has the worst performance. This is the result of the absolute privileging of natural diversity, and reveals the very serious conceptual flaw of this paradigm. Landscape Urbanism has no metrics to assess the urban side of the Transect. With only half the tools, the Urban Core's social diversity does not register except as impervious pavement and denatured heat island. Places like London and Manhattan are rated as enormously negative ecological footprints. Such urban patterns are considered part of the problem and not part of the solution.

Figure C: The New Urbanism assigns T-3 Sub-Urban the lowest value, as it has the lowest index in both social and natural diversity, thus correcting the assessment of the other two paradigms. With a declension of tools ranging from the urban boundary for

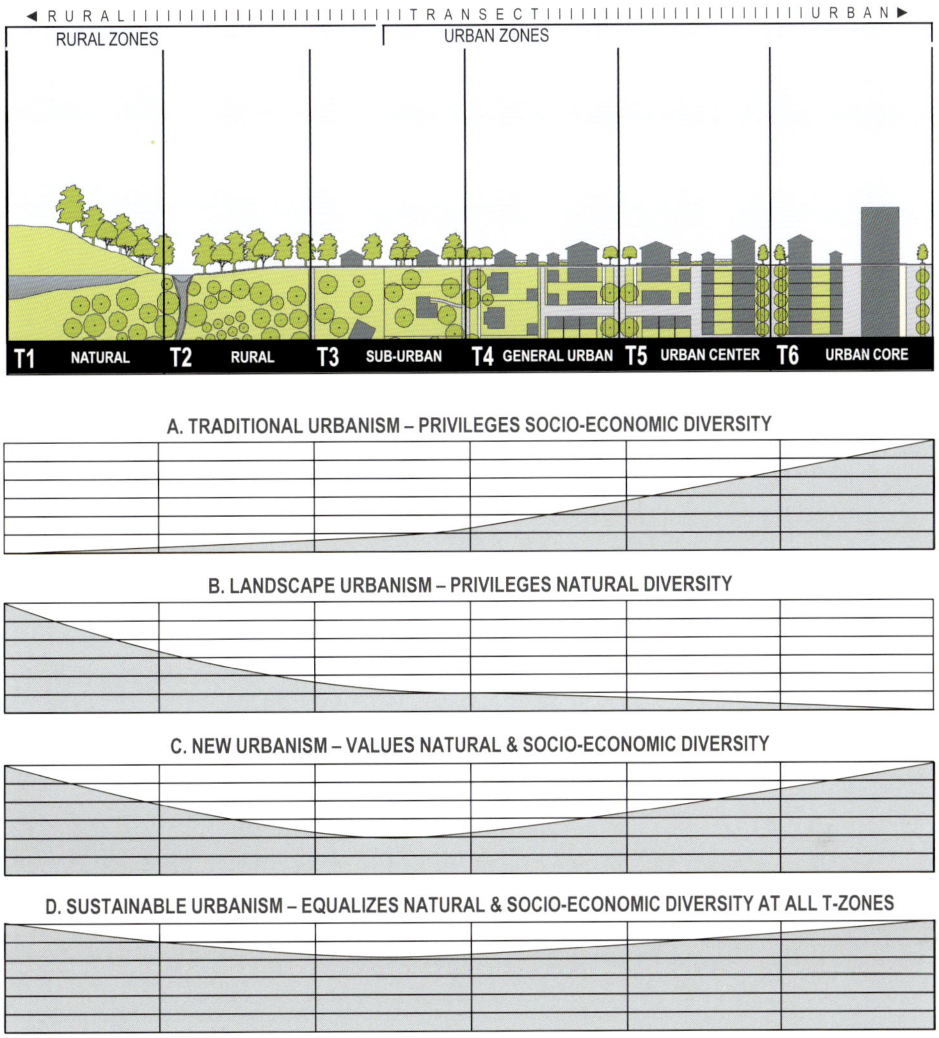

DPZ CODESIGN

the preservation of nature at T-1 and T-2, and a transit orientation enabling density and social diversity at T-5 and T-6, the New Urbanism is capable of selectively accepting or rejecting nature depending on the relative urbanity of the T-Zone. However, it is unable to justify the persistence of the suburban single-family house, except as driven by market preference—a regrettable necessity to implement its larger agenda elsewhere along the Transect. This flaw precludes the New Urbanism from becoming the paradigm for Sustainable Urbanism.

Figure D: Sustainable Urbanism retains the "correct" high points of social and natural diversity of the New Urbanism, but it improves the performance of T-3 Sub-Urban by integrating it technically to a green regime. T-3 is redesigned by definition to compensate for its higher land occupation and transportation impact with requirements for energy generation, water reuse, recycling/composting, and food production. The ability to do this happens to coincide with its higher allocation of land per capita. These mitigating techniques are better handled by a freestanding house than by the urban building types of T-5 and T-6. (An example of a food-production protocol can be seen on pages 82 and 83.) The suburban thus becomes T-3 Sub-Urban, with no opprobrium attached. A general theory of Sustainable Urbanism thus equalizes the environmental performance all along the Transect, retaining the choice that is integral to the politics of a market economy.

Summary

Both natural and social diversity are combined in various ratios along the Rural-to-Urban Transect. The high natural diversity of T-1 Natural establishes the ideal for Landscape Urbanism, while the high social diversity of T-6 Urban Core establishes the ideal for the Old Urbanism. But these two monovalent paradigms undervalue the positive consequences of the other, in the process assigning an unwarranted high value to T-3 Sub-Urban. The New Urbanism values both natural and social diversity at T-1 and T-6, while correctly devaluing the suburban point of T-3, which has the lowest indices of both. Sustainable Urbanism, according to the General Theory, equalizes the combined level of diversity of all T-zones, creating the Sub-Urban, so that all are justified environmentally, and the market can exercise its preferences. The equation of the General Theory can determine if a transaction to the urban can fairly justify the loss of nature.

This essay was orginally published in Ecological Urbanism*, 2016, Harvard University Graduate School of Design.*

1. See www.transect.org and "Regulating as if Humans Matter," Andrés Duany and David Brain, p. 293–332, *Regulating Place: Standards and the Shaping of Urban America*, edited by Eran Ben-Joseph and Terry S. Szold (Routledge, 2005).

2. This type of equation contains both immeasurables (indices of diversity) and incommensurables (the natural and the social). Unlike the hard sciences, approximate metrics may constitute equations in the social and environmental sciences as they serve to elucidate a trend. A discussion of this appears in "It Must Be Beautiful: Great Equations of the Modern Science" (London: Granta, 2002) by Graham Farmelo.

WHY SIX TRANSECT ZONES?

BRUCE DONNELLY

The Rural-to-Urban Transect is useful worldwide, but why are there six Transect Zones? How can the zones be observed everywhere, despite the radically different urbanism in each country? Each zone of the Transect is an immersive environment. Each one is to do with much more than building types. Among other things, thoroughfares, cultural expectations, and salient laws vary between Transect Zones. Moreover, each building type can be built in more than one zone. While we can observe that the building types typical of a Transect Zone tend to share certain qualities, no building type is exclusive to a single T-Zone. Yet, each Transect Zone has its own reason for being, and that reason makes it nearly universal in some form.

As Andrés Duany has shown, the Transect is adapted from landscape ecology. Ecologists draw transects across landscapes. Despite the natural world's variety, not everything varies from place to place. For example, although climates and ecological systems vary, ecologists will expect to find a fixed number of zones at almost any seashore: offshore, nearshore, foreshore, and backshore. Since there are only so many ways for the land to meet the ocean, there are only so many zones possible. It is the same with urban Transect Zones. For instance, just as the tides in the foreshore require animals to adapt to changeable conditions, dense urban areas require buildings, streets, and people to adapt to tight urban conditions.

The Transect Zones are similarly universal to the human realm. The stable zones in the urban Transect correspond to the conditions that reliably produce attached buildings, freestanding houses, and un-settled lands. These three zones are virtually universal.

Unsettled lands may be natural or cultivated. Mankind's first and oldest ambitions come from these landscapes. Even today, nomadic people usually live in temporary or portable huts and plant very little or nothing. Un-settled land requires laws governing the right to pass through, to graze animals, and so on. Although un-settled lands may have roads, laws governing enclosure and grazing leases still have enormous effects—notably in the American West.

Freestanding houses are individual dwellings on their own plots—generally built of wood and limited in height. Such houses are almost universal among settled people. Except in unusual communities, such as fishing villages built on stilts, freestanding houses sit on individual lots facing roads. The family makes a territorial claim on the land and on access to farm and market. Typically, each family keeps a fenced or walled plot for a little garden, some animals, or a work yard. Historically, laws often treat the house's enclosed plot as its curtilage, so that it is legally coupled with the house.

Attached buildings typically save space by filling the width of their lots and by extending upward two or more stories. In the city, direct access to frontage is valuable, so buildings often have separate entries to different parts—such as a shop, basement, and main entry. Such a building must face onto a street. It generates enough traffic to require strong, wide roadbeds and sidewalks. Although urban buildings have courts and yards, they generally do not permit much gardening. The laws regarding urban living are some of the oldest in the world. They must govern encroachments above and below the street, and often govern privacy from the street. Since abutting walls are expensive, laws sometimes permit one building owner to insert beams into a neighbor's wall, or allow two neighbors to build and maintain a party wall. Most urban buildings have historically been of masonry, because fire laws insist that the outside walls support themselves even if the floors collapse in a fire.

These three ways of inhabiting the land are millennia old. They are not only to do with building types; they touch on every aspect of the built and legal environment. Each of those environments requires specific laws and customs. Nomadic people occupy territories in un-settled land, and will fight over territory, even though they may have no notion of individual land ownership. Stationary houses on plots require individual land ownership and leasing (and, historically, servitude). They also require laws regarding static resources such as watercourses and wells. Urban locales with attached buildings require laws regarding encroachments, shared walls, liability, and maintenance.

These ways of inhabiting the land correspond to the Transect Zones T-1, T-3, and T-5. The oldest, T-1, includes natural land and some cultivated land. T-3 consists mostly of plots with mixed-use, freestanding houses. The historic pattern of burgage lots can be thought of as T-3, with what Douglas Duany calls a "rural weave." T-5 typically designates built-up plots for attached buildings. These are stable, age-old zones every bit as essential to the human landscape as forests and beaches are to the natural landscape.

But what about T-2, T-4, and T-6? Between the stable zones are zones of overlap. In a natural transect, the "nearshore" is the transition between the "offshore" and the "foreshore." It is an in-between condition, and urbanism has in-between zones, too. In landscape ecology, these are land-cover types called "ecotones," or overlapping zones. Where a mangrove forest encroaches onto a bay, it has the qualities of both land and water. There are trees, and there are fish. This sort of environment is inherently rich and varied, unstable, and fragile.

Our American heritage is bound up in the yeoman farmer inhabiting the land. We often forget that T-2 varies a great deal from place to place. Servitude on the land still exists—in the form of near-serfdom, land leases, sharecropping, and industrial farms with hundreds of employees. It is arguably more prevalent worldwide than the owner-occupied farm. Sometimes, as in parts of Spain, houses in T-2 are used only at mid-day when farmers tend their land. They return at night to city houses. Sometimes the workers who tend the farms have quarters in rows of rented houses or even live in dormitories. The historical American farm has stereotypically had a wall or fence surrounding a green plot topped by trees. It is as though the house and its plot were transported from a village to a field.

Similarly, T-4 is an area of complex overlap. The tragic conflagrations of Tokyo and London were due, in part, to a mismatch between flammable wooden houses and urban density. T-4 spans the gradient from the independent house to the urban building. As in T-3 and T-5, this is not just a matter of building types; it is an immersive habitat. The adjacent building may be freestanding or abut the lot; the balance between airiness and privacy becomes complex. Code requirements for setbacks, fencing, and other issues in the United States are most complex in T-4. Moreover, complex residential building types, such as side-by-side double houses, grouped town houses, Boston triples, and others come out of this compromise. We can sense just how complex and contested T-4 is by noting that it was not until the 17th and 18th centuries that London codified the fire-resistant town house.

The most urban zone, T-6, is an interesting case. It is not in between any T-Zones; it is above T-5. We can look at T-6 in two different ways: as a more intense version of T-5, or as something between T-5 and a hypertrophic T-Zone that is hostile to streets. Certainly, buildings typical of both T-6 and T-5 are attached. We could simply consider T-6 a taller, denser version of T-5, but that may be a dangerous way to think of it. T-6 seems to be an urban phenomenon made possible only by types of transit developed in the 19th century. It runs the risk posed by 19th-century building forms.

T-6 is an immersive environment just like all the other T-Zones. Yet it is the first in which the public realm is in danger of being sucked indoors. Office buildings, department stores, rail stations, and the glazed arcades of the 19th century are qualitatively different from ordinary attached buildings. They let people avoid the street. Perhaps these 19th-century inventions interbred with palaces and monasteries.[1] In any case, they share an unfortunate affinity with the earlier aristocratic and monastic ones. Like palace courts and cloisters, atriums, arcades, and floor upon floor of semi-public office corridors, bridges, and tunnels all bypass the messy streets. Today, bridges, tunnels, and other means of secession are dangerously commonplace in urban redevelopments. We can think of T-6 as being an ecotone between T-5 and a hypertrophic, street-phobic urbanism that ceases to be urbanism at all. Urbanists should remember that T-6 is not merely an enhanced version of T-5. If we do not handle it sternly, it can suck the public life of the city off the street.

The Transect, then, is a bounded range of distinct zones. They are not arbitrary, but grow out of ways of inhabiting land. Three of its zones have been with us for millennia: T-1, T-3, and T-5. Two of the remaining "ecotone" T-Zones, T-2 and T-4, are necessary transitions between the well-precedented three. The third "ecotone," T-6, is at the dangerous edge of urbanism. When we are faced with a new place, we can understand it better if we ask what role it has within the city. Each T-Zone has a role, be it stable or transitional. It is a question not just about building types and frontages, but about laws and customs, trade, and ways of living. When we are trying to keep an existing place happy, we may do well to institute policies for maintaining T-2, T-4, and T-6, so they don't lose their complexity. Otherwise, they might slip into their adjacent-numbered T-Zones.

1. Nikolaus, P. (1976). *A History of Building Types*. Princeton, NJ: Princeton University Press.

THE TRANSECT OF SPEED LIMITS

SANDY SORLIEN

I came to the Transect as a non-architect, non-planner, and non-scientist. For two decades I had been traveling America to photograph the built environment. Starting in 1988, I drove through all 50 states on the old national routes and byways, looking for houses. I wanted to see my country in some sort of entirety before it was gobbled up by sprawl. At the time, I didn't know what sprawl was made of: the zoning, the subsidies, the departments of transportation. I just knew it sucked.

My photography project took eight years of several journeys per year, traced afterwards with Sharpie on a big paper map in ever-expanding wiggly loops out from Philadelphia. The first trip, PA-WV-KY-IN-OH-PA, was the best, until the next one. I processed film in motel bathrooms, and had a blast talking to strangers. When I got to Alaska in 1995, I sent postcards home with "FIFTY!" emblazoned on the back.

A few years later, in 2000, the normative Rural-to-Urban Transect as systemized by DPZ CoDesign was brought to my attention by *The Geography of Nowhere* author James Howard Kunstler. He introduced it at a conference as an important concept for understanding existing communities, and for organizing new ones using Transect Zones, or habitats. Ecologists might call them patches. New Urbanists were simply calling this concept the Transect, capital T, for short.

This Transect had an elegant new six-zone model, but it wasn't a new phenomenon. I recognized it from my travels.

When I left my big city's orbit, the Transect was more evident than it was in the metropolis, though it's here too. Back in the 1980s and '90s, I'd approach small towns from the countryside, and began to notice a pattern. The speed limit signs would change predictably: first 55 mph, then 45, then as the houses appeared, 35, then as the houses got closer together and closer to the street, 25, and maybe even 20 on the main street. With a manual transmission, you couldn't miss the downshifts. I'd explore the town on foot or bike, photograph buildings, eat in a downtown diner, then drive on out. Then the signs went up: 25, 35, then 45 where you could see open country ahead, then 55 and a rural highway again.

Much later, in 2011, I drove coast-to-coast on US Route 50, which is mostly two-lane. Sprawl had gotten worse. But there it was again: the Rural-to-Urban Transect of speed limits. Because the major interstates bypass the towns, older thoroughfares like US 50 still respect the built context they pass through. More often than not, after the Speed Limit 25 sign, US 50 either becomes Main Street or intersects it. This occurred from Winchester, Virginia, to Chillicothe, Ohio; from Sedalia, Missouri, to Rocky Ford, Colorado; from Salina, Utah, to Eureka, Nevada. Along this Transect, you can see the symbiotic elements that make up the contexts, or habitats—what we now call Transect Zones. Around 35 mph, as village density and pedestrians increase, a rural swale becomes an urban curb, and sidewalks appear. The frontages change from lawns to porches to stoops, the setbacks from deep to shallow to zero. At 25 mph a few businesses start mixing in until it's mostly shopfronts, and the reverse on the way out. If the town has not been reamed out by the state DOT, nor the spatial enclosure of the street (shaped by buildings and trees) destroyed for parking lots, the speed limit signs aren't even necessary. The design of the public and private frontage would signal whether pedestrians take precedence in the habitat, and if they do, naturally drivers slow down.

These are the old small towns, not the new subdivisions where all the frontages are blank garages, nor the commercial strips where surface parking enfronts tedious overwide "stroads" [1] and the speed limit is the same 45 all the way, taunting the drivers stuck at light after light. The old towns settled and evolved before the automobile, and they all have a Rural-to-Urban Transect.

A Regularity of Nature

Andrés Duany and Emily Talen have written that the Transect can be the basis for a unified theory of urbanism. Some have gone even further to suggest the Transect might be a natural law, evident everywhere in nature and therefore ethically binding on society. Species symbiosis is already ethically binding to environmentalists, who take it for granted that specific plants and animals belong together in certain habitats. Transect proponents simply add humans to this calculus.

Still others have debated the possibility that the Transect is instead a law of nature, which is not considered obligatory or morally binding like natural law. A law of nature is merely observed, cannot be proved, and is subject to being disproved. It is, like all science, provisional.

Having consistently observed the Transect of speed limits making cars behave in walkable settlements, I became intrigued by these proposals and did more research. A law of nature applies when certain physical conditions are invariably found along with other physical conditions. We can say that in settlements that evolved pre-automobile, invariably we find a range of habitats from rural to urban; their food was not traveling thousands of miles by truck. In and around such settlements, the habitats usually range from woodland/prairie (T-1 Natural) to farmland/ranchland (T-2 Rural) to market town. The market town may have two or more habitats similar to the T-3 Sub-Urban, T-4 General Urban, and T-5 Urban Center zones, even if the center is just a produce shed and an inn. To recognize this, it helps to analyze habitats by their character, purpose, and function, not just by their relative form and density.[2]

Another characteristic of a law of nature is that it can be stated quite simply, perhaps like this: "A Rural-to-Urban Transect occurs wherever permanent settlements are based on the walking range of humans." I've yet to see this disproven. Just as gravitational force declines when dependent bodies swing too far from their orbit, the Transect dissolves when the fundamentals of human physical form are neglected. The consequence is the loss of symbiotic human habitats, and sprawl.

Nevertheless, I'm skeptical that the Transect or any other settlement pattern is a natural "law" of any kind, whether God-given or agnostic-scientific. We can argue whether a Transect pattern is something that we should be emulating in the 21st-century built environment. As a code writer, I think so. But codes are normative policies based on normative theory (i.e., what ought to be), positive law, not natural law.

The Encyclopedia of Philosophy states:

"Within metaphysics, there are two competing theories of Laws of Nature. On one account, the Regularity Theory, Laws of Nature are statements of the uniformities or regularities in the world; they are mere descriptions of the way the world is. On the other account, the Necessitarian Theory, Laws of Nature are the 'principles' which govern the natural phenomena of the world. That is, the natural world 'obeys' the Laws of Nature. This seemingly innocuous difference marks one of the most profound gulfs within contemporary philosophy, and has quite unexpected, and wide-ranging, implications."[3]

This gulf is the one between a religious natural law and a scientific law of nature. Usage varies from era to era and discipline to discipline, and the term "natural law" is sometimes confusingly used when a "law of nature" is described. Examples of "laws of nature" include Newton's laws of motion, of a type that requires a mathematical equation and rigorously repeatable experiments. But in one camp of the field of metaphysics, at least, a law of nature need only be a "regularity." Perhaps we can agree that the Transect is, if not a law, a regularity of nature.

Furthermore, the Transect persists as a regularity across eras, to the extent its pattern is compatible with current transportation modes. Still, in a time when the conventional design default is for automobiles, coding must be deliberate to avoid what we call, only half-jokingly, Transect Violations—the built version of invasive species.[4] Modern Transect-based plans and codes carefully accommodate the automobile and transit according to context. Even parking location is a symbiotic element that supports the character of each habitat from rural to urban.

Food Design

Since working with New Urbanists, I've learned that photographers and urban designers have a lot in common. We pay close attention to the form of the physical world. With the advent of form-based codes, of which the SmartCode is a comprehensive example, planners too are addressing form. This is important at every scale: the form of the building, the form of the block, the form of the community, and the form of the regional watershed.

We like metaphors, too. When the Transect was first widely debated on the lively listservs of the New Urbanism, there were food metaphors. This is probably Leon Krier's fault. The biggest objection to the Transect was that "the city is not a fried egg." In other words, skeptics said, it doesn't rise up symmetrically toward the center when viewed in section (transect), e.g., a relatively flat egg white of T-3 and T-4 to an elevated egg yolk of T-5 and T-6. Actually, the city usually does rise up that way, but only at the macro scale, from a great distance. (See the image of Chicago on page 20). The huge error that some critics and a few supporters make—and this book's many-scaled transects may not help—is to apply the normative Rural-to-Urban Transect at that vast scale. Instead, the six-zone model is based on the Transect of speed limits: the small town or neighborhood scale, the scale of the pedestrian shed.

In cities, therefore, we're really looking at a big frying pan full of quail eggs, plus one or more chicken eggs, abutting each other. My native Philadelphia is famously a city of neighborhoods with Center City as its chicken egg. Center City, like other large downtowns, is an intense neighborhood of T-4, T-5, and T-6, but a neighborhood nonetheless.[5] In contiguous neighborhoods, the centers usually spread out, becoming a connective T-5 corridor over time: Germantown Avenue, Passyunk Avenue, Erie Avenue, Broad Street, South Street. When quarter-mile radius pedestrian sheds, drawn as circles or lozenges, are centered on these corridors, there's a fine-grained Transect evident. The T-4 General Urban fabric supports the nearby T-5 Center and T-6 Core zones; those higher T-Zones in turn serve the residences.

Especially, They Serve Pedestrians

And that's the scale at which the SmartCode activates the Transect. If the T-Zones of the Transect are applied at too large a scale, they create sprawling and hypertrophic monocultures. Rather, the Transect, the universal regularity, reveals the compact, fine-grained, symbiotic habitats that occur everywhere in nature.

1. Charles Marohn of *Strong Towns* has popularized the term "stroad" to refer to those placeless thoroughfare types that are neither a true road (rural and fun to drive) nor a true street (urban and fun to walk). Everywhere there's a big box store in suburbia, there's a stroad.

2. A declension of mixed use intensity is clarified in the General Function table of the SmartCode, available for download at www.transect.org.

3. "Laws of Nature," Internet Encyclopedia of Philosophy, A Peer-Reviewed Academic Resource. http://www.iep.utm.edu/lawofnat/.

4. Transect Violations, like non-native species, can be accommodated as long as they don't become invasive and take over existing niches. A Transect Violation either jarringly urbanizes the rural, or ruralizes the urban, or suburbanizes either. A ruralizing type usually belongs in a lower T-Zone, like a T-2/T-3 post-and-beam fence appearing oddly along a T-5/T-6 sidewalk, or a meandering wetland that blocks the walking network. A 20-story hotel looming over T-2 farmland or T-3 bungalows would be an invasive urbanizing type. Suburbanizing species may invade any T-Zone. On a walkable urban T-4 block of porches and shared curbside parking, one garage-front "snout house" wouldn't destroy the block, but several of them would.

5. Dena Belzer, Transit-Oriented Development expert and President of Strategic Economics, has stated that downtowns should be thought of as neighborhoods, that in fact a downtown should be a city's best neighborhood.

THE SYNOPTIC SURVEY:

SANDY SORLIEN

The Rural-to-Urban Transect is a powerful framework for planning and zoning, but it is only a normative model. Its framing potential is wasted if the new plan and code are not calibrated, or customized, to a local Transect to support the community's historic patterns, favorite parts of town, and desired future evolution.

The model SmartCode is based on the six-zone model Transect. The launch of the SmartCode as a free and open-source document (in early 2005) led to widespread adoptions of its calibrations, and it influenced other Transect-based codes. It gives municipal planning staffs and urban design firms a coordinated set of normative standards to check against, developed by the top New Urbanist professionals in the fields of thoroughfare design, architecture, planning, retail, stormwater management, and more. It provides a head start for cities, saving time and money, because there are certain metric ranges and types that nearly all compact, walkable communities have in common.

Still, every town is as unique as its boosters claim. The model standards should be adjusted to reflect local character and civic goals. The versatility of the system has been tested by communities as different from each other as Jamestown, Rhode Island, an island village with about 5,600 residents, and Miami, Florida, a major urban center with more than 400,000. Code calibration teams literally walk each local neighborhood Transect, taking samples from its various environments (such as T-3, T-4, and T-5) by measuring and photographing the DNA of the urbanism to be protected and augmented. Jamestown's Transect is calibrated down from the model (overall more rural, i.e., less dense, with more rural thoroughfares and building types), while Miami's is calibrated up (overall more urban, with much taller buildings in the core).

A well-calibrated SmartCode will be as place-sensitive and local as a Transect-based code written from scratch. Both require a Synoptic Survey.

Code Calibration with the Synoptic Survey

The Synoptic Survey is a sampling method. It is typically used for environmental analysis to determine the characteristics of a given site by discovering the habitats (or "communities") that it contains. The intention is to determine the values of each habitat in order to recommend the degree of protection and type of restoration it might require. Each functioning habitat is a symbiotic community of micro-climate, minerals, humidity, flora, and fauna.

The Synoptic Survey begins with a systematic visual inspection that identifies typical habitats: a wetland here, an oak hammock there, a rocky outcrop elsewhere. The most representative locales are then analyzed in depth by means of the *dissect* and the *quadrat*. The *dissect* is a simultaneous analysis of the conditions above and below ground, and involves borings to determine soil condition, water table, archeology, etc. The *quadrat* involves taking a normative area (say 100 by 100 feet) where the component elements of flora and fauna are itemized and counted. (See pages 106 and 107.)

These techniques have been adapted by Transect planners for the human habitat in urbanized areas. The urban Synoptic Survey has three purposes: analysis, coding, and evidence. First, the analysis compares existing metrics and types with the existing zoning code, often showing that it doesn't support historic patterns or future goals. (If it does support them, a new code might not be needed.) Second, it records the DNA of desired patterns to be replicated in other parts of town or in new communities within municipal boundaries. The new code is written, or the model code calibrated, with this genetic material. And finally, the Synoptic Survey data sheets and photographs offer proof, during the political process, that the new code is based on local conditions.

The photography done during the initial stages of the Synoptic Survey is valuable as a resource for educating the community and discussing the character of the settlement to be mapped and coded. The photographic vantage point should be standardized so that frontage types and building types may be easily compared. Photographs illustrating the local Transect may appear later in slide presentations and printed reports, and images of architectural details may be collected into a pattern book to augment the code.

The Transect Collection, a free photographic image bank, is available at www.transect-collection.org for such educational purposes, and may be helpful to show citizens how their local Transect differs from those of other cities.

The following description of the process is adapted from a sequence written by Andrés Duany for the SmartCode Manual.

Step One: Begin a Synoptic Survey

Organize a visual inspection of the best existing urban areas, with the intention of extracting the Transect data necessary to evaluate the old code and write the new one.

SANDY SORLIEN

SANDY SORLIEN

Consultants and locals should work together to identify locations that could be representative of the new Transect Zones. The SmartCode Transect describes the basic patterns to look for, even though individual elements will vary from the model. Each zone has its own character, ranging from a mostly residential but compact and walkable T-3 to a T-5 Main Street or town square center. Consensus may be reached using visual preference surveys and aerial photographs, as well as by walking or driving through neighborhoods.

Step Two: Analyze the Transect Zone Components via Urban *Dissects* and *Quadrats*

An urban *dissect* involves taking cross sections across the public and the private realms. Photograph, draw, and measure the disposition and dimensions of the elements within the public right-of-way as well as private lots. Vehicular lanes, curbing, planter/planting, and the walkway are studied simultaneously with the setbacks, building frontage type, building heights, and location of parking.

An urban *quadrat* involves taking, at the same location as the *dissect*, the average measurements of about four acres of lots. From visual inspection and using available mapping, determine the collective ratios of paved and planted areas, lot coverage by building, number of on- and off-street parking spaces, areas dedicated to commercial use and/or the number of dwellings (usually by counting mailboxes or doorbells, as buildings that were once single-family may now contain multiple dwellings). Much of this information may be extracted from an aerial photograph.

Step Three: Create or Calibrate the Code

Decide how many zones to sample. Most municipalities do not have or desire a T-6 zone. Larger cities like Cincinnati and New Orleans do, and may also require sub-zones, such as varying T-4 zones to finely tune the heights, setbacks, and lot widths of different neighborhoods under the same zoning code. Using a set of standardized templates, one for each Transect Zone or sub-zone, enter the data. (See page 108.) This record becomes the basis for the standards of the code. After verification that the results are politically acceptable as outcomes of the proposed code, input the data into the appropriate tables and written standards (as on page 109).

Step Four: Prepare a Comparison Chart

Analyze the existing zoning code and organize the categories under those of the most similar Transect Zones. On a chart, replace and compare the zoning with the closest available Transect Zone. This will usually result in a reduction in the number of zones, and/or it will show that the Transect Zones address issues not covered in the conventional code, such as frontage type and parking location.

Step Five: Prepare a Translation Map (Preliminary Regulating Plan)

Prepare a map that translates the existing zoning map into the Transect categories, using the same zoning district boundaries, based on Step Four. This is an interim step for explanatory purposes. It gives citizens a basis from which to judge any changes that the finished Regulating Plan will represent; otherwise, everything looks like a drastic change, even if it is not. For example, a conventional zone numbered R-1 might translate closely to T-3, perhaps with additional benefits, such as allowing an Accessory Unit. Later on, the bigger changes, such as upzoning some areas to higher T-Zones, can be evaluated in relation to these baseline "translation" T-Zones.

Step Six: Add a Neighborhood Structure to the Regulating Plan

With citizen participation, select and assign important pedestrian destinations: transit stops, schools, retail shops, civic buildings, or civic spaces. Delineate pedestrian sheds around each destination. Group the sheds into a composite shed (if necessary) and translate that to a network pedestrian shed (actual walking time along streets and paths) to determine neighborhood boundaries. These boundaries may require adjustment according to local topography or traditionally understood neighborhood edges, such as zip code changes or catchments of civic associations. The resulting neighborhoods should allow the majority of residents to walk from their homes to the mixed-use center (Main Street) in approximately five to seven minutes.

Step Seven: Calibrate the Transect Zones and Adjust the Regulating Plan

Through analysis of existing conditions and with citizen participation, identify those areas where the urbanism needs to be preserved as it is, or intensified. For example, if open lands are to be preserved and growth focused toward existing urbanism, and demographics signal a market for smaller in-town lots and dwelling units, then some of the areas that are currently T-3 may accommodate T-4 zoning.

At this stage, mapping and code writing go hand in hand. Calibrate the standards for individual Transect Zones while adjusting the mapped Regulating Plan at the fine grain. Evaluate the zoned areas at the block scale to fine-tune their boundaries. In general, "like should face like" across thoroughfares to create an immersive environment and spatial definition in the public realm. Therefore, the T-Zone transitions should usually occur in the middle of blocks, i.e., along rear lot lines.

Step Eight: Incorporate any Special Requirements and the Identification of Thoroughfare Types into the Regulating Plan

This usually requires a second map. Special Requirements may include designations for Mandatory Retail Frontage, Recommended Terminated Vistas, A/B Grid of thoroughfares, etc. They allow designers to code at yet finer grain. The text in the SmartCode should be adjusted to include only the Special Requirements that are actually used. The final Regulating Plan is the zoning map, and as such is a legal part of the adopted code.

Final Steps: Customize the Tables and Text

Enter into the appropriate tables of the model code the numerical and typological standards derived from the Synoptic Survey and subsequent discussions. Delete any material pertaining to T-Zones that are not included in the final Regulating Plan. Add sub-zone standards as necessary, and review administrative procedures with the planning office. Code calibration also requires adjustment of legal language, and coordination of the various enabling authorities and documents, including the comprehensive plan. If sections of the model code are removed or supplementary Modules added, adjust the glossary accordingly.

GOVERNANCE ALONG THE TRANSECT

DANIEL K. SLONE

The boundaries of our daily existence are established by governance processes. As residents, we are subject to civil governance—the laws of our locality, state, and federal governments—whether or not we have agreed to the imposition. This governance is created through federal and state constitutions, laws, ordinances, and regulations. In contrast, we consent to private governance when we join an organization and agree to abide by its rules, or when we go to work for a company and agree to comply with its employee handbook. Property owners are also subject to private governance processes that result from legal documents that have been recorded in the land records. Courts have ruled that property owners agree to these governance processes just by purchasing their properties.

Private governance documents are sometimes preempted by civil governance. This preemption may be specific, as when a state legislature determines that prohibition of clotheslines will have adverse effects on energy use, or when Congress determines that private regulation of satellite dishes will disrupt communications. It may also be on general policy grounds, as when the courts determine it is against public policy to enforce racist provisions in private governance documents or to allow the prohibition of children in communities except in accordance with strict limits. Otherwise, the courts frequently assert that individuals can agree, through private governance documents, to curtail their rights.

There is a broad range of private governance documents, and the frequency of their use varies along the Rural-to-Urban Transect. This variation is not uniform, as some private governance documents increase in use in the same conditions that lead to the decrease in use of other types.

The simplest kinds of governance documents are agreements between property owners to share operation or maintenance. These include agreements for the construction and maintenance of shared roads or driveways, common walls or shared parking facilities, or for the creation and operation of shared water wells or waste water treatment facilities. Although these documents are often simple, involving two owners, they can also be complex, involving many owners and intricate financial arrangements. Similarly, easement agreements among property owners may include few parties or many. These private governance documents can give access across property, allow building footings to encroach, preserve a scenic vista, allow the use of a bicycle trail, assure a right to a parking space, or enable other similar relationships.

Another significant type of private governance document is the community association document. Homeowner and commercial owner associations are typically created through a mixture of corporate documents (articles and bylaws) and a declaration, which is filed in the land records. The declaration allows the association to put liens on private property for failure to pay fees. These documents create the election and governance process as well as allow the imposition of rules on the property owners. A corporate model for governance is more common than a civil governance model. For example, there is typically no bill of rights to protect individual rights in community association documents. These documents may enable the association to undertake a wide range of activities. Many of the details for these activities—the easements that permit them, the standards that govern things like architectural approval, and provision of utilities like voice, video, and data—are set forth in common companion documents called codes, covenants, and restrictions (CC&Rs). Sometimes the CC&Rs are included in the community association declarations, but they may also be used apart from associations to define typically complex relationships among multiple owners through detailed standards, procedures, and restrictions.

Finally, there are townhouses and condominium documents. Like homeowner association documents, state law may specifically require or limit many of the provisions of condominium documents, which create ownership parcels consisting of the individual units and an interest in the common areas. These and townhouse documents define the rights of owners in shared spaces and prescribe steps for accomplishing and paying for the maintenance of shared roofs, footings, walls, and facades. They describe any shared amenities and how they are used. Unlike homeowner association documents, which may regulate activities in the entire community, the detailed rules of these documents regulate only activities on the condominium or townhouse property itself.

There are some general trends in the use of private governance documents along the Transect. As shown in the chart on page 193, some governance documents occur with greater frequency in certain Transect Zones. The patterns are somewhat easier to identify in the diagram on page 194, which adds in a comparison with civil governance mechanisms. Other than when new towns are created (which always stimulates the need for associations, at least until municipal status is obtained), the property owners in the simplified terrain of T-1 and T-2 most frequently relate to one another using shared maintenance agreements (for such things as shared roads or wells) or easements (for issues such

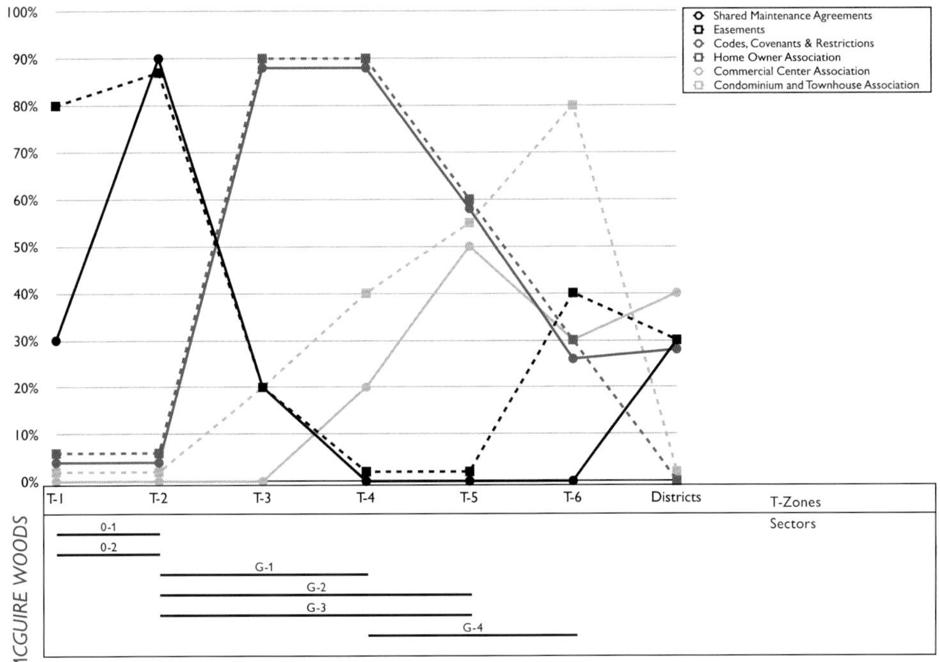

MCGUIRE WOODS

as access, protection of vistas, protection of natural resources, or rights to use). These two types of documents are not frequently used in other T-Zones, except for the complex environments of T-6 (where easements are used for such things as building subsidence or footings on tight lots, or maintenance of buildings along zero lot lines) and districts (where shared maintenance agreements may deal with issues such as cross-boundary parking or private areas that function as commons).

As density increases, the prevalence of condominium associations and townhouse associations and their building-level governance documents also increases, despite the decline in the need for community-level governance documents. The numerous multifamily or shared building elements that accompany increased density require the easements and shared maintenance schemes that are provided as a part of standard condominium and townhouse documents. These documents also provide the rules for the use of shared building space and amenities, as well as providing a mechanism for forcing participation in payment by all owners.

The need for associations of residents or businesses to provide governance is at its highest when existing civil government mechanisms are weakest. Civil government mechanisms tend to be weakest when background populations are lowest (and the available taxes and expectations for government services and oversight are reduced). As the existing population density increases, the need for homeowner associations or commercial owner associations declines. Consequently, community association documents have their highest use in the portion of the Transect from T-3 to T-5, and there is a greater

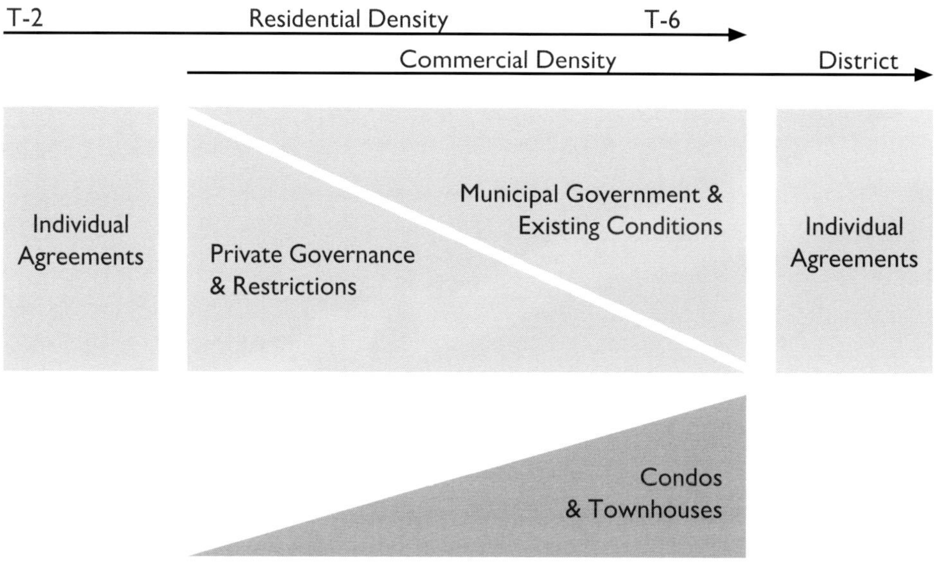

MCGUIRE WOODS

likelihood that association documents will be necessary in a new sub-urban setting than for a T-5 infill area. As density increases, so does the likelihood of an actual municipal government to maintain streets and parks, provide police, and resolve disputes. There is also an increased likelihood of public and private commercial recreation opportunities and a host of voluntary associations that provide political access or arts opportunities. In a more rural neighborhood that's mostly T-3, governmental services may be provided by a county government, with the sheriff providing law enforcement, services such as libraries centralized, if they exist at all, and volunteers responding to fires. Consequently, the home-owner association may maintain parks, build swimming pools, repair roads, regulate architecture, sponsor cultural events, and employ security guards. A neighborhood with T-5, in a more urban, municipal setting, may receive all of these services through a mix of municipal departments, non-profit cultural organizations, and voluntary neighborhood groups.

Under municipal governance, capital may be provided through neighborhood tax devices such as Tax Increment Financing Districts or Community Development Districts instead of special assessments under the association documents. Similarly, CC&Rs, often the favorite tools of associations, are typically replaced by detailed zoning and subdivision codes, light and sound regulations, building codes, historic preservation ordinances, and similar rules for humans living in proximity to one another. This likelihood can be undermined if the municipality refuses to provide normal urban services for the new neighborhood because of fiscal or physical constraints. For example, if the municipality refuses to take responsibility for parks, alleys, parking, or other elements of the neighborhood, then a private association will still be necessary.

There are, of course, other factors that affect governance documents in ways not predicted by the Transect. For example, almost any time a planned unit development (PUD) is undertaken, regardless of its mix of Transect zones, it results in the use of association-type governance documents. A PUD is a type of subdivision, allowed in designated zoning districts, that is not required to comply with the typical zoning and subdivision rules, allowing the creation of sections with non-uniform lot sizes, mixed uses located adjacent to one another or in the same buildings, and shared recreation areas and open spaces. Many traditional neighborhood developments have utilized PUD zoning categories, and many localities require PUDs to create homeowner associations, regardless of their settings or their intensity of development. Similarly, when multi-owner commercial development occurs at a significant scale other than in an existing business district or along an existing business corridor or main street, there will likely be some form of commercial owner association. Also, because of the attention to the architecture, any New Urban project is likely to have CC&Rs, no matter its location or characteristics.

The table on page 197 shows that even within the various types of documents, the kinds of services provided and issues addressed also vary by T-Zone. An easement may be used to preserve endangered habitat in T-1, but provide auto access in T-2, and it may support cross-property parking in T-6. Moreover, even similar uses can vary significantly according to T-Zone. CC&Rs may regulate community or front yard agricultural uses in T-3, but address green roof or green wall agriculture in T-5 or T-6. Similarly, a homeowner association may maintain T-3 stormwater ponds, but in T-5 provide maintenance and monitoring for stormwater infiltration devices, rain gardens, and bioswales.

Understanding private governance documents along the Transect helps us choose the right tools for the right setting, and it may also help us think about how these tools and their uses should be modified. As an increased amount of redevelopment and infill development takes place in already dense urban areas, developers should begin by surveying the functions already served by existing community organizations and strengthen those organizations as part of their development strategy rather than weakening them by creating competing homeowner associations to provide similar services. Homeowner associations and other community governance tools should be tailored to the level of governance necessary for their locations and types of communities. Thus, they should be equipped to provide town-like governance when necessary, but precluded from this level of governance when they are located in existing municipalities. When private governance mechanisms are used in the absence of public governance, those private mechanisms should operate more like civil governance, being more democratic and including checks and balances. The corporate form of contract governance is more appropriate when the documents create a more basic maintenance organization and civil government is otherwise adequate.

The shift from private to civic governance is an important part of becoming a real, functioning community. For example, new neighborhoods, such as TNDs in rural areas or TODs in suburban areas, almost always begin with extensive private governance documents. When appropriate densities are achieved in these new towns, villages, or neighborhoods, the private governance mechanisms should be replaced with civic government mechanisms. Because the PUD is a frequent tool for the creation of New Urban projects, sometimes in very urban existing settings, localities should move beyond an automatic requirement of the creation of homeowner associations for each PUD. They also should develop a deeper understanding of what they actually need the homeowner association to accomplish and not require more than this so they do not unnecessarily make the already complex urban environment even more complex. Wherever possible, localities should perform their expected functions of maintaining parks and streets and providing municipal services such as parking, and utilize other mechanisms for the fair distribution of costs rather than force the creation of homeowner associations.

Document Function	T-1	T-2	T-3	T-4	T-5	T-6	SD
Shared Maitenance Agreements							
Restoration	•	•					
Agriculture or Silviculture	•	•					
Paths	•	•					
Open Spaces	•	•					•
Roads		•					•
Utilities		•					•
Parking							•
Easements							
Protection	•	•					
Other Uses		•					
Access for Occupancy		•					
Access for Maitenance						•	•
Subsidence / Support of Shared Structure						•	•
Codes, Covenants & Restrictions (Used by Developers, HOAs & COAs)							
Regulation of Architecture			•	•	•		
Rules			•	•	•		
Services							
Utilities (Water, Sewer, Power, Reuse Water)			•				
Parking				•	•		
Voice, Video, Data			•				
Recreation			•	•			
Maitenance & Capital Improvements							
Paths & Sidewalks			•	•	•		
Roads			•	•	•		
Parking Lots			•	•	•		
Private Yards					•		
Common Areas			•	•	•		
Storm Water			•	•	•		
Agriculture			•	•	•		
Green			•	•	•		
Car & Bike Share Programs			•	•	•		
HOA							
Lien / Assess			•	•	•		
Political Action			•	•			
Community Events			•	•			
Dispute Resolution			•	•			
COA							
Assess					•		•
Political Action					•		•
Sales / Marketing					•		•
Security					•		•
Events					•		•
Dispute Resolution					•		•
Condo / Townhouse							
Lien / Assess				•	•	•	
Maitenance				•	•	•	
Rules				•	•	•	
Dispute Resolution				•	•	•	
Architectural Approval				•	•	•	
Political Action				•	•	•	
Recreation				•	•	•	

RETAIL AND THE TRANSECT

SETH HARRY

Traditional urbanism represents an outwardly simple, yet highly evolved system for human habitation that encompasses all of the necessary ingredients for daily living in a compact, efficient, and pleasing form. Of all the elements comprising traditional urbanism, retail has proven the most difficult to implement in a traditional urban format, particularly when applied in a primarily suburban context, and when held to contemporary standards of suburban retail planning and market criteria.

The Rural-to-Urban Transect, however, provides an effective tool for reintroducing traditional retail formats into a regional context. It does so by proportionally allocating land uses and transportation infrastructure in such a way that the retail uses can appropriately be distributed, in both scale and location, relative to the sources of demand for goods and services. This model is consistent with historical urban land use practices, generates a system that is optimized around locational efficiencies, and is, in effect, self-regulating.

This approach, when properly realized, effectively balances the convenient availability of retail goods and services with the frequency and level of consumer demand. In other words, the products that are most frequently needed and consumed are those that are most widely available, at appropriate increments of scale and distribution relative to that demand, throughout the region. Conversely, products that are purchased in a more discretionary fashion and/or with considerably less frequency, are appropriately clustered where they will be accessible to the largest possible concentrations of consumers (typically in the urban core), because those merchants need to capture the maximum incremental demand from the largest pool of customers possible, in order to generate a sufficient customer base to sustain themselves.

Traditional retail types have fundamental characteristics in common with contemporary conventional retail center types. Both evolved around recognized and historical patterns of consumer spending. Based on the size and composition of the merchandising mix, both are tailored to ensure the maximum theoretical capture of consumer potential within a given center's designated or assumed trade area. And in general, smaller trade areas typically focus on a more limited palette of goods, purchased on a frequent basis close to work or home, while large trade areas by definition encompass and present a much broader spectrum of consumer products.

The conventional retail types, which have been formally codified by the Urban Land Institute to represent standardized models for the purposes of financial and market feasibility analysis, are also applicable to a traditional urban setting. The equivalent traditional retail designations of the ULI classifications are described as follows:

1. Neighborhood Store: A retail business that provides a convenient location for quick purchases from a wide array of products (predominantly food). They are usually smaller than 5,000 square feet, with convenient access and parking, and with extended hours of operation.

2. Neighborhood Center: A collection of stores and commercial establishments providing personal services (dry cleaning, barber shop, shoe repair) and convenience goods (food, drugs and sundries). Usually anchored by a small convenience or drug store, and may include a local restaurant/café, it has a typical gross leasable area of up to around 20,000 square feet.

3. Main Street Shops: A supermarket-anchored center providing for a range of daily needs and personal services to the surrounding neighborhoods. Ideally sized around 50,000 square feet, it typically ranges in area from 30,000 to 80,000 square feet, and may include a junior department store and several food establishments at a variety of price points and service levels.

4. Downtown Shopping District: A regional center selling general merchandise (apparel, home furnishings and accessories) in significantly greater depth and variety than what might be offered in a Main Street setting. It offers a range of services and recreational facilities and a wide array of dining and entertainment options. It is typically anchored by one or more full-line department stores of not less than 75,000 square feet, with a total gross leasable area for the entire center ranging from 300,000 to 850,000 square feet.

Perhaps the most significant characteristic of a properly structured retail system in a Transect-based regional context is its propensity to evolve cumulatively, and in a successional fashion, consistent with its placement within the ascending zones of the Transect. It is cumulative because as communities grow and evolve, the retailers that are already in place continue to serve the same consumer market they have always served, while new retailers emerge to serve the needs of the growing market. And it is successional because the overall array of retail goods and services increases in both density and complexity, as the nature of the surrounding urban fabric does the same.

In this way, the diversity and sophistication of the retail offerings evolve along with the communities they serve: large towns can offer goods and services that small towns can't support, and cities can offer a range and sophistication of offerings that even large towns can't imagine. When this rational framework of urbanism and commercial activity is fully in sync, as represented by the Transect, the complexity and diversity of both the urban fabric and its attendant retail ecosystem evolve in complementary and predictable fashion, across the full spectrum of Transect Zones.

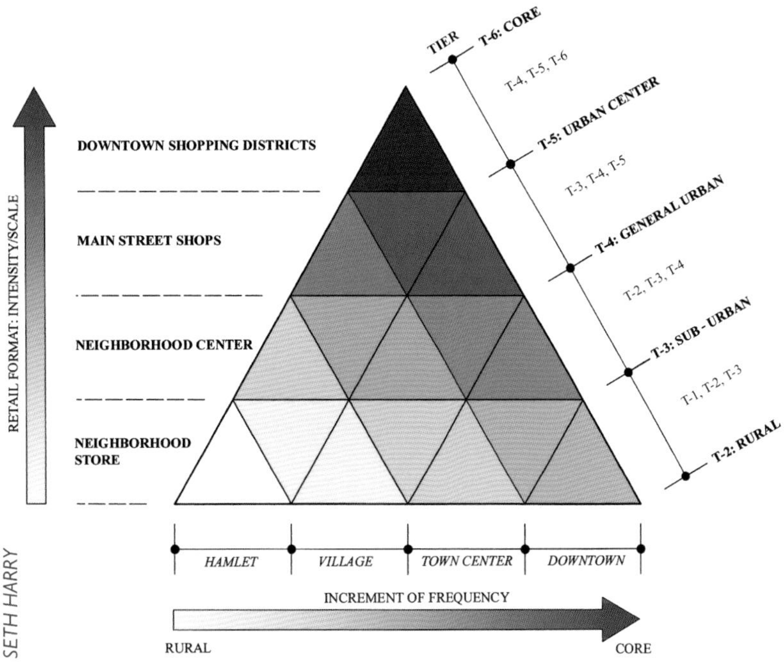

SETH HARRY

This relationship can be graphically depicted as in the diagram above, which shows the supply of retail increasing in both breadth and diversity as urban types evolve from small-scale settlements to regional centers. In a Transect-based regional framework, retail center types can be more closely aligned to the specific consumer patterns and spending potential of the communities they serve, resulting in more consistent economic performance and greater resilience to changing market dynamics for the centers as a whole, and for the individual retailers contained therein. The diagram conceptually illustrates an optimal relationship structure between retail center types and Transect-based community development types, as both ascend incrementally toward higher levels of complexity.

The diagram is pyramidal in form to reflect the fact that as the urbanism moves toward increasing levels of complexity and scale, it typically does so in a measured, incremental fashion, as indicated by the ascending order of community types along each side.

However, regardless of where any particular "place" lies along that continuum, in terms of its transformative trajectory, there is always a single, corresponding, "highest order" retail type representing the most evolved level of retail goods and services that can be supported in conjunction with that community type, and/or urban structure, at that stage in its evolution.

The largest retail type is usually referred to as a regional center, though large urbanized areas can often support multiple regional centers, and in limited cases certain urban centers can even be extra-regional, national, or even international-level in terms of their consumer base.

As a schematic representation of reality, the diagram suggests that retail activity rarely occurs in T-1. In T-2, it happens only sporadically, and in a manner usually related to the rural/agricultural nature of its regional T-2 context, such as a general merchandise or farm supply store. From T-3 through T-6, however, retail tends to occur in a more consistently rational and modulated basis—increasing in scale and diversity in correlation to the increasing density and complexity of the urban fabric around it, and completely consistent with the attributes of the consumer market that fabric includes.

One should also note that as retail grows cumulatively within the Transect (moving from T-2 to T-6), most of the retail types from the lower levels of the Transect will tend to reoccur, though at increasingly higher frequencies, in response to the greater population density and spending potential. This is suggested in the progression from Hamlet/T-2 through Downtown/T-6, as the lowest level of retail type, Neighborhood Store, might occur only at half-mile intervals in T-3, but would be present at increasing frequencies, for instance as the corner store, in T-4, T-5, and T-6.

This would again be the natural and appropriate response to the higher population densities and greater spending potential available at these more intensive urban levels. Also, each preceding increment of retail type will generally be embodied in the makeup of the subsequent one, such that the individual merchandise categories present in a Neighborhood Center will also be present in the tenant and merchandising composition of the Main Street Shops, and those present in Main Street Shops will be present in a Downtown Shopping District, and so on, until the highest order of retail type supportable by the market at any given point is achieved.

To understand how retail types mutate and evolve over time as cities grow within this framework, read the diagram starting from the lower left-hand corner and proceed toward the upper right-hand side. Each increment of growth progresses accordingly: a hamlet evolves over time into a village, and then a town, and finally a city. Consistent with that dynamic, each "higher-order" increment of urbanity results in a corresponding incremental rise to the next higher level of retail type (in addition to the new, full-spectrum layer of additional lower types below—another reason for the pyramidal form).

However, to remain within the hierarchical framework of the Transect, at no time should either the scale or fundamental characteristics of that "higher-order" retail level outpace, or otherwise be inconsistent with, the corresponding successional stage of the community as a whole.

An anomaly of this type usually occurs only if there is a distortion in the system, such as those routinely engendered through the dendritic road networks of the style favored in post-war suburban settlement patterns. These anomalies often enable and encourage inappropriate retail center types and/or formats to exist outside of the market parameters that would otherwise be appropriate for their immediate urban context, or T-Zone.

What this means, as a practical matter, is that the size and nature of the retail formats in a suburban market setting are more often dictated by the size of the road in front of the buildings than by the density and nature of the immediate surrounding fabric, as would typically be the case in a true urban consumer market context. The same is often true of the overall composition of goods and services in a suburban market.

The locational criteria for retail types in a traditional, extant urban fabric will be determined primarily by their placement within the transportation network and the number of households typically serviced by that network, both of which should bear a direct relationship to each other. Therefore, a full spectrum of street types and transportation modes, hierarchically deployed within a comprehensive regional urban framework, should also generate an equally full and diverse spectrum of retail types, serving everything from a neighborhood-oriented, pedestrian-based trade area to a full, regional-scale, retail consumer market. And, more importantly, all of these diverse types will likely be located precisely where they need to be in relation to their market contexts, in terms of frequency of need and increment of market share required to support them.

This arrangement is inherently efficient and self-regulating in terms of balancing location-specific retail demand and supply, as it encourages every retail type to locate in its most rational location within the urban structure, relative to its target market. It also encourages retail competition to take place primarily between retailers of similar sizes and resources, based on legitimate distinctions of quality, service, and value. And it reduces or eliminates unreasonable competitive advantages based primarily on the aforementioned distortions within the overall regional transportation network, which might otherwise encourage and permit over-scaled retail formats (i.e., big boxes).

In a conventional suburban market context, the trade areas of the retail center types often vary significantly due to variations in population density and household incomes (and hence spending potential). But the more typical determinant is the ability of particular retail centers to access the market by taking advantage of distortions in the existing transportation networks that occur when transportation planners, in an ongoing attempt to mitigate congestion, allocate an ever-increasing proportion of regional traffic flow onto a very limited network of over-sized arterials by simply increasing the number of lanes on those roads. This creates market dynamics that provide suburban retailers access to a larger consumer market potential than would otherwise be proximately available, resulting in disproportionately scaled formats relative to local demand.

This physical disconnect between community and retailer, exacerbated by our over-reliance on infrequently spaced, large-scale arterials, creates a regional population of automobile-borne consumers—easily aggregated at major intersections in sufficient quantities to sustain virtually any sized retail box imaginable. As a result, "standard" retail formats have increased steadily and dramatically in size and associated trade area for the past 50 years, compounded by single-use zoning, which has helped to effectively sever the intrinsic spatial relationship between retail and the community it traditionally served.

Unfortunately, this model affords no direct, proportional spatial relationship between the size of the retailer and its immediate physical and market context. Reilly's law of retail gravitation, which says, in effect, that larger concentrations of retail have larger spheres of influence (trade areas) than smaller concentrations, implies that all things being equal, in a generic physical context (suburbia) the larger box will always outperform a smaller box in terms of controlling market share. That reality, along with the aforementioned trends in land-use planning that have encouraged that outcome, have diminished the inherent advantages of efficiency and sustainability for compact, mixed-use development, thereby threatening the viability of true neighborhood-oriented retail.

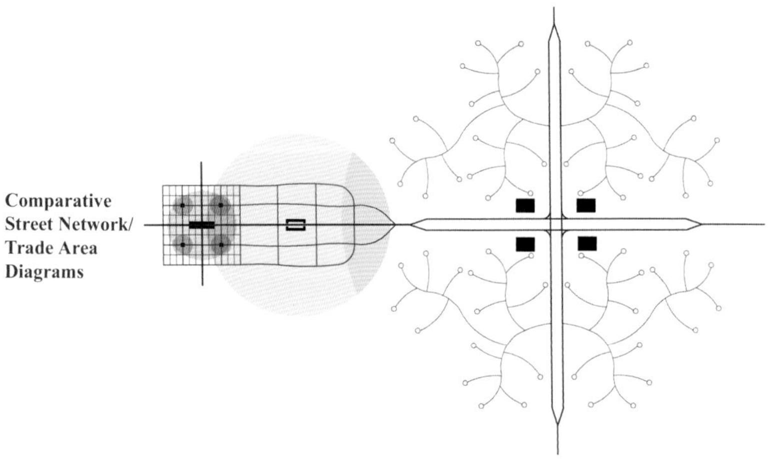

	T-4/6 Urban	T-3 Sub-Urban	Sprawl
Square Footage/ Residential Unit	Same	Same	Same
Relative Scale	1.0	1.5	3.0 +
Average Distance To Daily Needs	1/2 mile	2 miles	3 - 5 miles or more

SETH HARRY

A clear, empirical illustration of the effect is demonstrated by the conceptual diagram on page 204, which is based on a typical contemporary metropolitan area (in this case, it was empirically modeled on Omaha, Nebraska) and depicts the evolution of the traditional urban street network/retail hierarchy over a period of time, from pre-war urbanism to pre-war sub-urbanism, to post-war sprawl. It illustrates the change from urban to suburban retail models, based on the phenomenon described above.

The street network evolves from compact, walkable, mixed-use urban fabric on the left, to less dense residential neighborhoods in the middle, but with a still visible articulated street network, and a reasonably well-integrated commercial component. But then, to the far right, it changes into full-blown sprawl, with low-density residential development, segregated uses, and a dendritic residential street configuration that forces all trips for daily needs onto a single, large arterial network, around which is clustered a group of large-box retail responding to the correspondingly high number of traffic counts this model produces.

Because the basic merchandise categories haven't changed—only the scale of the retail formats, in response to their ability to capture a much larger number of residential units through the increased dependence on fewer, but much larger, arterials—the actual sales per square foot of the individual stores, as well as the square footage allocation per household unit, does not vary significantly across the three diagrams. However, the larger overall capture, combined with the much lower densities typical of sprawl, results in substantially larger trade areas, geographically speaking, and in proportionally and substantially more vehicle miles per trip to satisfy the same fundamental retail needs.

The use of a Transect-based model allows for the creation of regional plans that balance transportation infrastructure against regional consumer demand by means of a finely articulated urban fabric that both acknowledges and effectively responds to the specific needs of a community, regardless of scale, all the way from a rural hamlet to a regional center. When tied to appropriately coupled land use and transportation planning, it provides an ideal framework for integrating a full complement of uses, including retail, into a comprehensively vibrant, equitable, and sustainable human habitat. In other words, retail—in a traditional urban context—is by nature both self-regulating and self-correcting, thereby eliminating or avoiding many of the problems typically associated with large-box retail today.

Application of Transect planning at the regional level not only provides a clear framework in which new development may take place, but it can also help rationalize existing development by providing appropriate metrics to guide the recalibration of existing uses based on idealized standards: Where retail concentrations exist out of proportion relative to their legitimate places within the Transect, remedial actions can be justifiably pursued to help put the retail back into more appropriate balance and scale. This can be accomplished by gradually reducing the amount of retail, by adding additional density of other uses, or ideally by a combination of both.

GETTING A RETURN ON OUR INVESTMENT: USING THE TRANSECT TO REPAIR SPRAWL

GALINA TACHIEVA

Human settlements are resilient and successional in nature; they change, while going through cycles of regression, deterioration, and advancement. Even the most cosmopolitan cities started as meager hamlets on crossroads, but then grew and matured, while regenerating their physical environment multiple times throughout their histories. Today's image of American urbanism is inseparable from the image of sprawl—endless, soulless, wasteful and, most importantly, malfunctioning. However, this predicament may signal a pivotal point, when quantitative and qualitative changes converge, as has happened in previous civilizations, and the paradigm shifts toward better human habitats.

Sprawl is failing. It has underperformed for a long time, but its collapse has become obvious with the 2008–2010 financial meltdown and economic crisis, and its abundance magnifies the problems of its failure. Judging from history, the repair of sprawl is inevitable. Building more sprawl cannot continue, if only for a lack of capital and the failure of the financial instruments that enabled sprawl's proliferation. Abandoning existing sprawl is not possible either, as it represents too vast an investment (of money, infrastructure, time, human energy, and dreams). The existing sprawling physical environment cannot be simply discarded or demolished. Fortunately, it offers opportunities for reuse.

The only reasonable option is to repair sprawl—to deal with it straight on, by finding ways to reuse and reorganize as much of it as possible into complete, livable, robust communities. Pragmatism calls for the repair of sprawl through redevelopment that creates viable, human-scaled settlements, places that are walkable, with mixes of uses and transportation options. Pragmatism also demands, however, the acknowledgement that portions of sprawl may remain in their current state, while others may devolve, reverting to agriculture or nature.

There are several examples from urban history that show successful transformations of existing rural patterns "on the edges" into more urban and resilient environments. Camillo Sitte's work in the late 19th century demonstrates the redevelopment of rural hamlets into the next sequence of urbanism, denser urban villages. It was done in a sensitive manner, by keeping most trajectories of existing rural roads, as they contained the traces of the land and the wisdom of the first settlers. He also respected most of the property lines by subdividing the plots parallel to these lines. The result was complex and picturesque urbanism in contrast to the Beaux-Arts grand gestures prevalent at that time, which cut bold diagonals and formal public spaces through the existing fabric to achieve direct terminations and symmetry. The figures below contrast the more formal planning technique with Sitte's more sensitive approach.

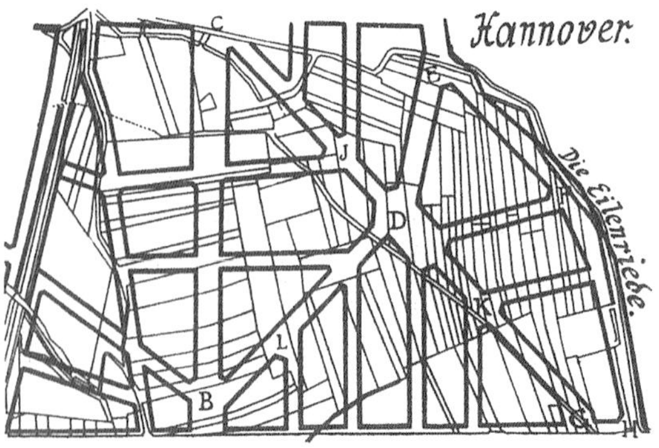

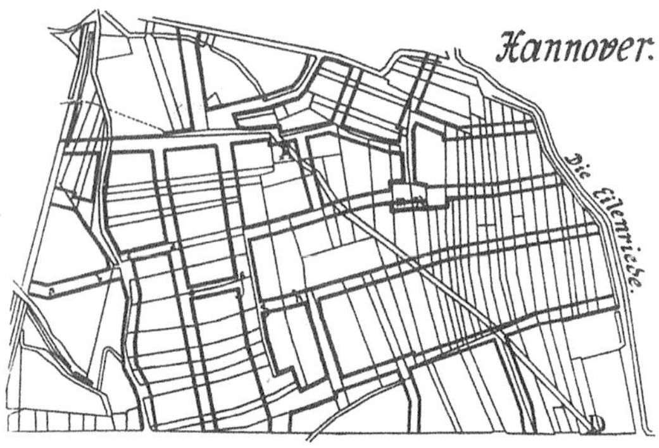

Other examples of generational transformation of human settlements are the "bulwarks," or fortification walls, around many European cities. For example, the image on the next page shows that when these defense installations became obsolete in Vienna, they were redeveloped into the grand perimeter boulevard of the Ringstrasse, to be used not only for circulation but also as grand public spaces accommodating civic buildings and parks. These examples are among many others that can give us confidence that any human-built artifact, including sprawl, can be redeemed through restructuring and reuse. The past six decades of American planning have achieved a dramatic transformation of compact and walkable environments into car-oriented, single-use, sprawling patterns. This is the time to start transitioning back to walkable, diverse, and human-scaled communities.

How to Achieve Sprawl Repair?

Sprawl has been aggressively promoted and encouraged, and the approach to repair must be the same. It should start soon, because the current situation is not sustainable. The operational and maintenance costs for existing sprawl are rising, straining government budgets that are already stretched. The previous model relied on new development to pay for those costs, but rising energy costs, scarce capital, and expensive credit have exposed the brittleness of that model. Settlements that have survived hundreds or thousands of years have proven to be adaptable. By incorporating essential characteristics of successful urbanism, we have the chance to make sprawl useful and to see a return on our

DPZ CODESIGN

vast investment. We need to act fast, however, to create new opportunities in these failing, sprawling places to house the 100 million people expected to be added to the U.S. population in the next several decades.

Sprawl repair should be pursued using a comprehensive method based on urban design, regulation, and strategies for funding and incentives—the same instruments that made sprawl the prevalent form of development. Repair should be addressed at all urban scales, from the region down to the community and the building—from identifying potential transportation networks and creating transit-connected urban cores to transforming dead malls into town centers, reconfiguring conventional suburban blocks into walkable fabric, down to the adaptation and expansion of single structures. The sprawl repair method should identify deficiencies in typical elements of sprawl and determine the best remedial techniques for those deficiencies. Rather than the instant and total overhaul of communities, as promoted so destructively in American cities half a century ago, this should be a strategy for incremental and opportunistic improvement.

Sprawl must be fixed. The good news is that we have the tools to do it. The Transect is one such tool.

Succession for the Future

Even though sprawl's poor performance has been proven, it is still difficult to approve and finance mixed-use, walkable, and diverse projects. Furthermore, it is impossible to repair sprawl using most existing zoning practices and policies, as they were designed to create sprawl. A total overhaul of current zoning practices is required for an effective intervention in suburbia. As this is impossible to do in a single, sweeping motion, new codes must be adopted one municipality—or even one project—at a time, as overlay districts, as parallel options for planning complete neighborhoods, or in place of existing codes. In all cases, these codes must powerfully incentivize smart growth rather than sprawl.

Many municipalities and cities have adopted form-based codes to overcome the difficulties related to building and maintaining sprawl. Form-based codes regulate the form of the built environment, allowing and encouraging good place making. One model form-based code is the SmartCode, a comprehensive ordinance that enables smart growth community patterns and the transformation of sprawl into walkable urbanism. A calibrated SmartCode may include a special sector (G-5 Sprawl Repair Sector) that is assigned to areas that are currently single-use and have disconnected conventional development patterns, but have the potential to be completed or redeveloped into neighborhoods and urban centers.

The Sprawl Repair Module, excerpted opposite, has been created as a special "plug-in" to the SmartCode to activate the technology for repair as a part of the code. The module presents a sequence of techniques for retrofitting the sprawl elements into complete communities. It operates at the scale of the region, community, block, building, and thoroughfare.

Some of the sprawl areas will be up-zoned to accommodate higher but well-designed density and allow the introduction of mixed uses and transit. This creates the regulatory basis for successional growth and the transformation of sprawl elements into viable neighborhoods with more transportation and housing choices. Conventional suburban blocks may be reconfigured to receive higher densities and additional uses.

At the scale of the building, the most important issues will be to allow flexible uses within existing structures (houses becoming live-work units, big-box retail becoming office space or civic buildings), and increased density within existing parcels and lots (a mansion turned into multifamily housing or an assisted living facility, or the addition of accessory units).

Another important task is to create standards to calm and repair dangerous thoroughfares and make them safe for walking and bicycling while creating connections between residential areas, shops, workplaces, schools, civic buildings, and recreation.

The lack of rural-to-urban logic in sprawl is one of the fundamental differences from traditional urbanism. The Transect is broken into zones, each representing a complex habitat of different building types, streetscapes, and public spaces. This is in contrast to sprawl, in which each element is a single-use agglomeration, usually a monoculture of a single building type.

SMARTCODE MODULE — SPRAWL REPAIR

Municipality

Author: Duany Plater-Zyberk & Co. Draft: October 12, 2018

TABLE SR3: Sprawl Types Repaired. This table provides descriptions of the necessary tools to repair the Sprawl Types into Community Units/ Walkable Place Types.

SPRAWL TYPES		T1	T2	T3	T4	T5	T6	TECHNIQUES	INCENTIVES/ BENEFITS	COMMUNITY UNITS	
S-3 RURAL SUBDIVISIONS	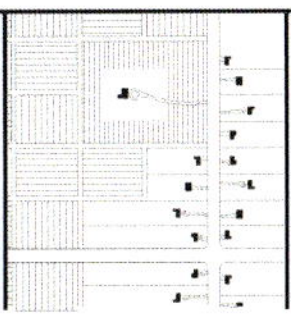	50% min.		10 - 30 %	20 - 40%			• Cluster at intersections through TDR, modified PDRs, purchase of Conservation Easement • Concentrate infrastructure • Create a rural Green • Introduce Live-Works, farmers market	• Deferred taxation; higher Density; permitting By Right • Packaged Sewer Service within 1/4 square mile • Hamlet growing into a village	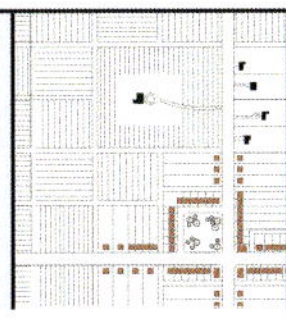	CLD
S-4 SINGLE FAMILY SUBDIVISIONS			No Minimum	10 - 30 %	30 - 60 %	10 - 30 %		• Introduce new building types and Retail/Office/Lodging/Civic uses • Connect Thoroughfares • Repair Thoroughfares; add pedestrian and bike Paths • Define and make usable Open and Civic Space	• Higher Density; additions; Outbuildings; permitting By Right • Infrastructure incentives • Transit potential • Neighborhood/Town Square	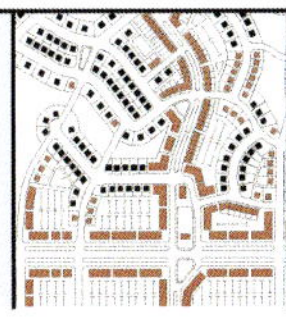	TND
S-5 MULTI FAMILY SUBDIVISIONS	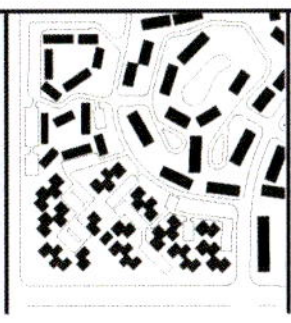		No Minimum	10 - 30 %	30 - 60 %	10 - 30 %		• Introduce new building types and Retail/Office/Lodging/Civic uses • Connect Thoroughfares • Rationalize parking; add garages • Repair Thoroughfares; add pedestrian and bike Paths • Define and make usable Open and Civic Space	• Additional development potential; permitting By Right • Incentives for infrastructure • Incentives for garages • Transit potential • Community gathering places	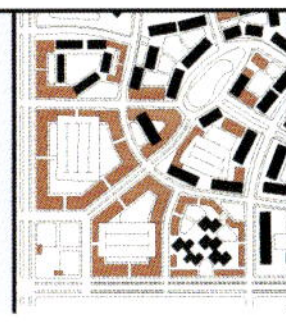	TND
S-6 SHOPPING CENTERS & STRIPS	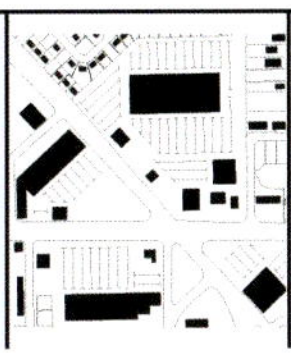				10 - 30 %	10 - 30 %	40 - 80 %	• Introduce new building types and Residential/Office/Lodging/Civic uses • Connect Thoroughfares; add Streets in front of stores • Rationalize parking; Add garages • Define and make usable Open and Civic Space	• Additional development potential; permitting By Right; TIFs, CDBG • Incentives for infrastructure • Incentives for garages • Transit potential • Community gathering places	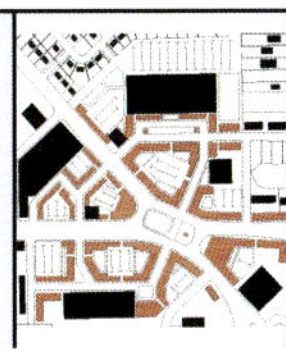	RCD / TND
S-7 BUSINESS PARKS & SUB. CAMPUSES	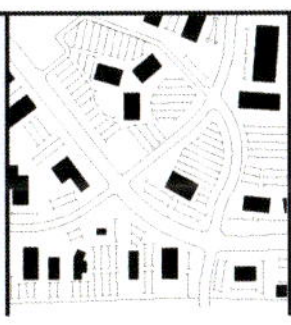				10 - 30 %	10 - 30 %	40 - 80 %	• Introduce new building types and Residential/Office/Lodging/Civic uses • Connect Thoroughfares; create urban Blocks • Rationalize parking; add garages • Define and make usable Open and Civic Space	• Additional development potential; permitting By Right; TIFs, CDBG • Incentives for infrastructure • Incentives for garages • Transit potential • Community gathering places	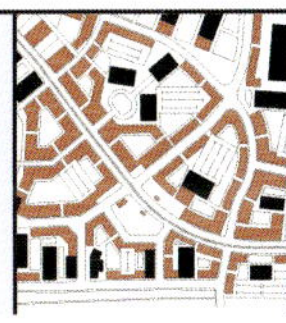	RCD / TND
S-8 MALLS					10 - 30 %	10 - 30 %	40 - 80 %	• Introduce new building types and Residential/Office/Lodging/Civic uses • Connect Thoroughfares; create urban Blocks • Rationalize parking; add garages • Define and make usable Open and Civic Space	• Additional development potential; permitting by Right; TIFs, CDBG • Incentives for infrastructure • Incentives for garages • Transit potential • Community gathering places		RCD
S-9 EDGE CITIES					10 - 30 %	10 - 30 %	40 - 80 %	• Introduce new building types and Residential/Office/Lodging/Civic uses • Connect Thoroughfares; Create urban blocks • Rationalize parking; Add garages • Repair Thoroughfares; resolve complicated interchanges and intersections into urban types • Define and make usable Open and Civic Space	• Additional development potential; permitting By Right; TIFs, CDBG • Incentives for infrastructure • Incentives for garages • Opening additional real estate for development; transit potential • Community gathering places	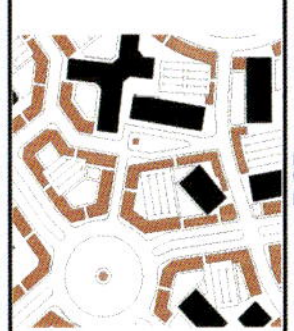	RCD

The Transect Zones represent zoning conditions that are similar to the ones administered by conventional zoning codes, except they include not only the building use, density, height, and setback requirements, but also how buildings relate to each other and how together they shape the public realm.

Sprawl elements cannot be repaired in isolation; they must always be considered in the context of the community and/or regional scale. Single-use and typologically monotonous areas need to be balanced with other required elements and uses to form the full range of Transect Zones appropriate to complete communities.

For example, the diagrams below show the sharp contrast between the conventional zoning map of an existing subdivision and the proposed Transect-based regulating plan. A residential-only suburban enclave, which accommodates only low-density housing, needs to be rebalanced with other uses and building types found in T-4 General Urban and T-5 Urban Center zones.

The existing zoning shows only one shade, as there is only one use allowed—the single-family residence on a defined minimum lot size. This is an outdated, coarse, and inflexible type of zoning.

DPZ CODESIGN

The proposed zoning diagram is based on different principles—maximum flexibility, a mix of uses, and inclusion of the full range of human environments, from rural to the most urban. Transect-based zoning allows for disparate uses to co-exist within walking distance from each other and be accommodated in building types that form harmonious street frontages. The new regulating plan shows several Transect Zones that include a range/hierarchy of building types according to their urban qualities. The most urban buildings—shops, apartments, lofts, and offices—are in the T-5 Urban Center Zone. Townhouses, live-work units, and smaller houses are in the T-4 General Urban Zone, and the larger houses, together with the existing ones, are in the T-3 Sub-Urban Zone.

The newly created public spaces are organized under CS (Civic Space), while the existing green spaces, together with the newly introduced agricultural lands, are grouped within the T-2 Rural Zone. The designation of Transect Zones within the plan will be defined by a process of local calibration based on an understanding of existing conditions and the relationship of the enclave to other close-by developments.

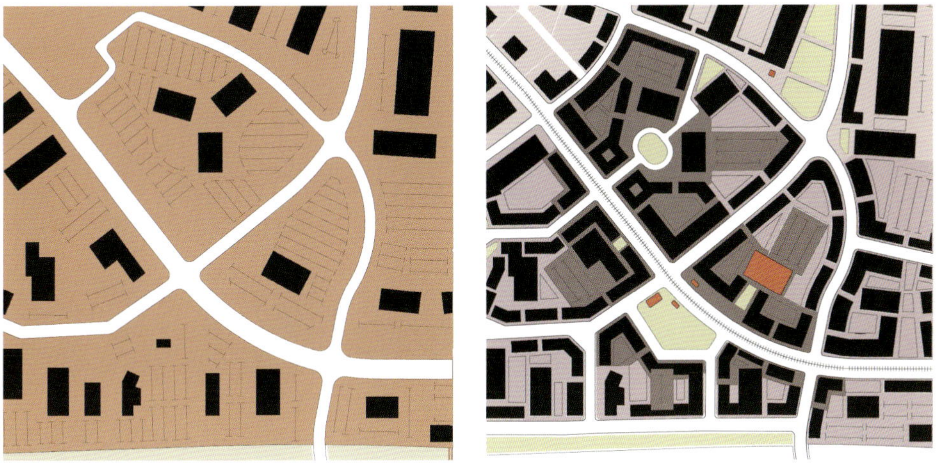

DPZ CODESIGN

In addition to single-use residential enclaves, commercial agglomerations, such as malls and office parks, also need to be rezoned, as shown in the diagrams above. They often exemplify intensities typical of the T-6 Urban Core Zone, and should be rebalanced with a mix of lower-intensity Transect Zones, also calibrated to local conditions, at the densities necessary for transit.

Transect-based zoning creates the flexibility needed to transform the business park into a mixed-use environment. The existing office use and the main square will be zoned T-6, with parking garages added to support high-density residential infill and retail. T-5 will include the next tier of urban intensity, incorporating live-work units, lofts, and townhouses. A variety of civic spaces will be zoned CS to accommodate civic structures such as a transit stop and farmers market. The mix of uses can also be accomplished vertically, in the new buildings, as the ground floors can be used for shops, daycare facilities, and so forth, with the upper floors used for residences.

The Sprawl Repair Module indicates the proportions of Transect Zones that need to be added or rebalanced to transform the sprawl repair target into a mixed-use, diverse and transit-ready community. The zoning modifications, together with the urban design adjustments, such as connecting streets and creating public space, are reflected in specific regulating plans.

Conclusion

The use of the Transect is essential for sprawl repair because it provides the framework for re-balancing and diversifying the mono-cultural environments of single-use zoning. The use of the Transect provides variety, not only in the practical sense of additional uses and building types, but also in other parts of the physical environment, through a variety of setbacks, a range of frontage conditions, building heights, etc. When utilized along with the proper design techniques, Transect-based zoning produces places of distinct character, creates landmarks, and delineates recognizable streets and public spaces.

By introducing the Transect, we can incorporate the existing sprawl elements, but embed them in a wider palette of urban fabric, experiences, geometries, and relationships between human-made and natural entities. The new system of zoning will provide gradients of complexity and organic character based on a rural-to-urban continuum.

That complexity and organic character, combined with the incremental change to smaller and more affordable lots and buildings, can also be very useful in adapting to changing economic conditions. Transect-based zoning provides more options to accommodate different people, incomes, and ages, and helps a community prepare for the future.

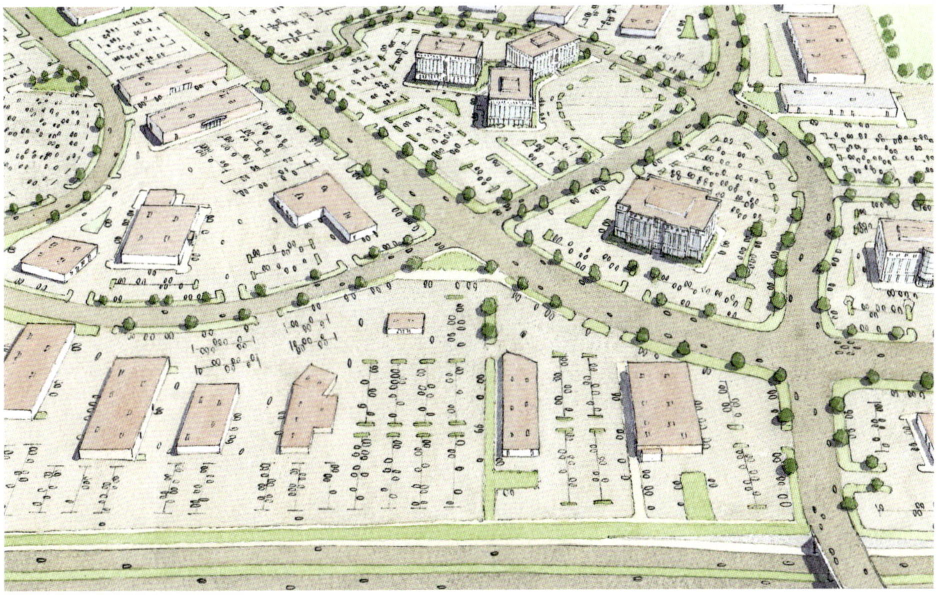

CHRIS RITTER FOR DPZ CODESIGN

These illustrations show an office park with dispersed buildings and over-scaled parking lots repaired to create a transit-oriented town center.

A TRANSECT OF ENGAGEMENT

SIDNEY BROWER

Few housing areas in the United States are designed as total residential environments; most consist of a patchwork of housing subdivisions, commercial developments, and public projects that are assembled piece by piece, without an overall plan. In part this is because we as a nation favor the interests of the individual over those of the collective.[1] And in part it is because, while we have models of area design (and have had most of them for a considerable period of time), we do not know which one is the best.

Some of our models, such as Ebenezer Howard's country towns[2] and le Corbusier's skyscrapers in the park,[3] were imported; and some were born or shaped in the United States—these include Frederick Law Olmstead's houses in a garden,[4] Clarence Perry's urban villages,[5] Frank Lloyd Wright's villas in the countryside,[6] Clarence Stein's Radburn idea,[7] and, most recently, the Neotraditionalists' version of 19th-century small towns.[8] Each of these models is, in essence, a reaction to conditions of its time: Olmsted's to the incursion of commerce and industry, Howard's to the spread of cities, Stein's to problems of living with the automobile, and the Neotraditionalists' to the sameness of suburbia. Two things characterize all of these models. First, while some include social elements (Howard's formula for collective land ownership is a notable example), it is the physical characteristics that have "taken"; the models are read as architectural prototypes. And second, each model is defended as the single best way to design a residential area. The fact that these ideal forms differ in so many important respects—density, spatial organization, housing types, distribution of land uses, and so on—and result in environments as different as Roland Park, in Baltimore,[9] the Greenbelt towns,[10] Columbia, Maryland,[11] Seaside, Florida,[12] and public housing projects of the 1950s and '60s—should be enough to raise questions about the notion that there can be a single ideal, and point to the need for a typology that consists of a number of models representing a range of good residential settings in which one is distinctively different from the other. The Rural-to-Urban Transect is such a typology.

Imagine ordering residential environments from highly rural at one end to highly urban at the other. You would come up with a continuum that stretched from country estates through sub-urban blocks to dense, inner-city areas. When you cut through this continuum at critical points you find that each segment (called a Transect Zone or T-Zone) varies in the degree and appearance of urbanity. Each T-Zone has its own particular range of densities, street profiles, open spaces, and building forms, a characteristic way in which houses address the street, a characteristic ratio of human-made to natural materials, and so on. Neotraditionalists argue that, ideally, the physical elements in each T-Zone should go together in the way that a Corinthian column and a Corinthian entablature go together.

The Rural-to-Urban Transect differs from earlier concepts of transects offered by people such as Patrick Geddes, with his Highlands, Foothills, and Shores,[13] and Richard Coleman, with his central city, older suburbs, new subdivisions, and rural areas,[14] in an important way. Historians and geographers use transects to describe the way things are, but urban designers and planners use the Rural-to-Urban Transect to prescribe an ideal—the way things ought to be. Implied in the Rural-to-Urban Transect is the belief that residents will be more satisfied living in places where all of the open spaces, fences, curbs, roof lines, landscaping, turning radii, and the like read as unified compositions.

However, a review of 36 neighborhood-satisfaction studies shows that what contributes most to one's satisfaction are the kind of people one lives with and the kind of social relationship one has with them.[15] Residents mention such things as: people who are like oneself or who are different, people who are sophisticated or down-to-earth, people who have a strong sense of community or who leave one alone. Physical elements are valued less for their intrinsic qualities than for their social implications. Places are valued because, for example, they are clean and tidy, or well kept, are used by local people or outsiders, are quiet or lively, restful or exciting, and because they provide opportunities for participation or for privacy. The studies do not support the idea that a unified composition leads to increased residential satisfaction. If the Transect concept is to be accepted as framework for designing more satisfying residential areas, if it is to be used as an instrument of public policy, it cannot consider only physical elements; it must take social concerns into account.[16]

In fact, transects that recognize only social concerns have more relationship to satisfaction than those that recognize only physical ones. The former include Warren and Warren's Integral, Parochial, Diffuse, Stepping-stone, Transitory, and Anomic areas,[17] and Moore's High-mobility/high-change, High-mobility/low-change, Low-mobility/high-change, and Low-mobility/low-change areas.[18] But these formulations are of little help to urban designers. Studies of cultural landscapes are more promising because they include both social and physical components. See, for example, Meinig's classification of New England Village, Main Street, and California Suburbia,[19] and Weiss' classification of

Urban Gold Coast, Young Influentials, Furs and Station Wagons, and Blue Chip Blues.[20] However, these, again, are descriptive rather than prescriptive.

What urban designers need is a Transect in which each zone offers a desirable but different residential experience, where the experience is supported, even heightened, by the physical setting. Imagine a continuum of residential environments ranging from High Social Engagement, where people are sociable and adventurous and there are many opportunities for meetings and interactions, to Low Social Engagement, where people are self-sufficient and independent and there are few opportunities for chance encounters. I am suggesting such a Transect. I call it the Transect of Engagement, and it has four component elements or TE-Zones:

> TE-Zone 1, Center: A place that is lively and busy, with lots to see and do. It has a mix of many different people and uses, and it attracts visitors from other parts of the city and beyond.
>
> TE-Zone 2, Small Town: A place that has the feeling of a small town, with its own institutions and meeting places. People who live here know one another and are able to recognize those who do not live here.
>
> TE-Zone 3, Residential Partnership: A separate residential area, a place for family and home life. Residents go to other parts of the city for work, shopping, and entertainment.
>
> TE-Zone 4, Retreat: A place where one feels removed from other people and their activities. People who live here tend to be independent and go their separate ways.

These four types of residential environments were tested in interviews with a sample of 96 residents in eight neighborhoods in Baltimore, Maryland.[21] Each interviewee was given descriptions of the four zones as stated above, and a list of 36 qualities that were found to be associated with residential satisfaction (see Table 1), and they were asked to indicate which of the qualities "went with" each zone. They were asked to describe people who would most likely choose to live in each zone, and whether they themselves had ever lived in each of them. They were asked to name places that fit each zone. The results show that interviewees associate each zone with a real place, a distinctively different set of qualities, and a different set of residents (see Table 2). While the zones prove to be distinctively different, some are more different than others. Small Towns share several qualities with Centers and a number with Residential Partnerships (Table 3).

The qualities of each zone have different implications for the design of the physical environment:

A Center is crowded, bustling, varied, ever changing, stimulating, and exciting, with many opportunities for people to see and meet one another. It supports what is best about in-town living. There is a fine-grain mix of activities, a dense pattern of development, and an efficient public transportation system. Theaters, concert halls, galleries, restaurants, promenades, and public spaces are active, inviting, and hospitable. The area is designed to bring people together so they can learn about one another without necessarily having to interact. Retail uses are visible and recognizable from the street, uninterrupted, accessible to the general public, and with closely spaced points of entry. There are many small stores, and there is considerable duplication and redundancy, with places that serve highly specialized users and offer novelty and variety. Housing is available for people of different ages, classes, and cultures, and because there is a high rate of turnover, there is rental accommodation at a range of price levels. The area is inevitably noisy, and so the housing units are designed with more than usual attention to sound insulation. Small squares, parks, and courtyards relieve the feeling of crowding. Because it serves nonresidents and new arrivals, a good Center has a clear spatial structure, good directions, and visible, legible functions. It is constantly changing, full of surprises, a work-in-progress rather than a completed set piece, and so it is likely to be somewhat chaotic. Because it is so open and varied, it is especially vulnerable to crime and acts of incivility, so good policing and defensible space design features are important.

A Small Town is a familiar, manageable, more-or-less self-contained world, one that is visually distinct, with clear boundaries and a generally agreed-upon name. It is small enough that residents know one another by name or reputation, and they enjoy a relationship that evolves slowly over time. Its residents are stable; they have a steady source of employment and a high rate of home ownership. Local businesses and institutions offer a full complement of services; they tend to be small and locally run, and they are oriented primarily to local people. Residents have a localistic attitude: they develop many contacts and interests within the neighborhood, and they remain loyal to the local stores. Nonresidents enjoy the local flavor and the feeling of authenticity, but they are treated as guests rather than as regulars. Some downtown neighborhoods function as Small Towns.

A Residential Partnership creates a cocoon of tranquility around the housing unit. It is a bedroom community (residents go out of the area for work and shopping) that emphasizes the recreational functions of home, and offers special amenities for the benefit of the residents. These are likely to be privately owned, included in the sale or rental price of the units, run by a formal organization of residents, and maintained by fees that are backed by covenants. A Residential Partnership may have its own system of governance, formal and informal procedures to screen out potential residents who may be unpredictable or disagreeable. It is a community in which social ties are fragile and easily ruptured. It is attractive to people who are fearful of conditions in the larger society, and for whom home rather than community is the center of domestic life. Residential Partnerships are the most common type of residential development being built today in the United States.

A **Retreat** reinforces one's identity as a unique individual rather than a member of a community. It is a private place, where one can be alone, quiet, rested, and contemplative, a place for creation, healing, comfort, and reflection. Housing units are largely self-sufficient. Privacy is enhanced by giving special attention to the placement of door and window openings, and the separation of potentially intrusive uses. Views are protected from being destroyed or blocked. The area has few shared facilities, and outdoor spaces separate people rather than bring them together. A good Retreat may be off the beaten track or difficult to find, or visitors may be excluded or screened by gatekeepers. Retreats may be found in the exurbs as well as on the upper floors of downtown buildings, on mountainsides, and on waterfronts—sites that dramatize isolation. Preference for a Retreat zone means abdication from a residential community, not necessarily from community at large.

Each of these TE zones offers a distinctively different residential experience: the Center is a place for new beginnings—diverting, changing, and open; the Small Town is a place of belonging—friendly, familiar, and enduring; the Residential Partnership is a place that is quiet, safe and predictable; and the Retreat is a place of escape—solitary and unspoiled.

An important idea underlying the Transect of Engagement is that an urban design must be evaluated by the way people experience it rather than its intrinsic appearance or form. This presents a number of non-traditional design problems, such as: how to design a public space so it brings people together or keeps them apart; how to design a cluster of housing units so it maximizes or minimizes chance encounters; how to design high-density housing so it does not feel crowded; how to design a residential area so it can be lively without being too noisy; how to design an environment that will instill a feeling of collective identity and responsibility; how to design a walk-to neighborhood center that residents will prefer over outlying shopping centers; how to encourage personal attention in neighborhood stores; how to design an environment so people will feel safe there; how to design an area that will attract compatible neighbors; how to attract a diverse group of people to some areas and like-minded people to others; and how to create areas for stable populations and areas for short-term residents. To address these kinds of problems, it is necessary to extend the traditional scope of what we call "design" to include the work of developers, economists, event planners, advertisers, community organizers, and sales people, as well as architects, landscape architects, and planners.

In short, I am suggesting a Transect that consists of four ideal residential environments, each distinguished from the other by the nature and extent of social interactions among residents, and the presence of facilities and features that generate and support these interactions. Neighborhood-satisfaction studies teach us that residents look not only for houses but for a level of community.[22] Design should be about more than creating houses and housing areas; it should also be about generating community, which may vary from intimate to casual. Its ultimate purpose should be to create relationships among people, not buildings. The Rural-to-Urban Transect is driven by a concern for the physical environment, with implications for social behavior. The Transect of Engagement, on the other hand, is driven by social concerns, with implications for the design of the physical environment.

Table 1. *Thirty-three qualities of good neighborhoods that were identified in 36 residential satisfaction studies done over about as many years. They offer quite different, often conflicting, views of a good place to live.*

A place that is clean and well maintained
A place that is quiet and relaxing
A place that is entirely residential
A place that has a definite center
A place that is right in the center of activity
A place where neighboring homes are close to one another
A place that is full of surprises
Living here, one can manage without a car
A place with convenient public transportation
A place where residents feel safe and secure
A place with world-class restaurants, stores, and cultural facilities
A place where there are many tourists
A place that suits the needs of newcomers
A place to meet new people
A place where one can have an active social life close to home
A place that offers a wide selection of goods and services close to home
Living here, you do not have to spend as much time caring for the house
A place where neighbors are outgoing and friendly
A place to put down roots and settle
A place where most people know one another
A place where one will always meets people one knows
A place where people take care of one another
A place where relationships are long lasting and personal
A place where residents are involved in community affairs
A place where there is no pressure to socialize or join anything
A place where residents are private and go their own ways
A place that has a reputation as a desirable place to live
A place where all residents have a similar life style
A place that is protected from the larger problems of society
A place to raise children
A wide diversity of people live here
A place where one can find sophisticated neighbors
A place where neighbors are genuine and down-to-earth

Table 2. *Residents were asked to identify and rate the importance of the qualities that "go with" each zone. The following qualities (listed from high to low ratings) were strongly correlated with a particular zone; they define each zone as a distinct type.*

Zone	Qualities
Center	A place with convenient public transportation
	A place with world-class restaurants, stores, and cultural facilities
	A place that offers a wide selection of goods and services close to home
	A wide diversity of people live here
	Living here, one can manage without a car
	A place that is right in the center of activity
	A place where one can have an active social life close to home
	A place to meet new people
	A place where there are many tourists
	A place that is full of surprises
Small Town	A place where neighbors are outgoing and friendly
	A place where people take care of one another
	A place where most people know one another
	A place where relationships are long lasting and personal
	A place where one will always meets people one knows
	A place where residents are genuine and down-to-earth
	A place where residents are involved in community affairs
Residential Partnership	A place to raise children
	A place that is entirely residential
Retreat	A place where residents are private and go their own ways
	A place where there is no pressure to socialize or join anything

Table 3. *The ratings for some qualities do not differ significantly between zones; some zones have more in common than others. Small Towns and Partnerships share many of the same qualities.*

Zones	Qualities
Centers and Small Towns	A place that has a definite center
	A place that suits the needs of newcomers
	A place where neighboring homes are close to one another
Small Towns and Residential Partnerships	A place that is protected from the larger problems of society
	A place to put down roots and settle
	A place where residents are involved in community affairs
	A place where neighboring homes are close to one another
	A place that is quiet and relaxing
	A place where all residents have a similar life style
Residential Partnerships and Retreats	A place that is protected from the larger problems of society
Retreats and Centers	Living here, you do not have to spend as much time caring for the house
	A place where one can find sophisticated neighbors

This essay was adapted from one orginally published in The Journal of Urban Design, *October 2002.*

1. For more on this, see Richard Tseng-yu Lai, *Law in Urban Design and Planning: The Invisible Web*. New York: Van Nostrand Reinhold, 1988.

2. Ebenezer Howard, *Garden Cities of Tomorrow*. London: Faber and Faber, 1945 (original publication 1898).

3. Le Corbusier, *The City of Tomorrow And Its Planning*. Cambridge, MA: MIT Press, 1971 (first English edition published 1929).

4. Frederick Law Olmsted, "Preliminary report upon the proposed suburban village at Riverside, near Chicago, by Olmsted Vaux and Co., Landscape Architects, Sept. 1, 1868." In *The Papers of Frederick Law Olmsted, Volume 6, The Years of Olmsted, Vaux and Company, 1865–1874*. David Schuyler and Jane Turner Censer (eds.), Baltimore, MD: Johns Hopkins University Press, 1992, pp. 273–290.

5. Clarence A. Perry, "The neighborhood unit." In *Regional Survey of New York and Its Environs, vii* (Neighborhood and Community Planning monograph 1). New York: Committee on the Regional Plan of New York and Its Environs, 1929.

6. Frank Lloyd Wright, *The Disappearing City*. New York: Payson, 1932.

7. Clarence S. Stein, Toward New Towns for America. Cambridge MA: MIT Press, 1966 (original publication date, 1951).

8. Andrés Duany, "A new theory of urbanism." *Scientific American, 283, Issue 6*, December 2000, p. 90–91.

9. James F. Waesche, *Crowning the Gravelly Hill: A History of the Roland Park–Guilford–Homeland District*. Baltimore: Maclay & Associates, 1987.

10. Clarence S. Stein, *Toward New Towns for America*.

11. Robert Tennenbaum (ed.), *Creating a New City: Columbia, Maryland*. Partners in Community Building and Perry Publishing, 1996.

12. Brooke, Steven. *Seaside*. Gretna LA: Pelican, 1995.

13. Sir Patrick Geddes, *Cities In Evolution: An Introduction to the Town Planning Movement and to the Study of Civics*. New York: Harper & Row, 1971.

14. Richard P. Coleman, "Attitudes towards Neighborhoods: How Americans Choose to Live." *Cambridge MA: Joint Center for Urban Studies of MIT and Harvard University, working paper no. 49*, 1978.

15. Sidney Brower, *Good Neighborhoods: A Study of In-Town and Suburban Residential Environments*. Westport, CT: Praeger, 1996, 2000.

16. Brain, David. "From good neighborhoods to the sustainable city: social science and the social agenda of the new urbanism." Paper delivered at the research symposium on New Urbanism and Smart Growth. National Center for Smart Growth Research and Education. University of Maryland, May 5, 2002.

17. Rachelle B. Warren and Donald I. Warren, *The Neighborhood Organizer's Handbook*. Notre Dame, IN: University of Notre Dame Press, 1977.

18. E. G. Moore, "A typology of neighborhood change" (resource paper no. 13). Washington, DC: Association of American Geographers, Commission on College Geography, 1972.

19. D. W. Meinig, "Symbolic landscapes: some idealizations of American communities." In D. W. Meinig (ed.), *The Interpretation of Ordinary Landscapes*. New York: Oxford University Press, 1979, pp. 164–192.

20. Michael J. Weiss, *The Clustering of America*. New York: Harper and Row, 1988.

21. For a full discussion of the environments and the methodology used, see Sidney Brower, *Good Neighborhoods*. Westport, CT: Praeger, 1996.

22. Sidney Brower, *Neighbors and Neighborhoods: Elements of Successful Community Design*. Chicago: APA Planner's Press, 2011.

THE POLIS AND NATURAL LAW: THE MORAL AUTHORITY OF THE URBAN TRANSECT[1]

PHILIP BESS

The Aristotelian-Thomist intellectual tradition's understanding of natural law—the broad, pre-modern tradition of western culture—is that there are certain foundational principles of morality that are (according to Thomas Aquinas) "the same for all, both as to knowledge and to rectitude;" in other words, principles of morality that are not only right for all human beings but also knowable to all human beings by reason alone without need for divine revelation. These foundational principles of morality, along with their first few rings of implications, are known as the natural law.

The Rural-to-Urban Transect is a heuristic device discovered, developed, and employed by New Urbanist theorists both to explain certain essential formal characteristics of traditional urban design and as the basis for alternatives to modern single-use-based zoning codes. The Urban Transect is defined here as that range of human habitats that support human flourishing, within which human settlements are part of a sustainable (albeit not necessarily locally bio-diverse) eco-system. These habitats, diagrammatically depicted as Transect Zones, range from less dense areas to more dense areas within neighborhoods; but each urban T-Zone denotes a walkable and mixed-use human environment wherein within each or from each urban T-Zone, many, if not most, of the necessities and activities of daily human life are within a five- to ten-minute walk for persons of varying ages and economic classes.

It is the thesis of what follows that, given this understanding and characterization of both natural law and the Urban Transect, the proposition "Human beings should make mixed-use walkable settlements" is generally valid for all human beings in all times and places—and therefore constitutes a natural law precept. If this were true, such a precept would be binding in conscience for—and acted upon with prudential judgment by—all persons who act in accordance with right (practical) reason; and most especially for and by persons who understand themselves to be a part of the Aristotelian-Thomist intellectual tradition.

The Moral Content and Agenda of the New Urbanism

Modern societies are pluralistic, and it is common wisdom among many architects that aesthetic and moral relativism are necessary implications of social pluralism. Part of my purpose here is to challenge the limits of this common wisdom; and specifically—the great variety of historic human settlement patterns notwithstanding—to ask whether and how it may be possible to defend the propositions that 1) some forms of human settlement are truly better than others in promoting human flourishing; and 2) all human settlements that succeed in promoting human flourishing share some common—and more importantly, identifiable—formal characteristics which, once understood, suggest a moral imperative to promote the creation of settlements possessing such formal characteristics.

I think it safe to say there would be widespread assent to these two propositions among both the architects and the non-architects who constitute the Congress for the New Urbanism. And yet, from much discussion with fellow New Urbanists in recent years, I find that we are divided over the issue of whether there is such a thing as objective standards of morality. The intellectual problem, therefore, is this: a general objection to the notion of objective morality calls into question New Urbanist claims for the objective goodness of traditional urban form. If it is true there are no objective moral goods, then how can the New Urbanist claim that traditional urbanism is itself an objective moral good be true?

I myself find New Urbanist arguments on behalf of the goodness of traditional urban form persuasive.[2] But taking New Urbanist arguments as a single cumulative argument for traditional urban form as a genuine human good both implies and requires a larger theoretical framework, one which makes plausible claims about what is genuinely good for human beings generally. And lest the reader be tempted to dismiss this issue as a merely internal matter, of consequence only to New Urbanists, be it noted that what is at stake is precisely the New Urbanist claim that traditional urban form is a genuine good for all human beings and that post-World War II sprawl is not. In other words, like it or not, New Urbanists are making a truth claim; indeed, New Urbanists are making a truth claim with moral implications. Since such a claim makes no sense in a theoretical context of epistemological skepticism and moral relativism—indeed, this is a primary reason for the hostility toward New Urbanism that exists within the architectural academy—in what kind of theoretical context does such a claim make sense?

I contend that New Urbanist arguments on behalf of traditional urbanism both rehearse the arguments of and only make sense in the broad intellectual and cultural context of natural law theory. But first, since I have been referring to the Congress for the New Urbanism (CNU), I would like to demonstrate how New Urbanism's founding document, the Charter of the New Urbanism,[3] presents itself as an appeal to reason on behalf of the common good.

From the Charter I excerpt the following passages that concern themselves primarily with the relationship between urban form, long-term sustainable eco-systems that accommodate human beings, and a social order grounded in justice:

> The Congress for the New Urbanism views disinvestment in central cities, the spread of placeless sprawl, increasing separation by race and income, environmental deterioration, loss of agricultural lands and wilderness, and the erosion of society's built heritage as one interrelated community-building challenge. [Intro.1]
>
> We stand for the restoration of existing urban centers and towns within coherent metropolitan regions, the reconfiguration of sprawling suburbs into communities of real neighborhoods and diverse districts, the conservation of natural environments, and the preservation of our built legacy. [Intro.2]
>
> We recognize that physical solutions by themselves will not solve social and economic problems, but neither can economic vitality, community stability, and environmental health be sustained without a coherent and supportive physical framework. [Intro.3]
>
> We advocate the restructuring of public policy and development practices to support the following principles: neighborhoods should be diverse in use and population; communities should be designed for the pedestrian and transit as well as the car; cities and towns should be shaped by physically defined and universally accessible public spaces and community institutions... [Intro.4]
>
> We are committed to reestablishing the relationship between the art of building and the making of community, through citizen-based participatory planning and design. [Intro.5]
>
> Where appropriate, new development contiguous to urban boundaries should be organized as neighborhoods and districts, and be integrated with the existing urban pattern. Noncontiguous development should be organized as towns and villages with their own urban edges, and planned for a jobs/housing balance, not as bedroom suburbs... [Section I.5]
>
> Cities and towns should bring into proximity a broad spectrum of public and private uses to support a regional economy that benefits people of all incomes. Affordable housing should be distributed throughout the region to match job opportunities and to avoid concentrations of poverty. [Section I.7]
>
> Many activities of daily living should occur within walking distance, allowing independence to those who do not drive, especially the elderly and the young. Interconnected networks of streets should be designed to encourage walking, reduce the number and length of automobile trips, and conserve energy. [Section II.3]

> Within neighborhoods, a broad range of housing types and price levels can bring people of diverse ages, races, and incomes into daily interaction, strengthening the personal and civic bonds essential to an authentic community. [Section II.4]
>
> Concentrations of civic, institutional, and commercial activity should be embedded in neighborhoods and districts, not isolated in remote, single-use complexes. Schools should be sized and located to enable children to walk or bicycle to them. [Section II.7]
>
> Civic buildings and public gathering places require important sites to reinforce community identity and the culture of democracy. They deserve distinctive form, because their role is different from that of other buildings and places that constitute the fabric of the city. [Section III.7]

In these eleven short paragraphs the word "should" occurs eleven times. Also occurring are the words "deserve," "require," "we stand for," "we advocate," and "we are committed to." From the Charter, and from observing the actions of New Urbanists in the world, one can infer that New Urbanists regard traditional urbanism as a genuine human good that human beings ought to pursue. The rest of this essay concerns itself with the nature and the status of that "ought."

Is traditional urbanism really good for all human beings everywhere, or not? Why ought human beings to make walkable mixed-use settlements—i.e., traditional towns and neighborhoods—instead of sprawl? Is the promotion of traditional urbanism a mere expression of preference, no different in its moral status than a preference for sprawl (a preference which today certainly seems wide-spread)? Or would one be correct in regarding the promotion of traditional urbanism in opposition to sprawl as in some tangible way morally obligatory?

These are the kinds of questions I propose to consider here, under the rubric of natural law; and I note that both the structure of the New Urbanists' founding document and their behavior in the world suggest that New Urbanists promote a substantive view of urbanism and believe it to be a genuine human good. The Charter does not say:

> The CNU views disinvestment in central cities, the spread of placeless sprawl, increasing separation by race and income, environmental deterioration, loss of agricultural lands and wilderness, and the erosion of society's built heritage as problems directly related to the triumph of the post-1945 suburban ideal—but we may be wrong. Should you disagree, well, we really can't say which of us (or whether either of us) might be right. But we really do like traditional cities, and we hope you will too....

On the contrary, the tenor of actual New Urbanist arguments is declarative and prescriptive, cumulatively both an ontological and a moral argument, an argument about the way things are as well as an argument about the way things should be. As such, the New Urbanist argument seems on its face to constitute an implicitly natural law argument—good or bad—on behalf of traditional urbanism; though this is a conclusion denied and rejected, often vehemently, by at least some New Urbanists.

Natural Law

My conversations with fellow New Urbanists have reminded me of the difficulty in an emotivist culture of achieving consensus about the meaning of natural law. Of necessity therefore I must begin to speak of natural law from out of a particular tradition of natural law thinking: in this instance the tradition that looks to Aristotle and Thomas Aquinas as intellectual touchstones for a community of inquiry that operates to this day not exclusively but most prominently in the intellectual tradition of the Catholic Church. But this tradition is not the only tradition of natural law theory. There is currently a revival of interest in natural law theory in both Protestant and Jewish circles; and there are strands of implicitly natural law thought in non-biblical/non-theistic religious and cultural traditions as well. Nevertheless, the Aristotelian-Thomist tradition has been particularly important if not foundational for natural law thinking throughout the whole of western culture. And although its methods are empirical and rational, I must nevertheless acknowledge here a point developed persuasively and at length by Alasdair MacIntyre, first in *After Virtue* and subsequently in *Whose Justice? Which Rationality?* viz.: that rationality is always rationality within a certain shared narrative structure, within a shared story—what sociologist Peter Berger has characterized as a "plausibility structure," another name for which is a tradition. Nevertheless, the fact that rationality can only be judged as such from within a tradition does not mean that truth claims made from within an intellectual tradition can not be universally true, as, for example we take the claims of science to be. But it does mean that the truth of such claims may or may not be apparent to those who are outside the intellectual tradition. In other words, considering here the example of natural law: although a tradition may make a genuinely rational and true argument on behalf of natural law and its universality, and although this argument may be understandable to some people outside the tradition, we nevertheless should not necessarily expect everyone everywhere to understand it. Something may be understandable but not necessarily understood; someone may possess the capacity to understand but not necessarily understand.

These caveats notwithstanding, the broad western understanding of natural law is that there are certain foundational principles of morality that are (according to St. Thomas) "the same for all, both as to knowledge and to rectitude"[4]—in other words, principles of morality that are not only right for all persons but knowable to all persons by reason alone (i.e., without need for divine revelation); and also at some level known to all persons who have attained the age of reason. These foundational principles of morality, along with their first few rings of implications, are known as the natural law.

The term "natural law" implies something about both nature and law. Of the two, "nature" seems the more difficult because of its multiple meanings. We speak of nature substantively, in the sense of everything that really exists (except God and other supernatural beings); or, alternatively, theists can speak of nature in the (slightly different) sense of "all created being/s." We say that it is in the nature of rocks to be hard or of turtles to be slow, in the sense of "characteristic of"; or we say that it is in the nature of male and female mammals to mate, in the sense of an instinct they possess. Likewise, we say that Michelangelo Buonarroti and Peter Paul Rubens personified the nature of a sculptor and a painter respectively, in the sense that they were exemplary of their kind, specimens of the full and appropriate development of a certain kind of artist.

In the case of the natural law, we generally mean that law is natural in two or maybe three different senses: first, in the sense of referring to something real, as in the judgment "murder is wrong" is not merely a subjective feeling or an illusion, but rather speaks of genuine knowledge about the objective moral character of a certain kind of act; and second in the sense that the purpose of the natural law is to help guide human beings from the way we are at any given moment in our lives toward our full and appropriate development as human beings, i.e., the achievement of our life's purpose, the fulfillment of our nature—per Aristotle's "the nature of a thing is its end, for what each thing is when fully developed we call its nature." We might also speak of a third sense in which law can be "natural": that such law is knowable by, authoritative for, and binding upon all human beings by virtue of the kind of beings we are by nature; and that while such law can be ignored or broken, we can do so only at peril to our own well being.

"Law" appears easier to define. St. Thomas contends that genuine law has four essential characteristics: law, he says, is "nothing else than an ordinance of reason for the common good, made by him who has care of the community, and promulgated."[5] In other words, Thomas argues first that genuine law is rational, something that right reason grasps as right; second, that it necessarily is for the common good rather than the good of a select few; third, that it must be initiated by the person or persons authorized to initiate it; and fourth, that it must be promulgated/announced/made known to those toward whom it is directed. And this is characteristic of all law, not merely the natural law.

To consider the adequacy of this definition of law, consider as a mental exercise item by item the negative of Thomas's definition. Most of us would object to a law that is unreasonable, or be suspicious of a law designed for special interests rather than the common good.[6] We would not recognize a law not both articulated and enacted; and we would not grant status to "laws" made by individuals who have not the authority to do so (which is but another way of saying that no human being is recognized by others as properly being, having, or making a law unto him or her self).

St. Thomas speaks of several different kinds of law, the relations between which are diagrammed in the digram below.[7] There are first the two broad categories of eternal law and human-made law (the latter of which is also called positive law). Under the category of the eternal law there are 1) the natural law, knowable through reason unaided by revelation; and 2) the divine law, known only by revelation and itself divided between the old law of the Hebrew scriptures and the new law of the Christian New Testament. The natural law consists of primary precepts, immediate precepts, and common precepts; and these in turn also inform the making of human/positive law (as do the old and new law in those human cultures existing within the biblical orbit and still influenced by it, here indicated by the dashed line linking the divine law to the positive law). The dashed arrows between the natural law and the divine law allude to some similarity and overlap between the natural and divine law, but also reiterate the idea that the natural law and the divine law are not identical.

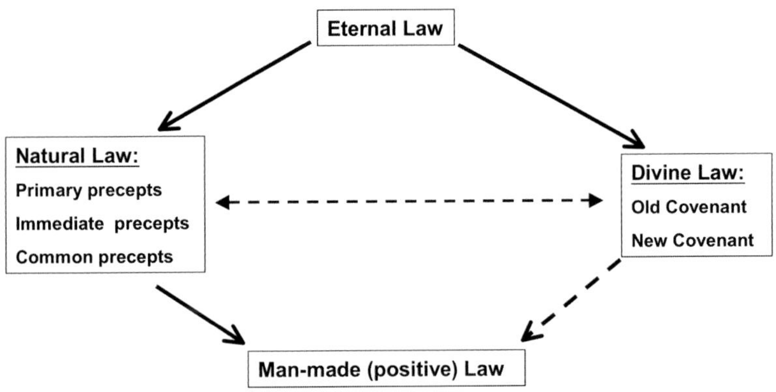

But let us consider St. Thomas's distinction between positive and natural law less abstractly. Positive law is made by man: 60-mph speed limits, life in prison for murder, zoning laws, and so on. The natural law is made by God. More specifically, the natural law is that part of the eternal law made by God that is immediately accessible to human reason without special revelation: e.g., that we know to not murder, to not steal, to be good, and so forth. The natural law, therefore, is discovered by human beings, whereas the positive law is made by human beings—but positive law is **made** by human beings always with reference to the natural law. Thus when a positive law contradicts the natural law, it is said to be an unjust law (e.g., a law requiring, or even allowing, all two-year old boys with, say, red hair or Down Syndrome to be killed). Likewise, although both natural law and positive law refer to property, the natural law does so in a general way (e.g., theft is wrong), while the positive law does so in a particular way (e.g., theft of a car will get you two years in prison). Positive law changes as circumstances change (you can't have a law against cloning until cloning is invented), while the natural law is eternal (deliberate killing of an innocent person is always and everywhere wrong).[8]

Most law that regulates human behavior is positive law; and positive law clearly differs not only from culture to culture, but even from city to city and town to town within the same larger culture. Nevertheless, any and all of these different positive laws can be truly legitimate so long as they are in accordance with and do not violate the natural law. Thus it is a mistake to think that in identifying the moral limits of human behavior (including human habitats) the natural law is somehow contrary to cultural pluralism. The natural lawyer simply maintains that there are certain behaviors that really are morally wrong for all persons in all places at all times. The contrary view is that there is no natural law, but rather only positive/human-made law. But if this latter point of view is true—if laws are made only by the powerful without reference to some constraining notion of right that I am here characterizing as the natural law—it follows that there are no human acts that are inherently and intrinsically wrong. If there really is no natural law, everything—at least potentially and in principle—is permissible.[9]

It seems important here to say a few things about what the natural law is not. The natural law is not "innate." We are not born knowing it, but rather with the capacity for knowing it and an inclination to it. A child is not born knowing that stealing is wrong; but as soon as a child is capable of understanding what is meant by "theft" and "wrong," he or she is capable of understanding that stealing in fact is wrong.[10] Natural law is not mere instinct; though it is not unrelated to certain biological realities of human beings as mammals and their implications for the practical requirements of love and child care in the context of families. Neither is natural law mere custom, though the customs of almost all times and places more or less acknowledge the natural law. Natural law is not simply a theory; rather it is a reality which theories attempt with greater or lesser success to describe. Finally, natural law is not a "law of nature" in the same sense that gravity is a "law of nature." Indeed, given Thomas's characterization of law, it is gravity that is a "law of nature" by analogy to natural law, since falling apples or rocks or other inanimate bodies are not freely and rationally aligning their behavior with a rule they know to be right.

With no Mosaic pretensions, here are ten precepts about which natural law theorists as well as ordinary people everywhere more or less agree,[11] to which I am going to propose an eleventh precept relevant to making human habitat (and eo ipso, New Urbanism). The first two are commonly regarded as primary precepts of the natural law—the moral axioms upon which all other moral precepts are based.

1) good should be pursued and evil avoided[12]
2) harm no one gratuitously

From these primary precepts are derived more or less by direct inference various immediate precepts, including the following (in no particular order):

3) render impartially what is due to every person (i.e., "be just")
4) do not take innocent human life
5) honor marriage and don't commit adultery
6) care for children and the elderly
7) be trustworthy
8) don't steal
9) treat others as you yourself would wish to be treated

The tenth precept is an example of a common precept of the natural law. More detailed than an immediate precept and more remote from the primary precepts, common natural law precepts are called "common" rather than "immediate" because there may be exceptions to them and because they may not be so widely known as the primary and immediate precepts. The tenth precept, concerning the principle of subsidiarity, is implicit in much of the Aristotelian–Thomist natural law tradition, but was not really recognized and articulated as a natural law principle until the first third of the 20th century, in response to the rise of the totalitarian state:

10) observe and obey the law of subsidiarity (viz., that—in the words of Pius XI's 1931 encyclical *Quadragesimo Anno*—it is wrong "to assign to a greater and higher association what lesser and subordinate associations can do"; i.e., larger institutions should not attempt to do what smaller institutions do better)

We remain some distance from a more detailed discussion of the Urban Transect. Nevertheless, insofar as the Urban Transect may be regarded not simply as a tool but also as a discovery, the historic specificity of its discovery and articulation is similar to the historic specificity of the discovery and articulation of the principle of subsidiarity, inasmuch as prior to the rise of sprawl the Urban Transect was likewise not in need of articulation. So here is an eleventh natural law precept, a new one describing something real but heretofore understood only implicitly. It is best thought of as a common natural law precept because it is not inferred directly from the primary precepts of the natural law, and because it requires arguments of the kind I am here offering—not least an argument about the Urban Transect—in order to recognize it as a natural law precept.

11) human beings should make mixed-use walkable settlements

Before I go into greater detail about why this eleventh precept should be considered a natural law precept, I must say just a bit more about what the natural law can and cannot do with respect to guiding moral behavior, both generally and with regard to the built environment. Note therefore that of the several natural law precepts I have proposed, some are formulated as positive admonitions and some as prohibitions. Alasdair MacIntyre has pointed out that most of us in the modern west have been taught either formally or informally to believe that moral behavior is primarily a matter of following rules. But this is not at all the meaning of moral behavior in the natural law tradition, which rather focuses upon the moral life as the development of good character habits, historically characterized as virtues or excellences.

It is impossible to overemphasize this point. To the list of natural law precepts I have cited one could easily add any number of positive admonitions: be courageous; be temperate; make good judgments; be magnanimous; be a friend; be steadfast; be faithful; be hopeful; love your neighbor. Moral behavior does entail prohibitions—against killing or harming the innocent, against theft, against bearing false witness—because certain acts are intrinsically destructive of those human communities necessary for individuals to discover and realize our good. Nevertheless, although obeying natural law prohibitions is obligatory, in the Aristotelian-Thomist intellectual tradition such rules are unquestionably secondary to the substance of the moral life. It is noteworthy, for instance, that Aristotle has no explicit theory of natural law; though he does have an extensively developed argument that the best life for individual human beings is the life of moral and intellectual virtue lived in community with others, and especially in a *polis.* Likewise, though St. Thomas develops a detailed theory of natural law in the *Summa,* his so-called *Treatise on Law* therein follows immediately after the *Treatise on Habits*—follows, that is, Thomas' detailed theory of the primacy of place in the moral life of virtues rather than rules.

Success in the moral life therefore entails not simply following rules, but, even more importantly, developing the habits of moral and intellectual excellence that enable us to live well both as individuals and as members of communities. Similarly, though it is necessary for urban designers, architects, builders and patrons to obey the natural law precept to make walkable mixed-use human settlements, this necessary obedience is not even close to being a sufficient condition for making good towns, neighborhoods, and cities. What is needed above all for making good urbanism is rather the productive reason and ability of artists (i.e., urban designers, architects, engineers, and builders), whose art is not only a matter of not breaking rules but much more of exercising skill and making good judgments, of knowing and being accountable to the highest standards of the art of urban design.

To engage in the making of something is to exercise "productive reason"; indeed, St. Thomas's very definition of art is "reason-in-making." In the Aristotelian-Thomist tradition the practices of architecture, urban design, or any other art at their highest levels have always been regarded as rational; it's just that the type of rationality they exhibit is not the speculative reason of the mathematician, scientist, or philosopher, but rather the productive reason of the artist. Discussion of the moral virtues, on the other hand, occurs under the rubric of "practical reason." Moral virtues are, collectively, the good character habits that enable human beings to negotiate our way successfully in the world; but whereas justice is the individual and corporate bond of human beings in political society, the foremost of the cardinal ("secular") virtues is prudence: the habit of making good judgments, especially in situations where virtues may be in conflict.

Thus when architect, principal of DPZ CoDesign, and CNU co-founder Andrés Duany says publicly, as he often does for rhetorical purposes, that New Urbanists both are and should be more interested in being practical than in being virtuous, he seems to be making a category mistake. The substance of Duany's argument may be summarized in the following variation of a familiar aphorism: prudential judgment requires that New Urbanists not allow the perfect to be the enemy of the good. Now there is nothing self-evidently wrong about this argument.[13] Duany's error is rather his apparent belief that in making pragmatic decisions he and we are acting outside the arena of morality, i.e., are not being "virtuous." This may be because Duany is failing to see prudential judgment as a virtue, or possibly because he is thinking of morality only in terms of rules.[14] Regardless, what makes prudence a virtue in the Aristotelian-Thomist tradition is precisely the necessity of good judgment not so much to decide between good and bad (such choices for most of us are relatively easy to determine, if not always so easy to act upon), but rather especially because good judgment is necessary to choose between conflicting goods in which no rule or set of rules can guarantee definitively the moral correctness of one's choice. Indeed, if we think of some popular films from the last twenty years or so—*Witness* or *The Fugitive* or *Babette's Feast*—what makes them dramatically compelling is less the conflict between good and evil found therein (but do note there is genuine evil represented in these stories, particularly in *Witness* and *The Fugitive*), but rather the conflict between goods: the rough justice of the Catholic Philadelphia cop who falls in love with the pacifist Amish woman whose son he is trying to protect; the conflict between the bulldog detective chasing down a fugitive who we (but not the detective) know to be innocent; the conflict between the self-chosen asceticism and good works of two rural Danish Lutheran pietist sisters and the urban Catholic sacramental sensibility of their Parisian housekeeper who unbeknownst to the sisters is a master chef. With whom does one identify and for whom does one cheer in these dramatic encounters? For me, it is hard to avoid identifying with and cheering for all of them; except that we recognize the inherently tragic circumstance that no single and contingent individual can choose and embody all these various goods, and that hard existential choices must be made.[15]

The Transect and Natural Law

The Congress for the New Urbanism has undertaken the revival and creation of traditional towns and neighborhoods in a physical context of sprawl and the legal and cultural context that promotes it. One of the ideas increasingly employed by New Urbanists is called the Transect, put forth by New Urbanists not only as a tool and intellectual construct, but also by some as a discovery and articulation of a general principle of both land use and historic human settlement.

Though several Transect diagrams exist, and many depictions are possible, the most common New Urbanist diagram of the Transect depicts six distinct Transect Zones (T-1 through T-6). Zones T-1 and T-2 refer to rural Transect Zones, but only in the most general way, insofar as such zones are considered with respect to the development of human habitat, with T-1 defined as uncultivated wilderness ("Natural") and T-2 as cultivated landscape ("Rural"). The Urban Transect—where human beings make settlements larger than the family—is described by zones T-3 through T-6, which together with zones T-1 and T-2 constitute the Transect proper. The Transect seeks and purports to describe some general conditions of good human settlements, and can itself be used as the basis for locally particular zoning codes. In this respect the Transect as a discovered principle is like the natural law, and particular zoning ordinances are like positive law—except that I am arguing here for identity rather than similitude. The Transect (or rather, the proposition that human beings should make walkable mixed-use settlements) is a natural law precept, and particular Transect-based zoning codes that promote walkable mixed-use settlements are positive laws.

Duany himself has referred to the Transect as a "natural law," adopting a dictionary definition of natural law as "a principle derived from the observation of nature by right reason and *thus* ethically binding in human society" (emphasis added); and likens natural law to Thomas Jefferson's references in the Declaration of Independence to "self-evident truths."[16] Duany's dictionary formulation of natural law seems to me almost but not quite right, better formulated had it said instead that a natural law precept is "a principle derived from the observation of nature and recognized by right reason to be ethically binding for individuals and human society." The problem with the formulation employed by Duany is the word "thus," which blithely purports to leap the huge chasm that in the modern world divides what we believe to be our extensive knowledge of what is from what we believe to be our excessively modest knowledge of what ought to be. But how we get from the "is" to the "ought" depends entirely upon our understanding of human nature: and specifically upon whether or not human beings even have a nature, and if there is a *telos* or end or good toward which all human beings are oriented that in fact defines our nature.[17]

Viewed in the light of New Urbanist efforts to recreate traditional urbanism in a modern legal, political, and cultural context, Duany's reference to Jefferson is particularly poignant. The Declaration of Independence refers at the outset to the separate and equal political station of a people "to which the Laws of Nature and Nature's God entitle them"; and continues with the assertion that all men are created equal and "endowed by their Creator with certain inalienable rights," including life, liberty, and the pursuit of happiness. Here we must note two things. The first is that although Jefferson is enumerating a list of inalienable human rights, he is careful to anchor them in an account of our divinely created status. In other words, for Jefferson and his colleagues the revolutionary implications of the idea of "inalienable (read 'natural') rights" follow from a traditional (if not in the Declaration extensively articulated) understanding of natural law. The second thing to note is the turn in modern culture subsequent to Jefferson, where increasingly we are confronted with assertions of natural rights (today more commonly characterized as "human rights") independent of their grounding in natural law. Thus there is no shortage today of persons appealing for recognition of their human rights; but what collection of intellectuals today—except for some religious intellectuals and (maybe) evolutionary psychologists—would or could in good intellectual faith write of "inalienable rights" and ground them in "the Laws of Nature"[18] (let alone "Nature's God")?[19] To so argue today would be (and is) perceived as a mark of cultural conservatism, not a dangerous political stance in a truly free society but unquestionably anathema in the secular academy and among the elites of modern high culture. Most human rights advocacy today is typically an appeal that some right be enshrined (or is already implicit) in positive law. But the authority of positive law itself—which has historically been grounded in natural law, and certainly was so at the time of the Declaration—is virtually nowhere articulated, but rather assumed as *sui generis*. Alas, this assumption represents a widespread cultural habit of mind that shrinks from the fact that rights created solely by positive law can likewise be invalidated solely by positive law—the very meaning of "alienable."[20] But even the Declaration itself originated at a moment in time where the understanding of "rights" and "laws" in western political philosophy, insofar as they increasingly were premised upon various social contract theories of human society, were being re-built upon faulty foundational mis-understandings of nature and human nature.[21]

But let us consider a Transect theory argument consistent with the way that New Urbanists actually use the Transect that also acknowledges two prominent contentions implicit in the Charter for the New Urbanism itself, previously cited: 1) that conventional post-war sprawl development is unjust; and 2) that conventional post-war sprawl is culturally and environmentally unsustainable. Taking these factors into account, I offer the following definition of the Urban Transect:

The Urban Transect refers to that range of human habitats that support human flourishing, within which human settlements are part of a sustainable eco-system.[22] These habitats, depicted diagrammatically as Transect Zones, range from less dense areas to more dense areas within neighborhoods; but each urban T-Zone denotes a walkable and mixed-use human environment wherein within each or from each urban T-Zone many if not most of the necessities and activities of daily life are within a five- to-ten-minute walk for persons of varying ages and economic classes.

This definition of the Urban Transect owes much to a larger discussion of the Transect that has been occurring among New Urbanists for several years now. Nevertheless, while I acknowledge my debt to that discussion, the definition of and claims for the Urban Transect that I am here putting forth may or may not find wider support among New Urbanists, in part because I am trying to make more precise what some New Urbanists perhaps prefer to leave ambiguous.[23] But while there are surely occasions when prudential judgment warrants ambiguity rather than precision, this appears to me not to be one of them, at least insofar as current New Urbanist ambiguity about the nature of our own claims on behalf of traditional urbanism and the Transect may more reflect intellectual confusion than justifiable strategy.

The first thing to note about this definition of the Transect, therefore, is its generality. The New Urbanist Transect diagrams, as well as the specific examples of T-Zones, are inevitably culturally specific; but the idea of the Transect is general and could be represented in a variety of cultural modes. Indeed, in this understanding, specific towns and cities in the world—each presumably reflecting a locally specific climate, within a locally specific culture and economy—relate to the Transect in a way exactly analogous to the relationship of culturally specific positive laws to the natural law.

The second thing to note is that this definition of the Transect is normative: it is intentionally defined not only to include good forms of human settlement but also to exclude bad forms of human settlement.[24] Although this definition of the Transect acknowledges and leaves room for a wide variety of human settlements—from the single-family house of the village T-3 to the dense mixed-use blocks of London T-6—it nevertheless does not include every form of human settlement; it makes distinctions. A normative definition of the Transect proposes that we really can distinguish between good and bad human settlements with respect to human flourishing and environmental sustainability. It suggests, for example, that large parts of late 18th-century Manchester, England—where human life expectancy was about one-half what it was in the adjacent countryside—really were bad human settlements, for both human beings and local ecosystems; that large parts of contemporary Mexico City really are bad forms of human settlement that need to be reclaimed and ought not to be emulated; that the post-World War II sprawl developments of, in and around the historic lowlands of New Orleans really are bad human settlements with respect to the long-term flourishing of local communities.

The tragedy in New Orleans from Hurricane Katrina in particular raises larger general questions about conventional post-war sprawl development. Following are some of the problems commonly associated with sprawl, problems that are either direct consequences or unintended byproducts of sprawl's physical patterns of development:

- sprawl systematically separates different human activities from each other and makes them accessible only by car, which makes it impossible for people to both live and work, shop, play, learn, or worship within the context of a walkable neighborhood
- sprawl effectively de-mobilizes and disenfranchises those without cars and those unable to drive, notably children (whose parents must become chauffeurs) and the elderly
- sprawl injures the common good by concentrating both wealth and poverty; by separating people by income, age, and race; and by failing to provide a genuinely public realm shared by all
- because sprawl separates housing settlements by class, it promotes extreme inequality of educational opportunity
- sprawl hastens the loss of agricultural lands and wilderness, and the monocultural single-use unwalkable settlements it creates are not worth the tradeoff
- sprawl, by its automobile-dependent lifestyle, both increases air pollution and discourages national energy self-sufficiency in a period of global political conflict
- sprawl, by its automobile-dependent lifestyle, contributes to North America's currently unprecedented rates of obesity
- sprawl is ugly, and produces nothing in the public realm worthy of civic and aesthetic contemplation
- although suburbia has become a cultural ideal, it is a contradictory ideal because sprawl consumes the landscape that is the very substance of its promise
- and finally, sprawl is culturally problematic and undermines the common good because its dynamic is self-contradictory. Sprawl is unable to deliver on its promise of convenience, mobility, natural beauty, individual freedom, and well-being for all. Hence the phenomenon that often the persons most recently arrived at the fringes of suburbia are also the persons most vociferously opposed to its continuing extension, the political phenomenon that has come to be known as NIMBYism—"Not In My Back Yard."

The inference to draw is that because the formal patterns of sprawl encourage unjust, ugly, and socially and environmentally unsustainable human settlements, therefore 1) sprawl development should not be emulated and perpetuated; and 2) sprawl development should not be regarded as part of the Transect.

I am contending here that the arguments New Urbanists already make on behalf of traditional urbanism cumulatively (if only implicitly) constitute a natural law argument: viz., that traditional urbanism is an objective good not simply by virtue of its aesthetics nor simply by virtue of its utility, but by virtue of its promotion of both the good of individuals and the common good as these goods are implied in the Charter. But as I have alluded, this contention meets resistance among some (by no means all) New Urbanists, mostly colleagues active on one or several New Urbanist related listserv discussion groups. So what exactly are the objections I encounter to my contention that New Urbanists both do and should argue for our urban objectives from natural law assumptions? Essentially, there are four:

1) that natural law arguments are "conservative" arguments (and therefore shouldn't be associated with the Congress for the New Urbanism);
2) that natural law arguments are used by those who oppose homosexual marriage and legalized abortion (and therefore shouldn't be associated with the Congress for the New Urbanism);
3) that natural law arguments presume that human beings have a "nature" (and therefore shouldn't be associated with the Congress for the New Urbanism); and
4) that natural law arguments imply the existence of God (and therefore shouldn't be associated with the Congress for the New Urbanism).

To the first objection I would say that although many if not most persons who hold the Aristotelian-Thomist view of natural law are indeed cultural conservatives, this does not necessarily make them political conservatives (which is what I take to be the underlying concern). Like New Urbanism itself, both support for and criticism of natural law theory come from across the contemporary political spectrum. "Conservative" Libertarians, for example, appear to have little use either for the positive estimation within the natural law tradition of the legitimate authority of government, or for the natural law notion that the common good—including the idea of a public realm—is something more than the sum of individual desires. Likewise, Martin Luther King Jr.'s "Letter from a Birmingham Jail," a foundational document of the "liberal" 1960s civil rights movement, is an explicit appeal for political rights grounded in a natural law understanding of justice. Again, prior to the Supreme Court's *Roe v. Wade* decision of 1973 and the contemporary Democratic Party's enthusiastic embrace of that decision and its implications, Catholics voted overwhelmingly Democratic; and about half of them still do today. But more importantly with respect to this particular New Urbanist objection—and setting aside the interesting if unspoken assumption that political liberals have a monopoly on correct thinking about the relationship of good urbanism to the common good—it is the natural law insistence upon objective standards of justice that offers the only non-theistic [sic] intellectual justification for protecting the weaker members of society from the stronger members of society, a concern that has traditionally been a moral cornerstone of the liberal social agenda.

To the second objection I would say first that because its *raison d'etre* is the formal order of a common public realm, it would be imprudent for the Congress for the New Urbanism to take any official or collective position at all on the issues of homosexual marriage and legalized abortion. That said, the more important point is that just because there is disagreement about the implications of the natural law when applied to one issue or set of issues does not mean that there cannot be consensus about the implications of the natural law for another issue or set of issues. Considering, for example, the fact that most of the arguments one hears in favor of homosexual marriage are also themselves either implicitly natural law arguments (well-conceived or badly) from justice or about "human (read natural) rights," the fact that there are natural law arguments against homosexual marriage clearly does not constitute a persuasive argument that therefore there is no such thing as natural law and that it is irrelevant to making human settlements.

The third objection—that natural law theory presumes human beings have a nature—is a much more serious and substantive complaint, because the history of much of the modern west is premised upon the idea that there is no such thing as human nature, and that human beings are both self-made and infinitely malleable. The unfortunate consequences of that belief for both global and domestic politics and human habitat in the 20th century are evident; and from these negative witnesses as well as positive witnesses from history, anthropology, natural law theory, biology, and traditional human habitats themselves, it is not unreasonable to infer that human beings do indeed have a nature—the existence of which does not in the least diminish the influence, significance, and necessity of good culture for human flourishing. If the idea implicit in the Charter of the New Urbanism that human beings have a nature is less clearly articulated in the Charter than in natural law theory, drawing out that implication from the Charter is both an immediate and long-term objective of this essay.

Finally, the fourth objection, which in fact is related to the third—that natural law theory implies the existence of God. I agree that it does. Nevertheless, this last New Urbanist objection to natural law and natural law theory is particularly problematic because recognition of the requirements of natural law by definition does not depend upon theological premises, even if one may draw theological conclusions from natural law requirements, precisely because one also may not draw theological conclusions from them. The objection appears, therefore, to reside in a fear among some (by no means all) New Urbanists of religious believers who bring their beliefs to bear upon law and public policy, a fear of "bringing God into civic affairs." But to the extent that natural law theorists make any theological claims whatsoever on the basis of natural law, such claims are *a posteriori* conclusions drawn from observed human moral beliefs and behaviors—including, possibly, the moral beliefs (cf. the Charter) and behaviors of New Urbanists who are atheists and agnostics as well as theists.

So here I would make two points: first, the lesser point that it's too late for New Urbanists to "keep God out of civic affairs" because for better or worse most human beings generally (and Americans in particular) have always brought God into civic affairs; and second, the more important point that—without any theistic arguments whatsoever, either *a priori* or *a posteriori*—New Urbanist arguments for traditional urbanism already have both the structure and the substance of natural law arguments. For some New Urbanists to deny that this is true because others—including other New Urbanists—may draw theistic conclusions from natural law theory seems to me a case of cutting off the New Urbanist practical nose to spite the New Urbanist theoretical face. New Urbanists are either making claims for the objective goodness of traditional urbanism—and hence a moral imperative to make good urbanism—or we are not. If we are, this has at the very least realist metaphysical implications.[25] New Urbanists can hardly make a credible intellectual claim that traditional urbanism is a genuine good, but all other goods are relative.[26]

Many of the leading architectural figures of the Congress for the New Urbanism have worked hard to overcome the dogmatic modernist architectural and urban ideologies they learned in architecture school. But although New Urbanists have begun to wean ourselves away from the ideology of modernist urbanism and to relearn the art of traditional urban design, to the extent that we still recoil from the notion of obligation—even as we evangelize others on behalf of the goodness of traditional urbanism—we have still not weaned ourselves from the individualist and emotivist moral sensibilities of the modern world. There remains, I fear, a modernist anthropology very near the heart of New Urbanism that I suspect is in fact incompatible with traditional urban culture and New Urbanism's own professed urban and cultural objectives; and the danger of this, as always, is that an incorrect understanding of human nature has detrimental consequences for the making of our cities. If we misunderstand human nature, we will surely not make good cities.

For New Urbanists, the merit of the natural law intellectual tradition is that it allows us to argue in good faith for why traditional urbanism is a genuine human good and why suburbia is objectively problematic. By attending to the complex inter-relationship between biology, culture, and human agency with respect to individual and collective human behavior, and without denying either our social or biological natures, the natural law intellectual tradition draws us away from modernist temptations to social and/or biological determinism by its dogged insistence that character is the key to civilization, not only in terms of social justice and human happiness, but also in terms of artistic production and aesthetics. It reminds us that it is a false objective to seek what T.S. Eliot called "social arrangements so perfect that they will make us good." And it allows us as architects and urban designers to steer ourselves away from sterile notions of the *zeitgeist* and personal "authenticity" in favor of the more fecund language of craftsmanship and of moral and intellectual and artistic excellence.

1. In the characterizations of natural law that follow I am particularly indebted to extended conversations with Jay Budziszewski, Benjamin Lipscomb, Randall Smith, Dino Marcantonio, Domiane Forte, and Michael Benedikt; though I do not assume they will necessarily agree with everything that follows.

2. Here I would encourage the reader to not confuse New Urbanism with the easy caricatures and mis-characterizations of its critics: e.g., that New Urbanism is primarily about front porches (which is characteristic of many New Urbanist projects but not all; and certainly in New Urbanist thinking not prerequisite for good urbanism), or primarily about traditional architectural styles (about which there is much debate among New Urbanists, and which is explicitly not an "article of faith" in the Charter of the New Urbanism), or primarily just a different form of suburban development. Because New Urbanism makes a conscientious effort to succeed in the contemporary marketplace—note well however that although the New Urbanist definition of "success" would include the notion of "success in the marketplace," its definition of success is hardly exhausted by this notion—these are all features of some New Urbanist developments. Nevertheless, the essential New Urbanist objective is to promote the creation of traditional towns, neighborhoods and cities; and specifically to do this in a cultural and legal context that currently at best discourages and at worst forbids the creation of such settlements. By the standards of excellence to which New Urbanists aspire, even the best New Urbanist projects at this point invariably fall short. What critics of New Urbanism generally overlook, however, is that no good traditional city or town ever became so overnight; and that today nobody other than the New Urbanists are even attempting to systematically challenge the legal regime and cultural habits and mind-set of post-WWII suburban sprawl development.

3. See the Congress for the New Urbanism web site: http://www.cnu.org/cnu_reports/Charter.pdf.

4. Summa Theologica, Part I of Second Part, Question 94. Article 4 (I-II 94, 4).

5. Ibid., I-II 90, 4.

6. This common sense of the nature of law as existing for the common good is of course very different from the way contemporary legislators, jurists, and legal theorists typically think about the law. Edward Oakes, in his review of Craig Bernthal's "The Trial of Man: Christianity and Judgment in the World of Shakespeare" in the June/July 2004 issue of *First Things* (p. 45–46) quotes Bernthal's characterization of law as it is understood in the modern west:

The prevailing theory of law in our time is that the law is rational, utilitarian and secular. Legislators create rules to accomplish policy objectives. Laws are the instruments used to promote the finite material interests of particular groups and individuals. Judges, in reaching decisions, use legal precedents to solve problems, not to propound universal truths or to make the will of God explicit. Laws are not evaluated with respect to any universal standard of right and wrong, but by workability.

Oakes contrasts this with the view of law that prevailed in Shakespeare's England (among both Protestants and Catholics). "For Elizabethans," writes Oakes, "positive law derives from natural law, which itself flows from the divine will. This means above all that a just verdict in a human court must in some way reflect, and be validated by, the divine verdict; and when the two diverge, divine judgment waits in the wings and will not ultimately be stayed or thwarted. For example...the great Anglican [legal theorist and] divine Richard Hooker asserts: 'The judgments of God do not always follow crimes as thunder follows lightning, but sometimes the space of many ages comes between...'"

Few if any New Urbanists describe traditional urbanism, the imperative to make traditional urbanism, and the deficiencies of post-WWII suburban sprawl environments, in such Elizabethan terms. Nevertheless, New Urbanist arguments for traditional urbanism are not substantially different from Hooker's: there is hell to pay (so to speak) both environmentally and socially for human beings who habitually and systematically make human settlements that are not mixed-use and walkable. Moreover, as I have already suggested, the Charter of the New Urbanism itself describes its traditional urban objectives not as a special interest but rather in terms of the common good. This suggests one of two things: either the Charter is an exercise in bad faith, presenting itself as something it is not; or its objectives are better described in terms of implicit natural law assumptions than by the utilitarian/interest-group understanding of law common to the modern age. New Urbanists will have to decide for ourselves whether we wish to represent ourselves as just another special interest group; and if not, whether we wish to be intellectually coherent.

7. My concern in this essay is only with the relationship of natural law to urbanism. St. Thomas, as a Christian, was concerned (as the diagram indicates) with explaining the relationship of the natural law to the revealed law of Christian scripture; but this particular issue, however interesting in itself, is neither essential nor opposed to the intellectual coherence of New Urbanism.

8. I am indebted to Dino Marcantonio for the succinctness and clarity of these characterizations.

9. A friendly critic—who I'll not identify here but who I promise does exist—objects to this formulation; and with some exasperation urges I drop it "because [it's] not true: Atheists, humanists, existentialists, evolutionists, Taoists, Zoroastrians, Confucians, Buddhists and secular moralists of all kinds—utilitarians, virtue ethicists, Kantians, Pragmatists—are all capable of arguing that certain actions really are bad and wrong from every point of view, and can do so without reference to a biblically styled (or any) God. (E.g., natural law may come from…nature, as sociobiologists argue.) Besides which, traditional western believers have the prevalence of evil in a God-ruled world to account for, as you well know, plus innumerable instances of God not seeming to obey his own natural/eternal law (e.g., not preventing the [deaths] of innocent human lives by the thousands a day world over….). Bottom line: you cannot here imply as self-evident the statement: Believe in Aquinas's God-endorsed natural law or 'everything is permissible.'"

Setting aside the issue of theodicy—which is a genuine problem for biblical religion, but not, I think, for natural law theory—and noting also that the provenance of natural law is human behavior, I think my critic's objection proves my point. For I did not say (though I do think) "if there is no God everything is permissible." Rather, more modestly, I said "if there is no natural law everything is permissible." In response I am advised of large numbers of non-theists who do not think everything is permissible. But it is exactly the human sense that not all things are permissible—objectively, "from every point of view"—that I am characterizing as evidence of and for the natural law. My point is not that one must believe in God in order to believe in natural law; my critic helpfully provides a whole list of persons who do not believe in God but do believe that some things are intrinsically bad and wrong. But since the notion that some things are intrinsically bad and wrong is one of the implications of natural law, my original point stands.

10. St. Paul writes that there is a moral law distinct from divinely revealed law which is "written on the heart" of every person (Romans 2:15), suggesting there is a correspondence between every individual's inner capacity for moral knowledge and the objective moral order of the universe. An obvious analogy here is with mathematics, which on the one hand seems purely a product of the human mind, but on the other hand seems to correspond in ways both observable and yet to be discovered with the physical structure of the universe. The reason this can be so—in the realms of both morality and mathematics—is because human beings are ourselves part of the same universe we are seeking to understand, and share its basic structure.

11. I am loath to suggest a putatively exhaustive list of natural law precepts. Both St. Thomas and John Calvin contend that one of the reasons that human beings require a specially revealed and specific divine law is because all but the most highly abstract principles of the natural law can be driven or obscured from the human mind by ignorance or by the corruption of sin (see, e.g., *Summa Theologica*, I-II 94, 4). Thomas also offers as one of the principal justifications for a positive divine law that people reason very imperfectly in matters of natural law (ibid., I-II 91, 4). And Calvin adds that "the Lord has provided us with a written law [i.e., the Torah, or old law] to give us a clearer witness of what was too obscure in the natural law, [to] shake off our listlessness, and [to] strike more vigorously our mind and memory" (*Institutes of the Christian Religion*, Book II, Chapter VIII, Section 1).

12. This first natural law precept is the equivalent in practical reason of the law of non-contradiction in speculative reason: that "a" cannot simultaneously be both "a" and "non-a" at the same time and in the same respect. See Thomas Aquinas, op. cit., I-II 94, 2.

13. At times of course the excellent does have to be defended tenaciously even in order to advance the good. European architect Leon Krier, the intellectual godfather of New Urbanism and a major influence upon Duany's work, once famously declared that he did not and would not build buildings in the context of the contemporary world of sprawl precisely because he—Krier—is an architect. Happily, Krier has reconsidered, in part because he has been provided the opportunity to design prominent buildings in the context of DPZ-designed traditional town plans. But ethically speaking, both Krier's strict position and Duany's more flexible posture can be defended as moral behaviors insofar as they represent exercises of prudential judgment: each is a penultimate and strategic position adopted in the service of the telos of good urbanism. My own sense, unavoidably informed by my own Catholic/catholic sensibilities, is that individual prudential judgments are necessarily related to and in part justified by the particular vocation (in the full religious/existential sense of that term) of the individual making the judgment—presuming both that the vocational end being sought is a genuine good and that the means employed in its pursuit is not in violation of the natural law.

14. Another possibility is that Duany is quite aware that prudence is both practical and a virtue, but simply appealing to the vestigial transgressive fantasies and emotivist sensibilities of his audience.

15. In a religious framework these tragic choices are redeemed, making the dramatic narrative in fact inherently comic—as "Babette's Feast" exhibits explicitly.

16. Andrés Duany, "Introduction to the Special Issue: The Transect," *Journal of Urban Design*, Vol.7, No.3

(2002), p. 253. Duany's dictionary source is uncited, but his own gloss on the idea of the Transect as a natural law is worth quoting: "The Transect...can be observed anywhere and everywhere. [It] emerged organically in human settlement, preceding any conceptual formulation. That it is timeless and cross-cultural can be easily observed by walking from the center to the outskirts of Pompeii. It is illustrated in Chinese scrolls and assumed by the Spanish Laws of the Indies. It is still inhabited in thousands of towns and cities in the United States. The Transect as a natural law may be immanent, but its suppression by modernist transportation and zoning has catalysed the current need to re-present it as a viable alternative theory."

17. The famous modern difficulty of deriving evaluative judgments from descriptive accounts—that is, to describe something that is as something that is good or is bad—only exists to the extent that moderns deny that human beings have a nature. In cultures and/or sub-cultures where there is greater consensus about the purpose of being a human being, there is no more trouble commonly recognizing from empirical observation a "good" human being than modern sports fans have recognizing that Derek Jeter is a "good" baseball player, or that Tiger Woods is a "good" golfer.

18. There are arguments from contemporary socio-biologists and evolutionary psychologists that purport to demonstrate that sociability and cooperation are "hard-wired" into the human brain as an evolutionary survival mechanism—a materialist hypothesis that to me seems merely to corroborate the Aristotelian observation that "Man is by nature a social/political animal" [emphasis added]. Thus we are to understand from the evolutionary psychologists that human beings have evolved "instincts" that dispose us to act in ways that pre-moderns would have characterized as virtuous; and that these instincts rather than some notion of natural law are or should be the natural foundation for morality and the positive legal codification of rights. The problem here is not the idea that morality, laws, and rights are properly grounded in our biological nature; or even the idea that our instincts (affected also by culture) have "evolved." The problem is rather that human beings cannot ground morality, laws, and rights in our instincts alone, because we in fact have warring instincts. By what instinctual criteria therefore do we determine which of our instincts to follow? Why ought I to be cooperative today when I am actually feeling more aggressive? I'm not sure what answer the socio-biologists can give in defense of cooperation (or even aggression)—or counsel about the same in any particular existential circumstance—other than in terms of some argument either about what is "really good" for me or in terms of what is "the right thing" to do. But really good and the right thing are themselves natural law categories that reflect a teleological view of human nature; and even though the moral force of doing the right thing that is really good for me is indeed grounded in human biology, it necessarily transcends any materialist assumption that the universe is nothing more than matter-in-motion and lacking a teleological structure. Nietzsche provided a different and more lucid argument on behalf of an ethic grounded solely in a materialist view of nature and instinct; but his conclusions about the primacy of the will-to-power were quite the opposite of (and to me more plausible than) the conclusions of the evolutionary psychologists, who take as a premise the goodness of the behaviors they wish to justify in strictly materialist terms. This is not to say that the evolutionary psychologists are wrong about either the goodness of the virtues or their grounding in human biology; only rather that Nietzsche better understood the moral and social implications of the materialist metaphysic.

19. This reticence of modern intellectuals suggests of course that the "self-evident truths" presumed by the signers of the Declaration are perhaps not so self-evident. But as Hadley Arkes has written: "[T]he founders never meant 'evident' to every 'self' who happened down the street. As Aquinas pointed out, 'it [is] true for all that the three angles of a triangle are together equal to two right angles, although it is not known to all.' A self-evident truth was something that could be grasped as true per se nota, as something true in itself, with the force of an axiom. When it came to 'all men are created equal,' it was a matter of grasping, with Aristotle, the distinctions that ran between humans and other animals. Even in this age of 'animal liberation' the partisans of animal rights still do not sign labor contracts with their horses and cows. Nor do they seek the informed consent of their household pets before they authorize surgery on them. But we continue to think that beings who can understand reasons over matters of right and wrong deserve to be ruled with the rendering of reasons, in a regime that elicits their consent." (Hadley Arkes, "The Rights and Wrongs of Alan Dershowitz," *The Claremont Review of Books, Volume V, Number 4,* Fall, 2005.) A similar line of reasoning, by the way, may be pertinent to the moral authority of the Urban Transect as a discovered principle: It may be true for all that human beings should make walkable mixed-use settlements, though it is not known to all.

20. This exact point is made succinctly by Fr. Edward Oakes, S.J. in his review of Rabbi David Novak's Natural Law in Judaism ("Nature as Law and Gift," *First Things* 93 (May 1999), p. 44–51): "[N]atural law... provides the only possible long–term grounding for human rights [because] only a theory of natural law can rescue the campaign for human rights from being anything more than disguised power politics or cultural imperialism. The idea of human rights has usually assumed that these rights can simply be posited without the enunciation of any ontology underlying them, that they create themselves as it were...But unlike the idea of human rights, [the concept of natural law] does not claim to be self–constituting. By its real assertion of nature, it indicates that it is rooted in an order that transcends any immanent society. Here is where it parts company with [modern] liberalism."

21. Again Oakes, ibid.: "[T]he modern problem really lies in the fact that so many Enlightenment thinkers

relied on a concept of 'natural' that was anything but a reflection of human nature as it actually exists... [T]oo much of natural law theory, especially that derived from those thinkers from Grotius on who transposed natural law into natural rights (which after the French Revolution usually became known as 'human rights'), relies on a concept of nature that is not natural. Vast swaths of political theory stemming from the Enlightenment speak of human beings as pre–social monads whose sociality stems from a subsequent decision to join a group from a prior isolation....This notion...is called the theory of 'the social contract.' Unfortunately for its advocates and despite its vast influence, it is a total fiction, a complete distortion of the nature of the social life of humans. The absence of any historically authentic social contract in the life of primitive man makes all political theories founded on this airy cloud equally fictional. Most people today categorize political divisions into the binary categories of liberal and conservative...A much more central dichotomy in modern politics, however, is rooted in those who accept the fiction of a social contract and those who see it for the fiction that it is. [The] view...that accepts the social contract theory leads to a hyper–individualism...The position that recognizes the social contract as a fiction, however, sees community as the locus for individual meaning...[H]ere is where an authentic theory of natural law proves to be indispensable...but only when the social contract theory is abandoned, a task that [quoting David Novak] 'requires radical criticism of the key political idea of the Enlightenment,...that human beings can construct their own primary society autonomously...' Once it is recognized that the notion of a social contract is a fiction and that human sociality is an essential component of human nature, it then becomes immediately clear that community takes priority, not over the individual as such...but over society... [A]ll contractual relationships are first founded on a prior community of kinship relations, which themselves are founded on ineluctable biological realities of mammalian life: mother/child, begetter/conceiver, infant/adult, and so forth. Human sociality is entirely an outgrowth and expression of these unavoidable relationships, which are no more 'agreed upon' by some hypothetical caucus of Australopithecenes than is human existence itself. No one chooses to be born, or to be born male or female, etc., nor does anyone in primitive communities choose the role of hunter, gatherer, and so on. Even later social identities of status—king, shaman, crone, warrior, matriarch, seer—are grounded in these more fundamental mammalian relations and not in some fictitious contract or verbal agreement. In other words...the individual always comes from society (in the wider sense), not to it."

22. A distinction between "sustainable" and "biologically diverse" eco-systems is important. Biologists and environmentalists tell us that preserving bio-diversity in the aggregate is important for preserving earth's eco-system as a whole. Hence the practical necessity of T1/Natural zones as part of the larger Transect, in addition to the aesthetic imperatives to preserve wilderness that together help shape our common and proper human understanding of the obligation of environmental stewardship. But it seems to me that the important environmental issue with regard to making human habitat is not that every local species of flora and fauna be preserved (e.g., that there must be trout streams in T6 zones; or that mosquitoes must not be harmed) but rather that the urban environment must be environmentally sustainable, in the sense that it is imperative that human habitat not disrupt or destroy the immediate environmental conditions that make human flourishing itself possible—literally and metaphorically, that human beings must not spoil our own air and water.

23. My positing in this essay of a normative definition of the Urban Transect in the interest of greater precision is only the most important of several thoughts about the Transect that I perhaps do not share with other New Urbanist Transect theorists. But if a normative definition of the Urban Transect seems to me fundamental (see note 24 below), the points that follow may be more like issues about which thoughtful urbanists of good will simply disagree. For example: I concur with most of my New Urbanist colleagues that urban T-Zones can be regarded as "locally calibrated,"—meaning that what is T3 ("Sub-Urban") or T6 ("Urban Core") in Italy or Indonesia may not be T3 or T6 in the United States. Nevertheless, I think that with regard to absolute density T-Zones should be regarded as similar; and also that it is not necessarily the case that every human settlement must have every one (or even most) of the urban T-Zones within its borders. (While the T3 Zone is rightly regarded as "sub-urban" and thereby dependent on one or more higher, more urban, T-Zones, some settlements, particularly in some cultures outside of the U.S., may thrive with only one or two of the more urban habitats.) Or to take a second example: Should the Urban Transect diagram include Districts (which are defined as large parcels of land devoted to a single-use, e.g., hospitals, colleges, power generating plants, modern convention/exhibition facilities, etc.)? In my opinion, it should not; not because single-use Districts are not to be permitted or because Districts don't occur or because Districts are not needed, but simply because Districts are exceptional whereas the Transect diagram is typical and normative. Or, to take a third example, with respect to what appears to be the temptation of some New Urbanists to view the Transect as the comprehensive organizing principle of all of life: Are some rural-to-urban "transects"—e.g., rural-to-urban gradients not merely of human habitat but of human artifacts such as shoes, hats, building styles—better understood as manifestations of custom and tradition (i.e., as cultural) rather than as natural? That is: are some rural-to-urban gradients more analogous to positive law than natural law? In my opinion, absolutely yes—considering, for example, that there may be local manifestations of the Rural-to-Urban Transect Zones in which the human occupants don't even have shoes or hats.

24. It is possible to define the Urban Transect descriptively rather than normatively, as a gradation of every conceivable human habitat. However, since we New Urbanists are obviously evangelists on behalf of a normative idea of urbanism, if we don't use the Transect as an intellectual tool to help us identify and promote normative urbanism, then we are going to have to find some other intellectual tool to describe and articulate our normative agenda. I would argue, therefore, that my proposal here to define the Transect as normative commends itself not least because a normative understanding of the Transect is so eminently practical.

25. I'm willing to pursue this point further here, not as an article of New Urbanist faith but simply in the interest of truth. The modern world's denials of human nature, natural law, and God together constitute a foundational dilemma the practical effects of which manifest themselves in numerous existential, political, and cultural dilemmas of modern life. The foundational dilemma can be described as something like this: If human beings have no nature, then we have no natural telos or purpose. And what this has meant in the modern world, where the belief that human beings have no nature is widespread, is that rather than the purpose of an individual life being to discover one's unique vocation—literally, one's calling from God; i.e., that work which an individual needs to do both for his or her own gladness and for the world's—rather than discovering one's own vocation (which in the modern view is an illusion) one instead makes an artifact of one's life. More precisely, one is forced to become the artisan of one's own life because one has no un-chosen obligations. The implication of there being no natural law (and eo ipso, no God) is that there are no un-chosen obligations; and therefore, as I've suggested earlier, that everything—genocide, murder, chattel slavery, cloning, totalitarian politics, abortion, sprawl—is in principle permitted, if only as an aesthetic and experiential "choice." To be clear, I am not suggesting that persons who deny the existence of natural law therefore favor any or all of these aforementioned practices; rather only observing that to the extent that such persons regard any of these practices as intrinsically (as opposed to merely situationally) wrong, they are thereby implicitly affirming the existence of the natural law. Nor is it germane for the non-believers in natural law to point out that some believers in natural law have at times supported some of these activities; because the obvious inference of this criticism is that the believers, by engaging in such practices, have themselves behaved immorally, i.e., in violation of the natural law.

26. In contending here that building in accordance with the Urban Transect—i.e., making mixed-use walkable settlements—is properly understood as a moral imperative, it is no part of my contention that individual urbanites (including New Urbanists) are necessarily and inherently "more moral" than persons who live in sprawl suburbs. It is my contention that acquiring the virtues necessary to living a good life generally does require communities of propinquity, which are both more numerous and more accessible in traditional urban environments than in sprawl environments. It is therefore by these criteria that efforts to build more of the former and fewer of the latter, as cultural and institutional conditions permit, should be regarded as morally obligatory to all persons possessing right (practical) reason.

THE SMART CODE AS TRANSECT TOOL

ANDRÉS DUANY & SANDY SORLIEN

Consider the most-loved towns of North America. They were either carefully planned, or they evolved as compact, mixed-use places because of their geography and the limits of the transportation and economics of their time. However, over the past 60 years, places have evolved in a completely different pattern. They have spread loosely along highways and haphazardly across the countryside, enabled by the widespread ownership of automobiles, by cheap gasoline and cheap land, and by a generalized increase in wealth.

Such patterns are enabled by zoning codes that separate dwellings from workplaces, shops, and schools. These codes include design standards that favor the automobile over the pedestrian, and are unable to resist the homogenizing effects of globalization.

These practices have produced banal housing subdivisions, business parks, strip shopping, big box stores, enormous parking lots, and sadly gutted downtowns. They have caused the proliferation of drive-by eateries and billboards. They have made walking or cycling dangerous or unpleasant. They have made children, the elderly, and the poor utterly dependent on those who can drive, even for ordinary daily needs. They have caused the simultaneous destruction of both towns and open space—the 20th-century phenomenon known as sprawl.

The form of our built environment needs a 21st-century correction. But in most places it is actually illegal to build in a traditional neighborhood pattern. The existing codes prevent it. In most places people do not have a choice between sprawl and traditional urbanism. Codes favor sprawl and isolated residential subdivisions. It is not a level playing field.

The SmartCode was created to deal with this problem at the point of decisive impact—the intersection of law and design. It is a form-based code, meaning it envisions and encourages a certain physical outcome—the form of the region, community, block, and/or building. Form-based codes are fundamentally different from conventional codes that are based primarily on use and statistics—none of which envision or require any particular physical outcome.

The SmartCode is a tool that guides the form of the built environment in order to create and protect development patterns that are compact, walkable, and mixed-use. These traditional neighborhood patterns tend to be stimulating, safe, and ecologically sustainable. The SmartCode requires a mix of uses within walking distance of dwellings, so residents aren't forced to drive everywhere. It supports a connected network to relieve traffic congestion. At the same time, it preserves open lands, as it operates at the scale of the region as well as the community.

Transect Planning

The SmartCode is a Transect-based code. A transect of nature, first conceived by Alexander Von Humboldt at the close of the 18th century, is an analytical cross-section of a region intended to reveal a sequence of environments. Originally, it was used to analyze natural ecologies, showing varying characteristics through different zones such as shores, wetlands, plains, and uplands. Its purpose is to study the many elements that contribute to habitats where certain plants and animals thrive in symbiotic relationship to the minerals and microclimate.

Human beings also thrive in different places. There are those who could never live in an urban center; there are those who would wither in a rural hamlet. Humans need a system that preserves and creates meaningful choices in their habitats. Near the close of the 20th century, New Urbanist designers recognized that sprawl was eradicating the pre-war American built environment. They began to analyze it and extract its "genetic material" for propagation. They extended the natural transect to include the built environment, thus establishing the Rural-to-Urban Transect, the basis for the SmartCode.

The Rural-to-Urban Transect (or simply "the Transect") is divided into six Transect Zones for application on zoning maps. These six habitats vary by the level and intensity of their physical and social character, providing immersive contexts from rural to urban. SmartCode elements are coordinated by these T-Zones at all scales of planning, from the region through the community scale and on down to the individual lot and building.

One of the principles of Transect-based planning is that certain forms and elements belong in certain environments. For example, an apartment building belongs in a more urban setting, a ranch house in a more rural setting. Some types of thoroughfares are urban in character, and some are rural. A deep suburban setback destroys the spatial enclosure of an urban street; it is out of context. These distinctions and rules don't limit choices; they expand them. This is the antidote for the one-size-fits-all development of today.

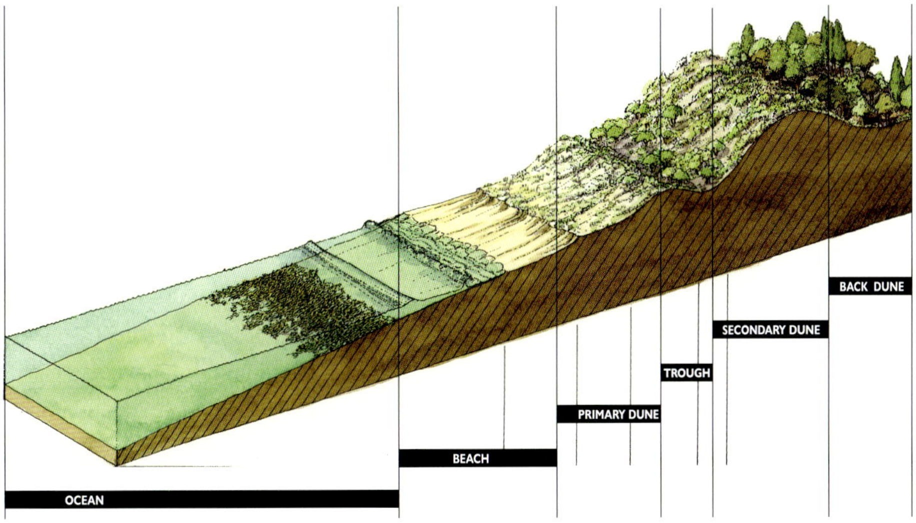

A Typical Natural Transect

EUSEBIO AZCUÉ FOR DPZ CODESIGN

The Transect is evident in two ways. Zones and communities exist as characteristic places on the Transect and they also evolve along the Transect over time. As places, the six Transect Zones display identifiable characteristics, based on normative American urban patterns. They also increase in complexity, density, and intensity over a period of years, until a "climax condition" is reached. This is a growth process analogous to succession in natural environments.

The best urbanism requires the sequential influence of many participants. A code allows buildings to be designed and built by many hands over years, or even generations. The single designer or committee leads to a lack of robustness, similar to vulnerable monocultures in nature. A parametric and successional code like the SmartCode allows experience to feed back and become integrated—the fourth dimension of time. Once adopted, it stays in place, allowing urbanism to evolve and mature without losing its necessary foundation of order.

It also ensures that a community will not have to scrutinize all projects as they are proposed, because the intentions of the citizens will have already been determined in the process that leads to the code. The SmartCode is a comprehensive framework for that process.

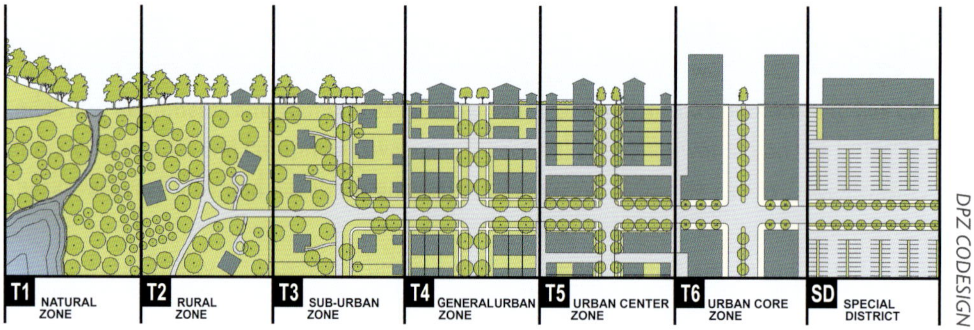

About the SmartCode and Manual

The SmartCode is a unified development ordinance that incorporates the transect-based planning principles of Smart Growth and New Urbanism. A publication, *SmartCode Version 9 and Manual,* has been prepared to assist those who are considering calibrating and adopting a SmartCode for a city, region, or project. It presents the entire SmartCode Version 9.2 with comprehensive annotations and other supporting materials.

The SmartCode is a model ordinance. It is not persuasive and instructive like a guideline, nor is it intentionally general like a vision statement. It is meant to be law, precise and technical, administered by municipal planning departments and interpreted by elected representatives of local government. As a model code to be calibrated, the SmartCode should be customized to regional characteristics by urban designers, planners, civil engineers, architects, and landscape architects—ideally with the participation of the local citizens. The code must also be connected by reference to local law by land use attorneys.

Because the SmartCode envisions only beneficial outcomes based on known components of urban design, it is a more efficient document than conventional codes. Version 9.2 is even more streamlined than previously, based on the the experience of several years of using the SmartCode in the field. Sections now appear as optional Modules. They are available to supplement the base code during customization. Because they are numbered by their correct place in the base code, they are easy to insert.

The publication also includes an extended Appendix offering sample plans, step-by-step procedures, illustrations, historical commentary, checklists, and resources. One particularly useful section is a submittal document.

The Annotations and the Appendix are support for the SmartCode: They are explanatory and advisory only. They are not legally binding and must not be included as part of the SmartCode itself when it becomes law. To distinguish them, the official text of the SmartCode itself appears in a sans serif font, and the commentary appears in a serif font, and items that should be considered for calibration are in green.

Summary: What the SmartCode Does

- It utilizes a type of zoning category that ranges systematically from the wilderness to the urban core.
- It enables and qualifies Smart Growth community patterns that include Clustered Land Development (CLD), Traditional Neighborhood Development (TND), Regional Center Development (RCD), and Transit-Oriented Development (TOD).
- It integrates the scales of planning concern from the regional through the community scale, on down to the individual lot and, if desired, its architectural elements.
- It integrates the design process across professional disciplines.
- It integrates methods of environmental protection, open space conservation, and water-quality control.
- It integrates subdivision, public works and Transfer of Development Rights (TDR) standards.
- It provides a set of zoning categories common to new communities and to the infill of existing urbanized areas.
- It is compatible with architectural, environmental, signage, lighting, hazard mitigation, and visitability standards.
- It establishes parity of process for existing and new urban areas.
- It integrates protocols for the preparation and processing of plans.
- It encourages the efficiency of administrative approvals when appropriate, rather than decision by public hearing.
- It encourages specific outcomes through incentives rather than prohibitions.
- It specifies standards parametrically (by range) in order to minimize the need for variances.
- It generally increases the range of the options over those allowed by conventional zoning codes.

LOOKING BACKWARD ON AMERICAN URBANISM

ANDRÉS DUANY & EMILY TALEN

In the middle years of the last century, Jose Luis Sert summoned designers and critics to Harvard with the intention of defining a discipline to be called urban design. Records of the annual meetings show reams of tentative disquisition.[1] That no conclusions were drawn, despite the presence of the exemplary urbanism of Cambridge, signaled from the outset that empirical evidence was to be held outside the discourse.

Not until 2010, with the semicentennial proceedings commemorating Sert's quest, did it become clear that his legacy to urban design, at least in the academy, had been the consensus to avoid consensus. This clarification arrived by way of contrast, as a replacement paradigm became visible—a focused academic agenda called Landscape Urbanism.

Meanwhile, outside the academy, another consensus had become dominant, this one based specifically on the empirical observation of places like Cambridge. It was called the New Urbanism.[2]

By the end of the century, the practicing professions had come to support the principles of the New Urbanism (by its several names) with remarkable unanimity: Americans should reduce driving and live more compactly because of concerns related to climate, health, economics, social equity, and energy use.[3] The particulars were still in debate, but that basic outline of the human habitat had largely been settled.

The instruments to achieve it would be based on the pedestrian shed—an urban pattern in which the basic needs of daily life are within walking distance.[4] Buildings would not be high rises or megastructures, but multiple, adjacent structures designed sequentially in response to evolving circumstances under the guidance of codes. From this combination would ensue all that is sustainable about the human habitat: the compactness, the complexity, the completeness, the connectivity, the conviviality, and the cost-effectiveness.[5]

The New Urbanism was at that time close to supplanting the tenacious paradigm of suburban sprawl, which had been the unintended consequence of a century's search for the "true synthesis" of the social and natural realms. The original proposition, called the Garden City, had long dissipated as the ubiquity of the automobile and planners' capitulation to it negated geographic discipline. The New Urbanism, especially through Transect-based codes and LEED-ND, was poised to become the standard. Rather than the defensive protection of nature, a new environmental strategy would be market-oriented and projective: an urbanism that humans needed and desired, and would therefore be loath to abandon. Those with a choice would not want to inhabit suburban sprawl.

The Congress for the New Urbanism led the campaign to overcome the procedural inertia. The effort seemed to provide enough intellectual content to support research, stimulate debate, and keep reform-minded designers well occupied: How much compactness should be expected, when driven also by market expectations? To what extent could natural processes be accommodated without undermining human prerogatives? How could the socioeconomic segregation enabled by the automobile now be reversed? Should urban growth be bounded as conceived by Howard, or channeled as proposed by McKaye? How to incorporate food production, energy sourcing, and the inevitable poverty into an urbanism adapted to the 21st century? These proposals would have to be implemented within the then-current bureaucratic protocols, in the friction of an angry and confused public, a venal political system, a development industry programmed for simplistic solutions, and—as it turned out—the opposition of the design academy.

But by the turn of the century it gradually became clear that the more intellectually compelling debate was no longer against conventional suburbia, but between the New Urbanism and the Landscape Urbanism, two paradigms with competing visions of nature and society. Landscape Urbanism had overcome the reflex that had kept the Academy uncommitted for half a century—not by challenging Sert's internal discourse, but by unifying it against an opponent, explicitly taking on the threat of New Urbanism, proposing to "undermine its certainties, explode its limits, ridicule its preoccupations."[6]

The initial challenge was not properly engaged by the New Urbanist side. Ann Spirn's early critique in *The Granite Garden* that there had been "a fundamental lack of understanding of how natural processes shape cities, towns and regions" was dismissed with the facile retort that Commonwealth Avenue, which appeared on the cover of her book, could not be built following the prescriptions of the text within.[7]

In retrospect, the New Urbanists' failure to immediately assimilate Spirn's prescient and reasonable message was the greatest strategic blunder on their part. Years of practice complying with mandatory federal standards had coarsened New Urbanism's ecological sensibility. The natural processes, which were accommodated or mitigated as required by law, had not been polemicized. Unimaginative designs of public space permitted the accusation that New Urbanism was dismissive of nature. New Urbanist designs, responding to the empiricism of William White, Jan Gehl, and Oscar Newman, were both socially and environmentally responsible, yet did not appear to be the latter.

This emergent challenge was overshadowed by a distracting debate over architectural style. It seemed that architects would not go along with a New Urbanist discipline of a contextual architecture cooperating toward spatial definition. The discipline of the urban street, for some an obvious necessity, was for many modernist architects a tyrannical constraint on their creativity. New Urbanists had underestimated this profound discontent. Not even a spectacular success of modernist buildings within a New Urbanist discipline, as had been made evident by 2015 with the HafenCity project of Hamburg, was convincing to them.

Providing refuge from an urban discipline privileged Landscape Urbanism among the many offerings of the architectural academy. Nature's "indeterminacy and flux," its "instability," would require "a resilient structure of voids."[8] This was understood to allow freely designed buildings as freestanding objects within a prioritized landscape. A brilliantly argued and lavishly illustrated agenda to restore unconstrained form-making was on offer—in exchange for the dominant position within Sert's old urban design triad of Architecture, Planning, and Landscape Architecture.[9]

Rather than spatial definition by buildings as the basis of an urban fabric, landscape would be the "structuring medium." "The look and shape of the city" was to be a matter of "open space within which buildings are set."[10] When Stan Allen stated that "designers can activate space and produce urban effects without the weighty apparatus of traditional space making,"[11] it was a radical proposition only against the near-consensus that a disciplined building frontage was the primary component of a successful urban outcome—and its absence the catalyst for social failure.

Landscape Urbanists had put an end to Harvard's 50 years of dithering by systematically asserting whatever positions were contrary to the New Urbanism.[12] The design syntax was to be the obverse: the avoidance of grids, blocks, sidewalks directly associated to building frontage, a primary ground plane, standard-issue pavement technology, trees coinciding with paths, multiple buildings accreting to define public space, and any of those disciplines (even typology) that could promote and reconcile the super-adjacency of disparate social and functional programs. By taking a "critical" position, Landscape Urbanism was forced to discard all the constituent elements of the dominant paradigm. The polemic of avoiding established tropes led to a *deformation professionelle*. With an aplomb unique to the academy, New (and Old) Urbanism was simply *hors le discours*. There would be an exploration of density and complexity, but without urbanism.

This was, at least, an unambiguous position—not Sert's feckless stance between coveting the forbidden traditional city, a mandatory distancing from CIAM and swerving from the glamorous but branded Team 10. The continuity with Sert's regime was that new propositions could ignore empirical evidence. By that time skepticism regarding success had become the "critical" method of academic research. Excellent design would mitigate the long-established evidence that attracting free-willed pedestrians required disciplined frontages. Until proven otherwise, there would be swarms of Zip-a-Tone pedestrians, then, later their Photoshopped equivalents.

Given the decisive failure of CIAM's *espace vague* in the late 20th century, the belief that street frontages were dispensable required the kind of deliberate amnesia that could be effected only within the academic discourse. The attempts to create a public realm in Vallingby, Stevenage, Toulouse-le-Mirail, Firminy-Vert, Don Mills, Brasilia, Pruitt-Igoe, Tyson's Corner, Columbia, Hansaviertel, Vauban, and Shenzen had, without exception, failed to support pedestrian activity at levels approaching those of the nearby corridor streets, which—unless they had been undermined or demolished—stood as permanent indictments.

New Urbanists believed that walkability was the essential element that made urbanism intrinsically sustainable—and that, conveniently enough, is also urbanism's greatest competitive advantage. Why would one choose to live in higher density if not for the street life? The compensation for the absence of a private yard out the back door was the vitality found out the front door. Even the omni-skeptical New York critic, Michael Sorkin, could not deny the primacy of the spatially defined street. In his autobiographical *Twenty Minutes in Manhattan*, there was nothing but the rue corridor to salve his quasi-penitential private realm.[13]

Unusually, the discourse of the Landscape Urbanists excluded Manhattan, otherwise *maison mére* of the architectural avant-garde. Had it not been so, the New Urbanist position would have quickly prevailed. Manhattan's urbanism, of course, has never been modernist in any respect. A list of its differences from CIAM principles would be quite long. Manhattan's streets are proportionally (building height to spatial width) the opposite of *espace vague*. Indeed, if within Manhattan (or any other historic core), a modernist object-building is seen to support pedestrian life, it is because it is embedded into and braced by the urban fabric. Note the case of the Seagram Building, or Foster's Gherkin, neither of which exterminated pedestrian activity. This was the reason that at the turn of the last century in London, Milan, St. Petersburg, Washington, and Paris, the star architects demanded inclusion in the historic areas—refusing available sites in modernist enclaves such as Crystal City, La Defense, and the Docklands. Modernist buildings succeeded only when they were parasitic on traditional urban fabric. When placed among other object-buildings, they coalesced into a *strada comica*, as Rem Koolhaas eventually demonstrated with his Starchitect Collage.[14]

Just as CIAM and Team 10 had done previously, Landscape Urbanists banned the *rue corridor* for ideological reasons, and the result eventually proved to be the same: a sterilized civic realm. As there could be no emulation of the world's stock of functioning urbanism, only the dreary social housing and suburban sprawl would have remained as the models. The disinterment of Usonia and Hilbersheimer had to follow. The "critical method" was duly applied.[15]

Like Sert, Landscape Urbanists avoided evidence. The demolition of the Robin Hood Gardens (the iconic Team 10 project) at the turn of the century was not permitted to have the devastating effect that Pruitt Igoe had on CIAM's legacy. As modernist housing schemes were martyred, the evidence of social failure was fortunately lost. A new justification, environmentalism, was brought into the avant-garde discourse (for the first time) as a life-support apparatus. The high proportion of *espace vague* became available, indeed was justified, not as social space (Landscape Urbanism never succeeded in conceptualizing an integral social agenda), but as the locus of environmental mitigation through the implantation of "nature." Surrogate hill and dale, prairie, woodland, and stream were deployed to embalm the otherwise moribund residue between "urban" buildings. The surrogate was highly appealing visually, and endowed Landscape Urbanism with the symbols of superior environmental performance.

While the social agenda was dissimulated, the treatment of nature was curiously honest: There was to be no pretending within the discourse that the plantings were natural. Landscape Urbanism's design tropes were careful: the insertion of "native species" would be on the artificial order of a plant nursery. Naturalistic planting, if provided, would be as quotation, to be framed—literally. Anything that might be confused with the reconstitution of the natural was proscribed. Olmstead was avoided in general and in detail.

This innovative environmental proposition was accompanied by an audacious attack on the New Urbanists' purported inability to deal with what were then thought to be the conditions of reality. Thus James Corner defined Landscape Urbanism as "a response to the failure of traditional urban design and planning to operate effectively in the contemporary city." The "out of control" metropolis was "not a weakness but its strength." A crossover vocabulary of "indeterminacy," "openness," and "flux" was developed to affirm the metaphor of synthesizing nature and urban design. The incompletion and temporality of landscape became the "antidote to the implicit finitude" of conventional planning tools, not excluding the technical synthesis proposed by the widely used Rural-to-Urban Transect. Seeing the environmental crisis not so much as a scientific reality to be affected, but as an incubator of metaphor, the agenda aligned well with the "critical" discourse then prevalent. James Corner dismissed even McHarg's overlay maps because they attempted to impose measures. In the absence of metrics, the technical arguments in favor of compact urbanism could be ignored.[16] There could be no accounting for suburbia's dismal environmental performance. Only one metric was retained—for the scientific gloss: hydrology. Water filtered to the aquifer, was elevated to a rhetorical position whose merits were beyond verification. Eventually this was implemented—ironically for those disapproving of top-down planning—by federal policy.

As an example, one proposal presented at a conference on Landscape Urbanism held at Harvard in 2010 involved the replacement of a street intersection in downtown Berkeley by a plug of landscape. That this intervention clipped the street grid, reducing transportation capacity and thereby density, was an unmentioned externality. The concept was to provide an explicit allusion to a coastal wetland some miles distant. This was understood as a metaphor by the *cognoscenti* present, but taken as effective environmentalism by others.

The perverse implications of such "day-lighting" of wilderness gradually became evident. New York City was the counterexample. What would the effect be on Manhattan's transportation network if the nearly 3,000 streams and wetlands then in pipes were to have been preserved as riparian corridors as per Landscape Urbanist praxis? How much street connectivity would be interrupted, thereby severely reducing density? How many thousands of square miles of actual, functioning, natural areas would have been consumed by the dwellings, stores, and offices of the millions of consequently dispersed Manhattanites—all adding their lower-density carbon footprints to the global crisis?

But these metrics missed the point. An ethical commitment to environmentalism was not essential within a relativistic discourse where power was the only objective verification. Landscape Urbanism was clear about this. It could not be fully understood as a design movement, or even an environmental reform strategy—the peculiar combination of intentions could be comprehensively understood only as a campaign to amass power.

Landscape Urbanism thrived with the support of constituencies that the New Urbanists had either ignored, annoyed, or anathemized. Among them were: 1) The profession of Landscape Architecture, whose formal concerns had been made subordinate to the social determinants of public space; 2) Environmentalists, specifically those impressed by the visual foregrounding of nature in designs; 3) Academic faculty who had been constrained by New Urbanism's research agenda, which privileged proof over speculation; 4) Architects, who would retain their prerogatives to formal innovation; 5) Infrastructure purveyors who, confronting NIMBYs could absorb the high cost of Landscape Urbanist visual mitigations; and 6) Suburban sprawl developers who would be made to, literally, "look good." These were all strategically embraced by Landscape Urbanism.

Foremost among these constituencies were the architects, to whom Landscape Urbanism offered a reprieve. They could retain the prerogatives of untrammeled formalism in exchange for ceding urban design to the Landscape Urbanists. This finally let slip the Beaux Arts assumption that architecture was the master art. Furthermore, there was something to be gained by aligning with an agenda that was exclusively environmental—there would be no further need to sustain the tiresome CIAM/New Urbanist commitment to social equity. They also re-discovered that interspersed "nature" could provide the visual shock absorber between the mutually destructive shapes of their buildings. The New Urbanist proposition required a collective discipline and a formal cooperation that was intolerably repressive to the modernist architects.

Thus there developed a very symbiotic relationship. Architects supported the "urban" claims of Landscape Urbanism by evolving a formal repertoire that was equivalently metaphorical. There was a look that identified the corresponding architecture: the quality of being carefully random, from an arbitrarily complex and diverse massing to a misalignment of details such as walls, columns, openings, and mullions. This architectural syntax, which had originally emerged to express the ambiguity of the relativist discourse, was surreptitiously re-branded as a surrogate for the complexity of urbanism. The visual multiplicity provided camouflage for what were in fact functionally homogenous buildings. The "critical" project privileged appearance, and verbalized intention—and so representation trumped metrics without undue stir.

The timing of the architectural alliance was fortuitous. At that time the post-modern architectural culture was just past the sequential infatuations with Edwardian, Art Deco, and Mid-Century Modern.

Students were no longer exposed to the necrotic European New Towns or the narcoleptic American Planned-Unit Developments. The social failure of the high-rises, no less than HUD's garden apartments, had extinguished what was left of modernist planning's reputation. The mercy killing came from every direction: *Collage City, Delirious New York, Townscape, Architecture Rationelle, The Golden City,* Jane Jacobs, the Krier brothers, *Defensible Space,* the Charter of the New Urbanism. It was a rare moment of consensus: the practitioners, the academy, the publications were all in agreement that whatever may still have been viable about modernist architecture, nothing remained standing in modernist planning.

But that consensus had occurred in the 1980s. A full generation of amnesia had since been applied within the academy.

"Cutting edge" design was essential to Landscape Urbanism's academic credentials, but it was a fiction that could not be indefinitely maintained, even within the highly edited history curriculum pioneered by Michael Hays at Harvard. One of its great achievements was the non-existence of the pioneers Diana Balmori, Anne Whiston Spirn, and Ian McHarg, even at the time they were all still alive and in Academia. Despite the suppression of memory, the students did eventually focus on Olmsted, and they finally did discover Team 10. But in the formative decades of Landscape Urbanism it was an urgent priority to control the precedent.

With Olmsted the problem was the evidence of indisputable success under a virtually identical agenda. Why innovate, instead of emulate? And regarding Team 10, if the formal repertoire of Landscape Urbanism could be distilled to a single source, it would be the Robin Hood Gardens by the Smithsons. Skewed slabs hovering over a rolling landscape of *espace vague*. "Streets in the air" providing a "thick matt" in lieu of ground plane. The randomly placed mullions marking an early apparition as complexity-surrogates for the socioeconomic and functional monoculture.

Charles Waldheim, the *eminence grise* of Landscape Urbanism, at first put forth three decoys: Andrea Branzi's Agronica, Frank Lloyd Wright's Usonia, and Hilberheimer's New Regional Pattern, taking recourse in three unbuilt concepts that could not therefore be challenged by objective measurement. But all three resisted resurrection until they were bundled with an emergent aspect of sustainability—food self-sufficiency. This coincided with an important New Urbanist initiative, becoming the first instance of agreement between the contending parties. The contemporaneous *Theory and Practice of Agrarian Urbanism* could have been Landscape Urbanism instead of New Urbanism had the buildings illustrated been flat-roofed. Yet another point of eventual agreement was when the crucially important hydrology agenda coinciding with the cost-effective Light Imprint technology formulated by Tom Low.

The trusty *rue corridor*, which was the one weapon the executioners all held in common, was slated once more for the trash heap of history.[17] (Further proof of Jane Jacobs' observation that the "pseudoscience of planning seems almost neurotic in its determination to imitate empiric failure and ignore empiric success.") Jane Jacobs herself was replaced by the refurbished reputation of her nemesis, Robert Moses—recalled not as destroyer of cities, but as the great builder of parks and infrastructure. His achievements would be tapped by Landscape Urbanists as another means of connection to the infrastructure constituency. This agenda was manifested in the aestheticizing of the existing systems of arterials, highways, stormwater facilities, and parking lots. The induced traffic and carbon emissions were externalities ignored by the discourse. If there was a gloss of "science," it was at the scale of advancing plant-bed technology in unnatural locations: on roofs, decks, walls, and high slopes.

Yet the principal players in the Landscape Urbanist constituency were the environmentalists—especially in the United States. The American environmental movement had emerged from the campaign for the creation of the National Parks toward the end of the 19th century. This agenda necessarily held wilderness as the ideal. Humans were conceived as outside of nature (per Woody Allen at the turn of the last century: "Nature and I are two"), and urbanism effectively came to rest outside of their discourse. As the toolbox defines and limits the craft, the extreme rustication of Landscape Urbanism was inevitable; while New Urbanism, with its prerogatives assigned to density, connectivity, and contiguity, could not be seen as anything but a clipper of green corridors, purveyor of impervious surface, and creator of heat islands. The evolving New Urbanist response was that the application of visual greening de-tuned the attributes of urbanism that supported walkability and hence lowered the environmental performance by fostering vehicular traffic. But the argument was complex and lacked the reflexive appeal of visual biophilia.

The "green" aesthetics proved to be an effective vaccine against NIMBYism, so suburban typologies were granted a reprieve. The Landscape Urbanist constituencies had long been adversarial to New Urbanism, but deploying this one was a direct affront. Conventional developers had nearly been cornered by the 30-year campaign of the New Urbanistm: penned in by the government-administered protocols of the SmartCode and LEED-ND. New Urbanism's technical progress against the sprawl machine was invisible to the avant-garde because it lacked *élan*. So sprawl became valued design fodder. Thus the superb designs—and not just the biophilia—of Landscape Urbanism managed to refurbish the reputation of suburban sprawl, a pattern that was not only failing economically and environmentally, but looked as if it were. Landscape Urbanists so skillfully aestheticized the sprawl that few recognized they were explicitly promoting the protraction of car-dominated, sociofugal places. The real effects of "unprecedented typologies" such as big-box retail were easily camouflaged by green roofs, screens, and porous-pavement parking lots.

Typically, Landscape Urbanism settled into arranging buildings in suburban settings that were urban in their statistical density, but not in their performance. Designers could now entertain the notion of "an expansive form of urbanism," disaggregated, not (only) to accommodate the automobile, but also to become "integrated with nature and agriculture," dispersed under a "sustainable energy grid" that would allow them to "keep our options open."[18]

And there was a further bonus for the architects: the unprecedented phenomenon of making modernism widely marketable. Landscape Urbanism delivered at long last the connection to the populus. It was no longer the environmental imperative of imposed acceptance: "Trust us, this is what green is supposed to look like." As any Visual Preference Study[19] will show—human biophilia is such that an image of anything with leaves will tilt the selection in its favor. Americans accepted "green" modernism from the same stimulus that had enamored them to a suburbia embedded in landscape: that modernist architects were being made acceptable to the middle class. As much as for the environmentalism claimed by its rhetoric, Landscape Urbanism was gratefully granted disciplinary preeminence in the academy.

Regulators of the scientific persuasion, principally at the Department of Environmental Protection, did not discern that the biophilic visuals of native plants, enhanced topography, and groundplane permeability had no measurable effect on performance. They had been seduced when their metrics were represented in gorgeous graphic formats and deployed as totems justifying the actions of the designers. (New Urbanists had done no more than follow the rules.) There evolved an astonishing escalation in the representational quality of scientific analysis. The once-lugubrious environmental reports were aestheticized; the statistical drones were promoted to protagonists. The Landscape Urbanists succeeded in avoiding the cost/benefit analysis that might have exposed the "critical method."

When the metrics came eventually to be analyzed, the benefits proved to be paltry, and—because of the extremely high cost of producing natural effects where they did not naturally occur—counterproductive. Vignetted nature was so expensive to install and maintain—the cost of the High Line was estimated at $32,000 per linear foot, or 40 times the unit cost of a walkable, tree-lined street[20]—that its effective environmental performance was revealed as not even remotely commensurate with its cost. This problem had been obscured for a time by the propensity to apply Landscape Urbanist technique only to civic space, which traditionally justified the higher investment. But with both the economic and environmental crises becoming truly serious, it was noted that natural systems were effective only where nature is preserved or restored in substantial areas—not as implants between buildings. Natural function proved to be resistant to Landscape Urbanist theories and techniques.

Undeniably, Landscape Urbanism made a substantial contribution to the design of civic open space, but it was incapable of delivering ordinary urban fabric, despite claims of being a comprehensive theory of urbanism. There was a rhetorical commitment to "process," but there were no means of coordinating the sequence of urbanization.

The technical problem was that when an infrastructure of nature permeates between, above, and beside, both the private buildings and public spaces must be designed and built simultaneously. There was no allowance for successional protocols: the coding that would have permitted the sequential generation of urbanism by many over time belonged to the New Urbanists and was therefore outside their discourse. The avowed aspiration to flux and indeterminacy was reduced to the prerogative of choosing sympathetic developers and architects to design the gray voids between the green areas on the plan—a methodology based on personality and power that could not in the long term be sustained, as the timeline of urbanism is much longer than the human.

In the meantime, more obvious flaws were being noticed. The conceptual "framing" of implanted nature gradually became a physical necessity. The puritanism of "native species" rather than the hardy urban ones required that the "frame" become actual railings and walls to keep humans from trashing the landscape by walking on it. The landscape could be gazed upon—that's all. An enormous amount of urban open space was thereby removed from its recreational purpose—at the very center of cities where it was most necessary. After the first sections of the High Line were completed, a plaque of "temporary" fencing and proscriptive signage became necessary. Subsequent sections had to include lawns that could be used by humans in the original, Olmstedian function. A well-known instance came out of Portland, Oregon, with the New Urbanist Jamison Square from the 1990s and the Landscape Urbanist Tranner Springs Park, one block away and a decade later. Jamison is usually packed with people of all ages, while Tanner is virtually devoid of human activity, as walking in that park would crush the prairie grasses. In yet another square in Portland, the restoration of "woodland" resulted in objections—not so much to the sexual activity which the rusticity made possible, but to the residue when found by the neighbors walking their dogs in the morning. Association with New Urbanist culture would have prevented such a romantic misconception of human nature.

The promise of Landscape Urbanism would have failed like the ethanol campaign, which arose concurrently—both driven by elegant intention rather than practical effect—had it not been subjected to the taxonomic engine of the New Urbanist Rural-to-Urban Transect, which absorbed Landscape Urbanism's techniques wherever they were relevant and functional. Not being ideologically proscribed, New Urbanists gradually assimilated Landscape Urbanism at the rural end of the Transect. They refurbished those aspects of their design repertoire where it had been weak. Urban Center and Urban Core Transect Zones remained, as Landscape Urbanism had never really engaged those. The rue corridor, which had always been exclusive to New Urbanism, survived.

New Urbanists assimilated the compelling vocabulary as well. Using Lars Lerup's "areas of stimulation," or "stim," within the "unfortunate economic residues," or "dross,"[21] was a more interesting way of polemicizing what New Urbanists had been calling "sprawl repair" and "districts." There arose an elegant and comprehensive language. Landscape Urbanism proved to be an important contribution to New Urbanism's evolution, having been made possible because the Landscape Urbanists had taken a firm position—quite unlike the "many urbanisms" which had been Sert's long legacy.

The Landscape Urbanist episode within the New Urbanist discourse shared the fate of other compelling counter-proposals: assimilation. Effective techniques were absorbed as a matter of pragmatism. There emerged an urbanism dealing with a greater range of constituencies, deploying a more complete technical repertoire, cultural as well as natural.

The alienation at Harvard continued as expected. The demands of the times do not necessarily coincide with the interests of the academies—nor should they, despite the very difficult century that is still upon us.

This essay was orginally published in Landscape Urbanism and its Discontents, *2013, New Society Publishers.*

1. Sert was president of the Congrès International d'Architecture Moderne (CIAM) from 1947 to 1956, and Dean of Harvard's Graduate School of Design from1953 to 1969. See Mumford, Eric. 2000. *The CIAM Discourse on Urbanism, 1928–1960*. Cambridge: MIT Press.

2. Krieger, Alex and William Saunders, Eds. 2010. *Urban Design*. Minneapolis: University of Minnesota Press.

3. Via irrefutable evidence, as reported in, e.g., Bartholomew, K. and R. Ewing. (2009) "Land Use-Transportation Scenario Planning: A Meta-Analysis," *Journal of the American Planning Association*, 75(1), 13–27; Ewing, R., K. Bartholomew, et al. (2008). *Growing Cooler: The Evidence on Urban Development and Climate Change, Urban Land Institute*, Washington, D.C.

4. Which meant: social diversity, well-used transit, informal visual supervision, third-place social cohesion, and the entertaining street theater of humans amused by other humans.

5. Mumford, Lewis. 1956. "The Natural History of Urbanization." In William L. Thomas, Ed., *Man's Role in Changing the Face of the Earth*. Chicago: University of Chicago Press. p. 382–400; Jacobs, Jane. 1961. *The Death and Life of Great American Cities*. New York: Vintage Books; Cronon, William. 1996. "The Trouble with Wilderness; or, Getting Back to the Wrong Nature." *Uncommon Ground*, W.W. Norton & Company. Pp: p. 69–90.

6. Koolhaas, R. (1995). "Whatever Happened to Urbanism?" In *On Landscape Urbanism* (p. 122–123). Austin, TX: Center for American Architecture and Design University of Texas at Austin School of Architecture. Quote, p. 123.

7. Spirn, A. W. 1985. *The Granite Garden: Urban Nature and Human Design* (1st ed.). Basic Books; Spirn, A.W. 2000. New Urbanism and the Environment. Places 13, 2: 2–79.

8. Corner, J. (2006). "Terra Fluxus." In *The Landscape Urbanism Reader*. New York: Princeton Architectural Press; see also Wall, A. 1999. Programming the Urban Surface. In On Landscape Urbanism (p. 182–193). Austin, TX: Center for American Architecture and Design University of Texas at Austin School of Architecture.

9. Mostafavi, M., Ed. 2010. *Ecological Urbanism*. Lars Muller Publishers.

10. Spirn, Anne Whiston. 1985. *The Granite Garden: Urban Nature and Human Design*. New York: Basic Books. quote p. xi–xii.

11. Allen, Stan. 2009. *Practice: Architecture, Technique and Representation*. London: Routledge.

12. To establish the ascendancy of the New Urbanism see *Urban Design* by Alex Krieger and William Saunders. A good kick at the New Urbanism is one of the few themes common among the 21 papers.

13. Sorkin, Michael. 2009. *Twenty Minutes in Manhattan*. New York: Reaktion Books.

14. Footnote: Ecological Urbanism.

15. Alan Berger, Drosscape.

16. Corner, James. 1991. "Landscape Architecture and Critical Inquiry." *Landscape Journal, Fall*, Vol.10, no. 2, p. 155–157.

17. At a jury at SciArch, Duany mentioned a similarity between a student's social housing project and Pruitt Igoe. The hapless student asked, "What is Pruitt Igoe?"

18. Margaret Crawford. 2010. In Mostafavi, M., Ed. 2010. *Ecological Urbanism*. Lars Muller Publishers. Quote p. 143.

19. See Tony Nelessen.

20. See quote by Paul Crabtree, in Sorlien & Donnelly, this volume.

21. Lerup, L. (1994). Stim and Dross: "Rethinking the Metropolis." In *On Landscape Urbanism* (p. 94–107). Austin, TX: Center for American Architecture and Design University of Texas at Austin School of Architecture. Quote, p. 101.

AUTHORS AND EDITORS

Philip Bess is a professor in the School of Architecture at the University of Notre Dame. He teaches graduate urban design and theory, with a particular interest in Catholic and classical humanist intellectual and artistic traditions in the context of modern American life. He is the author of numerous articles and books, including *Inland Architecture: Subterranean Essays on Moral Order and Formal Order in Chicago* and *Till We Have Built Jerusalem: Architecture, Urbanism, and the Sacred.* He holds a graduate degree in church history from Harvard and a graduate degree in architecture from the University of Virginia.

Charles C. Bohl is an associate professor and the director of the graduate program in Real Estate Development and Urbanism (MRED+U) at the University of Miami's School of Architecture, where he directed the interdisciplinary Knight Program in Community Building from 2000–2008. He is an expert on place making, mixed-use development, and the public process for planning and community design. He is the author of *Place Making: Developing Town Centers, Main Streets and Urban Villages,* a best-selling book published by the Urban Land Institute, now in its 5th printing.

David Brain is a professor of Sociology and Environmental Studies at New College of Florida, teaching courses that include urban sociology; the sociology of space and place in cities and suburbs; and sustainable communities. He earned an M.A. and Ph.D. at Harvard University, and taught at Harvard and Indiana University prior to New College of Florida. His practical experience includes consulting on planning and urban design projects, facilitating charrettes and visioning workshops, and directing neighborhood-oriented action research projects. As a member of the board and training faculty of the National Charrette Institute, he has trained architects, planners, public agencies, community leaders, and citizens.

Sidney Brower is professor emeritus in the Urban Studies and Planning program at the University of Maryland School of Architecture, Planning, and Preservation. His research focuses on ways in which people's attitudes and behaviors affect and respond to their physical surroundings, and on making research findings useful to planners and designers. He holds a Bachelor of Architecture degree from the University of Cape Town, and a Master of City Planning from M.I.T. He worked as an architect in Cape Town and for the City of Baltimore as Chief of the Comprehensive Planning section and then Chief of Design Research. His books include *Design in Familiar Places, Good Neighborhoods,* and *Neighbors and Neighborhoods.*

Bruce Donnelly is an urban planner, editor, and New Urbanist intellectual based in Cleveland, Ohio. His main work is in editing plans and published works, and in analyzing codes and documents and framing/explaining issues, problems, and solutions. He has collaborated on codes and comprehensive plans for several cities, has worked on the Louisiana Speaks recovery plan, and has authored essays in *Landscape Urbanism and its Discontents*.

Andrés Duany is an architect, urban designer, planner, author, and founding partner of DPZ CoDESIGN. He has influenced planners and designers worldwide, redirected government policies in the U.S. and abroad, and produced plans for hundreds of new and renewed communities. His leadership can be credited with the plan and code for Seaside, the first new traditional community; the Traditional Neighborhood Development (TND) zoning ordinance; the development of the SmartCode, a model form-based zoning code adopted by numerous municipalities and developments; and the definition of the Rural-to-Urban Transect, Agrarian Urbanism, and Lean Urbanism. His books include *Suburban Nation: The Rise of Sprawl and the Decline of the American Dream, The Smart Growth Manual, Garden Cities: Theories and Practice of Agrarian Urbanism,* and *The New Civic Art.*

Brian Falk is the director of the Center for Applied Transect Studies. He has overseen CATS' support of several publications, and was a contributing editor of the *Sprawl Repair Manual.* He also directs the Project for Lean Urbanism, a program of CATS. Dedicated to Making Small Possible, the Project for Lean Urbanism raises awareness of the value of small-scale economic development and helps municipalities enable it, allowing residents to participate in the building of their homes, businesses, and communities. He managed a series of pilot projects to test ways to enable small-scale development and oversaw the creation of a kit of tools, and now gives presentations on Lean Urbanism and provides technical assistance to enable it in municipalities.

Seth Harry is an architect and president of Seth Harry and Associates, Inc., an award-winning architecture, planning, and urban design firm. The company has been responsible for the master planning, design, and implementation of numerous civic, institutional, and mixed-use projects, new communities, and infill projects throughout the USA and overseas. He has written and lectured widely on the subjects of incremental infill redevelopment, suburban infill/retrofit, and sustainable commerce (regional-based retail and commercial development).

Elizabeth Plater-Zyberk is an architect, urban designer, and planner with more than 30 years of experience in a variety of projects at every scale, including regional plans and municipal zoning codes, downtown and neighborhood revitalizations, new towns and neighborhoods, streetscapes and building designs. A founding partner of DPZ CoDESIGN, she has initiated many of the firm's advances over the years. She is also an educator, and has maintained a career-long affiliation with the University of Miami School of Architecture, continuing to teach after 18 years as dean of the school. Her books include *Suburban Nation: The Rise of Sprawl and the Decline of the American Dream*, and *The New Civic Art*.

Daniel K. Slone is an attorney and partner in the Richmond office of McGuireWoods LLP. He represents property owners and localities developing innovative new land use strategies for more sustainable developments and open spaces, and he counsels product manufacturers regarding green products. He has represented numerous national and international nonprofits such as the USGBC, the Congress for the New Urbanism, the World Green Building Council, and EcoDistricts. He serves on the boards of several nonprofits, including the Congress for the New Urbanism, the Form-Based Codes Institute, and Bioregional North America (One Planet Communities). He co-wrote *A Legal Guide to Urban and Sustainable Development for Planners, Developers, and Architects*, and contributed chapters to *Developing Sustainable Planned Communities and Sustainable Development: The Practical Legal Guide*.

Sandy Sorlien is an urban code writer, editor, photographer, and teacher. She is former Director of Technical Research for the Center for Applied Transect Studies, and was the managing editor for the SmartCode and its Modules from 2005 to 2010. She wrote the Pocket Code in 2013. She is currently employed by the Philadelphia Water Department as an Environmental Educator at the Fairmount Water Works. She is completing a photographic book about Main Streets and has embarked on another about the Schuylkill River. In March 2014 she won a micro-grant from the Awesome Foundation for her public art project, Rescue H2O.

Emily Talen is professor of Urbanism at the University of Chicago. Prior appointments were at Arizona State University and the University of Illinois at Urbana-Champaign. She has a Ph.D. in urban geography from the University of California, Santa Barbara. Her research is devoted to urban design and urbanism, especially the relationship between the built environment and social equity. Her books include *New Urbanism and American Planning, Design for Diversity, Urban Design Reclaimed, City Rules*, and *Neighborhood*. She also has several edited volumes, including *Retrofitting Sprawl: Addressing 70 Years of Failed Urban Form*. She is the recipient of a Guggenheim Fellowship, and is a Fellow of the American Institute of Certified Planners.